CONTINUITY AND
CHANGE IN
ROMAN RELIGION

CONTINUITY AND CHANGE IN ROMAN RELIGION

J. H. W. G. LIEBESCHUETZ

OXFORD
AT THE CLARENDON PRESS
1979

Oxford University Press, Walton Street, Oxford OX2 6DP

OXFORD LONDON GLASGOW

NEW YORK TORONTO MELBOURNE WELLINGTON

KUALA LUMPUR SINGAPORE JAKARTA HONG KONG TOKYO

DELHI BOMBAY CALCUTTA MADRAS KARACHI

NAIROBI DAR ES SALAAM CAPE TOWN

Published in the United States by
Oxford University Press, New York

© *Oxford University Press 1979*

Quotations taken from I. D. Duff's translation of Lucan's Pharsalia *are reprinted by permission of The Loeb Classical Library*
(Harvard University Press: William Heinemann)

British Library Cataloguing in Publication Data

Liebeschuetz, John Hugo Wolfgang Gideon
Continuity and change in Roman religion
1. Rome – Religion
I. Title
200′.937   BL802   78–40499
ISBN 0-19-814822-4

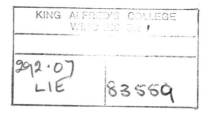
Printed in Great Britain
at the University Press, Oxford
by Eric Buckley
Printer to the University

IN MEMORY OF
HANS LIEBESCHUETZ

ACKNOWLEDGEMENTS

THIS book has developed out of an undergraduate course on Livy I and is in a sense an extended discussion of the third chapter of Professor P. Walsh's *Livy*. Dr. J. North allowed me to use his regrettably unpublished dissertation (J. North, 1968), a mine of valuable insights. Visits to London libraries and the preparation of the final text were aided by grants from the Research Board of Leicester University. Dr. M. Koerner, a helpful neighbour, translated and summarized parts of an important book written in Polish (J. Linderski, 1966). Conversations with Sheila Spire on the subject of Greek philosophy at Rome have left their mark on several chapters. Much of the book was typed by Linda Rayner. Rachel Liebeschuetz has helped me in various ways to get the text ready for submission. Professor P. Wiseman has read and criticized the opening chapters, and Professor A. Fitton Brown and Professor P. Walsh have gone through the whole text. So, from a stylistic point of view, has Margaret Liebeschuetz. Numerous errors, ambiguities, and infelicities have been removed by the editors of the Oxford University Press. I am extremely grateful to all who have helped to improve the book. The shortcomings that remain are my own.

J. H. W. G. L.

Leicester
October 1976

CONTENTS

ABBREVIATIONS

References in footnotes are to the author's name and date of publications as found in the bibliography. As a rule the title is only cited when an author has several publications in the same year.

A.J.A.	*American Journal of Archaeology*
A.J.Ph.	*American Journal of Philology*
A.N.R.W.	H. Temporini, ed. *Aufstieg und Niedergang der Römischen Welt*
B.S.A.	*Annual of the British School at Athens*
C.A.H.	*Cambridge Ancient History*
C.I.L.	*Corpus Inscriptionum Latinarum*
C.I.M.R.M.	M. J. Vermaseren, ed. *Corpus Inscriptionum et Monumentorum Religionis Mithraicae*, 2 vols.
C.J.	*Codex Justinianus*
C.Ph.	*Classical Philology*
C.Q.	*Classical Quarterly*
C.Rev.	*Classical Review*
C.S.E.L.	*Corpus Scriptorum Ecclesiasticorum Latinorum*
C.T.	*Codex Theodosianus*
Dar.S.	C. Daremberg, E. Saglio, *Dictionnaire des antiquités grecques et romaines*
E.P.R.O.	*Études préliminaires aux religions orientales dans l'empire romain*
F.I.R.	*Fontes Iuris Romani Ante Iustiniani*, vol. 2
F.R.A.	T. Hopfner, ed. *Fontes Historiae Religionis Aegyptiacae*
Gr. Christ. Schrift.	Die Griechischen Christlichen Schriftsteller der ersten drei Jahrhunderte, Leipzig
H.R.R.	H. Peter, *Historicorum Romanorum Reliquiae*
H. Theol. Rev.	*Harvard Theological Review*
I.L.C.V.	E. Diehl, *Inscriptiones Latinae Christianae Veteres*
I.L.S.	H. Dessau, *Inscriptiones Latinae Selectae*
J.H.S.	*Journal of Hellenic Studies*
J.R.S.	*Journal of Roman Studies*
J. Theol. S.	*Journal of Theological Studies*
M.A.A.R.	*Memoirs of the American Academy in Rome*
O.G.I.S.	W. Dittenberger, *Orientis Graeci Inscriptiones Selectae*
P.B.S.R.	*Papers of the British School at Rome*
P.G.	J. P. Migne, *Patrologia Graeca*
P.I.R.	*Prosopographia Imperii Romani*
P.L.	J. P. Migne, *Patrologia Latina*
Prl.	J. Marquardt, *Das Privatleben der Römer*
P.W.	Pauly-Wissowa (-Kroll), *Real Encyclopädie der klassischen Altertumswissenschaft*

R.A.C.	*Reallexikon für Antike und Christentum*
R.E.A.	*Revue des Études Anciennes*
R.E.L.	*Revue des Études Latines*
Rh.M.	*Rheinisches Museum*
R.H. Phil. R.	*Revue d'histoire et de philosophie religieuses* (Strasbourg)
R.I.C.	*The Roman Imperial Coinage*
R.R.	K. Latte, *Römische Religionsgeschichte*
R.St.	Th. Mommsen, *Römisches Staatsrecht*
S.E.G.	*Supplementum Epigraphicum Graecum*
S.E.H.R.E.	M. Rostovtzeff, *Social and Economic History of the Roman Empire*
S.H.A.	Scriptores Historiae Augustae
S.I.G.[3]	W. Dittenberger, *Sylloge Inscriptionum Graecarum*, 3rd ed.
S.M.S.R.	*Studi e Materiali de Storia delle Religioni*
Stv.	J. Marquardt, *Die Staatsverfassung der Römer*
T.A.P.A.	*Transactions of the American Philological Association*

INTRODUCTION

THIS book is about religious change and particularly about the interrelation between religious attitudes and the general political situation. Chapter I deals with religion in the disintegrating republic, its role in the political system, and its resistance to rationalism. Chapter II describes the changes of direction Roman religion had to undergo in order to adapt to the needs of the new semi-monarchical system of government. An attempt is made to explain how the innovations were accommodated to the Roman sense of religious propriety. Developments under the Julio-Claudian emperors are the subject of Chapter III. The fact that the nobles considered the empire an inferior, if inevitable, form of government alienated them from the Roman state and created the need for a system of values independent of the community. Stoicism provided this. Its deepening influence, together with the end of open politics, furthered the use of astrology and magic, which only now began to have a significant role in public life. In this respect, the empire introduced a retreat from rationalism as we would define it. Chapter IV centres on the crisis that brought down the emperor Nero. Lucan's *Pharsalia* is seen as expressing the poet's opposition to Nero, and his rejection of the institutions, religious as well as political, that had made his misrule possible. Prodigies recorded in Tacitus' *Annals* reflect (so it is argued) the religious uneasiness which contemporaries felt at Nero's behaviour. After civil war, Roman society had to be reconstructed once more. The *Punica* of Silius Italicus illustrate the ideology which influenced the Flavian rebuilding. Departures from Silius' Virgilian model reflect *inter alia* religious developments since the Augustan period. There had been progress in the moralization of religion. There was the beginning of a tendency to give supernatural embodiment to absolute evil. Above all, Stoic material had been given greater prominence at the expense of historical institutions and customs of Rome.

Chapter V bridges the third century when the empire was on the point of disintegration. Political and military anarchy had been preceded by what can only be described as the collapse of Latin literature. The emperor Marcus Aurelius wrote in Greek, while the writings of Apuleius, the last great non-Christian writer in Latin of the early empire reflect a new religious tendency which was to become increasingly important in the future. Political collapse followed in due course and towards the end of the third century there was once more a need for reconstruction. As always, reconstruction involved religion. Diocletian tried to revive the traditional religion. Constantine placed his hope in what was still largely a religion of outsiders: Christianity. Examination of the books of Arnobius and Lactantius shows how much ground Christians and educated pagans might seem to have in common. It was the existence of this common ground that enabled Constantine to choose Christianity as his personal religion, and emphasis by both parties of the common ground made it possible for pagans and Christians to co-operate, until towards the end of the fourth century Christianity became in the full sense the religion of the empire.

Two themes recur throughout the book: divination and the connection between religion and morality. The relative popularity of different techniques of divination changes, but belief in the possibility of divination is one of the constants of Roman history. In the course of the second century men became willing to accept as divinely inspired a much wider range of oracular material. This was perhaps the most fundamental change of religious attitude between the classical period and Late Antiquity.

As for morality, it is argued that Roman religion was never amoral. Its difference from the Judaeo-Christian tradition lay in the fact that neither the moral interest of the gods nor the moral rules (as opposed to laws) were defined in detail. As a result there could not be a code like the Ten Commandments backed by divine authority and sanctions. The Romans, nevertheless, so it is here maintained, took it for granted that the gods wished the Roman way of life to be preserved and would punish behaviour that threatened it. The Romans showed themselves particularly conscious of this divine interest when restoring their society after a crisis. In addition, Roman beliefs in this area were continually influenced by Greek philosophy which associated the divine and morality much more explicitly. According to these ideas, goodness was the essential quality of a divine being and imitation of divine goodness the principal service a god expected from an individual. The philosophical view came to be generally accepted and eventually was to provide an effective weapon for use by the Christians against the upholders of the old religion.

The book is based mainly on Latin literary sources. This means that the view of religious attitudes is a partial one. It is essentially the view of the Roman ruling class, and it is mainly concerned with the well-being of society as a whole rather than with the religious needs of individuals. Also, although there is much about Greek influence, there is no detailed examination of Greek writings. The reader may also miss the religion of that large number of Latin speakers who wrote no books but left inscribed dedications or tombstones. The fact is that the potential source material for the study of Roman religion is vast and the present author found it necessary to be selective. It is not suggested that the views of the people missing from this study were unimportant. After all, mystery religions and Christianity emerged from a lower level of society than that which created literature. But the religious attitudes of the Roman establishment are worth studying even in isolation. They represent, to some extent at least, a self-conscious and articulate version of the ideas which united Roman society. Moreover, the articulateness of this class enables us to study the relationship between political experience and religious attitude in a way which is impossible for other sections of society. Finally, the disintegration of the ancient religious system of the ruling class of an empire and the absorption of its remains into a new system of alien origin is a phenomenon of lasting interest.

I

THE LATE REPUBLIC

1. *A problem of religion in the republic*

FROM the second century, or even earlier,[1] the Roman nobility had proclaimed that Roman greatness was a reward sent by the gods for Roman piety. The Romans might be excelled by foreigners in other skills but in religious observance they were surpassed by none.[2] A visitor to the Rome of the late republic would still observe a vast amount of traditional ritual. Apart from numerous festivals, every public act began with a religious ceremony, just as the agenda of every meeting of the senate was headed by religious business.[3] Religion figured prominently in political controversy. Speaking to the people, Cicero linked his ability to detect the conspiracy of Catiline with the fact that he had set up a new statue of Jupiter on the Capitol not long before.[4] Cicero's career was long dogged by his feud with Clodius and this turned largely on religious issues.[5] He incurred Clodius' enmity by breaking the alibi which was Clodius' defence against an accusation of sacrilege.[6] In retaliation Clodius brought about the exile of Cicero and then did his utmost to ensure that Cicero should never get his house back by pulling it down and dedicating the site to Liberty.[7] Later the validity of Clodius' legislation was thrown into doubt. It was claimed that Clodius' adoption into a plebeian family, which

---

[1] *S.I.G.*[3] 601. 13 ff. (193 B.C.); 611. 23 ff. (189 B.C.).

[2] Cic. *N.D.* ii. 3 (8); *Har. Resp.* 19. Sall. *Cat.* 12. Liv. xliv. 1. 11; xlv. 22. 16; 39. 11. Posidonius *ap.* Athen. vi. 274. Dion. Hal. ii. 18. 1 ff. From first century A.D.: Plin. *N.H.* xxviii. 5 (24).

[3] Senate must meet in place inaugurated as temple: Dio, lv. 3; business begins with gods: Gel. xiv. 7.

[4] Cic. *Cat.* iii. 9; *Div.* i. 12 (17–22): privately he was more sceptical, ibid. ii. 21 (48). Ps.-Sall. *In Ciceronem*, 3 and 7 mocks Cicero's claims.

[5] For the personal circumstances see, for instance, E. Rawson (1975).

[6] Val. Max. viii. 5. 5.

[7] Cic. *Dom.* 37 (100) ff. *Har. Resp.* 5 (11) ff.

had made possible his election to the tribunate, had not been carried out in accordance with proper religious form and that this neglect of ceremony had rendered his consequent legislation invalid.[1] When Cicero was eventually recalled and got back the site of his house, Clodius argued that to restore a house which had once been dedicated was sacrilege, and exploited a widely known portent and its interpretation by the *haruspices* to support his point. Cicero had to admit that the portent gave warning of divine anger but insisted that the offences which had angered the gods had all been committed by Clodius.[2] It is clear that in Roman politics a charge of sacrilege could be extremely damaging.[3]

Much of the evidence for the importance of religion in the public life of the late republic shows it being manipulated for partisan political purposes. In fact religious manipulation can be said to have had a recognized place in the Roman constitution. So the Roman calendar, a semi-religious institution supervised by the *pontifices*, greatly limited the number of days on which the people could assemble, and consequently on which controversial legislation could be proposed.[4] In addition the *pontifices* could and did manipulate the insertion of intercalary months in such a way as to provide more or less time for legislation, or to extend or reduce the tenure of a particular office-holder, or the length of a particular public contract.[5] The time available for legislation or for political trials could also be affected by the proclamation of a period of public thanksgiving,[6] or the discovery that a festival had been celebrated incorrectly and must be performed again.

The electoral assemblies of the Roman people were accompanied by ritual of a kind that lent itself to political manipulation and was indeed so used. Before the day of a political assembly the presiding magistrate pitched a tent at the site where the assembly would be held and watched for signs. A report of unfavourable signs would stop the assembly. Other magistrates too[7] could prevent the assembly from being held by

---

[1] *Dom.* 15 (39). [2] *Har. Resp.* 10 ff.
[3] Cf. also charge against Gabinius: Dio, xxxix. 6.
[4] A. K. Michels (1967), 50–60.
[5] Censorinus, *De Die Nat.* xx. 6. Macr. *Sat.* i. 13. 2. Michels, op. cit. 145–72.
[6] L. R. Taylor (1949), 76 ff.
[7] Th. Mommsen, *R.St.* (1887), i. 89–116.

the announcement that they had been watching the heavens.[1] While the assembly was meeting augurs were present watching for signs from the gods. If lightning was observed the assembly would be dismissed, and even after the vote had been taken the college of augurs might declare it void on the ground that an unfavourable omen had been reported or that a mistake had been made in augural procedure.[2]

While there is thus an abundance of evidence that the Romans were even obsessively convinced of the need to placate the gods, belief in the gods seems to have had little effect on their conduct. The reader of Latin literature feels that fear of divine displeasure was very rarely a motive when a Roman decided on a course of action whether in a public or a private capacity; nor is there much evidence that a divine command was used as an excuse to justify any individual's behaviour retrospectively. If it were not for the descriptions of ritual a reader might conclude that the Romans of the late republic lived in as secular a world as our own.

This state of affairs is puzzling. Today religion is expected to be above party politics, and, if it is genuine at all, to have some influence on conduct. In consequence it has often been suggested that the religion of the late republic was dead, the fossilized shell of religion rather than the living organism.[3] Others have

---

[1] Ibid. 110–14. Cic. *Har. Resp.* 48; *Dom.* 40. It is usually argued that the announcement was sufficient because it was assumed that a magistrate looking for a sign would invariably see one. But the sources always describe the significant activity as 'having watched' and never as 'having seen'. It looks as if the watching by itself constituted the impediment. Perhaps the act of observation was regarded as a religious 'booking' of that day which would make it unavailable for use by other magistrates than the one who had 'observed'. It was presumably to prevent this that on election days the consul about to call the *comitia centuriata* forbade inferior magistrates to take auspices (Gel. xiii. 15. 1 'ne quis de caelo servaret'). The senate acted similarly on at least one occasion (Cic. *Sest.* 61 (129)). The earliest-known use of this device to stop the voting of an assembly took place in 59 B.C. (Other cases in Th. Mommsen, op. cit. 113, n. 2.) See also p. 14 n. 44 below.

[2] Cic. *Leg.* ii. 12 (31); iii. 4 (11); 19 (43). Liv. i. 36. 6. Th. Mommsen, *R.St.* i. 110, 115–16. Another striking use of religion for partisan political purposes is the consecration of the property of supposed public enemies, Cic. *Dom.* 38 (101); 47 (123) and notes in edition of R. G. Nisbet. Cf. also the use of auspices for preventing a magistrate leaving for his military command, Liv. xxi. 63. 5; xlv. 12. 2 (168). Liv. xxxii. 9. 28: Flamininus was kept at Rome most of 199 for expiation. Liv. xxxviii. 48 of 190 B.C.: Sibylline Oracle prevents Manlius from crossing the Taurus. Frontin. *Aqu.* i. 7 of 144 B.C.: *Xviri* prevent praetor from building an aqueduct.

[3] K. Latte (1960) heads chapter dealing with the period following the second

reduced it to a fraud practised by a sophisticated governing class on the credulous masses in order to ensure their continued subjection.

In the following chapters I am going to examine the social role of some aspects of Roman religion and in so doing to discuss how far concepts like 'decay' or 'political fraud' can be ustly applied to it.

2. *Ancient explanations*

Puzzlement at the nature of Roman public religion is not new. Already the Greek historian Polybius writing in the middle of the second century B.C. found it necessary to propound an explanation of the extraordinary amount of religious observance that was going on at Rome. 'The quality in which the Roman commonwealth is most distinctly superior is, in my opinion, the nature of their religious convictions. I believe that it is the very thing which among other peoples is an object of reproach, I mean superstition, which maintains the cohesion of the Roman state. My opinion is that they have adopted this course for the sake of the common people. It is a course which perhaps would not have been necessary had it been possible to form a state composed of wise men, but as every multitude is fickle, full of lawless desires, unreasoned passion and violent anger . . . it must be held in by invisible terrors and suchlike pageantry.'[1] It is clear that the meticulous attention to religious ritual which Polybius observed among members of the Roman ruling class was something that had no parallel among comparable circles in Greece.[2] It was also so 'unreligious' that Polybius could explain such behaviour only as political trickery.

There is something unsatisfactory about this explanation— even though it was formulated by an eyewitness. There is a contradiction in the fact that Polybius makes it clear that the

Punic war: 'der Verfall der römischen Religion', cf. ibid. 287 'für die Oberschicht hatte die römische Religion im letzten Jahrhundert der Republik jede Kraft verloren.' Similar views were already expressed by Warde Fowler (1923), 335–56.

[1] Pol. vi. 56. 6–11. Ibid. 12, which stresses the social value of beliefs about the underworld seems to be a generalization without specific reference to Rome.

[2] Cf. Liv. xxxv. 48. 13: Flamininus mocked by Aetolians for sacrificing before battle.

conduct of the nobility itself was affected by fear of the gods notwithstanding that they were supposed to have invented the whole business to cow the common people.¹ Then Roman religion is—or at least seems to be—singularly lacking in provisions to discipline 'lawless desires, unreasoned passion and violent anger'. One is tempted to conclude that Polybius' explanation owes as much to Greek theory as to observation at Rome.² Nevertheless Polybius' theory impressed the Romans themselves. Livy's description of how King Numa established the Roman state religion is obviously strongly influenced by Polybius. 'Rome was now at peace, there was no immediate prospect of attack from outside and the tight rein of constant military discipline was relaxed. In these novel circumstances there was an obvious danger of a general relaxation of the nation's moral fibre as a consequence of peace and inactivity [ne luxuriarent otio animi], so to prevent its occurrence Numa decided upon a step which he felt would be more effective than anything else with a mob as rough and ignorant as the Romans were in those days. This was to inspire them with fear of the gods. Such a sentiment was unlikely to touch them unless he first invented some marvellous tale. He *pretended* therefore that he was in the habit of meeting the goddess Egeria by night and that it was her authority which guided him in the establishment of such rites as were most acceptable to the gods.'³

Superficially Livy's account is open to the same objections as that of Polybius. Roman religion as we know it does not look like the first line of defence against immoral and aggressive behaviour. This might perhaps to a limited extent be seen as a function of religion at Athens⁴ but even there to nothing like the same degree as in the Books of Exodus and Leviticus of the Bible. Roman religion offers no sanction which might deter a potentially aggressive individual. But in fact Livy is not simply repeating Polybius' theory. He does not claim that fear of the gods deters men from antisocial behaviour. He defines the function of religion as a substitute for fear of the enemy and

¹ vi. 56. 14 it was the nobles who held office and therefore they were the people who kept their oaths and abstained from public wrong.
² F. L. Walbank (1957), 741–2.
³ Liv. i. 19. 4, trans. A. de Sélincourt.
⁴ See K. J. Dover (1974), 255 ff.; H. Lloyd-Jones (1971).

military discipline (metus hostium disciplinaque militaris).[1] This needs a little explanation. The substitution of fear of the gods for fear of an external enemy is clear enough: Livy, following in the intellectual tradition of which Sallust is the most eloquent surviving representative, believes that the cohesion and public spirit of the Roman state can only be maintained by the existence of an external threat. But what about military discipline? The discipline of a modern army is maintained by drill and the enforced and meticulous performance of a large number of in themselves insignificant tasks. This has, or is supposed to have, a decisive psychological effect on the soldiers subjected to it, and to instil subordination, cohesion, and comradeship. Livy seems to see the effect of religion as something like this. Finding out the right ritual for the circumstances and performing it keeps men busy in thought and act.[2] But this activity has the effect of imprinting the minds of the worshippers with a conviction that the gods take an interest in human affairs. This being so, society was securely founded on the inviolability of oaths and contracts which were made with invocation of the gods and whose breach the gods were expected to punish. Livy does not suggest that belief in divine concern increased men's knowledge of how to conduct their lives; he does, however, imply that it induced them to imitate the behaviour of their king and shape their manners by his example.

Livy's account, as far as it goes, is plausible. Roman religion was a discipline which yoked individuals and the people as a whole to the performance of an exacting round of duties, and obliged individuals to submit to the expert guidance of priests who were also leading figures in political life.[3] This did not by itself inculcate a code of conduct but it did provide some sort of underpinning for morality. This was strongest in the area of oaths and contracts, but extended, as we will see, over a wide range of behaviour.

Livy's account is plausible but obviously oversimplified. His explanation does not take account of the sense of human

[1] i. 19. 15.
[2] It is to counter *otium* (i. 19. 4) and its effect is that 'animi aliquid agendo occupati erant'.
[3] i. 21. 1.

inadequacy and helplessness in face of the universe which surely is one root of Roman as of all religion.[1] But even in the area of social organization the fact that it was a discipline did not exhaust the role of Roman religion. Many religious ceremonies undoubtedly made definable and quite specific contributions to the functioning of various institutions of Roman society. This is obvious in the case of the religious calendar, which provided the temporal framework within which the never-ending cycle of labours of the farmer's year had to be carried out. It is altogether appropriate that the calendar should head the list of Numa's religious innovations.[2] Similarly the ritual involving boundary stones played an important part in maintaining property rights.[3] The interrelation between religious ritual and social institutions is particularly easy to study in the area of divination.

3. *Public divination*

The Romans had three professions to provide divination for the community: *augures*,[4] the *haruspices*,[5] and the *quindecimviri*.[6] It was the function of the augurs to advise on religious aspects of meetings of popular assemblies, to ensure that the proper procedure was observed, and that the signs indicated divine approval. The science of augury was concerned with interpretation of the movements and calls of birds. Thunder or lightning before or during an assembly also fell within their province. *Haruspices* interpreted the entrails of sacrificial animals, and on the basis of their findings proclaimed whether a proposed course of action was favoured by the gods or not. The *quindecimviri* were the keepers of the Sibylline Oracles. When their advice was asked they would consult the books and make recommendations accordingly. The recommendations were usually of a ritual nature. Consultation of the *quindecimviri* formed part of the normal procedure for introducing new cults to Rome.

An essential feature in the working of Roman divination is

---

[1] On function of religion in society see, for instance: E. Dürkheim (1912); M. Weber (1922–3); A. Macbeath (1952).   [2] Liv. i. 19. 6.
[3] Ibid. 55. 3–4 with Ogilvie's notes (1965), 210–11. E. Marbach, P.W. 2 R. v, A1, 781–4, s.v. Terminus.   [4] G. Wissowa (1895).
[5] C. O. Thulin (1912).   [6] G. Radke (1968).

that the diviners provided very little factual information other than in the field of ritual. Their basic function was to proclaim divine approval, or its absence, and to suggest ritual by which it could be maintained or regained.[1] In theory augury, for example, might be exploited to obtain information, such as the whereabouts of hidden treasure.[2] In practice, public divination was not so used. When King Tarquinius Priscus wanted to test the skill of the first augur he did not ask him to divine what he was thinking about (cutting a stone with a razor) but whether what he was thinking could be done.[3] In other words he wanted the answer to be either yes or no. *Haruspices* sometimes made factual prophecies, of a kind, but their answers were stereotyped and general: forecasts of success or warnings of danger in war or politics.[4] Thus the nature of their responses ensured that Roman diviners could rarely be refuted by events. On the other hand, their scope for influencing public opinion was correspondingly limited.[5]

Public divination certainly performed the functions which Livy thought that Roman ritual had performed under Numa. It instilled the belief that the gods cared for what happened on earth, and that they might intervene with calamitous consequences to the community. In fact it provided a mechanism for tracing the temper of the gods in much the same way as radar traces the dangerous obstructions which lie in wait for shipping. It also provided a discipline, a discipline for politicians. It

---

[1] The root function of divination everywhere is to assist decision-making one way or another but Greek oracles, especially Delphi, gave more information—if ambiguously. See W. R. Halliday (1913); R. Flacelière (1965), H. W. Parke (1967).
[2] Cic. *Div.* i. 17 (31).   [3] Ibid. 17 (32).
[4] Forecasts of success would create a warlike spirit among citizens about to be asked to vote for war or soldiers being led into battle (Liv. xlii. 30. 8–10; xxxvi. 1. 3; xxxi. 5. 7. Obseq. 56b). Warning of the danger of ambush would help a commander to restrain the over-confidence (Liv. xxvii. 16. 15; xxvii. 26. 14); but was sometimes ignored xxv. 16. Frequently *haruspices* predicted civil strife. No doubt this helped to rally the defenders of civil order and excused more vigorous dealings with trouble-makers. (Obseq. 29. App. *B.C.* i. 71 (322). Plut. *Sull.* 7. Cic. *Div.* i. 44 (99); *Har. Resp.* 25 (53 ff.); *Div.* i. 12 (20).)
[5] In the Roman republic, divination was employed within a limited and well-defined area. It was not used to obtain information which could be gained through the senses, or through arts and sciences like music or medicine, or astronomy, or to establish moral judgements, or to lay down principles of conduct, or discover constitutional arrangements. So Cic. *Div.* ii. 3–5 (9–13). This is derived from Carneades and therefore in the first place about Greece. But it was true of the Roman republic, perhaps even more true than of Greek cities.

bound them to the rules of a strict procedure and compelled them to submit to the superior authority first of the priestly diviners, and then of the senate which in this field as in others had the ultimate say. In this respect the effect of Roman divination might be compared to that of the procedure of the House of Commons.

But definition of the social role of divination can go beyond Livy's analysis. I suppose that the central function of Roman divination was the maintenance of public confidence or, negatively, the avoidance of panic. The diviners scanned the state of relations between the gods and Rome and provided reassurance that the 'peace of the gods' was being maintained, or at least restored. This being so, the people could expect prosperity to continue or calamity to end. The so-called expiation of portents furnishes an example. Striking and unusual phenomena—not necessarily miraculous—were reported. Javelins had caught fire, shields had sweated blood, strange lights had been seen in the heavens, reapers had collected bloody ears of corn, a hen has changed into a cock.[1] The sights are reported to the senate, the senate takes official notice and consults the experts. The latter indicate which gods are angry and how they can be appeased ritually. Their advice is then fully and publicly carried out. When this procedure took place, as it normally did, before the consul and the armies left the city at the start of the campaigning season, the effect must have been to establish confidence that heavenly diplomacy was being maintained and that sons and fathers going to campaign would have powerful supernatural allies.[2]

It was well known that prodigies were reported more frequently and more sensationally in times of stress—for example, while Hannibal was invading Italy and winning his victories.[3] Moreover disastrous events such as flood, fire, disease, or defeat might themselves be treated as portents.[4] Thus the institution

---

[1] Liv. xii. 1. 8.
[2] On expiation: P. Händel (1959), 2290–5 F. Luterbacher (1904), 33–43.
[3] Liv. xxii. 10.
[4] Disease: iv. 21. 25; v. 13. 4; vii. 2; xxxvii. 44. 7; xl. 19; but ibid. 37: after three years of plague poisoners (i.e. scapegoats) were sought as well as ritual appeasement. Earthquakes: Liv. xxxiv. 55. On ritual measures taken after defeats in second Punic war see Warde Fowler (1923), 316–29. On expiation of Tiber floods, famines, etc., see L. Wülker (1903), 21 ff.

was employed most intensely when public anxiety was at a peak
and reassurance most needed. The ancients were helpless in
many situations. Helplessness creates tension and fear, and
since the world was thought to be governed by supernatural
forces the tension took the form of religious fear—in fact it is
precisely the situation described by the Latin word *religio*.[1] In
the circumstances sensational and dramatic ritual measures
might bring relief. Thus after the Romans had lost the battle of
Lake Trasimene to Hannibal it was decided after consultation
of the religious authorities that a vow to Mars must be performed afresh and more fully, great games vowed to Jupiter,
and temples to Venus Erycina and Mens, that a supplication
and *lectisternium* be held, and that the people should be asked to
vote a 'sacred spring'. The vow of the 'sacred spring' involved
the offering-up of 'whatever the spring should produce from
herds of swine, sheep and oxen' to Jupiter in five years' time if
the Roman state should have got through the war safely until
that date. The great games were to cost no less than 333,333
asses. As many as 300 oxen were to be slaughtered for Jupiter,
and other oxen for other deities. All the inhabitants with their
wives and children processed through the streets of the city to
make supplication at the couches of the gods set out as for
dinner.[2] The combination of massive sacrifices, processions,
and vows must have made a deep impression: something was
being done. This would calm the emotions, reduce defeatism,
and obviate the search for scapegoats. An atmosphere was
created in which senate and people could decide on future
strategy in a rational manner. Without such an atmosphere the
republican institutions could hardly begin to work.

It was of course a feature of Roman divination that it was
employed not merely in special circumstances but constantly.
The constitutional authority which entitled a Roman magistrate
to give orders, the *imperium*, had a religious counterpart, the
auspicium, which entitled its holder to receive divine communications on behalf of the community by taking the auspices.[3] The
relevant signs were mainly seen in the flight of birds or in

---

[1] Definition of *religio*: Gel. iv. 9. Another definition, Cic. *N.D.* ii. 28 (72); cf.
pp. 117 and 270 below.
[2] Liv. xxi. 9–10.
[3] Th. Mommsen, *R.St.* i. 96–7 lists occasions when auspices were taken.

meteorological phenomena but breaches in formal business procedure (e.g. of the voting process) would also be considered significant.[1] No doubt in the great majority of cases the auspices revealed divine approval so that the ceremony was little more than an impressive formality.[2]

With the British constitution in mind Bagehot wrote: 'In constitutions there are two parts—not indeed separable with microscopic accuracy, for the genius of great affairs abhors nicety of division: first those which excite and preserve the reverence of the population—the dignified parts, if I may call them so; and next, the efficient parts—those by which it in effect works.' Divination certainly contributed to the 'dignified part' of the Roman constitution, helping to gain popular reverence for decisions reached by constitutional process. If an assembly was held after favourable signs had been seen, and if no unfavourable signs were observed during the meeting, the decision voted, whether judicial, legislative, or electoral, would be deemed to have received divine approval.[3]

Important decisions of magistrates too were preceded by consultation of the gods. No doubt the ceremony was usually a dignified formality—but not always. In war a general's decision whether or not to fight a battle would inevitably be a difficult one taken in an atmosphere of apprehension. Divination enabled the commander to share responsibility with the gods and to avoid the subsequent charges, whether of irresponsible foolhardiness or of cowardice.[4]

The auspices also provided a procedure which ensured that

[1] Ibid. 78–87 lists signs.

[2] The extreme of formalism was reached when a recently elected magistrate took the auspices for the first time and an *invented* report of lightning was taken to signify divine approval. See Th. Mommsen, *R.St.* i. 81 on Dion. Hal. ii. 6. 2. Another once important ceremony, the 'departure auspices' of a commander leaving the city for a campaign went out of use in the last years of the republic (perhaps after 53–52): Cic. *Div.* ii. 77; *N.D.* ii. 9 and R. M. Ogilvie, *J.R.S.* lix (1969), 280–1. On auspices in general see Th. Mommsen, *R.St.* i. 76–116, E. Meyer (1961), 123–6. It is characteristic that the mandate to communicate with the gods is conferred by the senate or, strictly, the patrician senators and only confirmed by the gods. A. Magdelain (1964), 198–203; id. (1962), 226; id. (1968).

[3] W. Bagehot (1964), 61. On circumstances of divination see Th. Mommsen, *R.St.* i. 101 ff.; before judicial assemblies: Liv. xl. 12; Cic. *Har. Resp.* 18 (45).

[4] In the field, consultation of chickens (*auspicia ex tripudiis*) and of the entrails of sacrificial animals was used. See *R.St.* i. 83–4. Divination before battle: Liv. viii. 6. 12 (340); ix. 14. 3–4; xxii. 42. 7–9; xliv. 37. 12; xxxv. 48. 13. The gods were also consulted before the army crossed a river.

after conspicuous failure by magistrates their successors could start with an absolutely clean sheet. It was called 'renewing the auspices' and its effect was not only the emergence of new leaders but a renewal of the system of communication with heaven. The consuls resigned and successors were elected without any participation of the discredited leaders, under the presidency of a nominee of the senate, an *interrex*. The interposition of an *interrex* not only prevented the unsuccessful leaders from influencing the election of their successors but was also thought to confer on the new magistrates a more effective and reinvigorated *auspicium*. This happened, for instance, in 392 at a time of plague and threatening prodigies, and again in 389 when the procedure prevented the consular tribunes (during whose term of office Rome had been captured by the Gauls) from presiding at the election of their successors.[1]

An important occasion for taking the auspices was when a magistrate left Rome at the beginning of a campaign. It was obviously of great concern to everybody that the army should march with divine approval. A commander who had omitted the ceremony was not in possession of the full authority to command troops. This did not mean that the soldiers would necessarily refuse to obey him, but it could cause difficulties. The institution was used by the senate to maintain control over the consuls, and it also provided a certain safeguard against usurpation of command in the field: since the ceremony had to be performed at Rome itself, the full divinely sanctioned power to command troops could not be seized on campaign.[2]

A paradoxical effect of the regular use of divination may well have been to make possible a very secular, and therefore seemingly modern, form of politics. Divination freed the state from fear that its agents were irritating the gods, and so made possible the taking of decisions by objective considerations, unhampered by taboos or religious scruples. A Roman Nicias need

---

[1] v. 31–2 (392); vi. 1 (389). Cf. also vi. 5–6 (387) 'ab recenti clade superstitiosis principibus'; viii. 3. 3 (340); ix. 7. 12–14; xxiii. 19. 3 (216).

[2] Th. Mommsen, *R.St.* i. 99; E. Meyer (1961), 125. Used to control a consul: Liv. xxi. 63. 5. Required by soldiers: Liv. xli. 10. 7 (177 B.C.). Even as late as 47 B.C. the republican opponents of Caesar did not feel entitled to create new magistrates overseas, i.e. otherwise than at Rome (Dio, xli. 43. 2)—although they had consecrated an *auguraculum*; but Octavian 'auspicated' his imperium at Spoletum in 43 B.C. (*I.L.S.* 112).

not have been deterred by an eclipse of the moon from starting a withdrawal that was essential for the safety of his force.[1] He would have sacrificed until his *haruspices* were in a position to announce divine approval. A Roman magistrate was elected with divine approval and kept testing divine approval as long as he was in office. As a result he had no need to base his public acts on anything other than law, precedent, or public advantage.

Divination was intimately linked with the taking of decisions. Normally it did little more than provide routine confirmation. But from time to time its use resulted in postponement, prevention, or reversal of a decision. The effects of this were most far-reaching and controversial when the decision reversed was the vote of a popular assembly.[2] The most notorious examples occurred in the last years of the republic when divination was used *inter alia* to obstruct legislation.[3] But if we look at the history of the republic as a whole this was not typical. For most of republican history divination was used not against legislative decisions[4] but electoral ones.[5] Even this happened only rarely, perhaps on eight or nine occasions in a century. Numbers might be increased slightly if we include indirect religious intervention

[1] Nicias need not have been deterred either: Thucydides, vii. 50. 4 with K. J. Dover's note in A. W. Gomme, A. Andrewes, and K. J. Dover, *Commentary on Thucydides*, iv. 428–9. An eclipse was capable of various interpretations. The real obstacle to departure lay in Nicias' inhibitions. For Greek attitudes in general, see W. K. Pritchett (1971), chs. viii 'Sacrifice before Battle' and ix 'Phases of the Moon and Festivals'.

[2] Cic. *Leg.* ii. 12 (31): the formidable powers of the augurs; ibid. iii. 12. (27): the political function of the auspices: 'ut multos inutiles comitiatus probabiles impedirent morae'. Divination provided three ways of preventing a meeting from reaching a decision: (1) the presiding magistrate (other than a tribune) would take the auspices early in the morning. If the signs were unfavourable, there could be no meeting. (2) In the course of the meeting an individual might observe a sign indicating divine displeasure. If the magistrate accepted it, the meeting would have to be dismissed. If the sign was seen by an augur it *had* to be accepted. (3) Another magistrate might observe lightning. Again the meeting would come to an end. I am sure that this system of checks would only survive as long as it was used sparingly. See E. Meyer (1961), 194–5.

[3] See A. W. Lintott (1968), 132–48 (annulment of laws passed by violence).

[4] All examples known to me are from the first century. The possibility may have been created by the *leges Aelia et Fufia*. A. E. Astin (1964), 421–45 suggests that the laws were intended to prevent legislation such as had enabled Scipio Aemilianus to stand for the consulate though not qualified, and that the device was used instead of a tribune's veto when a vetoing tribune was likely to be deposed by the assembly. Also on *leges A. e. F.*: W. McDonald (1929), 164 ff., G. V. Sumner (1963), 337 ff.

[5] See Appendix, p. 309, below.

through manipulation of the calendar[1] or the institution of games.[2] Even so religious interference in the results of voting remains exceptional.

In the earlier republic from time to time the election of a magistrate was 'vitiated', that is, it was declared invalid on the grounds that it had in some way contravened the auspices. Like the sighting of prodigies, the 'vitiation' of elections occurred most frequently in times of stress, when political conflict was intense, or when war was threatening, or going badly, notably while Hannibal was in occupation of part of Italy.[3] It is probably significant that the office vitiated most often was the dictatorship. For a dictator was not (with the famous exception of Fabius Maximus in 217) elected by the people, but appointed by a consul on the advice of the senate. His vitiation did not therefore overthrow a popular vote. Moreover the appointment of a dictator was something like a proclamation of emergency. He held exceptional powers for an exceptional task, to deal with a military emergency or, more frequently, to hold an election. There was bound to be controversy about such an appointment, and if opposition was too strong vitiation might conceivably provide a retreat without loss of face.[4]

The use of divination for obstruction extended beyond the annual elections. It could be used to delay the start of a campaign,[5] or to keep troops at home, or to stop a trial before the assembly, or to prevent a victorious commander from advancing too far, or to prevent an aqueduct from being built.[6] This kind of thing did not happen very often, but it was one of the weapons at the disposal of the senate if it wanted to keep magistrates in their place.

In theory, the field for the use of divination for obstructive purposes was unlimited, but in practice this was far from being the case.[7] Religious obstruction appears to have been acceptable

---

[1] Manipulation of calendar: Censorinus, 20. 7; Dio, xl. 62. 1. Use of festivals to postpone *comitia*: Cic. *Ad. Q. Fr.* ii. 4. 4; *Ad Fam.* viii. 11. 1. Caesar, *B.G.* ii. 35. Plut. *Sull.* 8. 3. App. *B.C.* i. 56. 5; 59. 6.

[2] Liv. xxxii. 9. 28; xxi. 63. 5.

[3] See Appendix.

[4] On the dictatorship see Th. Mommsen, *R.St.* ii. 141–72; E. Meyer (1961), 158–60; J. Jahn (1970). See also E. S. Staveley (1954–5).

[5] Liv. xlv. 12. 12 (168).

[6] xl. 42. 10; cf. Cic. *Dom.* 17 (45); Liv. xxxviii. 48 (190); Frontin. *Aqu.* i. 7.

[7] G. K. Park (1963), 196: 'for every society in which divination is practised

in some areas but not in others. We never hear that divination interfered with a meeting of the senate. I know of no trial before a magistrate being interrupted for religious reasons. The new type of jury court of the later republic, the *quaestio*, seems to have been similarly immune. We have seen that for the greater part of republican history the inhibiting capacity of divination was used against individuals not against policies. It was not a means of cowing the masses. It was rather a device by which the nobility as a whole, as represented in the senate, could exercise control over individual nobles. In the post-Gracchan period the political scope of divination was extended. A number of laws were vitiated on grounds which were at least formally derived from divination, inasmuch as the claim was made that the laws had been passed contrary to the auspices (*contra auspicia latas*).[1] The most important occasion when this claim was made was in 91 B.C. when it was put forward by the opponents of Livius Drusus' proposal to enfranchise the Italians. The annulment of the law led directly to the disastrous social war. In this case the infringement of the auspices consisted of a breach of procedure rather than neglect of a heavenly sign: in contravention of a recent law Livius Drusus had made his franchise proposals part of an omnibus-bill.[2] Other laws were annulled as *contra auspicia latas* in 99 and 60.[3] But a new chapter in the history of religious obstruction began in the last decade of the republic. It was now used regularly both against elections and legislation,[4] employing the seemingly new device of *spectio*.[5] In practice this seems to have become something of a substitute for the tribunician veto.[6] In this period religious obstruction was not used as an instrument of the nobility as a whole, now hopelessly divided,[7] but by factions or individuals. While it had some effect on public opinion, it was not successful in blocking the opposed measures.[8]

there is a proper list of its occasions. Such a list may say much about the sources of strain in that society.'

[1] A. Lintott (1968), 134.   [2] Ibid. 142 on Ascon. 68–9C.
[3] *Lex Titia* of 99 B.C.: Cic. *Leg.* ii. 14 and 31. Obseq. 40. *Lex Manilia* of 66 B.C.: Dio, xxxvi. 42. 2–3; Ascon. 46C. Perhaps also Saturninus' law in 100 B.C.: App. *B.C.* i. 30. 1 and 6; Aur. Vict. *Vir. Ill.* 73.
[4] A. Lintott (1968).
[5] See E. Marbach, P.W. 2 R. iii, A2, 1570–83.
[6] See above, p. 13 n. 4.
[7] D. R. Shackleton Bailey (1960).
[8] For the facts see E. S. Gruen (1974).

At a time when secular constitutional checks proved inadequate, religious reinforcements were sought—but to bridge differences which were too wide to be bridged. The new use of religion is an aspect of the collapse of the political institutions of the republic. It is no coincidence that the breaking of the last frantic wave of political divination coincides with the first triumvirate.

To sum up: a principal purpose of the institution was to preserve morale and to prevent panic among the populace at large in times of stress. More specifically, divination contributed to the reverence and confidence with which the political institutions were regarded. It gave greater authority to the magistrates elected by the people and to the decisions made by them. More intermittently, divination supplied a means of controlling the political process. It made possible from time to time the reversal of a constitutional act, a vote by the people, or the appointment of a dictator without destroying the constitutional rule.[1] Even if a magistrate's election was not vitiated, divination might be used to hamper him in the exercise of his office. Control was carried out by the senate in co-operation with the colleges of priests. But it would be a mistake to conclude that divination, or indeed religion, provided the only, or even the principal, means of control. The religious safeguards were paralleled by numerous equally elaborate and significant secular ones. One need only mention the way group voting favoured the countrymen as against the city dwellers, or the rights which enabled the presiding officer to influence the outcome of voting. Compared with these, religious obstruction could have only a very limited effect on the Roman political process. After all, the utmost that the diviners could do was to propose the postponement of a vote. This was not insignificant because the composition of the popular assemblies, and hence

---

[1] Breaches of rules sanctioned by divination: In 42 B.C. a Sibylline oracle ordered celebration of Caesar's birthday to be transferred from 13 July, the principal day of Apollo's Games, to 12 July. In this way Apollo was placated without 'loss of face' to Augustus: Dio, xlvii. 18. 6. In 44 B.C. a *Xvvir* was to report a Sibylline oracle that the Parthians could only be conquered by a king: Suet. *Caes.* 79. 3; Cic. *Div.* ii. 54 (110). This was no doubt meant to induce someone to offer Caesar a crown without Caesar's asking for it, cf. Weinstock (1971), 340. See also G. K. Park (1963): 'among the Yoruba of Nigeria, the diviner provides a legitimizing sanction upon a process of structural realignment which depending as it does upon a voluntary act would be difficult to sanction otherwise.' Problems such as inter-racial marriage in a contemporary multi-racial society would be helped by a working system of divination.

their political interest, varied from day to day and season to season. Divination provided not a blocking but a delaying mechanism. It might prevent hasty decisions from being taken by a temporary majority under the influence of passing emotion. But it could not be used to thwart permanently even a well-supported individual, let alone an overwhelmingly powerful group such as Pompey, Crassus, and Caesar made.

The above account of Roman divination appears to assume that every religious intervention in politics was purposive and represented manipulation in a particular interest. This was certainly very often the case, but it cannot be the whole story. There must have been some examples of religious obstruction which were purely accidental, or at least not manœuvred by any interested group. It is of course very difficult to distinguish such cases from those whose instigation was political. But in fact religious checks and balances could only work because they were thought to be at least in part above conflicting interest.[1] The theory was that the augurs, *haruspices*, and *quindecimviri* were practising a science bound by strict rules of evidence, that based its interpretations on a large body of empirically confirmed precedent.[2] Without some such belief in the independence of the signs and their interpretation, soldiers would not have been encouraged or restrained by them, and politicians would not have been induced to overlook the breaking of constitutional rules.

From time to time the institution is likely to have demonstrated its independence, when naturally occurring signs coerced a magistrate, as it were, out of the blue. Perhaps the voting of a law was postponed one day,[3] or an election unexpectedly reversed.[4] Even in the rationalist age of the late republic striking signs that had indubitably been noticed could not be ignored. For example, a startling and puzzling noise was heard near Rome and provoked a consultation of *haruspices*.

---

[1] On the need for independence see G. K. Park (1963), 198; also K. Thomas (1971), 423 ff. Pure accidents may be represented by instances of magistrates obliged to 'seek again' their auspices, e.g. Liv. viii. 30. 14; x. 3. 6; xxiii. 19. 2.

[2] Cic. *Div.* i. 3 (6); 14 (25); 57 (131); *Dom.* 2. 4.

[3] Liv. ix. 38. 5–39. 1.

[4] Election vitiated by death of a returning officer: Cic. *N.D.* ii. 4 (10–11); *Div.* ii. 35 (77). In 152 *prodigia* brought about resignation of all magistrates (Obseq. 152).

The soothsayers' response duly provided Clodius with a political weapon against Cicero.[1] It enabled him to reopen[2] the question of the validity of the restoration of Cicero's house, although the affair seemed to have been finally and authoritatively settled by a law of the assembly and a decision of the *pontifices* confirmed by the senate.[3] Turning to a different context one also wonders if Cassius would have reduced the circumference of his camp if a swarm of bees had not settled in part of it.[4] Unfavourable signs were observed at inconvenient moments, and Julius Caesar was exceptional in his readiness to ignore them, or to improvise a far-fetched but favourable interpretation.[5]

Even a suspect sign might develop independent power of its own. The famous Sibylline oracle that the king of Egypt was not to be supported with 'a multitude' was widely thought to have been invented by political opponents who wished to prevent Pompey from being given the mission of restoring the king.[6] The oracle nevertheless achieved its object, and Pompey was not sent to Egypt. Eventually the king was restored by Gabinius, and his restoration was followed by an unusually damaging flood of the Tiber. This seemed to confirm the genuineness of the oracle, and among the people religious worry rose to a high pitch. Gabinius was in great danger. He was accused in court, found guilty, and driven into exile, while his property was confiscated.[7]

But if divination occasionally introduced an unpredictable element into Roman public life,[8] its rules were drawn up in such

[1] Cic. *Har. Resp.* 10 (20).

[2] Ibid. 7 (14).

[3] Ibid. 6 (11–13). On circumstances see P. T. Wiseman (1974), 137. An essential precondition of the reopening was that Cicero had recently offended Pompey: *Ad. Q. F.* ii. 6. 1; *Ad Fam.* 1. 9. 8.

[4] Obseq. 59. Of course he might have realized only after the camp had been fortified that the long periphery was not defensible.

[5] S. Weinstock (1971), 98, 116, 342, on signs at Caesar's departure against Pompey (Dio, xli. 39. 2); his departure for Africa (Cic. *Div.* ii. 52; Suet. *Caes.* 59); on arrival in Africa (Suet. ibid.); before Munda (App. *B.C.* ii. 116 (488); Polyaen. viii. 23. 33; Suet. *Caes.* 77).

[6] Cic. *Ad Fam.* i. 1. 1; 4. 2.

[7] Dio, xxxix. 12. 3; 15–16; 57; cf. also *Ad Fam.* i. 1. 3; 2. 1; 7. 4; 9; *Ad Q. Fr.* ii. 2. 3. Cf. also the Vestal scandal of 114: Plut. *Quaest. Rom.* 83 (284); Oros. v. 15. 20–2; Obseq. 37; Dio, xxvii, fr. 87 when the prodigium of a girl killed by lightning happening at a time of stress led to a witch-hunt, executions, and even human sacrifice. On this, E. S. Gruen (1969), 131; id. (1968), 59 ff.

[8] Surely nobody foresaw that the *augurium salutis* of 63 B.C. would be stopped by

a way that it could not seriously divert the state from the course
on which its leaders had set it. This was partly a result, as we
shall see, of the composition of the boards, but even more of the
fact that the working of the institution was supervised by the
senate, who made the decision as to whether the experts in
divination would be consulted and how far their recommendations were to be carried out.[1]

I think it can be accepted that by and large the working of
the institution of divination was sensitive to the needs of the
state.[2] One must assume that diviners' interpretations were
influenced by the circumstances as they saw them. Frequently
divination will have been rather like tossing a coin before a
match: it did not matter which decision was favoured provided
there was a clear recommendation. But when the decision was
of far-reaching inportance, such as the appointment of consuls
during the Hannibalic war,[3] or the right moment to begin
a battle, interpretation was surely determined by the diviners'
reading of the needs of the situation.

It was not for nothing that augurs were selected from the best
families,[4] and that good personal relations with members of the
college was an important qualification for the priesthood.[5] As
a result their advice will have tended to reflect the consensus of
the nobility. When the nobility was deeply divided in the last
years of the republic, the institution could not work. *Haruspices*
were Etruscans, men of leading Etruscan families but not
necessarily Roman citizens. One would expect their answers to

the augur Appius Claudius (Dio, xxxvii. 24. 1; Cic. *Div.* i. 47 (105)). But for all his
well-known piety Appius would presumably not have taken the sign so seriously if
he had not been aware of an imminent threat to public order.

[1] Senatorial control of divination: Th. Mommsen, *R.St.* iii. 2. 1059–62.

[2] E. Rawson (1974) deals with extension of popular control to the election and
disciplining of priests, in order to bring constitutional position of priests closer to
that of magistrates.

[3] See Appendix.

[4] D. Hahn (1963), 73–85. As a general rule the colleges were recruited from
young men of good families with no more than one man from each, and no more
than one priesthood per man. The priests thus represented noble houses rather
than themselves. Some outstanding men never became priests. See also M. W.
Hoffmann Lewis (1952), 289 ff.; C. Bardt (1871). On recruitment see Th. Mommsen, *R.St.* ii. 24 ff.; L. R. Taylor, *A.J.Ph.* lxiii (1942), 385 ff.; also *Class. Phil.*
xxxvii (1942), 421; A. Klose (1910).

[5] Good relations with colleagues: see G. Wissowa (1895), 2319, on Cic. *Ad Fam.*
iii. 10. 9; also Hahn, op. cit. 82 n. 30. L. R. Taylor, *Party Politics* (1949), 90, 94–5,
shows how a divided college lost effectiveness.

correspond fairly closely to the expectations of the men who consulted them.[1]

It is not suggested that signs and their interpretation was a conscious fraud in which experts conspired with the authorities to deceive the credulous multitude. It is likely that while the institution was working properly, that is up to the first century (and perhaps even after that) the priests were sincere.[2] That this is psychologically possible is shown by the working of divination in contemporary primitive societies. Among the Ifa of Nigeria, for instance, it is important for a practising diviner to be thought honest and objective, and the system has safeguards to ensure his honesty. At the same time, it is necessary for divination to produce socially beneficial advice. In fact, the system employed enables the questioner to choose his own answer, while both he and the diviner think that the answer is provided by the deity. Divination enables the client to think out his own solution to the problem, but owing to a 'kink' in human psychology, the real working of the system is not scrutinized.[3] Roman divination recognized a vast number of trivial warning signs. In normal times they were ignored, but the pressure of a particular situation would draw attention to any sign that happened to be observable and to be relevant. It is not necessary to assume insincerity. As for conscious deception of the credulous masses, the persons restrained by divine prohibitions were as a rule not the public in general, but members of the most sophisticated part of it, the nobility itself.

It has often been suggested that the political exploitation of religion in the late republic is a symptom of religious decay. That is probably a mistake. There were changes in the way religion was exploited in Roman politics, but the fact of its exploitation goes back as far as our information about the politics of Rome. The Roman calendar for instance was at least a semi-religious institution. It laid down the dates for religious festivals, it was maintained by a college of priests, the *pontifices*, and failure to comply with it by hearing a lawsuit on a so-called *dies nefastus* had to be religiously expiated with a *piaculum*.[4] But

[1] Cic. *Div.* i. 41 (92); cf. *N.D.* ii. 11; *Ad Fam.* vi. 18. 1. See also J. Heurgon (1953).
[2] H. H. Scullard (1951), esp. 28, has it otherwise.
[3] W. Bascom (1969).
[4] On political manipulation of the calendar see above, p. 2 nn. 4–6. Lawsuits on *dies nefasti*: Varr. *L.L.* vi. 30, 53.

the calendar was also an institution of the greatest possible political significance, as it limited the number of days on which a popular assembly could be held. Festivals were days on which the people could not meet. Moreover, very soon after the Roman calendar had been published in writing, it was decided to reduce the number of days available for assemblies still further by establishing a separate category of *dies comitiales*. The intention must have been to limit the scope for popular politics. But this was probably as early as 287 B.C., when presumably there can have been no question of religious decay.[1]

It is practically certain that the patricians used religious arguments during the Struggle of Orders. The plebeian claim to the consulate was countered with the assertion that only patricians were qualified to communicate with the gods through the auspices. Indeed, long after the plebeians had won their claim it was thought that the patrician senators were the real custodians of the auspices, plebeian magistrates merely the users of them.[2] But this religious fortification of patrician privilege must antedate the Licinian-Sextian legislation of 366. It is likely that religion was used to maintain patrician claims from the beginning.

The Romans lacked any sense that religion is sullied if it is exploited for sectional interest, and that the gods must be fair to all sections of society. Also they do not seem to have thought that the gods resented having their names taken in vain. Roman religion was in many ways different from the religion of the Bible. Roman gods could be laughed at.[3] An individual might be compared to a god[4] even to the god's disadvantage,[5]

---

[1] A. Michels (1967), ch. 3 '*dies comitiales* and *dies fasti*'.

[2] Speeches like that of Appius Claudius, *Liv.* vi. 40. 4 ff. of 368 are of course not historical, but his claim 'nobis adeo propria sunt auspicia ut non solum quos populos creat patricios magistratus non aliter quam auspicato creet sed nos quoque ipsi sine suffragio populi auspicato interregem prodamus' remained part of the constitution even though plebeians became eligible for patrician office. See Th. Mommsen *R.St.* i. 90–1.

[3] Comedy has not only the plot of Plautus' *Amphitruo*, which might be explained away as Greek, but numerous examples of the comic use of Roman ritual language, e.g. *Cist.* ii. 1. 45. Other references in J. A. Hanson (1959). Cf. also Cic. *Dom.* 34 (92) and various elaborations of the Bona Dea myth, on which see T. P. Wiseman (1974), 185–6; also the humour of Hor. *Sat.* i. 8. 2–3: 'faber incertus scamnum faceretne Priapum, . . . deus inde ego'. See also Pliny, *N.H.* xxxiii (24) 83.

[4] See J. A. Hanson (1959), 69 and Cic. *Red. Sen.* 4 (8); cf. also Cicero's use of *divinus* set out in H. Merguet (1887).   [5] e.g. Cic. *N.D.* i. 28 (79).

and benefits received from a man might be praised as superior to divine benefits.[1] In Roman religion, as opposed to Greek-influenced literature, the personalities of even the great gods are of no practical consequence.[2] As a result the Romans could arrange their relationships with the gods without worrying about so personal an attribute as divine jealousy. Certainly there is no evidence that anybody was ever shocked by the use of the gods to defend a political position.[3] The Romans of the late republic were only too eager to point out how far their own generation fell short of the ancestors. The tale of degeneration includes the neglect of religion but not its political abuse.

The question of decline in belief is a very difficult one. The development of religion at Rome is not simply a matter of the growth of rationalism, but also of the decline of one kind of belief being balanced by the growth of another.[4] One such change is clearly observable in the Roman attitude to divination. In the middle of the second century Cato had wondered how a *haruspex* could pass a colleague in the street without winking,[5] and about the same time Tiberius Gracchus the Elder had rejected a recommendation of these same soothsayers with the words: 'Who are you Tuscan barbarians to know the Roman constitution?'[6] The *haruspices* were Etruscan foreigners, not yet entirely part of Roman religion. But in the course of the second century consultation of *haruspices* became more frequent, and of the other diviners relatively less so, and this trend continued to the end of the republic and beyond. The emperor Claudius was the first to organize *haruspices* in a college, and their science played an important part in the last revival of paganism in the late fourth century.[7] The college of augurs on the other hand, traditionally the most influential, was consulted

---

[1] *Red. Quir.* 8 (18); *Red. Sen.* 1 (2); cf. 4 (9).

[2] This does not necessarily mean that they had no personalities (cf. below p. 177 n. 5), but ritual treated the gods pimersonally like remote and powerful officials.

[3] Speeches like Liv. iv. 2. 5; iv. 6. 1 ff.; v. 14. 2; vii. 6. 7 ff.; x. 6. 3 are not historical but show the kind of arguments that later Romans thought would have been made in the situation. Livy was not in the least shocked by this use of religion, but neither did he think that such arguments ought to be decisive. Cf. also Cic. *Amic.* 96; *Pis.* 9–10; *Vat.* 23.

[4] Cf. G. K. Park (1963), 99, on fashion in divination among the Yoruba of Nigeria.

[5] Cic. *Div.* ii. 24 (52).   [6] *N.D.* 2 (11).

[7] See above, p. 20 n. 1, also P.W. vii. 2, 243–4, 246–7, s.v. Haruspices.

less frequently in later years and in this case it is clearly correct to talk of loss of belief.[1] Cicero writing as a philosopher was convinced that augury as carried out in his time did not communicate with the gods.[2] The science had once been known but was now forgotten.[3] Marcellus, a fellow augur, went as far as to maintain that the science had never existed.[4] A third colleague, Appius Claudius, was a believer[5] but in this he seems to have been unusual.[6] Now in the decline of faith in augury (the social prestige of the college remained as high as ever) rational arguments such as those found in Cicero's *De Divinatione* presumably played a part. But if we look at the development in a wider perspective, it is obvious that other factors were involved. Augury as practised on campaign observed the feeding habits of caged chickens which were carried with the army. It is perhaps not surprising that it should have been superseded by haruspicy. It was easier to take seriously the entrails of sacrificial animals than the feeding of hens.[7] Another weakness of augury was its close association with the popular assemblies at Rome. A great part of the professional knowledge of the augurs concerned the circumstances and procedure of the assemblies. The decline in the use and prestige of augury must not be seen in isolation from the contemporary disorganization of the popular assemblies, and from the fact of their eventual loss of power. Haruspicy had no special relationship with the meetings of the Roman people.[8]

The period of the early empire also saw a great increase in the importance of astrology. It will be argued later that this was not a coincidence. The decline and rise of religious institutions at Rome kept step with that of the political institutions of which they formed part.[9]

---

[1] *Div.* i. 15 (26); 16 (28).

[2] ii. 33 (70): retinetur autem et ad opinionem vulgi et ad magnas utilitates rei publicae . . . ius augurium collegi auctoritas. Ibid. (71): haec certe, quibus utimur, sive tripudio, sive de caelo simulacra sunt auspiciorum auspicia nullo modo. See also ii. 36 (77). [3] *Leg.* ii. 13 (32) of 52 B.C. or later.

[4] Cic. *Leg.* ii. 13 (32-3); *Div.* ii. 33 (70-1). [5] *Leg.* ii. 13 (32).

[6] *Div.* i. 47 (105): 'quem irridebant collegae tui'. At marriages augury had become an empty formality, the *auspex* being no more than a witness. (Cic. *Cluent.* 14.)

[7] In private ritual haruspicy largely replaced augury, *Div.* i. 16 (28). Even this was used less than formerly.

[8] Cf. p. 8 n. 4 above. [9] See below, pp. 125, 136-7.

In fact the Roman system of divination, like all such deeply rooted institutions, seems to have contained a very effective inbuilt mechanism to shield it both from rational criticism and from refutation by events.[1] To a considerable extent Roman divination was protected by the vagueness of its theoretical principles. At first sight it appears to be a technique for receiving indications of the state of mind of gods. But its working often implied that the divine state of mind revealed by the diviners had no objective existence at all. It was for instance a principle of Roman divination that a sign only became significant when it had been recognized and accepted.[2] In the teaching of augurs it was a fundamental principle 'that neither evil omens (*dirae*) nor *auspices* affect those who at the outset of any undertaking declare that they take no notice of them. No greater instance of the divine indulgence of mercy could be found than this boon.'[3] Romans behaved accordingly. We read that Marcellus drove into battle in a closed carriage in order not to notice unfavourable signs. During a crisis in 193 the senate forbade the reporting of earthquakes. Another time the senate ordered that no one should watch the heavens while the bill for Cicero's recall from exile was passing through the assembly.[4]

Similarly, the reporting of a sign which involved the dismissal of a popular assembly had to be made personally by the magistrate who had seen it to the magistrate who would preside over the assembly. When the consul Metellus wished to hold an election, and the tribune Milo wished to prevent it by *obnuntiatio*, the two men engaged in a ridiculous game of hide-and-seek, the one to serve formal notice, the other to avoid it.[5] Clearly, what made the *obnuntiatio* effective was not the sign itself, nor even the fact that a magistrate had asked for a sign,

[1] The following owes a great deal to the excellent article by H. D. Jocelyn (1966).

[2] G. Dumézil (1966), 128–9 points out a resemblance to court procedure, where it is the decision of the presiding magistrate which creates a new situation.

[3] Plin. *N.H.* xxviii. 4. 15: 'neither evil omens (*dirae*) nor auspices affect those who at the outset of any undertaking declare that they take no notice of them.' *Exemplum* to same effect: Liv. x. 40. 9 ff. The rule applies not to divination alone: contact with death disqualified a man from performing a sacrifice, but it was possible to evade disqualification by not acknowledging the death—*funus non agnoscere*: Servius, *in Aen.* xi. 2; Liv. ii. 8. 7 (dedication of temple of Jupiter).

[4] Marcellus: Cic. *Div.* ii. 77. Earthquakes: Liv. xxxiv. 35 (193 B.C.). Senate forbids *obnuntiatio*: Cic. *Sest.* 129; cf. *Ad Att.* i. 16. 13.

[5] Cic. *Ad Att.* iv. 3. 4.

but the formal announcement correctly made by the magistrate making the objection to the magistrate who was to be restrained.

The same form of thought is implied in the practice of the 'forced portent'. It was quite in order to starve sacred chickens so that at the right moment they should snatch their food greedily with the result that some of the corn would drop out of their beaks. This was the required favourable omen and would be formally announced to the troops.[1]

From the 'forced portent' it is not far to the transformation of incidental words or actions into a sign by the mere ceremony of formally receiving them as such. After Rome had been sacked by the Gauls, the senate was debating whether the city should be transferred to the site of Veii. An officer was heard halting his troops with the command 'We will remain here'. The words were immediately received as an omen and the proposed move to Veii given up.[2]

On the other hand, a chance word or deed might have portentous significance even if it was not accepted. This was particularly worrying if the potential significance was unfavourable.[3] In that situation a Roman would almost automatically seek to avert or divert the unhappy outcome. Late in the second Punic war, Fabius Maximus warned the senate that if Scipio was allowed to invade Africa, Hannibal might exploit the situation to attack Rome itself. Then, worried that his very warning might bring about the feared event, he added 'may the gods turn aside the omen'.[4] A similar precaution was taken by Thrasea Paetus, the famous champion of senatorial freedom. When he had cut his veins in accordance with a decree the senate had voted on the orders of Nero, he sprinkled some blood on to the ground and, turning to the quaestor who had brought the death sentence, he said, 'This is a libation to Jupiter the Liberator. Watch me, young man, for you have been born into an age in which it is advantageous to strengthen one's resolution with examples of fortitude.' But while he was speaking the thought struck him that this gesture might cause another to

[1] Th. Mommsen, *R.St.* i. 83–5; Cic. *Div.* i. 15 (28); ii. 34 (72–3).
[2] Liv. v. 55. Other examples of accepted omens: i. 55. 4; i. 7. 11; ix. 14. 8; xxii. 37. 5–12; xxix. 27. 12.
[3] e.g. Liv. xli. 18. 7.
[4] xxviii. 42.

suffer his own fate and so he included the phrase, 'May the gods prohibit the omen'. In due course Thrasea's son-in-law, Helvidius Priscus, also died the victim of an emperor. The gods had allowed the omen to take its deadly course.[1] There is evidence that fear of potentially ominous chance situations was widespread and deeply rooted in Roman society.[2]

The Roman annals also contain tales that show how favourable or unfavourable consequences of a chance event might hang in the balance to be turned in one sense or the other by the right word spoken at the right time. When the Romans were digging the foundations of the temple of Jupiter they found a head. Taking this to be an omen, they sent an envoy to consult a famous Etruscan seer, Olenus Calenus. He immediately saw that the find was of immensely favourable significance and tried to transfer the benefit to his own people. He drew an outline of the temple in the soil in front of him and asked the Romans: 'So what you are saying is this: *there* the temple of Jupiter is arising, *here* we found the head?' The Roman saved the situation by a prompt reply: 'We are not saying that the head was found *here*, but at Rome.'[3]

When the Roman tunnelling party emerged into the Capitol of Veii, they heard a *haruspex* promising victory to whoever would cut out the entrails of the newly slain victim. The Roman seized the entrails and thus diverted the support of the omen from the Veiians to themselves.[4] The examples are legendary but they express a real attitude. When Octavian (later the emperor Augustus) was besieging Perusia the entrails of a victim sacrificed in his camp seemed to be unfavourable. A sudden sally of the besieged captured the victim with all apparatus of sacrifice. Immediately the *haruspices* announced that since the enemy now held the unfavourable entrails the disaster would fall on them. So it proved.[5]

---

[1] Tac. *Ann.* xvi. 35. Helvidius executed by Vespasian: Suet. *Vesp.* 15.

[2] Cic. *Div.* i. 45 (102–3): precautions taken at ceremonies, especially inaugurations, so that only words of favourable omen spoken, e.g. leaders of processions and the first recruits to be called up are selected so that their names have auspicious meanings.

[3] Plin. *N.H.* xviii. 15. cf. Liv. i. 56. 6 and Ogilvie ad loc. A comparable incident: Liv. x. 27.

[4] Liv. v. 21. 8.

[5] The Perusian incident: Suet. *Aug.* 96. On this class of omens see J. Bayet (1937) and (1949).

The preceding paragraphs have illustrated the vagueness and lack of definition of the Roman belief in omens. Auspices were sometimes said to be sent by Jupiter,¹ but for a sign to be significant it was not necessary that it could be traced to a particular, or indeed to any, god. There was, as we have seen, considerable ambiguity as to whether the sign became effective when it had happened, or only when it had been formally reported, while the act of reporting could actually reverse the apparent meaning of a sign. This brings in a further ambiguity —do signs forecast or do they actually *cause* events? Sometimes Romans behaved as if this were an open question. In 54 the triumvir Marcus Crassus set out on a campaign against the Parthians in spite of an *obnuntiatio* of unfavourable omens. He duly met with disaster. Thereupon A. Claudius, the censor of 50, censured the tribune who had announced the omens on the ground that he had falsified the auspices.² The implication is that if the signs had not been announced the disaster would not have happened. Cicero disagrees. Unfavourable omens do not cause disaster, they merely foretell what will happen unless precautions are taken.³ The point here is not that Cicero was a free thinker while Appius Claudius was a believer in augury. For the purpose of the argument both take the validity of signs for granted—but their interpretations of how they worked were opposite. The tribune himself seems to have been worried by the uncertainty. Not content to wait for the effect of the neglected auspices to work on Crassus he accelerated matters by cursing him as well.⁴ But some common practices definitely implied that portents cause disaster. Why else should it have been essential that certain prodigious births, especially hermaphrodites, should be utterly destroyed?⁵

Thus the principles on which divination rested were hopelessly vague, and consequently very hard to refute. Related beliefs have survived into our times. The practice of 'touching

¹ Cic. *Div.* ii. 36 (78); i. 47 (106). Divination conceivable without a god: *Div. i.* 6 (10).

² Liv. x. 40. 9–14. Cic. *Div.* i. 16 (29). On the same incident also Cic. *Ad Att.* iv. 13; Plut. *Crass.* 16; Dio, xxxix. 35, 39; Vell. ii. 46. See *inter alia* J. Bayet (1960).

³ Cic. *Div.* i. 47 (105).

⁴ Plut. *Crass.* 16. 4–8; Vell. ii. 46; The combination of bad omens and curses also found in reports of departures of Piso and Gabinius to their provinces in 56 and 58 (Cic. *Sest.* 71). Cf. A. D. Simpson (1938).

⁵ Obseq. 59, 84, 86, 91, 93, 96; Liv. xxvii. 37. 6; xxxi. 12. 7; xxxix. 22. 5.

wood', reluctance to walk under ladders, avoidance of the number thirteen, all resist rationalism just because they are not based on precisely defined, and therefore refutable, principles. It is not easy to refute such beliefs empirically either. To be conclusive the demonstration would require the assembly of a complete statistical record of signs and their fulfilment or non-fulfilment. This would have been unthinkable in Antiquity. In the absence of statistics the proof or disproof must be based on memory which is inevitably selective. Significant successes of divination would be remembered,[1] and embodied in edifying *exempla* for school use;[2] failures could be explained on the ground that the technique had not been properly carried out,[3] or they were simply forgotten.[4] As a rule the mechanical performance of ritual would receive little attention. Neglect of some detail would scarcely be noticed, except retrospectively in the case of a disaster following.[5] Then any defect would be remembered and the importance of meticulous observation would be confirmed. It is also certain that a great many apparently successful forecasts reported in history books were invented after the event.[6] This did not prevent them from testifying to the soundness of the techniques that purported to have produced them. All in all, it is not surprising that belief in divination—if not always in the same techniques of divination—was one of the persistent features of the Roman scene.

But to state the problem in terms of belief and disbelief is too simple: quantity and quality[7] of the belief must be assessed as

[1] e.g. Cic. *Har. Resp.* 9 (18).

[2] e.g. *Div.* i. 16 (29): Publius Claudius and Lucius Junius lost fleets by going to sea after auspices were unfavourable. Crassus' catastrophe (see above, p. 27 n. 2) surely confirmed the validity of the omens reported to him. The fate of G. Flaminius (*Div.* i. 35 (77)) confirmed the validity of omens and divination through sacred chickens, and (according to Liv. xxi. 63) of the need to take auspices and offer *vota* at Rome before departing on campaign. On this phenomenon in Tudor England, see K. Thomas, op. cit. 641.

[3] *Div.* i. 55 (125); or that the prophet had eaten or drunk too much, ibid. 51 (116).

[4] Ibid. ii. 24 (32-3); 65 (134).

[5] Liv. v. 17: *vitium* recognized after military failure and oracle, cf. xli. 18.

[6] S. Weinstock, op. cit. 21-2 examines the *post eventum* prophecies of the greatness of Augustus found in Suet. *Aug.* 94-5 and Dio, xlv. 1. 3-5. See also F. Taeger (1960), 211. F. Münzer, P.W. 2 R. ii, A2, 1783-6, s.v. Servilius (Caepio) 49 shows how the story of the disgrace suffered by Caepio for appropriating booty and losing his army was developed into an *exemplum* of divine punishment for temple-robbery.

[7] Logically, one ought to distinguish between belief in the institution as a genuine

well. Some belief in the results of divination there must have been as long as the rites were more than empty ceremonies and while they were able to produce concrete effects on the lives of the Romans. In any political context for the institution to work belief must be stronger than opposition to the decision which it is invoked to favour. In some situations divination will have required no more 'belief' than the tossing of a coin. In other situations only a quite improbably strong belief would have produced acquiescence in a decision on the sole ground of it being supported by divination. Quantity of belief can be measured in terms of its political weight.[1]

It has been the purpose of this section to show that divination played an integral part in the functioning of the institutions of the republic right up to its end. The political exploitation of divination was not a symptom of decay. On the contrary, belief in divination continued unshaken among the great majority of the Roman people including the governing class. Belief in augury declined but not in divination as such. The attitudes of Lucretius and of Cicero, when he wrote *De Divinatione* ii, were exceptional in the radicalism of their rationalism.[2]

4. *Rationalism of the late republic*

There is no denying that the late republic was an age which, like our own, was not markedly concerned with the possibility that supernatural powers might intervene in its day-to-day affairs. Correct observance remained very important. But it was important only in the same way as the maintenance of constitutional procedure. This apparent secularity of the Roman

instrument of communication with heaven and belief in it as a useful constitutional device. Cicero was in no doubt that even augury was politically useful. But psychologically the distinction is less absolute. If a religious institution was undoubtedly beneficial politically this could be taken as proof of its supernatural basis; cf. also G. K. Park (1963), 99: 'the drama of the ceremony creates its own authority.'

[1] It would be worthwhile to assemble a complete list of decisions known to have been affected by divination with a view to establishing how (or whether) the persuasive power of divination changed over the years.

[2] *Div.* ii. 52 (148–9) rejects totally all forms of divination as superstition and 'superstitiones stirpe omnes eiiciendae'. The whole passage is—apart from the reference to 'praestantem aliquam aeternamque naturam'—close to the spirit of Lucretius.

attitude to religious observance was not of recent origin. Already towards the middle of the second century the authors of the *leges Aelia et Fufia* had used the same enactment to deal with both religious and secular restrictions on the holding of public assemblies.[1] But the bulk of the evidence for this attitude comes from the speeches of Cicero. For instance, Cicero lists the villainies of his enemy Clodius: Cicero's own exile, the attacks on Pompey, 'abolition' of the censorship and of tribunician *intercessio*, provinces handed over to the consuls, his partners in crime, and more of the same kind. In the middle of the list we find the 'destruction' of the auspices.[2] This is in no way singled out as being more outrageous than the constitutional and political changes. Elsewhere Cicero violently attacks a law of Clodius which restricted or abolished *obnuntiatio*, but he attacks it in secular terms, as the removal of a necessary safeguard against the *tribunicios furores*.[3] The alternative to observance of the religious safeguards is not divine punishment but political violence.[4]

Roman nobles of the late republic, unlike Jews in the client Kingdom of Judaea, felt the prospect of divine punishment to be remote. Of course, they were very familiar with the idea expounded in *exempla*, that the neglect of quite minor signs, and small ritual omissions, could have catastrophic consequences. The Roman armies were unsuccessful at Veii because magistrates whose election had been 'vitiated' had improperly mounted the Latin Games.[5] *Vitia* ignored at a later election resulted in plague.[6] A *vitium* in a dictator's appointment brought about a deep antagonism between him and his *magister equitum*.[7] Failure to fulfil a vow to Apollo was followed by civil discord.[8] Even a religiously neutral action, the election of a substitute for a deceased censor, might entail terrible consequences.[9] But this was history. In the politics of the late republic fear of divine punishment was not very evident. Perhaps the masses might fear for the food supply of Rome,[10] but in time of crisis their hope was more conspicuously centred on Gn. Pompeius than on

---

[1] See above, p. 13 n. 4. [2] *Har. Resp.* 27 (58).
[3] *Red. Sen.* 5 (11); cf. *Sest.* 15 (134); *Vat.* 7 (18); *Pis.* 5 (8–10).
[4] *Phil.* i. 25. [5] Liv. v. 17. 2.
[6] Ibid. viii. 23. 10. [7] Ibid. 30. 1.
[8] Ibid. v. 25. 4 (speech of Camillus).
[9] Ibid. ix. 34. 20. [10] Cic. *Red. Quir.* 18.

supernatural powers. The reader of Cicero's address to the senate, *De Haruspicum Responsis*, a tale of charges and counter-charges of sacrilege, is not left with the impression that fear of the gods' reaction to the various acts of sacrilege mentioned in the speech weighed heavily with Cicero. Cicero wanted to keep his house. He clearly did not believe that Clodius had brought the state into great danger of divine punishment by the actions with which he charged him. The real danger to the state, and the one of which the gods were giving warning, was the bitter division within the ranks of the senators.[1]

Again Cicero's correspondence informs us quite fully of the reaction of the senate to Clodius' violation of the rites of Bona Dea. There was no question of turning a blind eye, and the senate set up a special court to try Clodius. But many senators saw the outrage in purely political terms, and were reluctant to proceed against a member of the Claudian *gens*. Cicero was indignant, but not so much because he feared the state would suffer divine chastisement as because he thought Clodius' action had been an example of dissipated and disrespectful conduct on the part of young nobles, which should, in his opinion, be stamped out. We might say he saw the situation as a conflict of generations.[2]

The late republic was an age of rationalism, certainly as far as the Roman nobility was concerned. But this tendency was never taken to its logical conclusion, rejection of traditional religious practice. Three men whom we know comparatively well and who were all in their way rationalists, Cicero,[3] Caesar,[4] and Varro,[5] all favoured the full performance of traditional ritual. This was also the attitude of Cotta, Cicero's sceptical spokesman in the *De Natura Deorum* who insisted that no

[1] Ibid. 28 (63)—but then *furor* and *dementia*, the qualities which cause division, can be divine instruments of punishment: ibid. 18 (39).

[2] Cic. *Ad Att.* i. 13. 1; 14. 5; 16. 1; 16. 5; 16. 7; 16. 12; 18. 2–3; 19. 8. He had suspected the gilded youth of sympathy with Catiline: *Cat.* ii. 4–5; 22–3. *Cael.* 10; cf. Sall. *Cat.* 17. 6. On the whole affair see T. P. Wiseman (1974), 113–17.

[3] Cicero wrote not only the rationalist *Div.* ii and *N.D.* iii but also the religious laws of *Leg.* ii. 8 (19)—27 (69).

[4] On Caesar's rationalism: Suet. *Caes.* 7; 81; but S. Weinstock (1971), 26–8 and *passim* shows its limits, cf. *C.I.L.* ii. 5439: Caesar's religious calendar for a new city.

[5] On Varro's rationalism see below, p. 37; his aim to preserve cult of gods: Augustine, *C.D.* vi. 2. Practical aim of antiquarianism also shown by his sending a pamphlet on senatorial procedure to Pompey on the latter's election to consulate (Gel. xiv. 7).

amount of philosophical argument would induce him to desert the religious practices of his ancestors.[1] Such respect for ancestral authority would assure the continuity of the traditional ritual, just as childhood associations, family tradition, and the peculiar nature of pagan beliefs would tend to preserve traditional mental attitudes. Nevertheless there were now fewer situations which seemed insoluble without divine aid, and in consequence the ritual will often have seemed a mere formality. The sphere of the gods was more remote, the awe and uncertainty about their intentions weaker. Cato could use the terms 'gods' and 'chance' synonymously.[2] The Commentaries of Caesar and the historical essays of Sallust are concerned almost exclusively with secular events;[3] this is a matter of literary form as much as of outlook but the choice of form is significant.[4] Secular acts deserve commemoration, their religious counterparts might be taken for granted. But from taking for granted it is not far to forgetting.

Of the causes of this rationalism, perhaps the most important was the greatness of the Roman state. Members of the Roman nobility held positions of immense power and their decisions often determined the lives of thousands. Similarly the decisions of the popular assembly could have extremely far-reaching effects. It is not surprising that there developed among Romans, and particularly the nobility, a feeling of immense self-confidence, a sense that the fate of the world lay in their hands. The situation might be compared with that of England of the later seventeenth century when an active and confident society reduced its reliance on supernatural means of influencing the environment some time before advancing technology had significantly increased control by mechanical means.[5]

Rationalism was fortified by literary education. Educated Romans, the authors of surviving literature and their readers,[6] were familiar with rationally coherent systems of Greek

---

[1] Cic. *N.D.* ii. 3 (5); cf. *Har. Resp.* 9 (18).

[2] Cic. *Ad Fam.* xv. 5. 2.

[3] Caesar's account is completely secular but his continuator, the author of the *Bellum Alexandrinum*, alludes to divine help: 'adiuuante deorum immortalium benignitate' (75) or 'deis adiuuantibus' (76).

[4] The proposals of Ps.-Sall. *Epistulae ad Caesarem* (ed. K. Vretska (1961)) are also altogether secular.

[5] Cf. K. Thomas (1971), 558 ff.

[6] E. Auerbach (1965), 237–61.

philosophy which pointed out that everything that happened in the world was the result of a long chain of cause and effect, and that natural causation allowed no scope for the arbitrary intervention of gods moved by wrath or favour, or responding to ritual.[1] Moreover, if the systems (of which Stoicism was eventually to be the most important) had a place for the divine, they were monotheist or pantheist rather than polytheist.

Both reading and personal experience made Roman nobles exceptionally clear-sighted about the social function of religion.[2] They were perfectly ready to concede that if religion was not true it would have to be invented, and even that the state religion of Rome had been deliberately invented for a political purpose.[3] Roman intellectuals were aware that religions had a history. Since Ennius had translated Euhemerus in the second century they were familiar with the theory that gods had been great men who, after death, came to be worshipped as benefactors of mankind.[4] This view was widely accepted.[5] Strangely enough it could be held without in the least invalidating the worship of the deity thus given a human origin.[6]

But it is easy to over-estimate the significance of the rationalism of the late republic. First of all, the authors on whom we depend for our knowledge of the period, Cicero, Caesar, and Varro, were not necessarily typical even of the nobility.[7] The great mass of the people was certainly much more directly in awe of the gods. In speeches to the people Cicero gave credit for the discovery of the conspiracy of Catiline to the gods. He felt no need to make such a claim to the senate.[8] In the civil wars

[1] See the arguments for Epicureanism, Stoicism, and the sceptical New Academy in Cicero's *De Natura Deorum*. *De Divinatione* represents a dispute between Stoic and New Academic views.

[2] Cf. Mucius Scaevola consul of 95 in Augustine, *C.D.* iv. 27; 31. Cicero in *Div.* ii. 72 (148); 12 (28); 18 (43); 34 (70); 35 (75); 72 (148). *Leg.* ii. 12 (30); *Rep.* i. 36 (56).

[3] Liv. i. 19. 4–5; Dion. Hal. ii. 62. 5.

[4] I. Vahlen (1928), 223–9; E. H. Warmington (1935), 414–30; G. Dumézil. (1966).   [5] Verg. *Aen.* vii. 47 ff.; 178 ff.

[6] Liv. i. 16 is a carefully written psychological study of how Romulus came to be thought a god after his death. Livy makes clear that he *is* a god.

[7] Of the previous generation Marius and Sulla were personally pious. On Marius and a Syrian prophetess, see Plut. *Mar.* 17. 2; Val. Max. i. 13. 4; Frontin. *Strat.* i. 11. 12. Marius' personal interpretations of signs: Plut. *Mar.* 38. 6; 40. 7. Vow to Magna Mater at Pessinus: ibid. 31. 2. On Sulla's attitude: Plut. *Sull.* 9, 20, 27–9. Vell. ii. 24; ibid. 25. Cic. *Div.* i. 33 (72). Augustine, *C.D.* ii. 24.

[8] D. Mack (1967), 76.

which destroyed the republic all parties assumed in their propaganda that religious hopes and fears exercised a powerful influence.[1] In 168 B.C. before the battle of Pydna when Roman soldiers were frightened by an eclipse of the sun, their officers could calm them by providing a naturalistic explanation. But in A.D. 14 an eclipse could still terrify mutinous soldiers.[2]

But even the rationalism of men like Cicero had significant limits. Intellectually it rested on philosophies which agreed that everything in the world happened by natural causes, but which were mutually incompatible. Each philosophy was adept at displaying the weaknesses of the others, but none could be conclusively shown to be true. Moreover, all included doctrines which offended common sense. Natural philosophers had not learnt to accept that some phenomena remained unexplained, and preferred to weaken convincing theories by juxtaposing them with fantastic ones.[3]

The progress, or even maintenance, of a scientific world view was also hampered by the difficulty of establishing what was in fact the case. Not only was there no tradition of experimental testing of the theories of the great philosophers, there was no discrimination in the use of authorities claiming to describe the facts of nature.[4] The Elder Pliny who died in A.D. 79 cites Valerius Antias, the notoriously unreliable historian, as evidence that Lake Trasimene had once been on fire.[5] He quotes Sophocles as an authority on plants,[6] asserts on the authority of Cicero that a certain man had been able to see 135 miles, and adds on that of Varro that the same person had been able to count ships leaving the harbour of Carthage from a viewing point in Sicily.[7] Pliny agrees that experience is the best teacher.[8] But in practice he finds it impossibly difficult or perhaps excessively troublesome to distinguish genuine experience from mere hearsay. Worst of all, he simply passes on a vast amount of information without stating any authority at all. As a result his *Natural History* reinforces a great deal of nonsense. In spite of

---

[1] Hence religious propaganda of all sides in civil war. See P. Jal (1961)
[2] Cic. *Rep.* i. 15. 23; Liv. xliv. 37; Tac. *Ann.* i. 28.
[3] K. Thomas (1971), 644 ff.
[4] On the following, see L. Thorndyke (1923).
[5] Plin. *N.H.* ii. 111.
[6] Ibid. xxi. 8.
[7] Ibid. vii. 21.   [8] Ibid. xxvi. 6.

Pliny, birds do not die if they fly over Lake Avernus.[1] Nor would an egg-shell have continued to withstand the imposition of a heavy weight until it was tilted a little to one side.[2] In this way belief in innumerable phenomena incompatible with a 'scientific' world picture could survive without refutation.

Many did much more than survive. They provided hope in sickness and the basis of countless remedies. It was thought that substances were linked by mysterious sympathy or antipathy[3] and this could be harnessed to provide cures. An antipathy was said to exist between stags and snakes. It was thought that stags would track snakes to their holes and extract them.[4]

The customs of popular healing preserved numerous practices which had quite antirational implications. For instance: when one plucks a medicinal herb it makes a difference when and how it is plucked, by day or by night or under what phase of the moon, with what hand or what finger.[5]

Such beliefs were helped by the formalism of Roman religion. Roman life was accompanied by innumerable ritual acts, each of which had to be accompanied by precisely the right form of words. The implication is that words have power. This implication may be rejected by the wisest as far as their individual beliefs are concerned, but collectively all men have always had confidence in the power of words, even though sometimes unaware of it.[6] Belief in the power of religious words was maintained by a complex of feelings, aesthetic, associational, and even empirical, the sense that Rome had fared well while these formulae had been used. But the outcome must have been an open-mindedness towards the possibility of practices that sought to move matter at a distance through a combination of words and gestures.

Moreover the Greek philosophy which eventually became the most influential at Rome could be used to explain the efficiency of such practices, and this helped their survival and even expansion. Stoicism was a monistic system but it could be interpreted either as materializing the gods or as spiritualizing

---

[1] Ibid. xxxi. 11.
[2] Ibid. xxix. 11.
[3] S. Sambursky (1959), 41–6; T. Hopfner (1928), 311.
[4] Plin. *N.H.* viii. 118, cf. xi. 278; xxviii. 149.
[5] Ibid. xx. 14; xxiv. 82; xxv. 92.
[6] Ibid. xxviii. 3. 11: an extremely important passage.

matter.[1] Both tendencies helped to support traditional state religion and the possibility of divination. By what George Orwell would have described as double-think,[2] Stoicism provided the gods with a place in the philosophical universe by identifying them with parts of the material world. Jupiter was the sky, or the divine universe as a whole, Neptune the sea, etc.[3] Thus the gods could be thought of as material whenever their existence or their function in a law-abiding universe was in question, only to become spiritual beings once more when they were to be placated by sacrifice or prayer. There was thus no reason at all why a Stoic should abandon the worship of the gods. The spiritualizing of matter had more revolutionary implications. If the universe was conceived as one huge living and feeling organism of which each part was aware of what happened in every other, changes in one area could induce reations elsewhere even at a great distance.[4] Thus the door was opened for astrology and the systematic magic of the Greek East.

In the late republic Stoicism had not achieved anything like as dominating an influence as it was to do under the empire. In fact, the philosophical system with most professed adherents may well have been that of the sceptical New Academy. But this was not antagonistic to traditional religion either, and had taken over part of the Stoic rationalization of religious beliefs. Varro is the outstanding exponent of Neo-Academic support for the worship of the old Roman gods.[5] Like the *pontifex maximus* Mucius Scaevola he believed that religion could be classified under three headings, the religion of the poets, the religion of the state, and the religion of the philosophers. The religion of the poets is the invention of the poets. The state religion is a

[1] A. H. Armstrong, ed. (1967), ch. 7 (P. Merlan), esp. 125–9.

[2] George Orwell, *Nineteen Eighty-Four* (1954), 171: 'Doublethink means the power of holding two contradictory beliefs in one's mind simultaneously and accepting both of them . . . To tell deliberate lies while genuinely believing in them, to forget any fact that has become inconvenient, and then, when it becomes necessary again, to draw it back from oblivion just as long as it is needed, to deny the existence of objective reality and all the while to take account of the reality which one denies.'

[3] e.g. Cic. *N.D.* ii. 24 (65–6).

[4] e.g. ibid. 4 (119); cf. below, p. 37.

[5] See F. Altheim (1938), 335–7; H. Dahlman (1935), 1234–6. P. Boyancé (1955) = (1972), 253–82. K. Kumaniecki (1962). B. Cardauns, *M. Terentius Varro: Antiquitates Rerum Divinarum*, 2 vols. (Mainz, 1976).

political artefact exactly like the secular machinery of government, and it came into existence after the state.[1] Only the
religion of the philosophers is, objectively speaking, true.[2]

Varro stated that it was his aim to preserve and restore the
state religion.[3] Roman religion was concerned not only with the
worship of a limited number of great divinities, but also with
winning the co-operation of whatever spirit might be needed
for the successful performance of each of the infinite number of
tasks of public and private life. With the aid of his antiquarian
scholarship Varro sought to establish the divinity responsible
for every conceivable activity in order to make it once more
possible to call on the correct specialist in every situation.[4] In
doing this, he recovered a great deal of ritual that had gone out
of use and been forgotten.[5] But truth was important. Varro
believed that in an ideal community the state religion would
accord with natural philosophy. The existing religion could not
be made so to accord, but it ought at least to contain an element
of the religion of the philosophers.[6] Consequently Varro proceeded in the manner of Stoics, systematically to ascribe to
each of the Roman divinities a place in the structure of the
universe.[7]

Philosophical justification did not leave traditional practices
unaltered. This can be illustrated once more from divination.
In his *De Divinatione* Cicero gives the Stoic explanation of the
effectiveness of traditional practices of diviners. 'In the beginning the universe was so created that certain results would be
preceded by certain signs which are given sometimes by entrails
and by birds, sometimes by lightnings, by portents and by
stars, sometimes by utterances of persons in a frenzy. And
these signs do not often deceive the persons who observe them.'[8]

[1] Augustine, *C.D.* vi. 3–4. See G. Lieberg, 'Die "theologia tripertita"', *A.N.R.W.*
i. 4. 66–115.
[2] Augustine, *C.D.* iv. 3.
[3] Ibid. 2: ut in eo ipso opere dicat se timere ne pereant [dei] non incursu hostili
sed civium neglegentia.
[4] Ibid. 22.
[5] Cic. *Acad. post.* i. 9.
[6] The religion of the philosophers did not include animal sacrifice (Varro *ap.*
Arnob. vii. 1), or images (Varro *ap.* Aug. *C.D.* iv. 21). Varro thought that Roman
religion had originally been imageless (ibid. iv. 31; vi. 10). This idea was probably
a mistake: Boyancé (1952).
[7] Augustine, *C.D.* vii, 6 and probably (accepted by K. Latte *R.R.* 272) iv. 1.
[8] Cic. *Div.* i. 52 (118).

This does not mean that gods are responsible for the occurrence of single signs and portents. 'Things which are to be do not suddenly spring into existence but the evolution of time is like the unwinding of a cable: it creates nothing new. This connexion between cause and effect is obvious to two classes of diviners: those who are endowed with natural divination, and those who know the course of events by the observation of signs. They may not discern the causes themselves, yet they do discern the signs and tokens of these causes. The careful study and recollection of these signs, aided by the records of former times, have evolved that sort of divination which is known as artificial, which is divination from entrails, lightnings, portents and celestial phenomena.'[1] We see that divination could have been reconciled with even a godless philosophical system.

But in the process of being reconciled with the Stoic system divination has changed its character. Traditionally divination provided warning of misfortune which would come unless it was prevented. Conscientious observation of signs would enable magistrates either to avoid potentially calamitous actions or to avert calamity by ritual. But if signs were mere markers attached to stages in an endless chain of cause and effect, it would not be easy to say how the chain could be broken by ritual. One would expect a tendency to see signs as an indication of the inevitable. This did indeed happen.

Divination continued to evolve as it had always done in response to new circumstances. In previous centuries Rome had changed from a small country town to a huge urban conglomeration. In the city some rural techniques of divination through flight of birds or animals' movements became impractical. The remaining techniques, for instance, divination from thunder or lightning, became all the more important. Public divination at Rome had once been in the service of agriculture. A truly urban population was no longer concerned with the details of the farmer's work.[2] On the other hand, the intense political strife of the late republic encouraged extensive use of divination in connection with the legislative or electoral assemblies of the people.

Not only divination, but Roman religion as a whole, showed remarkable power of adaptation to changing conditions. In

---

[1] Cic. *Div.* i. 56 (127–8). [2] Th. Mommsen, *R.St.* i. 76–85.

general, the success of the Roman state maintained belief in the efficacy of an institution so intimately linked with all public action. In the words of Cotta in Cicero's *De Natura Deorum*: 'The religion of the Roman people comprises ritual, auspices, and the additional division, consisting of all such prophetic warnings as the interpreters of the Sibyl or the *haruspices* have derived from portents and prodigies. Well, I have always thought that none of these departments of religion was to be despised. Our state could assuredly never have been as great as it is had not the fullest measure of divine favour been obtained for it.'[1] On the other hand, the stresses and strains in the political system would be reflected in the religious institutions too. We are particularly well informed about stresses and innovations at the time of the Hannibalic war,[2] but they were also a feature of other periods of crisis. The late republic was such a period, when public religion was affected by the general breakdown of Roman institutions. This did not mean that the ancestral cults were rejected. On the contrary, the crisis itself came to be seen as a punishment for neglect of religion and a religious renewal as an essential part of political reconstruction. Needless to say, the religious renewal included, as it had done in earlier times, a good deal of innovation.

5. *Morality and religion*

Much of Roman literature had a moral aim. History, Historical Epic, Satire, no less than popularizing Philosophy, were written to a considerable extent for moral edification.[3] This mass of moral guidance contains remarkably few references to the gods in the role of supervisors of morality. The contrast with the Bible is very great. Roman literature does not, for example, present the gods as originators of the moral code. There is nothing to compare with the Ten Commandments or the Sermon on the Mount. It also appears that Roman morality was sanctioned to only a very limited extent by expectations of divine reward or punishment. Cicero illustrates what seems to be the central concern of Roman religion: 'Jupiter is called

---

[1] Cic. *N.D.* iii. 2 (5).   [2] Warde Fowler (1923), 314–39.
[3] But as G. W. Williams (1968), ch. 9, shows, moralizing is only one of many ways of treating a moral theme.

Best and Greatest not because he makes us just or sober or wise but healthy and rich and prosperous.'[1] Roman gods are called upon to help men in difficulties or to assure their well-being, not to make them morally better.

The gods were not thought of as watching man's moral conduct. It is significant that in the plays of Plautus hundreds of passages state the superior power of gods while only four refer to their superior knowledge.[2] Maintenance of morality was of course thought essential for the well-being of the republic, but its maxims were not presented as religious duties, and, with a few precisely defined exceptions, moral offences were not treated as offences against the gods. The moral code was upheld by family tradition, public opinion, and the peculiar institutions of the censorship. To quote J. A. Crook: 'the small aristocratic society of early Rome, valuing above all overt esteem (*existimatio, dignitas*), dreaded its loss exceedingly. The disapproval of a man's peers was channelled through the censors, the customary guardians of public morality, who provided a sharp extra-legal sanction against bahaviour that offended accepted canons by their "censorial mark".'[3] The moral traditions of Rome were handed down from generation to generation in historical *exempla*, in which the advantage of morality and the disadvantages of immorality were demonstrated through incidents of Roman history.[4]

As a rule the moral was taught on an entirely secular level. So, the over-conscientious father in Terence's *Adelphi* (413 ff.): 'I spare no pains, let slip no chance and give him a sound training; in fact I am always telling him to look at other men's lives as in a mirror, and choose from them an example for himself. "Do this" I say . . . "Avoid that".'[5] Or a responsible brother, indignant at money being wasted on buying a slave girl: 'Oh Aeschynus. Fancy you doing this! Think of the disgrace to the family.'[6] Terence normally simply translated his Greek source, but it may be that sometimes he subtly Romanized an incident.[7]

---

[1] Cic. *N.D.* iii. 36 (87), cf. ibid. i. 41 (116); Epict. iv. 1. 60–1. R. M. Ogilvie (1969), 17: 'Roman religion was concerned with success not sin.'

[2] J. A. Hanson (1959).   [3] J. A. Crook (1967), 83.

[4] On Regulus see below, p. 175. Polybius on Roman *exempla*, vi. 54–5.

[5] Ter. *Ad.* 413 ff. Surely a parody of Roman education? Cf. Liv. i, *praef.* 10.

[6] Ter. *Ad.* 407.   [7] So *And.* 282 ff. and G. W. Williams (1953), 20–1.

If Terence is thought to reflect Greek conditions, Horace's evidence is undoubtedly Roman. 'My best of fathers taught me this [habit of preaching], when to enable me to shun every kind of wrong doing (*vitiorum quaeque*) he condemned them in living examples (*exemplis*). Whenever he encouraged me to live thriftily, frugally, and be content with what he had saved for me, he would say: 'Surely you see in what a bad state the son of Albus has got himself and how poor Baius is? A striking lesson not to waste one's inheritance.' When he would deter me from an affair with a prostitute he said: 'Don't be like Scetanus.' And to prevent me courting loose married women, when I might enjoy licit love, he would say: 'The reputation of Trebonius who got caught is not nice.' A philosopher will give you theories for shunning this or seeking that. Enough for me if I can uphold the rule our fathers have handed down, and if . . . I can keep your health and name from harm . . . The tender mind is oft deterred from vice by another's shame (*opprobrium*).'[1]

Republican moralizing makes a secular impression. Neither Cicero[2] nor Sallust[3] felt it necessary to introduce the gods when they suggested moral reforms. Cicero had frequent occasion to castigate real or supposed immorality in public life, but as a rule he did so without trying to arouse fear of divine punishment.[4]

If Roman moral comment was often remarkably secular, it would nevertheless be mistaken to conclude that Roman religion was entirely separated from morality. There is definite evidence for a moral side to Roman religion. If it is rather vague it is also consistent. The plays of Plautus written early in the second century tell essentially the same story as the literature of the late republic.

Offences that may be punished by the gods fall under a strictly limited number of heads. One class involves a direct affront to a deity, like the omission of a regular rite or theft from the deity's sanctuary.[5] Another is concerned with the breaking of an oath or a less formal agreement.[6] Incest was considered

---

[1] *Sat.* i. 4. 105–19.
[2] The moral advice of *De Officiis* is without reference to gods. Cf. also D. Daube (1956), 62–4 on Roman ethical rules.
[3] Sall. *Cat.* 1–5, 7–13, 53–4. [4] e.g. *In Cat.* i. 6–7 (14–18).
[5] e.g. Cic. *Verr.* ii. 72 (184); *Leg.* ii. 9 (22). J. D. Cloud (1971), 8 n. 7.
[6] Perjury: Cic. *Leg.* ii. 9 (22). In every oath a god was *called in* to punish the

a religious offence.[1] It may be that for the late republic kin-murder should be added to the list.[2] Of these offences those involving the breach of an undertaking (*fides*) were the most important from the social point of view. At the centre of the group was perjury, which was punished by the god in whose name the oath had been sworn.[3] But divine involvement was thought to extend to less formal agreements and to situations of mutual trust such as that between patron and client.[4] The gods were also expected to punish the breaking of a treaty with a foreign state and the waging of unjust war.[5]

It is difficult to be certain why some aspects of conduct should be thought to be under divine guardianship while others were not. Incest and parricide (kin-killing) certainly aroused deep abhorrence. These offences also shared the characteristics that they were difficult to investigate, and perhaps awkward to punish, since they were committed in the depths of the family.[6] The doctrine that such offences are punished by the gods at the

---

oath-breaker. See K. Latte *R.R.* 122–3 on Liv. i. 24. But divine supervision was thought to extend over all contractual relationship involving *fides*. Cf. P. Boyancé, 'Fides et le serment' (1962); 'Fides Romana et la vie internationale' (1972); 'La Main de *Fides*' (1964); 'Les Romains, peuple de la *Fides*' (1964).

[1] Cic. *Leg.* ii. 9 (22); *Clu.* 6. 15; Tac. *Ann.* xii. 5. 5; 8. Roman horror of incest expressed by fact that slaves could be tortured to give evidence against their masters on this charge: Cic. *Part. Or.* 118; *Pro. Mil.* 59. Otherwise this was only allowed when the charge was treason: Cic. *Part. Or.* 118, and from the time of Marcus Aurelius, adultery. See F. Garnsey (1970), 215 n. 5. The gods who punished incest were the *penates*, Cat. lxiv. 412. Judging by their reaction to incestuous behaviour in the Claudian *gens* (T. P. Wiseman (1974), 104–18), including the behaviour of the Emperor Gaius (Suet. *Gai.* 24), nobles could take a lenient view.

[2] The punishment of drowning a parricide in a sack, introduced around 200 B.C., looks like the expiation of a prodigy, i.e. a ritual designed to restore the threatened *pax deorum*. See J. D. Cloud (1971), esp. 26–36.

[3] Cic. *Leg.* ii. 9 (22): periurii poena divina exitium, humana dedecus. But if *dedecus* was equivalent to *infamia* or *ignominia* it carried considerable legal disadvantage. See J. A. Crook (1967), 83–4 with reference to literature on p. 303 n. 77. An example? Plaut. *Mil. Glor.* 521: the condition of being *intestabilis* is a consequence of *infamia*.

[4] Patronage is certainly a relationship involving *fides*, cf. Gel. v. 13. 2: clientes qui sese itidem *in fidem* patrociniumque nostrum dediderunt. Their claim on their patron is only less than that of his *parentes* and his wards.

[5] S. Weinstock (1971), 243–5. Two notorious disasters, the capture of Rome by the Gauls and the surrender of a Roman army at the Caudine Forks, were made into *exempla* of the punishment of broken *fides*: Liv. v. 21 and ix. 1. Caesar's Gallic war treated as unjust and risking divine punishment: Plut. *Caes.* 22. 4 (Cato's speech).

[6] See A. S. Diamond (1971), 223 f.

same time asserts the moral rule and avoids difficulties which might arise in enforcement.[1] In the case of perjury the god intervenes in the first place not because he is offended at a particular action, but because he has been called in to supervise the agreement. Divine supervision of the other relationships involving *fides*, and indeed of the so-called *leges sacratae*, seems to have originated in the same way as supervision of oaths.[2] In all these situations the interest of the gods is not so much an aspect of their moral concern as of the fact that their power was thought to be to some extent at the disposition of worshippers who might make use of it to safeguard arrangements which could otherwise be maintained only with great difficulty, if at all.

The concern of the Roman gods did, however, extend beyond these specialized areas, even if the wider concern is not easy to define. It can perhaps be said that the Roman gods in a vague way favoured respectable conduct, and disliked conduct that was disreputable. So we read in Plautus' *Captivi*: 'There surely is a God who hears and sees what we do: and according to your treatment of me here will he look after your son there. He will reward the deserving and requite the undeserving.'[3] Or in Terence's *Adelphi*, 'Father . . . you pray to the gods. They'll be more likely to listen to you I know, you're so much better than I.'[4] A passage in Plautus' *Rudens* informs us that Jupiter is interested in the deeds of men, their customs, their dutifulness, and their reliability (*mores, pietatem et fidem*). It is punishment of perjury that is used to exemplify Jupiter's interest, but the

---

[1] In Cicero's *Laws* some religious offences are not sanctioned by human punishment. Perjury: ii. 9 (22). Impure approach to gods: ibid. 8 (19): Ad divos adeunto caste . . . qui secus faxit deus ipso vindex erit, cf. ibid. 10 (25). Failure to perform vows made to gods: ibid. 9 (22). This is ambiguous but 16–17 (42–4) shows that punishment by gods is understood. Only for incest is capital punishment laid down: ii. 9 (22). The religious nature of the offence is shown by fact that the *pontifices* inflict punishment. Generally speaking Tiberius' words 'deum iniuriae dis curae' (Tac. *Ann.* i. 73) apply to the religiously sanctioned offences.

[2] So the Law of XII Tables, 8. 21 *patronus si clienti fraudem faxit sacer esto* is an example of a social relationship sanctioned by a curse. At Athens curses were regularly pronounced against political corruption, deception of courts or assembly, or treasonable activities. References in K. J. Dover (1974), 251. In the Bible Deuteronomy 27 is sanctioned by a curse, while the similar laws of Leviticus 20 are sanctioned by human penalties. See also J. Bayet, 'L'organisation plébéienne et les *leges sacratae*' in *Tite Live*, ed. Budé, vol. iii (1942), 145–53.

[3] 313–15.

[4] Ter. *Ad.* 703–5: melior multo.

generalization covers a much wider area of behaviour.[1] Elsewhere we are told that the pious are more likely to have their prayers answered.[2] This would hardly be worth noticing if piety simply described performance of religious duties. But in fact the Latin word embraces dutiful behaviour not only to the gods but also within the family,[3] so that the gods' interest in pious people might well be thought to embrace, for instance, conscientious parents or grateful children.[4] But the range of meaning of *pius* is wider still. Even when performed for a parent an act is *pius* in a strict sense only if it is also moral.[5] It is *pius* not to appropriate lost property whose owner one does not know,[6] and no doubt the gods rewarding piety would take this kind of conscientiousness into account too.

It is clear that in rewarding *pietas* and punishing *impietas* the gods might react to a wide range of moral conduct. But this must not be exaggerated. First, the plays are more or less free translations from Greek originals. This in itself does not matter a great deal: Greek ideas were being assimilated by the Romans throughout their history. Then the comparatively few passages showing the wider moral concern come mainly, but not entirely, from two particularly 'religious' plays: *Rudens* and *Poenulus*. Again, *pius* seems to have a wider moral connotation when it is contrasted with its opposite, *scelestus*, a word of general moral disapproval. But in three examples the *scelus* turns out to be perjury, so that we are once again within the central area of divine concern.[7] The reader of Plautus might conclude that the Roman gods were believed on the whole to favour the good and to punish the wicked, but it is clear that, outside the three special areas, individual behaviour was mainly determined by non-religious influences.[8]

---

[1] Plaut. *Rud.* 90.

[2] *Rud.* 26–7; 1193–4. *Poen.* 869, 1137, 1190, 1252 ff., 1277.

[3] On *pietas* see K. Latte *R.R.* 39–40. Also C. Koch, P.W. xx. 1. 1221–3, s.v. pietas. P. Strack (1931–7), i. 75; 244. Th. Ulrich (1930). H. Wagenvoort (1947), 142. M. P. Charlesworth (1943). J. H. Hanson, op. cit. 89–95, discusses *pius* and *pietas* in Plautus. The two principal areas of *pietas*: si erga parentem aut deos me impiavi, *Rud.* 192.

[4] Ibid. 190–7.   [5] Asin. 504–10.   [6] *Rud.* 1230–6.

[7] *Pseud.* 355–6; *Rud.* 26–7; ibid. 198 the *scelus* or *impietas* is *periuria*. Ibid. 618–19: *impii* are dragging girl from temple. *Bacch.* 1176: man addressed *mea pietas* refuses to enter a brothel. *Most.* 504: a haunted house, the site of (supposed) murder is *impius*.

[8] Cf. Alcmene's defence in *Amph.* 820. 'Istuc facinus, quod tu insimulas

When we come to the much more abundant and varied evidence of the late republic, the picture of divine concern for morality is basically the same as that of Plautus and Terence. In the poems of Catullus, for instance, there is unambiguous evidence that the gods are interested in morality.[1] In the 'reserved area' they punish perjury and offences against *fides*.[2] Beyond this, they may favour 'the pious'.[3] As in Plautus 'pious' and its opposite 'impious' are sometimes used in a wide sense, approaching our good or wicked. The magic of Persia is impious,[4] so are incest[5] and kin-murder.[6] The last two offences are within the 'reserved area' but impious is applied to behaviour which lies well beyond this. Injustice is described as impious,[7] as is theft,[8] and the flattery of childless old men for the sake of their property.[9] By implication such actions would tend to alienate the gods. On the other hand, a man who has lived a 'pure' life has a claim on the gods' pity.[10] It is not clear that standards of conduct would qualify, but in this poem at least Catullus seems to assume that his affair with the married Lesbia will not disqualify him.

There are indications that Catullus sometimes thought of adultery as a religious sin. Hymen is a god and marriage his rite.[11] But of course in this respect, marriage need be no more—and no less—holy than the other innumerable everyday activities supervised by a specialist deity which must be appeased to ensure success. More significant is that Catullus describes marriage as a treaty (*foedus*)[12] and of course supervision of treaties was definitely a concern of the gods. But Catullus never takes the final step of proclaiming a divine sanction for marital fidelity. He approaches this view most closely in lxviii.[13] In this poem Catullus' irregular affair with Lesbia is juxtaposed with

---

nostro generi non decet.' Such behaviour as you accuse me of does not become members of my family.

[1] T. P. Wiseman, 'Dis Invitis', Collection Latomus, ci (1969) = *Mélanges Renard*, i. 778–84.

[2] lxiv. 131–5; xxx. 12–13. [3] lxxvi. 26; lxviii. 154.
[4] xciv. 4. [5] lxvii. 25. 29; lxiv. 401–4.
[6] lxiv. 399–400. [7] lxiv. 398.
[8] xiii. 10. [9] lxviii. 123.
[10] lxxvi. 19. Cf. xv. 9.

[11] lxx. 71. Hymen was a literary god; the sacrifices at marriages were made to quite other deities. Marquardt (1886), 50–2.

[12] lxiv. 335; 373. [13] T. P. Wiseman (1974), 77–103.

the brief marriage of Protesilaus and Laodamia in such a way that the reader cannot help looking for parallels between the situations of the two couples.[1] Now the marriage of Protesilaus and Laodamia involved impiety. Laodamia had been in such a hurry to consummate the marriage that she had entered her husband's house before the proper sacrifices had procured the gods' favour. Punishment followed. The couple were at once separated. Protesilaus was obliged to join the campaign against Troy,[2] where he was the first to be killed. Next we are told that Troy brought bereavement to Catullus also. It was there that his brother died and was buried.[3] The reader is bound to ask[4] whether this too was a punishment for impiety. But the only conceivably impious act mentioned in the poem is that Lesbia was married and her love affair with Catullus adulterous.[5] The poem thus quite clearly suggests that adultery is punished by the gods.[6] But one can define the offence more closely. Just as passion induced Laodamia to omit the sacrifices, so it drove Lesbia to come to Catullus[7] to give him 'stolen gifts taken from the very lap of her husband'. As the situation is described in the poem the active guilt was that of the married woman,[8] and what the gods punish is adultery, not in the English meaning of the word, but in the narrower Roman one. The offence is not sexual relations outside marriage[9] but depriving a husband of his wife, and responsibility is thought to lie rather on the side of the passionately aroused woman than on that of her lover.[10]

---

[1] 70–104 (30–64).   [2] 75–84 (35–44).   [3] 91–100 (51–60).

[4] The two stories are interwoven in such a way that the reader expects to find all the main features paralleled. The union of one pair is flawed by impiety so presumably the other is. The creaking sandal of 72 (32) is an omen.

[5] 145–6 (105–6) shows the affair to be simultaneously marvellous and morally shocking. 103 (63) *moecha* condemns the adulterous Helen.

[6] Catullus lost a brother. Troy became the common tomb of Europe and Asia.

[7] 73 (33): coniugis ut quondam flagrans advenit amore . . . Laodamia. 131–2 (31–2): aut nihil aut paulo cui tum concedere digna lux mea . . .

[8] The stress is on Lesbia's coming to Catullus not vice versa, and on Laodamia's passion not on that of Protesilaus.

[9] 138–41 (98–101): Juno puts up with Jupiter's infidelities.

[10] 77–8 (37–8):

nil mihi tam valde placeat, Ramnusia virgo
quod temere invitis suscipiatur eris

imply that Catullus does not think that *he* has so far been moved by passion to do anything against the will of the gods. Appropriately he is not suffering agony as a result of Lesbia's behaviour to him in this poem 135–42 (95–102) although he does in others, e.g. lxxviii.

That the man is less guilty than the woman is suggested by other poems in which Catullus implies that his affair with Lesbia has not made his own life *impurus*, and indeed that the love of Lesbia had once been something for which he might pray to the gods.[1] But if guilt is unevenly distributed, divine punishment strikes both parties, and not them alone. Catullus lost his brother, Paris his life, not to mention the countless victims of the war provoked by the adulterous affair. Behaviour of married women leading to adultery is shown to endanger the whole of society. This is an attitude which we meet again, explicitly formulated, in certain Odes of Horace and in the marriage legislation of Augustus.[2] In Catullus these ideas are merely suggested. When Catullus felt the need to justify marital fidelity explicitly he did not refer to divine punishment which must follow infidelity but he pointed out the vital importance of the institution of marriage. Marriage ensures that the pleasures of love are enjoyed without loss of reputation, that the family continues and that the state does not run short of defenders.[3] These reasons are weighty, but they fall within the usual secular justification of morality.

When Catullus had occasion to mention the area of morality traditionally associated with the gods he was altogether more explicit. In the concluding section of lxiv he explains why the gods who once visited 'the chaste homes of heroes' are no longer seen by men on earth.[4] The reason is the contempt with which men now treat piety, and this is expanded to mean a decline in worship, fraternal slaughter, incest, and, more generally, the confusion of right and wrong, *fas* and *nefas*.[5] Impiety, kin-murder, and incest are traditional religious offences. Perjury is missing in this place, though it is duly condemned elsewhere in the poem. But we must also note that the divine interest is not sharply limited, *fas* and *nefas* can be applied to a wide range of behaviour, and the statement that the mind of the gods is just (*justificum*) allows their interest to range widely.

We meet belief in the wider moral concern from a different point of view in Lucretius' *De Rerum Natura*. It is a principal object of the poem to assure men that they cannot possibly

---

[1] lxxvi. 19, 23.   [2] See below, pp. 93–5.
[3] lxi. 61–75.   [4] lxiv.
[5] On *nefas* see J. Hellegouarc'h (1963), 127 ff.

experience unpleasantness after death, and the suffering which the poet has particularly in mind is punishment in the underworld. Now this is Greek Epicurean doctrine and, it might be argued, not necessarily applicable to Roman conditions. But this will not do. Lucretius is nothing if not a proselytizer, and the principal message of the poem must have meaning for himself and his potential readers.[1] One must conclude that in some circles at Rome, perhaps as a result of Greek philosophical influence, perhaps of more popular beliefs mediated through slaves and freedmen of eastern origin, the doctrine was prevalent that the sins of life would be punished after death.[2]

That public religion has a moral aspect is an assumption made in Cicero's *De Legibus*. The religious rules of Cicero's model community are essentially identical with the traditional system of Rome.[3] It is significant therefore that what Cicero says about the moral concerns of the gods agrees, if allowance is made for the public context, with what we found in Catullus and even in Plautus. The most important effect of fear of the gods is the sanctity of agreements and oaths.[4] Incest is to be punished by the *pontifices* and is therefore presumably a religious offence.[5] But Cicero assumes a penumbra of wider concern. The gods in a vague way prefer morally pure worshippers and the presence of temples and shrines is an inducement to moral behaviour.

The code of religious laws begins with the commandment *Ad divos adeunto caste*: 'They shall approach the gods in purity.'[6] The purity is in a sense ritual. It is required for the purpose of making the worshipper acceptable to the god, not for its own sake. But it is moral as well. As Cicero later explains, purity of mind is more important than purity of body. Water will wash off a stain of the body, but nothing will remove a mental stain.[7]

---

[1] Otherwise R. M. Ogilvie (1969), 86: 'Lucretius was tilting against a windmill since his readers were not scared of the proverbial punishments of Hell which he set out to ridicule.' He can cite dismissals of these beliefs as 'old wives' tales' in Cic. *Tusc.* i. 48; Juv. *Sat.* ii. 149; Prop. ii. 34, 53–4. But they are likely to have been part of Etruscan religion. See R. Bloch (1958), 158–60.

[2] The class correlation of different beliefs about the life after death seems not to have been fully explored in such works as F. Cumont (1922) and (1942) and F. Bömer (1963).

[3] *Leg.* ii. 10 (23).   [4] Ibid. 7 (17).
[5] See above, p. 42 n. 1.   [6] ii. 8 (19): Ad divos adeunto caste.
[7] ii. 10 (24).

One might compare the ruling of Scaevola that men who had failed to observe the restrictions on working during a holiday could appease the gods if they had offended by oversight, but not if they had acted knowingly (*prudentes*).[1] Later Cicero lays down that an impious man must not venture to appease the gods.[2] Again Cicero takes a wide view of piety, for he explains the law with an example, taken from Plato, that a good man will not receive presents from a wicked one.[3] Cicero undoubtedly thought that belief in the moral concern of the gods was useful: 'Who will deny that such beliefs are useful when he remembers how often oaths are used to confirm agreements, how important to our well-being is the sanctity of treaties, how many persons are deterred from crime by fear of divine punishment.'[4] There can be no doubt that much of the moral interpretation of the religious laws is derived from Greek sources. Purity in mind as well as in body is insisted upon in Greek religious laws,[5] and Cicero has a Greek source for the view that thinking of the gods makes men better, since he refers to the saying of Thales, the wisest of the Seven Sages, that 'men ought to believe that everything they see is filled with gods, for all would then be purer, just as they feel the power of religion most deeply when they are performing religious rites'.[6] Nevertheless the attitude of these chapters is more than mere theorizing. It recurs in a speech to the senate in which Cicero states that nothing unjust or disreputable should be sought from the gods in prayer.[7] In any case Cicero's explanation of the social utility of religion must have been credible in a Roman context. It would have been absurd for Cicero to assert that 'many persons are deterred from crime by fear of divine punishment', or that men would live purer lives if they saw temples all around them, or that the destruction of religion would bring about the end of justice also,[8] if his readers were convinced that the gods were totally indifferent to the purity and justice of mankind. The conclusion is inescapable that at Rome the sight of sacred

---

[1] ii. 15 (37), cf. Macr. i. 16, 10; Varro, *L.L.* vi. 30.
[2] *Leg.* ii. 10 (22). [3] Ibid. 15 (14).
[4] ii. 7 (17).
[5] L. Ziehen (1906): 91 (Delos), 148 (Rhodes).
[6] *Leg.* ii. 10 (26). [7] *Dom.* 107.
[8] *N.D.* i. 2 (4); on *iustitia* see Weinstock (1971), 244. For one divine punishment of bad, reward of good see Ps.-Sall. i. *Ep. ad Caesarem*, 12. 1.

places and the performance of religious ritual was thought to further morality, no matter how vaguely the area of divine concern for morality might have been mapped out.[1] Further, the evidence of comedy suggests that in essentials this attitude goes back to the early second century, that is, as far as the earliest surviving Latin literature. It may well be that it goes back much further still.[2] After all, the gods, or some of the gods, were patrons of Rome, and as such interested in conduct that had a bearing on the survival of the community. But if there was anything Romans were agreed about it was that the success of the community depended on morals.

Roman gods certainly took an active interest in a wide variety of actions which in some way or other affected the future of Rome. Aeneas was thought to have fulfilled a religious obligation when he toiled to make possible the founding of the city. It would have been impious of him to refuse this duty.[3] After the sack of Rome by the Gauls the Romans decided not to transfer their city to the site of Veii. The motive, at least according to Livy, was religious. The holiness of the public sanctuaries was attached to their present locations. The move to Veii would necessarily have meant deserting the sanctuaries and this would have been impious.[4] The fact that their worship was tied to Rome itself gave the gods a strong interest in any behaviour that might conceivably endanger the city.

The gods' concern for Rome, and hence their detailed interest in the doings of Roman public figures, was assumed and exploited in political controversy. Political actions which were presented by their opponents as offensive to the gods included the execution of Manlius Capitolinus who had saved the Capitol from the Gauls,[5] the attempt of a censor to remain in office after his colleague had died,[6] the fact that for the first time both consuls were plebeians,[7] the exiling of Cicero,[8] and failure to

---

[1] See below, pp. 98–9, 82 n. 3.

[2] On the other hand, *pius* may well have been a religious concept from the beginning. According to Weinstock (1971), 248 n. 4 *pium est* like *fas est* is what can be done without committing a religious offence.

[3] e.g. *Aen.* iv. 226–37. The thought is already in Naevius (*ob.* 191 B.C.). B. Snell (1967), 160.

[4] Liv. v. 52 ff.　　　　　　　　　　　　　　　　　　　　　[5] vi. 20. 16.

[6] ix. 33.

[7] Liv. xxiii. 31. 13.

[8] Cic. *Red. Quir.* 8 (18).

help the authorities in civil war.[1] An epidemic of adultery among matrons was something that seemed to call for appeasement of a divinity; at least a temple of Venus, the earliest in the city, was erected out of the fines.[2] This list is a medley, but it shows that speakers could hope to persuade people that a wide range of conduct, which in some way might affect the well-being of the community, was of interest to the gods.

If the patron gods of Rome resented behaviour which would injure their chosen city, other divinities would react to conduct that affected their particular speciality. As almost every conceivable act of ordinary life required the co-operation of a competent deity, the scope for supernatural interest in human behaviour was unlimited. Of all the deities none were more generally worshipped than the *penates*.[3] No Roman home was without a shrine dedicated to these supernatural protectors. Nothing is more likely than that any action which endangered the household, and one thinks particularly of murder within the home, or incest, would be considered an offence against the *penates*.[4]

Temples dedicated to public moral virtues were found in Rome from the mid fourth century[5] when the temple of *Concordia* (civil concord) was dedicated in 367.[6] Later there were built temples or altars to *Honos* (military honour) and *Virtus* (courage),[7] *Fides* (reliability),[8] *Spes* (public confidence),[9] *Pietas* (piety),[10] *Pudicitia* (conventional sexual behaviour),[11] and

---

[1] Obseq. 56a: the lightning is not explicitly linked with Pompey's neutrality.

[2] x. 31. 8–9. As in viii. 22. 3 Livy uses *stuprum* in sense of *adulterium*. Cf. also the events of 114 B.C., Obseq. 37; Ovid, *Fast.* iv. 85–164 with F. Bömer's note on 133 concerning Venus Verticordia as goddess of love withheld, citing Val. Max. viii. 15. 12.

[3] Not a proper name but a collective description of all gods worshipped in the home. Serv. on *Aen.* i. 378, cf. K. Latte, *R.R.* 89.

[4] Cat. lxiv. 404 with Fordyce's note on the MS. reading *parentes*; also Liv. i. 48. 7; *penates* of Servius cause downfall of Tarquinius Superbus. See also Gel. iv. 3: A concubine living with a married man offends Juno, though the offence only demands expiation if she has been in contact with a temple of Juno.

[5] K. Latte, *R.R.* 232–42.

[6] Plut. *Cam.* 42; Ovid, *Fast.* i. 637.

[7] Cic. *N.D.* ii. 61; Liv. xxvii. 25. 7; xxix. 11. 13; Val. Max. i. 1. 8; Plut. *Mar.* 28; Plut. *Rom. fort.* 318d.

[8] Cic. *N.D.* ii. 61.

[9] Cic. *Leg.* ii. 11 (28), Tac. *Ann.* ii. 49.   [10] Liv. xl. 34. 4 dedicated 181.

[11] Ibid. x. 23. 3 shrines of *Pudicitia plebeia* and *Pudicitia patricia*. Women who had been once married were the only ones allowed to offer sacrifices. But in

Libertas (freedom).[1] To dedicate a temple to an abstract deity
was of course to make a public affirmation of the importance of
that particular quality.[2] But if cult has any meaning the worship implied that a supernatural power was interested in a
particular kind of behaviour, and would help to make it prevail
among its worshippers. Moreover, worship of moral abstractions could not logically limit itself to ritual: respect for the
deity had to be shown in behaviour also. A man who wished to
honour *Libertas* ought to uphold the republican constitution.[3]
A statue of *Concordia* in the senate house could be expected to
restrain the aggressiveness of the speakers.[4]

An approach to a belief in a supernatural moral order is also
implied in the Roman treatment of prodigies. A deed that
aroused violent moral indignation might be considered a *prodigium*,[5] i.e. an indication that something was wrong in the
relations between the Romans and their gods, and that a
piaculum, usually ritual, was needed to set it right. This does not
mean that the gods were necessarily thought to condemn the
deed (after all, most prodigies were morally neutral) but it does
mean that the shocking deed, if ignored, would be followed by
disaster and thus in a sense would have brought about its own
punishment.[6] This belief hardly required the intervention of
a god, but nevertheless implied a moral order built into the
natural world.

I have tried to show that the nature of Roman religion was
such that it was bound to be involved in the rules governing

Livy's time the cult was no longer practised. Cf. K. Latte, *R.R.* 239 n. 3. See
also, p. 51 n. 2, above.

[1] Liv. xxiv. 16. 19 dedicated in second half of third century. K. Latte, *R.R.*
256.

[2] When Marius founded a temple of *Virtus* and *Honos* he was clearly asserting
the value to the state of merit (shown by himself) as opposed to birth, the qualification of the nobility.

[3] Cic. *Dom.* 42 (110).

[4] Ibid. 51 (131), cf. also the religious protection of property boundaries implied
in the worship of Terminus and proclaimed in the prophecy of Vegoia.

[5] That deeds as well as unusual phenomena were thought of as prodigious
is implied by the application of *prodigium* and *monstrum* to people, e.g. Catiline or
Cleopatra.

[6] Admittedly this is speculation. I have no certain examples, but the sack
penalty, see above, p. 42 n. 2, suggests that this fear became attached to parricide.
In a quite different context Prop. ii. 6. 19–22 suggests that Romulus by organizing
the rape of the Sabine women was responsible for later immorality and all the
evil resulting from it.

behaviour. This was so, quite apart from Greek influences. The
latter were of course very strong over centuries, and favoured
the close involvement of religion in morality in several ways.
Basically, the relationship between religion and morality at
Athens was very similar to that prevailing at Rome, but the
Athenian gods seem to have had a wider and more prominent
part in the sanctioning of morality than the Roman gods.[1] Then
the Greeks, and again especially the Athenians, developed a
philosophical concept of a divine nature that was essentially
good, and whose worship required moral conduct above all.[2]
In particular, Stoic philosophy[3] taught that God must be
imitated. The Stoic god was pure reason, but since the philosophy taught that conduct guided by reason would *ipso facto* be
good and moral, the Stoic could be said to worship God through
the conduct of his life rather than through ritual. But the peak
of Stoic influence was reached only around A.D. 100.

It is difficult to assess the practical significance of the vague
penumbra of moral concern that surrounded the Roman idea of
the supernatural. Normally, I would imagine, thoughts of the
gods did not loom largely in the minds of the individual Roman
when he was wondering whether to perform or to omit a particular action. The moral effect of religion was moderated by
the absence of a formulated code of divine commandments; and
by the fact that the ancient gods were thought of as most
effective when they were actually present, and as more effectively present in their temples than elsewhere. It is likely
that the fact that a man would have to perform a sacrifice, or
other religious act, would sharpen his conscience and induce him
to consider whether any recent conduct of his might be thought
reprehensible.[4] Romans had to perform sacrifices of some kind
or other on many occasions, but no doubt sacrifices and related

---

[1] See K. J. Dover (1974), 246–68; esp. 252: 'it becomes difficult to think of
any context which would attract any kind of secular valuation and yet could not
be called pious and impious.' Also the 'reserved area' of divine interest was wider
and beliefs about punishment after death more conspicuous.

[2] e.g. Plato, *Rep.* ii. 18 (379). Philosophers also emphasized much more the
'spiritual' part of worship. This was true even of the Epicureans: pietas . . .
pacata posse omnia mente tueri (Lucr. v. 1197–203).

[3] See below, p. 114.

[4] In *De Domo* Cicero argued against the validity of the consecration of the
site of his house by Clodius on the ground (among others) of Clodius' immorality
(esp. 139); cf. R. J. Goar (1972).

soul-searching were most frequent in times of crisis, whether individual or national. It is at such times that one would expect the link between morality and religion to be most apparent. At such times, also, religious fear would be most likely to give strength to a demand for moral reform in the community.

II

THE AUGUSTAN REVIVAL

1. *Restoration after disaster: a two-pronged approach*

THE civil wars that followed the murder of Caesar were long drawn-out and calamitous. Many died in battle. Thousands were killed in the proscriptions. Very many all over Italy lost all or some of their property, which was handed over to the veterans of the huge armies of the victorious side. There was much fighting between soldiers and civilians before the new distribution of land was accepted.[1]

The emotional impact of these events can still be felt in the works of a great generation of Roman writers. The experience of the war years shaped the literary personalities of Virgil, Horace, and Livy, and to a lesser extent Propertius. Sallust wrote during the period of civil war, and his basic theme is civil strife, but his outlook had been formed earlier. The art of Ovid already reflects the Augustan peace.[2]

In both Horace and Virgil we can feel the hopelessness engendered by the age of civil wars that would never end. 'Already a second generation is being ground to pieces by civil war, and Rome through her own strength is tottering. The city that neither the neighbouring Marsians had power to ruin nor the Etruscan host ... nor Hannibal ... this self-same city we ourselves shall ruin, we an impious generation of stock accursed.' In this poem written between 42 and 38 Horace, seeing no hope in the actual world of politics, counsels retirement to private life and literature.[3] Virgil found an impressive image:

> The wicked war-god runs amok through all the world:
> So when racing chariots have rushed from the starting gate,

---

[1] Dio, xlviii. 5–15. Proscriptions: App. *B.C.* iv. 2–6; confiscations iv. 2–3.
[2] F. Klingner (1961), 274–311; H. D. Meyer (1961).
[3] *Epod.* xvi, cf. J. V. Pöschl (1956), 16. E. Fraenkel (1957), 42–53. See also *Epod.* vii. 17: acerba fata Romanos agunt.

They gather speed on the course and the driver tugs at the curb
rein,
His horses run away, car out of control, quite helpless.[1]

When looking for a cause and related remedy for disasters of
this kind the Romans had traditionally sought a double explanation, a religious and a secular one. Each was as important
as the other and both would have to be put right if the state was
to recover.[2] It was so during the civil wars after Caesar's death.
We will examine each remedy in turn.

2. *Religious reform*

The traditional religious explanation of public disaster was that
divine anger had been provoked by incorrect or neglectful
ritual. The corresponding remedy was to establish what ritual
fault had been committed and to put it right. During the civil
war the Romans felt that they were being punished by angry
gods, and even after Octavian had defeated Antony and Cleopatra, and peace seemed in sight, men continued to worry
whether the 'peace of the gods' had really been restored. This
feeling of unease is expressed in a poem of Horace's, written in
28–27 B.C. after a spell of exceptionally bad weather. Snow,
hail, lightning, and flooding seemed to indicate that the gods
remained angry, and that resumption of civil war was still
likely. The question was, how could the gods be appeased?
'Which of the gods shall the Roman people call to the aid of
a collapsing empire . . . To whom will Jupiter assign the role
of expiating our guilt?'[3] An answer is given in another poem:
'You will continue to pay for the sins of your fathers, Roman,
though innocent yourself, until you restore the crumbling
temples and shrines of the gods and their statues filthy with
black smoke.'[4] The Romans' sufferings will continue until the
neglect of the gods has been made good.

Livy tells us how the Romans traditionally reacted to a situation like this. After a Roman army had been wiped out by
Hannibal in the battle of Lake Trasimene, Fabius Maximus
was appointed dictator to deal with the emergency. He

---

[1] *Georg.* i. 511–14, trans. C. Day Lewis.   [2] Liv. xxii. 9–11; xxiii. 57.
[3] *Hor.* i. 1. 25–30.   [4] iii. 6. 1–4.

immediately announced his diagnosis, neglect of the gods. The senate ordered a consultation of the Sibylline oracles so that the omissions and their appropriate remedies might be established. The *decemviri* looked up the oracular books and published what they found, a long and various list of spectacular religious performances. The senate accepted the advice of the priests and all the ceremonies were in due course carried out. At the same time a new strategy, the famous Fabian strategy, was adopted. But this was only thought to have a chance because the gods had been previously appeased.[1]

For the generation of Romans that lived through the civil wars which destroyed the republic the old procedure was no longer available. The record of prodigies observed at Rome, as far as it can be reconstructed from Obsequens and Dio, suggests that this technique for monitoring the divine state of mind was being abandoned.[2] No portents were recorded for 51. There is a brief notice for 50. A long list of portents is said to have been seen at Rome at 49, but no expiation was undertaken because republicans and Caesarians both thought that the prodigies threatened the other side.[3] Lucan describes an expiation ceremony after what might be the portents of 49, but his list of prodigies seems to be a reconstruction. Certainly the procession which includes the *sodales Titienses* looks anachronistic.[4] There is no record of Roman portents for 48 or 47, and only a brief one for 46. The year 45 has signs seen in Spain before the battle of Munda,[5] and 44 only signs specifically linked with the murder

---

[1] Liv. xxii. 9. 7–11, cf. the religious response to the defeats and misfortunes in 114 B.C. and following years described by E. Rawson (1974), 198–203.

[2] Obsequens has the fullest record, ultimately based on Livy (P. L. Schmidt (1968), 11 ff.). This can be supplemented from Dio, and Pliny's *Natural History* and Appian's *Civil Wars*. It may be that even in the earlier republic prodigies were not reported every year: we have records for 80 years out of 120 between 200 and 80 B.C. (J. North (1968)). But assuming that the surviving lists are ultimately, or to a considerable extent, based on lists of prodigies officially reported and expiated (P. L. Schmidt (1968), F. Händel (1959), and, sceptically, E. Rawson (1971)) it looks as if this practice was fading out in the last decades of the republic.

[3] Dio, xli. 14. 6.

[4] Luc. i. 522–605. According to M. W. Hoffmann Lewis (1955), 113–14 there is no reference to the *sodales Titii* in republican sources. It is likely that Augustus had to revive the college.

[5] These were not *prodigia* of the kind officially expiated by the consuls; for such had to take place on *ager Romanus* (Liv. xliii. 13; xlv. 16; Diod. xxxii. 12. 2; xlii. 19. 2). It is likely that the *prodigia* at Munda are part of the historical tradition— perhaps even *post eventum*—of the battle.

of Caesar.[1] After the death of Caesar there is a revival: there are lists for 43, 42, 39, 38, 37, 32, 31. There was a portentous Tiber flood in 27.[2] After the constitutional settlement of 27 the Roman lists of general warning almost cease.[3] Henceforth portents are only related in connection with particular events, mainly the births and deaths of princes. Livy can regret that portents are no longer reported or appeased.[4]

Various explanations are possible. We have seen that men were beginning to look at portents as indications of what would happen, rather than as warnings of what might happen unless the gods were adequately appeased.[5] Moreover the procedure for dealing with portents was intimately linked with the republican system of government and the management by the senate of sovereign popular assemblies. When that system collapsed, traditional ways of maintaining the *pax deorum* lost a principal reason for existence.[6] It may be that in a deeply disturbed state it was hopeless to try to restore confidence by ritual means alone. When Augustus emerged as the *de facto* ruler of Rome he was probably reluctant to leave to the senate the influence over public opinion that resulted from the recognition and expiation of prodigies. He himself used different techniques, administrative as well as religious.[7]

Thus the traditional ritual for dealing with the religious aspect of national disaster was not available, and fundamental

---

[1] See Weinstock (1971), 342–6. The signs are *post eventum* and therefore not derived from a list of expiated signs.

[2] 43 B.C.: Dio, xlv. 1–17; 42 B.C.: Dio, xlvii. 40. 1–5. Obseq. 70 notes that these were expiated. Dio, xlvii. 40. 6–8 has unfavourable signs of a different kind. 41/40 B.C.: no Roman signs. 40/39 B.C.: Dio, xlviii. 33. 3–4; 39/38 B.C.: Dio, xlviii. 43. 4; 38/37 B.C.: Dio, xlviii. 52. 1; 37/6–34/3 B.C.: no Roman signs. 33/32 B.C.: Dio, l. 8. 1–6; 32/31 B.C.: Dio, l. 10. 2–6; 27 B.C.: Dio, liii. 20.

[3] Perhaps in 23 B.C. (Dio, liii. 35. 5), or are these linked with the death of Marcellus? 22 B.C.: Dio, liv. 1. 1–3. 17 B.C.: Obseq. 71; Dio, 54. 19. 7. They result in prayers for the return of Augustus. 11 B.C.: Obseq. 72; Plin. *N.H.* xi. 18 (55). This notice seems linked with a campaign rather than urban history.

[4] Liv. xliii. 13. 1: non sum nescius ab eadem neglegentia, qua nihil deos portendere vulgo nunc credant, neque nuntiari admodum ulla prodigia in publicum neque in annales referri.

[5] See above, p. 38.

[6] If Obsequens more or less accurately reflects the taking-up of prodigies at Rome the institution ceased to work in the traditional manner as early as the Social war (91 B.C.). After this there are notices for fewer years, and of the prodigies reported many have reference to particular events.

[7] See below, p. 96.

reform was needed. The Romans, like other ancient societies, always preferred that reform should at least seem to involve the revival of good old customs and this tendency was never stronger than in the Augustan age, whose entire literature displays deep emotional attachment to the historical institutions of Rome. Virgil never allows the reader to forget that he is reading about practices and customs which, countless generations later, were still shaping life in his city.[1] The romantic attitude to traditional institutions found its fullest expression in Livy's *History*,[2] which is, among other things, a painstaking reconstruction[3] of a traditional society and its ethos.[4]

The theme of reconstruction is built even into the structure of the *History*. In contrast to Sallust,[5] who had published his *History* only a few years before Livy began to write, Livy went back to the very beginnings of Rome, and proceeded to give his work a traditional appearance by composing it in the form of *annales*.[6] This meant that the main division of the narrative would correspond to the annual elections at Rome, and not to the pattern created by the events themselves. Thus the traditional institutions are placed in the centre of the picture. The framework also ensures the regular inclusion of religious notices. In the annalistic manner the account of each year is preceded by a list of divine signs and the means by which they were ritually expiated.[7] This is the point of view of the old *pontifices* who had given the divine messages to the Roman people a pre-eminent place in their historical record of the year.[8]

In the narrative the spirit of religious revival is represented

---

[1] For references see C. Bailey (1935); W. Warde Fowler (1917); A. G. McKay (1971), 121–46.

[2] Cf. xliii. 13. 2: mihi vetustas res scribenti nescioquo pacto antiquus fit animus.

[3] But Livy was not an antiquarian: P. G. Walsh (1961), 110 ff.; id. (1974), 13–14. He probably did not even consult Varro's *Antiquities*: R. M. Ogilvie (1965), 6–7. Some of his documents are pastiches: ibid. 111 on i. 24. 7; ibid. 127 on i. 32. 4 ff. (fetial formula).

[4] Needless to say it remains an expression of Augustan sensibility.

[5] On Sallust in *preface* see Ogilvie (1965), 23 ff.

[6] Walsh (1974), 23; ibid. 8–9 shows that Livy used composition by decade to bring out the principal stages in the growth and subsequent internal decline of the Roman state.

[7] Bibliography in P. G. Walsh (1974), 13 n. 3. The material is displayed in E. B. Kraus (1930).

[8] J. E. A. Crake (1940); E. Rawson (1971).

by the exemplary piety in word and deed of heroes of the past.[1]
A number of episodes are elaborated to teach the advantages of
piety, and the disastrous consequences of its absence. Of these
the most elaborate is the account in Book V of the capture of
Veii and the Gallic invasion. Its message is summed up in
Camillus' speech: 'Consider the course of history during these
last few years: you will find that when we followed the gods'
guidance all was well; when we scorned it all was ill . . .'[2]

The religious passages in Livy's History—like the political
ones—look backward. The presentation is unproblematical.
The gods are the traditional gods. There is the traditional
suspicion of foreign innovations. The gods demand the traditional worship. They make no explicit moral demands on the
worshipper or on the community, except in the area of *fides*,
i.e. of oaths and contracts[3]. They make demands, which are
revealed by the interpreters of signs, but these are formal, the
draining of a lake, the repetition of a festival, the performance of
a new rite.[4] The gods are meticulous but they are not greedy.[5]
They do not demand expensive gifts. They expect exact performance—but respect legal quibbling.[6]

Religion is unemotional. Emotional religion, particularly
when kindled in the masses, is objectionable and dangerous,[7]
and among foreigners a sign of barbarism.

Secular and religious measures are in a peculiar way separate but complementary. The capture of Veii episode is used to
illustrate most vividly how success can be achieved by the
Romans only when they employ a combination of religious and
political or military measures. To a rationalist reader the detail
of the account of, for instance, Camillus' generalship might
provide a self-sufficient explanation of the Roman victory, but
this is not what Livy wants to suggest. The whole episode, as
well as the following one of the capture of Rome by the Gauls,
is composed to show that generalship and other secular factors

[1] P. G. Walsh (1961), 82–109.
[2] Liv. v. 51. 5.
[3] See W. Liebeschuetz (1967), 46 n. 11, 48 n. 46.
[4] e.g. Liv. xxix. 10. 4.
[5] Such at least was the theory: Liv. x. 42. 7; cf. Dion Hal. ii. 23. 4–5; Cic.
Leg. ii. 9 (22). But public sacrifices could be on a massive scale.
[6] Liv. x. 40. 11.
[7] W. Liebeschuetz (1967), 49 nn. 53, 56.

are not enough unless accompanied by religious support.[1]
After making this point strongly in Book v, Livy came back to it
only occasionally in later books. But this is natural. Ritual was
repetitive. Normally it was less picturesque than the draining
of a lake, which had contributed to the capture of Veii. There
are very many descriptions (particularly in the later books of
the history), of campaigns in which military factors, generalship
and the qualities of soldiers alone are described, but it would be
wrong to conclude that Livy had changed his mind and how
thought ritual measures insignificant.[2] On the other hand, the
detailed (if not always expert) accounts of military operations
illustrate the fact that for Livy, and Romans in general,
insistence on the importance of the co-operation of the gods
never implied that military science was unimportant: quite the
reverse.

As has been said earlier, Livy's advocacy of religion is un-
problematic: religion is presented with the tacit assumption
that it works, that the gods if treated in the proper way will
assist the Roman state. This does not necessarily mean that
Livy really believed that the proper working of religion would
or could be restored. To the present writer at any rate it
appears that Livy viewed the possibility of restoring ancestral
virtues pessimistically.[3] Nevertheless such unconditional assent
to the Roman tradition could be made the theoretical basis of
a revival. After all, it provided a diagnosis of the ills from which
Rome was suffering, and challenged a contemporary leader to
imitate the heroes of the golden age of the republic. In the same
way Virgil's great pageant of history in the Sixth Book of the
Aeneid quite naturally culminates in the reign of Augustus.[4]
Livy was much less committed to the *princeps* than Virgil, but
occasionally he too hints at parallels between the achievements
of the 'founders' Hercules, Romulus, Numa, Camillus, and
those of Augustus himself.[5] In due course the *princeps* was to

[1] e.g. the combination of ritual and Camillus at the capture of Veii: Liv.
v. 19. 1–2; or of the *devotio* of Decius and the generalship of Manlius in the great
Latin war: viii. 6 ff., cf. W. Liebeschuetz, op. cit. 47–8.

[2] A partial explanation is that much of the military history outside Italy is based
on Polybius who did not shape history into *exempla* of piety.

[3] W. Liebeschuetz, op. cit. 54–5 nn. 126–8.

[4] *Aen.* vi. 791–805.

[5] Use of adjective *augustus* with Romulus—i. 8. 3, with Hercules—i. 7. 9, cf.
R. M. Ogilvie (1965), ad. loc. Numa shuts gate of Janus: i. 19. 23.

make the same point, for he built a great temple of Mars Ultor
and decorated its precinct with statues of the great Romans.[1]
His aim, like Livy's, was educational. Every young man entering the army for the first time was to worship here and to be
impressed by the *exempla* in stone all around him.

While Livy revived the spirit, or what he thought the spirit,
of old Roman religion, he had not familiarized himself with it
by antiquarian research. Even passages which seem to re-
produce the quaint diction of an ancient document have been
shown to be archaizing reconstructions.[2] Livy's History could
not serve as a self-sufficient blueprint for a religious revival. But
Varro's great work 'The Religious Antiquities of Rome' could
so serve. Of this Cicero had said: 'We were wandering and
straying about like visitors in our own city, and your books led
us, so to speak, right home and enabled us at least to realise
where we were. You have revealed the age of our native city,
the laws of its religion and its priesthoods, the terminology,
classification and moral and rational basis of all our religious
and secular institutions.'[3]

Thus Augustus had the information he needed and duly went
ahead. 'In my sixth consulate I repaired 82 temples in the city
at the instigation of the senate.'[4] The proud words touch only
one aspect of his policy. Augustus also revived or radically
reorganized various religious colleges: the *fetiales*, whom he
employed to declare war on Cleopatra, the *Salii*, the *Sodales
Titi*, the *fratres Arvales*.[5] He revived the ceremony of the
augurium salutis.[6] On three occasions he marked the establishment of peace over the whole Roman world (more or less) by
ceremoniously closing the Gates of Janus.[7] He found and re-
consecrated the original wolf's cave for the festival of the
Lupercalia.[8] A good deal of ancient ritual was brought back,
allusions to which Augustan authors have tactfully worked into
their writings.[9]

[1] Aug. *R.G.* 20. 1 (2 B.C.); Dio, lv. 10. 2.   [2] See above, p. 59 n. 3.
[3] Cic. *Acad.* i. 3. 9 trans. H. Rackham, cf. Augustine, *C.D.* vi. 2 and iv. 3.
[4] Aug. *R.G.* 20. 4.
[5] M. W. Hoffmann Lewis (1955); G. Wissowa (1895), 1963–85.
[6] See J. Liegle (1942).   [7] K. Latte, *R.R.* 13 (45).   [8] Aug. *R.G.* 19.
[9] Besides Livy see Prop. iv. 1. 19–37 with references to Parilia (on which see
Weinstock (1971), 175 ff. Weinstock (1971), 175 ff., 184 ff.), Vesta, cult at the
compita, Lupercal; id. iv. 10: Jupiter Feretrius; iv. 9: Ara maxima; id. iv. 6: Apollo
of the Palatine. Also Ovid, *Fast.*: *passim*.

While restoration figures prominently in the *Res Gestae*, Augustus' own memoirs, and in the surviving literature, innovation was at least as important. To take an example, Augustus not only brought up to strength some priestly colleges and revived others,[1] but he also transformed the role of the colleges. The part of the great colleges in the process of political decision-making came to an end. After 44 B.C. we know of only four consultations with political implications of the *pontifices*.[2] We hear of only one case of the use of auspices to block an election, temporarily, and of two consultations of the Sibylline books.[3] The standing of the *fratres arvales* was higher under the empire than it had ever been before, but the function of the college was different. Rites addressed to Dia Dea to ensure a good harvest[4] came to occupy only a very small part of the college's time. Its main function now was to petition or thank gods on behalf of the emperor and his family.[5] The same was true of the other colleges. We are told for instance that the *pontifices* performed annual rites at the altar of *fortuna redux*.[6] The consuls and the four major colleges took turns every four years to produce games for the welfare of Augustus.[7] On 17 January the four major colleges sacrificed at the *ara numinis Augusti*.[8] The colleges jointly made annual offerings at the *ara pacis*.[9] On various imperial anniversaries the major colleges combined to take part in a procession which culminated in sacrifices on behalf of the emperor.[10] The minor colleges too were almost entirely occupied with rites of loyalty.[11]

[1] M. W. Hoffmann Lewis (1955), 7–23, 111–17 is fundamental for the following section.

[2] Dio, xlviii. 44; Tac. *Ann.* i. 10. in 38 B.C.; Dio, xlviii. 53. 4–6 in 37 B.C.; Tac. *Ann.* xi. 15 in A.D. 47. Ibid. xii. 8 in A.D. 49. They continued to be consulted about family religion and burials. See G. Rohde (1936); P. Preibisch (1878).

[3] Dio, liv. 24. 1 (14 B.C.): aediles resign. Dio, xlviii. 43. 4–6 (38 B.C.): Sibylline Books order purification of statue of Magna Mater. Tac. *Ann.* xv. 44 (A.D. 54): Books consulted after fire. Ibid. i. 76: Tiberius refused to consult Sibylline Books.

[4] G. Wissowa, 'Arvales Fratres' (1895).

[5] *Acta fratrum Arvalium*: Henzen (1874); A. Pasoli (1950); E. M. Smallwood (1966).

[6] Aug. *R.G.* 11.

[7] M. W. Hoffmann Lewis, op. cit. 19 n. 57.

[8] *C.I.L.* i. 231, 308; M. W. Hoffmann Lewis, ibid. 58.

[9] Aug. *R.G.* 12.

[10] Suet. *Gaius* 16; Tac. *Ann.* vi. 5; xii. 68.

[11] On activities of *fratres Arvales, sodales Titii, fetiales, luperci, salii, sodales Augustales* see M. W. Hoffmann Lewis, op. cit. 111–17.

Socially the major colleges remained extremely exclusive. A quite disproportionate number of patricians, whether descendants of the original patrician families or of recent creation, were found among the priests. Thus the colleges provided an instrument for involving the aristocracy in practical demonstrations of loyalty to the emperor, while at the same time they enabled the emperor to reward the most distinguished of his more humbly-born assistants with entry into the best society.[1] Augustus boasted that he had helped no fewer than 170 supporters into priesthoods.[2] Humbler followers were given a chance to display loyalty and to make social contacts in appropriately less exclusive associations. The *Luperci* were reserved for knights,[3] and freedmen formed the membership of the *Augustales* or *seviri Augustales*,[4] colleges that were found in many cities in the West, and whose duties comprised mainly the performances of rites in honour of the emperor.

The transformation of the colleges was of religious as well as political significance. Under the empire the peace of the Roman world and the well-being of the city of Rome was thought to depend, and did indeed depend, very largely on the actions of the emperor. The greatest service the gods could perform for the Roman people was to preserve and aid him. Hence the reign of Augustus witnessed the invasion of the religious calendar of the Roman people by a large number of imperial anniversaries. For example, prayers were offered to various gods on the anniversary of Augustus' first holding a magistracy of the Roman people (7 January), of his receiving the title Augustus (16 January), of his election as *pontifex maximus* (6 March), of his first victory (14 April), and on very many similar occasions.[5] Anniversaries of the empress and of leading members of the imperial family were celebrated in the same way. This part of Augustus' policy was of course maintained by his successors. The number of imperial anniversaries grew steadily and from

---

[1] See analysis of membership of colleges in M. W. Hoffmann Lewis, op. cit.

[2] Aug. *R.G.* 25.

[3] M. W. Hoffmann Lewis, op. cit. 115.

[4] They must be distinguished from the highly select *sodales Augustales* (M. W. Hoffmann Lewis, op. cit. 116). The creation of colleges for freedmen recognized the fact that they formed a large proportion of the population of cities, cf. P. Brunt (1971), 386-7. On colleges see L. R. Taylor (1931), 219 ff.

[5] See the conflation of epigraphic calendars in V. Ehrenberg and A. H. M. Jones (1949), 44-54. For later periods see W. F. Snyder (1940), 225 ff.

time to time the calendar had to be purged of obsolete com-
memorations.[1] Under the empire, the calendar thus bore witness
to a radical change of front of Roman public religion. Henceforth the most important aspect of the *pax deorum* was the gods'
protection and support of the *princeps*. This is most clearly
illustrated by the development of the public vows. In the
republic the consuls offered vows at the beginning of each year
for the preservation of the republic. Under the emperors the
consuls continued to make their vows on 1 January but these
were supplemented and overshadowed by the vows for the
safety of the emperor on 3 January. The same vows were
undertaken on the same day by all provincial governors,[2] so that
the date became something like an empire-wide day of prayer
for the emperor. It was the change in the object of worship,
with the result that intercession was made for the ruler rather
than the commonwealth which was the essential transformation
of the state religion in the reign of Augustus.

That the ruler, or a deified predecessor, might receive
religious honours was merely one aspect of this reorientation of
public religion. To us the offer of worship to living or dead men
may seem absurd. It is clear that it did not seem so to Romans.
A cult of Julius Caesar arose, it seems spontaneously, soon after
his murder,[3] and was thought to have received supernatural
confirmation when a comet was seen during seven nights while
the *Ludi Victoriae Caesaris* were being celebrated. This provided
an opportunity for Octavian (the later Augustus) to proclaim
that the comet was Caesar's soul, and to give wide publicity to
the claim by attaching stars to statues of Caesar.[4] Thus Octavian
could begin his political career with the unique advantage of

[1] Charlesworth (1937), 58 ff.

[2] Vows taken by magistrates in the republic Th. Mommsen, *R.St.* i. 244–6,
616. A formula: Si res publica populi Romani quiritium ad quinquennium proxi-
mum . . . servata erit . . . tum donum duit populus Romanus quiritium quod
ver attulerit . . . (Liv. xxii. 10. 2). The consuls on 1 January sacrificed in fulfilment
of the vow for the last year and renewed it for the year to come (Dio, fr. 102. 12;
xlv. 17. 9; li. 19. 7; Ovid, *Fast.* i. 79). Caesar was the first individual to be included
in the annual vows (Dio, xliv. 6. 1). Vows for the *princeps* were moved to a separate
ceremony on 3 January in A.D. 38. For the terms of the vow see, for example, *Acta
fratrum Arvalium* (Henzen), 107. On the whole subject see K. Latte, *R.R.* 314;
H. Mattingly (1950); S. Weinstock (1971), 217–20, with many references.

[3] Weinstock (1971), 364–7.

[4] Servius in *Aen.* viii. 681. Augustus' private view: Plin. *N.H.* ii. 94; Serv.
in *Ecl.* ix. 46.

having a god for a father. It is not surprising that among the first acts of the Second Triumvirate was the establishment of a formal state cult for the dead Caesar.[1]

Deification of rulers dead or alive did not form part of the Roman political tradition, but there is no reason to suppose that it was repugnant to Roman feelings. Worship of a deceased benefactor might arise spontaneously among the humbler classes.[2] Deification was something which could not be ruled out as impossible by even the most sophisticated. After all, there was general agreement that some of the unquestioned gods, e.g. Hercules, Asclepius, Romulus-Quirinus, had once been men.[3] Virgil has expressed the spirit in which the deification of the dead Caesar was accepted in the hope that he would use his influence for lasting peace. 'See how Olympian Caesar's star has climbed into the sky, the star to gladden all our corn with grain and paint the grapes with purple on the sun-bathed hills. Graft your pears, Daphnis, now; your children's children will enjoy the fruit.'[4] It is significant that the deified Julius Caesar, the deified Augustus, and all the other emperors who were consecrated by due process after their deaths, became part of the official pantheon of the Roman people.[5] This was not a status ever conferred on a living emperor.

Nevertheless, the sophisticated were ready to confer divine honours even on a living benefactor notwithstanding that this meant transferring the ritual and even the titles of religion to a person who could not be seriously thought to have supernatural powers. Virgil again furnishes an example. 'Ah Meliboeus a god made possible this happy leisure of mine, for he will always be a god for me, and blood of a young lamb from my fold will often stain his altar.'[6] That gratitude should take this form was unusual at Rome but far from unprecedented.[7] That the

---

[1] Weinstock, op. cit. 385–401.

[2] e.g. to the Gracchi on sites where they had been killed: Plut. *C.G.* 18.

[3] Cic. *Leg.* ii. 7 (19); *N.D.* ii. 24 (62). But no tax exemption could be claimed on behalf of a god who had once been a human being: *N.D.* iii. 19 (49). This was not always upheld in court: *S.I.G.*[3] 747.

[4] *Ecl.* ix. 47, trans. E. V. Rieu.

[5] C. Habicht (1972), 70.

[6] *Ecl.* i. 6–8.

[7] Humorously: Plautus, *Pers.* 99: 'O mi Iuppiter terrestris, te coepulonus compellat tuos.' Hanson (1959), 64 shows that identification of an individual with a deity is frequent in Plautus; obviously not sacrilegious but funny. Gratitude to

offering of religious honours to a ruler should be a normal part
of the ceremony of government was Greek rather than Roman.

To Greeks the idea of the cult of a man had never been
completely blasphemous. It was for instance regularly given to
a founder of a city, usually after death, but sometimes in his
lifetime. Up to the end of the fifth century Greek cities had
aimed at self-sufficiency, owing their security to the virtue of
the citizens aided by the support of their gods. In the course
of the fourth century the cities came to depend on great rulers
in the way they had previously depended on gods and began to
show their gratitude for particular benefits by honouring their
ruler in ways previously reserved for gods. Once started, the cult
might be continued in the hope that it would elicit further
favours. Eventually divine honours became a conventional
means of showing respect. The Greeks offered them, among
many others, to Roman provincial governors.[1] When the republic collapsed Roman citizens in Italian municipalities and indeed
in Rome itself found themselves to be similarly dependent on
a great ruler. The Roman poets show that the readiness to use
the forms of worship as a means of showing gratitude existed in
Italy.[2] The scene was set for the transfer of the Hellenistic
ritual to Rome and Italy when Julius Caesar was progressing
towards deification in his lifetime. But this development, like
the development to monarchy, was interrupted in 44 B.C. by
Caesar's murder.

It looks as if the deepest objection to ruler worship among
those Romans who objected to it was that it was monarchical.
It seems to have been this which inhibited Augustus, if not from
the start of his career,[3] at least after he had defeated Antony

consul who has supported Cicero's recall from exile: *Red. Sen.* 4 (8): 'P. Lentulus,
parens ac deus nostrae vitae, fortunae, memoriae, nominis.' Cult for Marius in
houses after victory over Germans: Plut. *Mar.* 27. 9; to Marius Gratidianus after
a popular edict: Cic. *Off.* iii. 20 (80). See A. D. Nock (1928), 31 n. 51 = A. D.
Nock (1972), 145. Also M. P. Charlesworth (1935), a most illuminating article.
S. Weinstock (1971), 293–6. A *triumphator* traditionally dressed up as Jupiter.
See R. M. Ogilvie (1965), 272–3, 679–80. Weinstock (1971) has a wealth of material
on religious honours conferred on Julius Caesar. See also the review of Weinstock's
book by A. Alföldi (1975), and by J. North in *J.R.S.* lxv (1975), 171–7.

[1] C. Habicht (1970); D. Roloff (1970); K. Dover (1974), 75–81.

[2] Deification of Augustus by the poets: references in Weinstock (1971) 304–5.
Cf. Plin. *N.H.* ii. 18–19: Hic est vetustissimus referendi bene merentibus gratiam
ut tales numinibus adscribant.

[3] That Octavian the triumvir was less inhibited as far as deification was

and Cleopatra and was seeking to re-establish constitutional government. Determined not to suffer the fate of Caesar, he ostentatiously rejected the role of monarch. His professed purpose was the restoration of the republic, and he took care that his position should be defined as far as possible, in terms of the republican constitution. Augustus was *princeps,* first citizen, not king or dictator. 'Henceforth', to cite his autobiography, 'I excelled all in influence but of power I had no more than my colleagues in whatever office I was holding.'[1] It followed that he could not receive honours like Caesar and the Greek kings. The conditions of first citizen and god were not compatible. Among his fellow citizens official apotheosis would have to await his death.

But this did not alter the fact that the use of religious ritual to express gratitude or loyalty to the ruler had become part of the political vocabulary,[2] and that there was no equally expressive alternative. Cities and organizations and, very occasionally, private individuals would take up this ritual language to proclaim their loyal feelings. Such behaviour was far too expedient to be suppressed. It remained for Augustus to regulate the use of the language so that it reflected the image of his rule which he wished to present to a particular group of subjects. Thus it is clear that at Rome and to Romans in general, Augustus stressed his position as first citizen, and therefore at least after 27 B.C. checked direct deification.[3]

In Rome or Italy, when Augustus permitted or encouraged ceremonies which might appear to approach worship of the living ruler, he normally ensured that they were developed from traditional ritual which had no associations with kingship. Among the honours voted to Augustus by the senate after his victory over Antony and Cleopatra was that libations should be

concerned than Augustus the *princeps* is argued by P. Lambrechts (1953), also T. Taeger (1957), 162.

[1] *R.G.* 34. 3. On refusal of direct worship by Augustus and successors see M. P. Charlesworth (1939).

[2] It was a flexible vocabulary, since it could be adapted to a large number of imperial situations: victory, illness, absence, birth of an heir. Worship of a dead emperor could express loyalty to the Roman state, but loyalty or absence of disloyalty to the reigning emperor could only be demonstrated through some kind of deification of the living ruler.

[3] On this topic, L. R. Taylor (1931) is still fundamental.

poured to his *genius* at all public and private banquets.[1] This looks like worship of Augustus as a god, but in fact it was merely a development of the cult of the *genius*,[2] which was part of the regular worship of the household. It was customary for a man's friends to make libations to his *genius* on the occasion of his birthday.[3] The honour voted for Augustus was merely an extension of this practice, and did not therefore imply deification. Already Plautus' use of the word shows ambiguity as to whether *genius* simply describes a man's personality,[4] or whether it refers to a supernatural guardian spirit separate from the individual.[5] Accordingly, a libation to the *genius* of an individual could be interpreted either as a rite addressed to that individual or, alternatively, as one performed to a divine spirit on his behalf. Thus, even a noble could pour a libation for the *genius* of 'his friend' Augustus without undue abasement.

It looks as if the libations at banquets were intended to express and foster loyalty among men of the upper class. But Augustus was determined to be the representative of the people as well as the nobles of Rome. Ever since the thanksgiving for his great victory at Actium, Augustus patronized local festivals and the theatricals produced by subdivisions of the city at the

---

[1] Dio, li. 19: 'ἐν τοῖς συσσιτίοις οὐχ ὅτι τοῖς κοινοῖς ἀλλὰ καὶ τοῖς ἰδίοις πάντας αὐτῷ σπένδειν'; and Hor. iv. 5. 35 (13 B.C.), taking *numen* to refer to the *genius* of Augustus.

[2] On the cult of the *genius* see Warde Fowler (1914), 17–22; G. Wissowa (1972), 78 ff., 175 ff.; A. D. Nook (1947), 108–72; K. Latte (1960), 333 n. 3; D. Fishwick (*H. Theol. Rev.* 1969); id. (*J.R.S.* (1969)); M. Bulard (1926), 23 ff. Basic questions as to the original significance of the cult of the *genius* (or *genii*) in the home are still without certain answer. See F. Bömer (1966), 88 ff. There is also the problem of how far *genius* and *numen* can be identified, as they are by Latte (1960), 333 n. 3. There was considerable overlap. But under Augustus the cult of the *numen* seems to have been thought more suited to public religion, while the *genius* belonged to the household or smaller subdivisions of the city.

[3] Tib. iv. 5; ii. 2 and (without mentioning *genius*) Hor. iv. 11. 6–7 (of patron); Ovid, *Trist.* v. 5. 2 (of wife). On birthday celebration see W. Schmidt P.W. vii, 1. 1145, s.v. γενέθλιος ἡμέρα. On link between birthday, cult of *genius*, and imperial cult see D. M. Pippidi (1941), 39 ff. Another precedent for the libations to the *genius* of Augustus was the placing of an image of a benefactor among the domestic *lares*, so that the benefactor would be honoured with the household gods (Suet. *Vit.* 2. 5); S.H.A. *M. Aurel.* 3. 5. On *lararia* at Pompeii see G. K. Boyce (1937).

[4] Phrases like *Pers.* 263: genio meo multa bona faciam. Cf. *Aul.* 725; *St.* 622; *Truc.* 182; or *Curc.* 628.

[5] In this sense *genius* is near to supernatural patron: *Capt.* 879; *Curc.* 307; *Men.* 138.

compita or crossroads. Eventually he reorganized the local government of Rome. But in Antiquity the creation of new administrative units was invariably accompanied by the creation of corresponding religious cults. In the case of Augustus' new organization the cult was provided by a reformed version of the worship of the *compita*. Instead of, or in addition to, being a celebration of the end of the year, the cult became a means of expressing the feelings of loyalty of the urban *plebs*. As a result of the reform the old divinities of the crossroads, the Lares and Liber Pater of the *compita*, were replaced by (or modified into) the Lares Augusti and the Genius Augusti.[1] Once again a community ritual became focused on the emperor and his family[2] without becoming worship of the ruler and his family.

In fact, the inhabitants of Rome were being asked to join in Augustus' family worship. Augustus had been very careful to take preliminary measures so that this extension of his family worship would be formally proper. When Augustus became *pontifex maximus* in 12 B.C. he did not move into the official residence of the head of Roman religion, but instead made part of his house on the Palatine hill public land.[3] There he dedicated a shrine of Vesta which contained in addition to an image of that goddess the *lares* and *penates* of Augustus' home.[4] Thus the domestic worship of Augustus' household became a public cult and citizens in general could be asked to join in. In the case of ordinary household worship of the *lares*, the actual ritual was usually carried out by freedmen or slaves. This practice too was adopted for the worship at the *compita*. Freedmen (*magistri*) were

---

[1] On the original character of the *compitalia*—to mark the end of the agricultural season?—see M. Meslin (1970), 41 ff. On Augustus' early patronage of the cult see Boyancé (1950) = (1972), 291–7. Cf. Prop. ii. 22. 13–14; Suet. *Aug.* 31. 4; 57; Verg. *Aen.* viii. 715–18. On Augustus' reform see L. R. Taylor (1931), 184–90; F. Bömer (1957), 707. *C.I.L.* xi. 3200 = *Dessau* 89 dates the reform to 7 B.C. Ovid, *Fast.* v. 145–8; Dio, lv. 8. 6–7 describe the reorganization. For games see M. Bulard (1926), 151–70 and *Delos*, ix (1926), on paintings at Delos.

[2] Dedications *laribus Augustis et genio Caesaris*, *C.I.L.* vi. 445–59, 30957–62; ii. 1133, 4293, 4297; iii. 5158. A similar cult, also looked after by freedmen, might exist in great houses: Tac. *Ann.* i. 73: 'inter cultores Augusti qui per omnes domos in modum collegiorum habebantur, Cassium quendam mimum corpore infamem adscivisset.'

[3] Dio, liv. 27. 3.

[4] *C.I.L.* i². 313; Ovid, *Fast.* iv. 949; *Met.* xv. 864. On the sanctuary see K. Ziegler, P.W. xviii. 3. 60–3, s.v. Palatium.

in charge and they were assisted by slaves (*ministri*).[1] This was appropriate since freedmen formed a high proportion of the population of Rome.[2]

The worship at the *compita* did not figure on the national religious calendar. It nevertheless marked an important stage in the Augustan reorganization of Rome. The new form of worship symbolized the fact that Augustan order had come to the city itself. In 58 B.C. Clodius' political activation of the colleges formerly responsible for the worship at the crossroads had symbolized, as well as accelerated, the breakdown of law and order in the last years of the republic. Julius Caesar had suppressed the colleges.[3] Augustus with his usual tact was slow to interfere in the administration of Rome. But after the settlement of 21 B.C. he began to do so, reluctantly it seemed, but with decisive effect.[4] The people already looked upon him as their patron. By organizing essential services, and later local administration, Augustus 'deserved' the clientage of the people. The cult at the *compita* was a religious corollary of the *princeps'* patronage of the people of Rome.

Once the *genius* of Augustus had become the object of religious honours of various kinds its use to confirm oaths followed. Bömer has proved that this practice did not have precedent in oaths supposedly taken by slaves[5] by the *genius* of their master.

---

[1] On the part of freedmen and slaves in the worship of the *lares* (not *penates* or Vesta) see F. Bömer (1957), 32–6. The inscriptional material including the *vicomagistri* and *vicoministri*, ibid. 37–52. Freedmen worshipping the *genius* of their masters, *C.I.L.* ii. 1980; v. 1868; vi. 257–9, 3684, 30883; x. 860–1; xi. 356, 818, 6806. Cf. Ruggiero, *Dizion. Epigraf.* iii. 453 ff.

[2] P. A. Brunt (1971), 386.

[3] On the *vici* and their colleges and their political exploitation or suppression, see A. Lintott (1968), 77–83; S. Treggiari (1969), 198. Suet. *Div. Jul.* 42; Ovid, *Fast* v. 145 and the commentary by Bömer, *Ed.* ii. 302.

[4] A. H. M. Jones (1960), 12–15; R. Syme (1939), 402–3.

[5] F. Bömer (1966), esp. 104–5, points out that the two passages from Plautus and Terence usually cited are not examples of oaths sworn by members of the *familia* by the *genius* of their master. In each case a suppliant appeals to the person he is petitioning by the latter's *genius*: Plaut. *Capt.* 997; Ter. *Andr.* 289. In Augustan authors invocation of the *genius* is still used in appeals: Tib. iv. 5. 8 (*genius* of beloved in appeal for love); Hor. *Ep.* i. 7. 94 (*genius* of patron in appeal for assistance). In Tib. iv. 13. 5. Ps.-Tib. swears his love by his beloved's Juno; ibid. iii. 6. 48, a girl swears her love by her own eyes, her Juno and her Venus. Even in a straightforward oath of a farm manager to his master (Sen. *Ep.* 12. 2), where the oath is by the *genius* of the master, the context is an appeal for sympathy. The oath by the *genius* of the ruler, as it may have been sworn by the *genius* of Caesar (Dio, xliv. 6.1, 50.1), and eventually was sworn by the *genius* of the reigning

But the oath by the *genius* of the emperor arose spontaneously—
or at least not in response to an explicit order.[1] This is shown by
the fact that Tiberius refused to recognize it.[2] Gaius was the
first emperor to impose the oath, and it was later still that
the genius of the emperor[3] came to figure regularly among the
gods called upon to sanction the official oath of loyalty.[4]

Whether we are justified in treating the cults of loyalty as
religion is a question which is not easily answered. In the first
place, the definition of religion is notoriously difficult.[5] It is
practically impossible to formulate a definition which will
embrace all phenomena to which naïve usage might attach
the adjective religious.[6] Secondly, the cults of loyalty were of
different kinds. A single definition of religion would not cover
every one of them, but I suspect that each aspect of the cult
could be caught by at least one commonly used definition.

There is little difficulty about the religious nature of cult
offered for the emperor. After all, the emperor stood between
the inhabitants and the chaos of civil war. It was in the interest
of almost everybody that the gods should preserve all but the
very worst of emperors.[7] As we have seen, a great part of the

emperor, could not have evolved from this tradition alone. The influence of oaths
by the τύχη of Hellenistic rulers must have had a decisive influence. F. Bömer
(1966), 82–7; P. Hermann (1968), 46–7.

[1] Hor. *Ep.* ii. 15 (12 B.C.) suggests that it was widespread—if *numen* here as
in Odes iv. 5. 33 refers to the genius. But Weinstock (1971), 213 suggests that
there was an abortive attempt in *c.* 13 B.C. to introduce an oath by the *numen*.

[2] Dio, lvii. 8. 3; lviii. 2. 8. Ibid. 12. 6 suggests that oaths by (the *genius* of?)
Tiberius and Sejanus had nevertheless been made unofficially.

[3] Suet. *Cal.* 27. 3, cf. Dio, lix. 14. 7.

[4] In Dometianic municipal charters: *Lex munic. Salp.* (A.D. 81–4), 36; *Lex munic.
Malac.* (A.D. 81–4), 59. Wax tablets from Herculaneum show its use in private agreements under Vespasian. G. P. Carratelli, *Par. d. Pass,* iii (1948), 174 no. 19, 173 f.
nos. 17 f. 171 no. 16, 177 no. 22, 179 no. 24. V. Arangio-Ruiz and G. P. Carratelli,
Par. d. Pass. ix (1954), 64 no. 65 is Neronian. The oath has been able to coexist
with Christianity, cf. the report from Addis Ababa in *The Times* of 18.9.75,
p. 6: 'The solemn oath of truthfulness, *Haile Selassie Yimut*, (I swear by the name
of Haile Selassie) is still used.' In the Christian Roman empire soldiers swore *per
deum et per christum et per spiritum sanctum et per maiestatem imperatoris* (Veget. i. 5).

[5] W. R. Comstock (1972), 18–27; C. Geertz (1966), 1–46.

[6] Defined as reference to the superempirical, C. Y. Glock and R. N. Stark
(1965); as reference to the sacred, E. Dürkheim (1912) and M. Eliade (1961);
as a reference to ultimacy, P. Tillich (1960).

[7] Particular groups, e.g. senators, might find the rule of a particular emperor
intolerable. But for the bulk of the population almost *any* accepted emperor was
better than a disputed succession. Most of the empire ran itself—provided that
war, civil or external, did not intervene.

religion of loyalty prayed for rather than to the emperor. But there was also a good deal of ritual which implied that dead emperors had become gods or even that the living emperor was a god.

Here one must distinguish between ritual addressed to living rulers and ritual addressed to dead ones. About such of the emperors as had been officially consecrated after their deaths there could be no question: they were gods and their worship part of the state religion of Rome. As we have seen Romans were ready to believe that a great public benefactor might in fact become one of the gods.[1] Thus the deification of Augustus, or of some of his successors, was not inherently impossible, and these dead rulers could be enrolled among the gods of the Roman people in a way that living men could not. But of course while it was conceivable that a ruler might become a god after death, some independent evidence was needed to prove that he had in fact done so.

The attitude of mind needed to make worship of the deified ruler a practical possibility was created by a ceremony of confirmation. Whenever the situation required the deification of a deceased emperor, a witness came forward to testify on oath to the senate that he had seen the soul of the departed emperor rise from the funeral pyre. The senate then proceeded to enrol the deceased *princeps* among the gods of the Roman people.[2] This ceremony might occasionally seem as absurd to Romans as it does to us. But not entirely.[3] After all, the evidence for the apotheosis of the emperor was being treated in the way prodigies had been received since time immemorial. It had always been the rule that it was the act of official acceptance, whether by a magistrate or by the senate, that turned an unusual event into a prodigy, and this rule had been followed to the point that the public announcement could turn even an invented event into a valid divine manifestation.[4]

In the second century the ceremony was on at least two occasions modified in an interesting way. In these cases apotheosis was as it were enacted. Some time after the emperor's

---

[1] Cic. *Rep.* vi. 16, 24.

[2] Dio, lvi. 46. 2, cf. Suet. *Aug.* 100. 4 (Augustus). Dio, lix. 11. 4 ff. (Drusilla).

[3] Sen. *Apocolocyntosis* mocks the ceremony but Liv. i. 16 anticipates it in his description of the death and apotheosis of Romulus, and takes it entirely seriously.

[4] See above, pp. 24–5. The rule: Liv. x. 40. 11.

body had been cremated or buried, a second funeral ceremony took place. This time, a wax image of the dead ruler was burnt on an elaborate funeral pyre. From the uppermost story of the pyre an eagle was released and as the bird rose it was said that the soul of the emperor was rising into heaven.[1] This very strange ceremony can be interpreted in the light of Roman beliefs concerning omens and prodigies. The second funeral was in a sense an omen of the apotheosis of the emperor, and since it was left obscure whether omens merely foreshadowed the future or actually caused it, spectators of the funeral[2] had no need to decide whether the show they were watching was actually bringing about the deification of their dead ruler, or only foreshadowing it. In any case, the ceremony did not entirely force the hands of the gods: they could frustrate it by sending rain to put out the fire or inducing the eagle to be unco-operative.

No ceremony ever took place to deify a living ruler since as far as the state religion of the Roman people was concerned, the emperor was not part of the pantheon. This did not, of course, mean that individuals, or more usually groups or communities, were prevented from honouring the living ruler as if he was a god. Occasionally this even happened in Italy, but it was very common in the provinces, especially the eastern provinces whose inhabitants had been familiar with ruler cults since Hellenistic times. Since ruler cult was supposed to be an expression of gratitude, it was normally offered by the governed not ordered by the ruler. There certainly could be no question of supervising every aspect of it.[3] But Augustus made an attempt to control its most prominent manifestations,[4] especially in the

---

[1] Bickermann (1929), (1973), (1974). Bickermann argues that this form was usual after Trajan but the only cases recorded are those of Pertinax and Septimius Severus. The fullest account is Herodian iv. 2; see also S.H.A. *Pertinax*, 15. 1. According to Hohl (1938) these were the only cases. A *funus imaginarium* was given by a college to a slave who had been refused burial by his master (*I.L.S.* 7212).

[2] See above, p. 27.

[3] On variety of cult see C. Habicht (1973), 42–50.

[4] L. R. Taylor, op. cit. 205–14. In the East Augustus 'permitted' the dedication of temples to himself provided his name was linked with that of Rome (Suet. *Aug.* 52). For provincials he allowed temples of *Augustus and Rome* at Pergamum and Nicomedia, but for Roman citizens at Nicaea the dedication had to be to *Divus Julius and Rome* (Dio, li. 20. 6). But there are numerous references on inscriptions to the god Augustus alone, e.g. Ehrenberg and Jones 106 = *I.L.S.* 9495;

ritual of provincial assemblies. Presumably it would have been impossible to have one policy in Italy and a totally different one in the provinces.

There is no evidence that a normal Roman believed that the living emperor had supernatural power. Emperors were not thought capable of influencing the weather, or the harvest, or of acting at a distance, or of hearing and answering prayer.[1] Vows were made on behalf of the emperor, but not to the emperor, and as a rule the emperor was not thought to have the gift of healing.[2] Domaszewski noted that in army camps the statues of reigning emperors were most often inscribed with their official titles, omitting any suggestion of divinity.[3] The emperor was not thought to be divine in the same sense as Jupiter. In fact, only two emperors are known to have applied the term 'god' to themselves.[3]

Romans were quite aware of the differences between a human emperor and a god. They also knew that while Augustus[4] had been worthy of posthumous apotheosis as a second founder of Rome, some of his deified successors were far less deserving.[5] The cults of loyalty at all times must have involved an appalling amount of hypocrisy.[6] How then did they survive? First, the

107 = *Ann. ép.* (1939), 113; 108 = *Ann. ép.* (1921), 2; 110 = *C.I.L.* x. 1613; 115 = *B.S.A.* xlii (1947), 222, no. 9; 118 = Wilcken, *Chrestomathie*, no. 112. On adoration of imperial images see A. Alföldi (1970), 68–79.

[1] K. Latte, *R.R.* 308; A. D. Nock (1952), 237 ff. (1957), 115.

[2] The incidents involving Hadrian (S.H.A. *Had.* 25) and above all Vespasian. (Suet. *Vesp.* 7; Tac. *Hist.* iv. 81 ff.; Dio, lxvi. 8) were quite exceptional, and in the case of Vespasian are portents of divine support rather than royal miracles. See A. D. Nock (1957), 117–19. But see S.H.A. *Carac,* v. 7: garlands taken from imperial statue to be used as remedies.

[3] On imperial statues in camps see A. V. Domaszewski (1895), 68. His nos. 143–52 are inscribed only with titles, while 139–40 are dedicated to the emperor's *genius*. See also F. Blumenthal (1913), 328: in Egypt the emperor was not a god officially. F. Millar (1973), 158 on Gaius (Philo, *Leg. ad Gaium*, 353) and Domitian (Suet. *Dom.* 13; cf. Mart. v. 8 and Dio Chrys. xlv. 1). See also G. W. Bowersock (1972), 182–6, who argues that a provincial priesthood was not considered a religious duty. According to Dio, li. 20. 8 no emperor even if worthy of deification dared claim the honour in his lifetime. This is only slightly exaggerated.

[4] On the humanity of the emperor see M. P. Charlesworth (1939). Seneca, *Clem.* i. 10. 3: (*Augustum*) deum non tamquam iussi credimus. Augustus' (supposed) birthplace was felt to have a 'numinous' atmosphere (Suet. *Aug.* 6 and 94).

[5] Seneca wrote the *Apocolocyntosis* to mock the deification of Claudius—but then the reigning emperor (Nero) had tried to annul the deification (Suet. *Claud.* 45).

[6] See some of the references in F. Sauter (1934) or K. Scott (1933); (1935).

ritual offered scope for a certain amount of double-think; for example, in the case of the cult of the *genius*[1] or of other imperial abstractions, there was some ambiguity as to whether the worship was offered to the emperor or on his behalf. Then it could be argued that the individual to whom the gods had given the rule of the world had become in some basic way different from ordinary men.[2] Men might persuade themselves that the emperor was bound to be in close contact with a powerful divine protector,[3] or that he owed essential qualities of character to particular divine inspiration.[4] No doubt fear and ambition were powerful motives for conforming to the rules once they had been established. But all this does not take us to the heart of the institution. One would imagine that the ruler cult would have collapsed under the weight of its own absurdity, if it had not been for imperative social need. The empire simply could not do without a language of loyalty. The emperor needed to cultivate the loyalty of his most powerful subjects and to assure himself that it existed. The subjects, whether for reason of gratitude, or ambition,[5] or just to avoid suspicion of subversive intentions, needed a means of demonstrating loyal sentiments. All these motives can be seen at work in the beginnings of emperor worship in the provinces. In the Asiatic provinces worship of Augustus by provincial assemblies began immediately after the defeat of Antony and the end of civil war, largely on the initiative of the provincials.[6] No doubt the Greeks of Asia felt gratitude for peace; certainly these former subjects of Antony wished to convince their new ruler that they would now be loyal to him. It is well known that emperor worship by provincial assemblies in the Western provinces came later, and was imposed by the government. Moreover, it was first intro-

[1] A. D. Nock (1952), 239–42 noted that occasionally votive offerings were made to the *genius* of even an inanimate object. De Ruggiero, *Diz. Epigr.* iii. 475 ff.; *Thes. L.L.* vi. 1836.

[2] C. Habicht (1973), 65–9.

[3] A. D. Nock (1947). One might compare *fortuna*, a divine quality which might be attached to certain men as Cicero argues in *Imp. Gn. Pomp.* 47–8.

[4] H. Mattingly (1937), esp. 111–15; M. P. Charlesworth (1937); A. D. Nock, *C.A.H.* x. 489; Dio Chrys. iii. 52.

[5] Provincial priesthoods as stepping stones to imperial honours: A. Stein (1927); a means of personal display: Epict. i. 19. 26–9.

[6] The council of Asia existed in republican times: J. Deininger (1965), 14 ff., origin of cult of Octavian ibid. 16–19. In Bithynia the cult began at the same time: Dio, li. 20. 7.

duced in the most recently conquered provinces: Lugdunese Gaul, Germany, Britain. This looks like a device for getting the conquered nobility to make public demonstration of their acceptance of Roman rule. A number of the more settled provinces received provincial assemblies and a provincial cult of the emperor as late as the reign of Vespasian. It is probably no coincidence that this emperor who had gained power in civil war should create new institutions to assure himself of the loyalty of his subjects.[1]

The whole Roman system turned on loyalty and under the principate the object of loyalty had become personalized in the emperor. How to evolve and communicate loyal attitudes among people spread over a vast area and to keep them focused on a remote ruler who was scarcely ever seen was a problem which a great territorial empire had to solve.[2] 'Norms do not live by themselves but must be recreated by ritual ceremony.'[3] The loyalty of the inhabitants of the Roman Empire was re-created by the ceremonies taken from religion: festivals, processions, temples, statues,[4] altars, sacrifices, even very occasionally mysteries,[5] focused men's attention on their remote sovereign as in their original context they had focused it on the remote gods.[6]

Educated Romans were conscious of the nature of the imperial cult. Roman law provided no penalty for perjury except disgrace. As we have seen, it was treated as an offence against the god.[7] But the breach of an oath sworn in the name of the emperor was frequently (according to the predilections of the

---

[1] J. Deininger, op. cit. 27–33.

[2] See A. H. M. Jones (1964), 1061 on the absence of active patriotism in the later empire.

[3] G. K. Park (1963), 200.

[4] L. Robert (1960); H. Kruse (1934); R. H. Bauman (1974), 82–92. *P. Oxy.* 2130. 1. 18: petition deposited at feet of imperial statue. Also on imperial statues: M. Wegener (1939); H. G. Niemeyer (1968).

[5] H. W. Pleket (1965).

[6] F. Millar (1972), 147, 161, 164, stresses 'the way in which the emperor takes his place among the other gods', and that 'a large proportion of the cult acts directed towards the pagan gods were addressed also to the emperor'. But surely as long as the 'worshippers' were aware that they were not placating an immortal being or one capable of miraculous intervention at a distance, their act was not fully religious.

[7] Cf. above, 42. Tac. *Ann.* i. 73: deorum iniurias dis curae. A. D. Nock (1941), 94, shows that divine sanction was adequate to safeguard the sanctity of tombs.

ruling emperor) punishable as treason.[1] The fundamental objection of the Roman government to the Christians was probably religious: they did not worship national gods and dissuaded others from doing so.[2] But they also refused to worship the emperor and this was considered evidence of disloyalty and therefore, at least potentially, treasonable.[3] The cult of the emperor was fundamentally a secular institution, but this would not prevent men who believed in survival of the empire from being sincerely and emotionally involved in it.

A. D. Nock has compared the imperial cult with the cult of the standards, which were kept with images of gods and emperors in the sanctuary of a Roman camp, and were in a sense the peculiar gods of the army. 'No homage was too great for these austere embodiments of the professional and personal sanctities . . . their loss was the ultimate disgrace and any insult to them would no doubt have evoked an indignation seldom aroused by ordinary sacrilege. Yet they were perishable material objects to be replaced and not restored, even as the Emperor was a mortal man.'[4] As the cult of the standards gave ritual expression to the *esprit de corps* and collective sense of honour which was necessary for the military functioning of the unit, so the imperial cult in its various aspects expressed the feelings of subordination, loyalty, gratitude, and concern for the safety of the emperor that had to be prevalent if the system was not to dissolve into chaos. The language of the cult of loyalty was frequently debasingly servile. But at the root of it was the widespread and justified feeling that there could be no peace for anybody unless there was an undisputed and divinely supported (a *felix*, 'lucky') emperor.

In practice the religion of loyalty affected mainly the organ-

---

[1] Perjury by the name of the emperor was normally punished: Dio, lvii. 8. 3; Tac. *Ann.* i. 73. 2; Min. Felix, *Oct.* 29. 5; Tert. *Apol.* 28; *Dig.* xii. 2. 13. 6. But not all emperors prosecuted on this charge (*C.J.* iv. 1. 2). See Th. Mommsen (1899), 586; K. Latte (1931), 346–57.

[2] Argued most clearly by G. E. M. de Ste Croix (1963).

[3] Tert., *Apol.* 28 shows that in an informal sense Christians were charged with treason; ibid. 35 shows that non-participation in the imperial cult was one reason for the charge, cf. Th. Mommsen (1890).

[4] A. D. Nock (1952), 239. On camp sanctuary of standards and its contents see A. V. Domaszewski (1895), 9–14. On standards see Tac. *Ann.* i. 39, iv. 2; Suet. *Tib.* 24; Tac. *Hist.* i. 36; Joseph, *B.J.* v. 6. 1. Tert. *Ad Nationes*, 12; *Apol.* 16. 8.

ized sections of the community. There were few dedications by private individuals.[1] At Rome, priests, magistrates, and senators were mainly involved and, to a smaller extent, colleges of humbler citizens and freedmen. In municipalities the rites were the concern of magistrates, priests, local councils, and colleges. But apart from the Roman colleges, the men most continuously occupied in ritual of loyalty were imperial officials and soldiers.

We know most about the annual round of ritual in the case of the college of the *Arvales* because their records happen to have survived,[2] but there is every reason to suppose that the other colleges performed a similar programme. We know, for instance, that at Rome all the priestly colleges celebrated the emperor's birthday[3] and from time to time made vows for his health and performed games in fulfilment of their vows.[4] In each case the ritual only involved a few performers, but it was witnessed by the other members of the officiating body. There was, for instance, a full turn-out of colleges and magistrates when the annual *vota* were offered for the emperor at Rome. Away from Rome the corresponding ceremony was attended by local magistrates, decurions, and priests.[5] Other celebrations were

[1] See E. J. Bickermann (1973), 5–7: archaeologists have found few statues of emperors other than on public buildings, and very few dedications by persons without any public status. But according to Fronto there were numerous paintings and carvings of Marcus Aurelius in the shops of Rome (*Ad. M. Caes.* iv. 12. 4 = Haines, p. 206).

[2] G. Wissowa, P.W. ii. 2. 1463–85, s.v. Arvales fratres. They make *vota* at beginning of the reign and of every year, for campaigns, illnesses, childbirths. They perform sacrifices at imperial birthdays and anniversaries of accession or of taking particular powers, on the birthday of divus Augustus, etc. For the *acta* see above, p. 63 n. 5.

[3] On birthdays generally see above, p. 69 n. 3. Imperial birthday celebration by colleges: *C.I.L.* x. 8375; banquet on capitol, Dio, liv. 26; sometimes presents to people and/or games in the circus. According to Dio, xlvii. 18. 5 all citizens were required to wear laurel wreaths and make merry at the celebration of the birthday of *divus* Julius. Senators and their sons failing to do this were fined, the punishment of others left to the gods. [4] *R.G.* 9.

[5] On *vota* at Rome see H. Mattingly (1950, 1951); also L. Marghitan and C. Petrolescu (1976). Pliny's report from Bithynia suggests that a considerable number of people were involved in the celebration of Trajan's accession (28 January). 'We have celebrated with *appropriate rejoicing*, Sir, the day of your accession . . . and have offered prayers to the gods to keep you in health and prosperity. We have also administered the oath of allegiance to your *fellow soldiers* . . . and found the *provincials* eager to take it too . . .' (*Ep.* x. 52, trans. B. Radice). Similarly on 3 January Pliny and *the provincials* made and discharged annual vows for the emperor: ibid. x. 34–5. See Sherwin-White's notes on the letters. Tert. *Ap.* 35. 1–4 shows

perhaps less well attended, although the extent to which they drew spectators is difficult to estimate. But since most of the imperial occasions were *feriae* and therefore, at least in theory, free from work[1] there was nothing to stop people from watching, and listening, not necessarily with indifference. It is easy to underestimate the emotional impact of the sacrificial rite. It was an impressive spectacle which had associations with all the most solemn moments of a Roman's life. Above all, there was the primordial emotion aroused by the act of killing.[2] On many occasions more than watching was called for, since a considerable proportion of thanksgivings took the form of *supplicationes*.[3] A *supplicatio* requires the participation of everybody. All temples were opened to the people for general prayers. People attended in festive clothing wearing garlands, and made an offering of wine and incense,[4] which was perhaps sometimes issued for that purpose.[5] In the same way means of purification were issued to all inhabitants of Rome before the Secular Games.[6]

that some imperial days were genuine popular holidays and occasions for merriment. Blumenthal (1913), 344, shows that Roman officers and the local *strategoi* were present at celebrations. See also F. Millar (1972), 151–2. On ceremonies and procession at imperial *decennalia* see E. W. Merten (1968).

[1] On *feriae* see K. Latte, *R.R.* 198–9; id. (1950), 328–40; A. D. Nock (1952), 188 = (1972) 738; Cic. *Leg.* ii. 29. Pollution could be avoided if work stopped when a procession came near the work site (Macr. i. 16. 9–12; Serv. in Verg. *Georg.* i. 268; Festus, 292). Cicero seems to have taken little notice of the traditional festivals, so J. P. V. D. Balsdon (1969), 73–4.

[2] On impressiveness of animal sacrifice see R. M. Ogilvie (1969), 50–2. W. Burkert (1972), esp. 45 ff. tries to explain the emotional effect of the killing rite, and its appropriateness as a symbol of group solidarity.

[3] *R.G.* 4: dies autem per quos ex senatus consulto supplicatum est fuere DCCCLXXXX; ibid. 9: privatim etiam et municipatim universi cives unanimiter continenter apud omnia pulvinaria pro valetudine mea supplicaverunt. *Supplicationes* on the calenders in V. Ehrenberg and A. H. M. Jones (1949), 44–54: 7, 16, 30 January; 6 March; 14, 16 April; 12, 29 May; 9 August; 3, 4, 23 September; 7, 18 October; 16 November; 15 December. Most come from the *feriale Cumanum*, *I.L.S.* 108. They were probably more frequent in municipalities than at Rome.

[4] G. Wissowa, P.W. 2 R. iv. 942–51, s.v. Supplicationes. Liv. xxx. 17. 6: ut aediles aedes tota urbe aperirent, circumeundi salutandique deos agendique grates per totum diem populo potestas fieret. x. 23. 1: wine and incense put at people's disposal. iii. 5. 4 and others: men and women participated. xl. 37. 3: participants wreathed and holding twig of laurel. Under the empire *supplicationes* were rarely held for urgent petitions, much more often for public thanksgiving.

[5] V. Ehrenberg and A. H. M. Jones (1949), 100 = *I.L.S.* 112, 20–34.

[6] P.W. 2 R. i, A2, 1712, s.v. saeculares ludi. Wine and incense issued for libation to population of Narbo for cult of *numen Augusti*: V. Ehrenberg and A. H. M. Jones, op. cit. 100 = *I.L.S.* 112.

The festival did not, of course, end with the sacrifice. Celebrations of another kind followed. Sometimes there were public games.[1] Before the games, images of gods were carried in procession to be cheered or hissed at according to the individual's attitude to the activity patronized by the particular god. The atmosphere was not reverent but not indifferent either. One might compare the progress of the statue of the local saint on the occasion of his annual festival through the streets of a village of modern Italy.[2] Even if the sacrifice was not followed by games, it usually concluded with a banquet of some kind.[3] A banquet was a normal part of birthday celebrations,[4] including of course those of the emperor.[5] Banquets were held at anniversaries of temples[6] and after the sacrifices of the great Roman colleges.[7] On a lower social level banquets were associated with the ancient sacrifices of the *curiae*.[8] Senators had the privilege of attending banquets held on the Capitol at Rome.[9] One supposes that local senates and perhaps other corporations had similar privileges in provincial towns. When a large number of animals had been slaughtered it would certainly have been convenient if a correspondingly large number of men were invited to eat the victims. There is evidence that soldiers attended official sacrifices and duly shared in the meal.[10] It is also known that in municipalities there might be provision for feeding the whole population, or at least for the distribution of

[1] References in G. Wissowa (1912), 456–8. Vows for Augustus' health resulted in *ex voto* games (*R.G.* 9). Games at *feriae* of thanksgiving for the victory at Actium (Dio, liii. 1. 5); at *natalis* of emperor (Dio, liv. 26. 2). Also Jos. *B.J.* vii. 2.

[2] Ovid, *Ars. Am.* iii. 2; cf. Cic. *Ad Att.* 13. 44. 1. *Pompae circenses* of republican times: Dion. Hal. ii. 71. 4; vii. 72. 48–9. Tert. *De Spect.* 10. 1–2; *Ad Nat.* 1, 10; K. Latte, *R.R.* 248–9; P. Wiseman (1974), 160.

[3] Macr. *Sat.* i. 16. 3; J. Marquardt, *Stv.* iii. 268 n. 10; J. P. Waltzing, *Corporations professionelles*, i. 235; K. Latte (1960), 391.

[4] Mart. x. 27, cf. Cic. *Phil.* ii. 6. 15; Gel. xix. 9.

[5] Dio, liv. 26; Ehrenberg and Jones, 101 = *I.L.S.* 154. 10.

[6] *C.I.L.* xii. 3058.

[7] On *Arvales* G. Wissowa (1895), 147 ff.; on banquets of *Salii*: Suet. *Claud.* 33. Plin. *N.H.* x. 45: first peacock ever killed for table at Rome was for banquet of augurs.

[8] R. E. Palmer (1970), 120. Dion. Hal. ii. 23. 2 and 65. 4, cf. also thanksgiving combined with banquets by tribes and *vici* after victory of Vespasian, Jos *B.J.* vii. 4. 1.

[9] Suet. *Aug.* 35; Dio, liv. 14; Th. Mommsen, *R.St.* iii. 894–5.

[10] Jos. *B.J.* v. 4: return of Titus marked by ritual thanksgiving in presence of troops, followed by banquet for soldiers. Amm. xxii. 12. 6: troops the worse for drink after sacrifice.

the special delicacies, honey wine, and pastry.[1] Of course, taking part in a banquet after a sacrifice was not necessarily morally uplifting. It was not thought to bring the diner into spiritual communion with the divinity.[2] But the diners' feeling of human community might be heightened by a sense of the solemn nature of the occasion.[3] To sum up, the ritual of loyalty never involved its spectators in the intense mental participation of the congregation at a Jewish or Christian service, but it was not just a cold ceremony performed by a few professionals either.

There was another way in which Augustus associated Roman public religion with his own position: he gave prominent status to the cult of gods who were particularly linked with his own career. In this, too, he followed the precedent of the great figures of the late republic, who had believed, or at least asserted, that they had enjoyed the special patronage of a particular deity. In Augustus' case, the patronage was that of Apollo and Mars. Augustus proclaimed his faith in Apollo early: 'Apollo' was the watchword of the Caesarian army at Philippi.[4] In Virgil's Eclogues, Apollo has been given a prominence which was surely calculated to be agreeable to Virgil's patron. In the 5th Eclogue Apollo shares annual *vota* with Daphnis-Caesar.[5] In the 7th Eclogue the reign of Apollo marks the beginning of a new age.[6] The poems were probably written around 40 B.C. In 36 B.C.

---

[1] Ehrenberg and Jones, 101 = *I.L.S.* 154: natali Ti Caesaris perpetue acturi decuriones et populus cenarent . . . natali Augustae mulsum et crustlum mulieribus vicanis . . . dedimus.

[2] A. D. Nock (1944), 152 ff. and 167 f.

[3] The sharing out of the sacrificial meat among the delegates at the festival of Jupiter Latiaris represented a symbolic strengthening of the Latin league: G. Wissowa (1912), 124; Cic. *Pro Plan.* 23; Varro, *Ling. Lat.* vi. 25; Dion. Hal. iv. 49. 3; Plin. *N.H.* iii. 69. See also Livy's description of the neighbourly and generous atmosphere at the open-air banquet following the first *lectisternium* (v. 13. 6 (399)). Ogilvie notes that *iurgiis ac litibus temperatum* is borrowed from prohibitions in force at sacrifices (Cic. *Div.* i. 102). Valerius Maximus relates how Scipio Africanus and Tiberius Gracchus settled a quarrel at the *epulum Iovis* on the Capitol: quasi diis immortalibus arbitris . . . dexteras eorum conducentibus (iv. 2. 3). A non-religious and earlier version is given by Livy (xxxviii. 57. 5). Ovid, *Fast.* iv. 743 describes something like the presence of the god following the sacrifice to Pales; cf. ibid. vi. 305–8: ante mos erat et mensae credere adesse deos.

[4] On Sulla and Venus see (*inter alia*) J. P. V. D. Balsdon (1951); on Caesar and Venus Genetrix (e.g. Dio, xliii. 43. 3) see S. Weinstock (1971), 84 ff.; for Sextus Pompeius and Neptune see Dio, xlviii. 48. 5. Apollo watchword at Philippi: Val. Max. i. 5. 7.

[5] *Ecl.* v. 66.   [6] *Ecl.* iv. 10.

Augustus (Octavian) narrowly escaped being killed by lightning. For this escape he showed gratitude to Apollo and proceeded to consecrate land on the Palatine to the god.[1] Five years later the great victory over Antony and Cleopatra was won in the neighbourhood of a well-known sanctuary of Apollo at Actium. Forthwith Augustus proclaimed his conviction that Apollo had helped him to win this decisive success. He rebuilt the sanctuary and founded games.[2] After this, he built a great temple of Apollo on the land which he had consecrated on the Palatine.[3] Here he housed the Sibylline books transferred from the temple of Jupiter Optimus Maximus. Finally, the Secular Games, the great festival that set a seal on Augustus' work, by ceremoniously concluding the past and solemnly introducing a new and better age, culminated in a ceremony in the temple of Apollo.[4]

Apollo had not previously been worshipped as a powerful supporter of the Roman state. His rather minor role was that of a god of healing. Unlike the other Olympians he retained his Greek name at Rome.[5] The choice of precisely this patron god cannot have been made with an eye to tradition. Jupiter would have been the obvious patron of the would-be successor of Aeneas. The choice of Apollo must have had a particular reason.[6]

It looks as if Augustus genuinely believed that Apollo was his personal protector. The belief would have been encouraged by the fact that Vediovis, who was traditionally worshipped by the Julian *gens*, was commonly identified with Apollo.[7] Nevertheless Augustus' promotion of the cult of Apollo was also a political act, and as such requires more than a personal explanation, all the more because this thoroughly Greek God was promoted in

---

[1] Dio, xlix, 15. 3.

[2] J. Gagé (1935); Prop. iv. 6. 29; Dio, li. 1; Suet. *Aug.* 18; Strabo, vii. 7. 6. Part of the booty was kept in boat-houses built on the site.

[3] Dio, liii. 1; Suet. *Aug.* 31.

[4] *C.I.L.* vi. 32323; Th. Mommsen (1913), 567–626; I. B. Pighi (1965); Hor. *C.S.*

[5] K. Latte, *R.R.* 221–5; G. Wissowa (1912), 293–7. A full, if wordy discussion: Gagé (1955).

[6] P. Lambrechts (1953).

[7] S. Weinstock (1971), 8 and 11; Gel. v. 12. 12. A Julius in 431 dedicated the first Apollo temple at Rome: Liv. iv. 29. 7. On Julian worship of Apollo see also Servius in *Aen.* x. 316.

a context of a revival of Roman institutions. It is certainly relevant that already Sulla had fostered a special relationship with Apollo[1]—at least until his final victory—and that he publicized the fact that an ancestor of his had established the *ludi Apollinares* in 212.[2] It is also significant that two of his opponents made a similar claim.[3] Julius Caesar may have spread the tale that his prospective heir Octavian had been fathered by Apollo.[4] After Caesar's murder, Brutus paid for the *ludi Apollinares*[5] and later, when they were leading their army in Greece, the conspirators issued coins bearing a bust of the god.[6] At Philippi, however, it was the Caesarian party which made a bid for Apollo's support,[7] and henceforth as we have seen the support of Apollo was consistently claimed by Augustus (Octavian).[8]

It is certainly not chance that in both the 4th[9] Eclogue and the Secular Games[10] Apollo is associated with the end of one age and the beginning of another. We know that there was thought and talk of the beginning of a new age. This was natural enough, in view of the war and the insecurity that was filling the present. It is perhaps no coincidence that precisely in 88 B.C., the year of Sulla's consulate, *prodigia* were interpreted as announcing the opening of a new saeculum.[11] Later in 63 expectations of cataclysm encouraged one of the fellow conspirators of Catiline.[12] The beginning of a new era was announced in 49 on the verge of the civil war between Caesar and Pompey,[13] and in 44 after Caesar's murder.[14]

The context in which this thought occurred is very obscure. We really know very little about the deeper religious currents of the age. But the 4th Eclogue suggests that in some circles

---

[1] S. Weinstock (1971), 13; Plut. *Sull.* 29. 11; Front. *Strat.* i. 11. 11.

[2] Macr. 17. 27.

[3] Macr. loc. cit. Liv. xxv. 12. 9 ff.; xxvii. 23. 5 show that Sulla prevailed.

[4] Weinstock op. cit. 14 on Dio, xlv. 1. 2; Suet. *Aug.* 94. 7.

[5] Cic. *Att.* xv. 18. 2; 26. 1; *Philip.* i. 36; ii. 31; App. *B.C.* iii. 24. 90; Plut. *Brut.* 21. 3.

[6] M. H. Crawford (1974), ii. 741.

[7] Val. Max. i. 5. 7.   [8] P. Lambrechts (1953).

[9] *Ecl.* iv. 10.   [10] See below, p. 18 n. 1.

[11] Weinstock, op. cit. 192 on Plut. *Sull.* 7. 7. In 65 *haruspices* interpreted portents as indicating the possible end of the city and the world: Cic. *Cat.* iii. 19. See A. Alföldi (1971).

[12] Cic. *Cat.* iii. 9; iv. 2, cf. Weinstock, op. cit. 98 n. 1.

[13] Dio, xli. 14. 5.   [14] Servius in *Ecl.* ix. 46.

Apollo was given a special role in the birth of a new age which would be a second golden age; he was for this purpose identified with the sun (Sol or Helios).[1] Augustus undoubtedly presented himself as the restorer of the golden age.[2] By demonstrating that he had been regularly assisted by Apollo, he confirmed that he was indeed the man to whom the transformation of the world had been divinely assigned. It may be that the expectation of a new golden age as well as the association of its coming with Apollo belonged to the Greek world rather than to Rome or Italy.[3] But there were numerous freedmen of Greek origin at Rome,[4] and at the other extreme of society many Roman nobles were as much at home in Greek literature as in Roman. If oracles circulated among the Greeks, they would surely soon become known to everybody, and since there was no certain criterion by which an oracle could be rejected as false,[5] the circulating prophetic literature is likely to have made a considerable impression in so disturbed a time.[6]

It is probably also significant that in the writings of Stoic philosophers the sun was described as the ruler of the other heavenly bodies and through them, by mysterious influences, of all things. The sun was the King of Heaven, as the ruler was King on Earth.[7] In a philosophy which favoured monotheism the sun was an obvious visible symbol of the supreme deity, or perhaps even the deity itself. This being so, it was natural that an educated young man setting out to become a ruler of the world should seek to win the favour of the sun or of the deity of which it was an image.[8]

---

[1] *Ecl.* iv. 6 and Serv. ad loc.: saecula per metalla divisit, dixit etiam quis quo saeculo imperaret et Solem ultimum, id est decimum voluit, cf. E. Norden (1924), esp. 55 and 144.

[2] Verg. *Aen.* i. 281; vi. 789.

[3] *O.G.I.S.* 458 and *S.E.G.* iv. 490, and the legends surrounding Augustus' birth: Suet. *Aug.* 94.

[4] See above, p. 71 n. 2.

[5] The unofficial oracles could be drawn upon to replace the Sibylline Books destroyed by fire.

[6] On the effect of circulating oracles in Tudor England see K. Thomas (1971), 389–432 on 'ancient prophecies'.

[7] Warde Fowler (1914), 58–9 on Cic. *Acad.* ii. 126; Varro, *ap.* Censorinum, *De Die Nat.* 8; Cic. *Div.* ii. 89.

[8] If Augustus was influenced by this tendency he was ahead of his time. The sun only became a regular part of imperial theology much later. See Cumont (1923). On the radiate crown on coins see Weinstock (1971), 381–4.

Augustus also promoted Mars. Mars was worshipped by many Italian peoples and he had always figured in the religious history of Rome, but in a special way. He had no temple within the *pomerium*. He was treated as a wild spirit, whose help was needed but who had to be kept at a distance.[1] His help was needed on campaigns—but outside the city. Augustus brought him into the city and made his temple a memorial to the qualities that had made Rome great. He built the temple on land owned by himself. This was appropriate because his motives for honouring the god were in the first place personal. He was honouring the god who had helped him to avenge his father's murder. The fact that Mars as consort of Venus was sometimes treated (in defiance of mythological genealogy) as ancestor of the Julian *gens*[2] surely also provides part of the explanation for Augustus' special devotion to the god. This was first shown to the world in 42 B.C., before the battle of Philippi, when Augustus vowed a temple to Mars if the battle should result in the avenging of Caesar.[3] In 20 B.C. he built a small shrine on the Capitol to house the standards of Crassus which diplomacy had recovered from the Parthians.[4] Finally, in 2 B.C. he consecrated the great temple in the new forum.[5] The temple was intended to become one of the chief sanctuaries of Rome. The forum was decorated with statues of the great generals of Roman history, inscriptions recording their honours. It was an *exemplum* in stone to inspire the young who in future would come there to be entered on the role of men of military age. From this temple generals were to set out on campaign, there they were to return victorious, and after they had dedicated spoils to Jupiter on the Capitol they would also dedicate a crown and sceptre to Mars.[6] Clearly Mars the ancestor of the Julii and the avenger of Caesar was to be given a share in the role of Jupiter. Augustus had performed two great acts of *ultio*. He had avenged Caesar by legal process (*iudiciis legitimis*)—he insisted—before being compelled to fight the murderers—and he had 'avenged'

---

[1] Warde Fowler (1923), 133.

[2] S. Weinstock (1971), 128 ff.; K. Latte, *R.R.* 302.

[3] Suet. *Aug.* 29. 2.   [4] Dio, liv. 8. 3.

[5] Ovid, *Fast.* v. 545 ff.; Dio, lv. 10. 1; lx. 5. 3; Vell. ii. 100. 'In privato solo Martis Ultoris templum forumque Augustum ex manubiis feci': Aug. *R.G.* 21. No doubt the land became public when the temple had been dedicated.

[6] Dio, lv. 10. 2.

Crassus by recovering the lost standards through diplomatic means.[1] For this he showed gratitude to Mars. Perhaps he saw Mars and Apollo as complementary deities. Apollo favoured the creation of a new world order; Mars assisted essential preliminaries, the righting of unbearable wrongs of the old order. This would be a personal interpretation on Augustus' part, but as we have seen it was Augustus' policy to give public status to his personal religious predilections.

The 'cult of loyalty' in its various forms flourished exceedingly. Its festivals came to dominate the calendar and it produced thousands of dedications all over the empire. In view of this it is impossible to call it a failure.

It is easy to underestimate the long-term effect of Augustus' religious policy.[2] This is a consequence of judging it by the moral and spiritual standards by which the effects of a Christian revival like the Reformation are judged. In fact it had numerous lasting consequences only some of which would be thought properly 'religious' by Judaeo-Christian criteria. I imagine that the least significant in the medium term was Augustus' promotion of Apollo and Mars at the expense of Jupiter.[3] The revival of forgotten cults of the city of Rome may well have had no lasting religious significance; after all, agricultural cults lost their meaning in a large city with a fully urbanized population. In the country similar cults had never lost their meaning, as we can still feel when reading poems of Virgil and Tibullus.[4]

On the other hand, the feeling of attachment to institutions because they were ancient and because they were Roman was now enshrined in a classical literature, the works of Livy, Virgil, Horace, Tibullus, Ovid, and Propertius, and thus became an essential part of a literary culture which was transmitted with little change from generation to generation. While Roman cities were being established in numerous places in the West, and participation in the government of the empire was

---

[1] *R.G.* 29.

[2] e.g. K. Latte, *R.R.* 309.

[3] For the worship of Sol, see below, pp. 282-3. As for Mars the fact that under the empire the army was permanently stationed along the frontiers meant that there was much more scope for temples and dedications. It was only then that Mars became the god of the Roman army according to A. V. Domaszewski (1895), 115–21; I. Toutain (1907), i, 191 ff.

[4] C. Bailey (1935), 34–42; Tib. i. 1. 11 ff.; ii. 1.

spreading to the upper classes of an ever-widening area, attachment to 'Romanism' was surely an essential factor in the cohesion of the empire. Cults were established imitating those of Rome in numerous provincial towns and military units.[1] How worshippers felt is very difficult to deduce from inscriptions which have preserved merely the fact that they worshipped. But the fact is important, for the cult of the traditional gods, public and domestic, remained the core of Roman religion. New cults of abstract deities or of eastern gods might be introduced to meet special needs. Stoic philosophy might influence how some men interpreted the reality behind the worshipped images. But all this was mere elaboration of the ancestral worship as long as the traditional religion survived at all.

On a secular level the cults of loyalty, and especially the imperial cult, offered a ritual which mirrored while it strengthened the constitution of the empire.[2] It provided an opportunity for expressing in ritual the attitudes of subordination, loyalty, and concern which were necessary for the maintenance of the system. At the same time, the procedure at the great festivals demonstrated the social hierarchy, with the emperor at the top, followed by the provincial governor, the local aristocracy, and the ordinary people. Moreover, the provincial assemblies convened to celebrate the imperial cult were designed to provide a channel of communication between emperor and provincials.[3] Within each city there were various

[1] The traditional public rites of Rome were bound to particular sites at Rome (Liv. v. 52. 2). In colonial foundations new rites were created on the pattern of Roman ones. A. D. Nock (1952), 186–252 = (1972), 736–82 notes that the following Roman festivals were recorded in the *feriale Duranum* of the cohors XX Palmyrenorum: natalis Martis patris victoris, quinquatria, natalis urbis Romae, circenses Martiales, Vestalia, Neptunalia, circenses salutares, Saturnalia. The unit also celebrated two military occasions, the day of *honesta missio* and the *Rosaliae signorum*. On the latter see I. Richmond, *Arch. Ael.* iv (1943), 162 ff.; also Fink, Hoey, and Snyder (1940). A different selection of festivals was kept at Theveste in N. Africa: *C.I.L.* viii. 1859; S. Gsell, *Inscr. Lat. Algérie*, i. 3041. W. F. Snyder (1940), 297 ff. According to the *lex coloniae Genetivae Juliae* decurions would lay down once and for all what festivals would be celebrated (*I.L.S.* 6087. 64). Colonies are described as *quasi effigies parvae* of Rome in Gel. xvi. 13. 8.

[2] They dominated the calendar of the cohort at Dura and at Theveste. Evidence for imperial anniversaries, etc., is assembled in W. F. Snyder (1940). On the imperial cult in various provinces see D. Fishwick (1961) and (1964); R. Etienne (1958); G. Herzog-Hauser (1924).

[3] E. Kornemann (1900) and (1924); J. A. O. Larsen (1955), 106–61; P. A. Brunt (1961), 189–227; J. Deininger (1963).

cults which gave scope to display loyal feelings to organizations and individuals of different social status.[1] Inevitably, the cults lent themselves to hypocrisy and adulation. But political exploitation had always been a feature of Roman religion and it had never devalued the ceremonies in Roman eyes. Roman religion had always been compatible with some humour at the expense of gods. Humour flourished at the expense of the deified emperors. The Emperor Caracalla, for instance, is said to have ordered the deification of a brother whom he had murdered with the comment 'Let him be a god, provided he is dead'. The Emperor Vespasian actually joined in the mockery, when he died with the words: 'I think I am becoming a god.'[2] But this did not undermine the institution. As long as people believed in the empire, they believed in the institutions which were seen to hold it together. There was no need for anybody to delve into the reasons for the effectiveness of the cults of loyalty, to question whether they were effective because they gained supernatural support for the emperor, or only because symbolic acts of loyalty fostered the real thing. Accordingly, a considerable part of the ritual and language of the cults survived the emperor's conversion to Christianity and the deposition of the gods.[3]

It may well be that the most important long-term effect of the Augustan revival was literary, a reshaping of the religious imagination of the Romans as a result of the religious colouring of Augustan literature. Henceforth generation after generation read, learnt, and imitated the writers of the Augustan period. If literature affects the mind at all, this prolonged concern with Virgil, Horace, Livy, and the rest must have had a profound influence on the imagination of the Romans. It surely contributed a great deal to the personalization of Roman ideas of deity. I am thinking particularly of the majestic presentation of Jupiter in the *Aeneid*, a supreme god whose majestic personality

[1] See, for instance, R. Meiggs (1973), 353–4 and 378–80 on Ostia. Colleges of artisans all over the empire used the whole range of loyal gestures, dedications and statues to the emperor as a man or as a god, or to his deified attributes, or dedications on behalf of the emperor, or celebration of imperial occasions. See Waltzing, *Corporations professionelles*, i. 495–508; ibid. 234–6, and the index, v. 585–608.

[2] Suet. *Vesp.* 23. 4; S.H.A. *Geta*, 2; D. Fishwick (1965).

[3] A. Alföldi (1970); F. Burdeau (1964); L. Homo (1931); S. MacCormack (1972).

shapes history. The Empire of Rome is part of a great divine plan.[1] A similar vision of the god is found in Horace:

> What shall I sing before the wonted praises of the Father,
> Who directs the destinies of men and gods,
> Who rules sea and lands and sky with its shifting seasons
> From whom is begotten no other greater than himself
> Nor doth aught flourish like or even next to him.[2]

3. *Moral reform*

The commonest secular explanation of the political instability of the late republic was moral degeneracy. Already the elder Cato had warned against luxury and its inevitable consequences.[3] It was generally agreed that moral decay had begun in the course of the second century, though different starting points were proposed. The historian Piso seems to have suggested that degeneration set in when the soldiers returning from Asia in 187 brought home the extravagant and demoralizing habits they had caught there.[4] Writing a little later Polybius traced the decline of Roman morals from the end of the second Punic war and especially the destruction of Macedon.[5] About the same time there was a famous debate in the senate on whether Carthage should be destroyed. In the course of it Scipio Nasica argued that Carthage must be allowed to survive, so that fear might discipline the national character. Eventually Carthage was destroyed, and in the view of Sallust it was the destruction of Carthage which started Roman morality on its downward course. Freed from external fear the Romans developed a passion for wealth and the self-indulgence which wealth made possible. Nothing was allowed to stand in the way of men striving for riches and power.[6] It was this that made the civil wars of Sallust's lifetime inevitable. Sallust wrote in the years following the murder of Caesar.[7] The practical application of

[1] *Aen.* i. 254 ff. and *passim.* On the earlier history of the idea, B. Snell (1967), 160.

[2] Hor. i. 12. 13–19, trans. C. E. Bennett.

[3] A. W. Lintott (1972), 626–38.

[4] Liv. xxxix. 6. 7. probably based on Piso, cf. H. Peter, *H.R.R.* Piso fr. 34 (Plin. *N.H.* xxxiv. 14) and 38 (Plin. *N.H.* xvii. 244).

[5] Polyb. vi. 51. 3; xxxi. 25. 3.

[6] Sall. *Cat.* 10.

[7] R. Syme (1964), 216.

the doctrine was obvious. If civil wars were to be ended the downward trend of Roman morals must be reversed or, in the words of Horace,

> Whoever wishes to abolish unholy slaughter and
> insane civic strife, if he is eager to have
> statues inscribed with the title father of cities,
> let him have the courage to bridle our
> unrestrained licentiousness.[1]

Moral reform could be, and was,[2] advocated without reference to religion on the ground that a self-controlled person would be a better citizen than a self-indulgent one. But there is evidence that this is not how the problem was seen in the decisive early years of the principate of Augustus. In the History of Livy, religion and morality are closely linked in the important chapter on the establishment of the state religion by King Numa. We have seen that Livy presented Roman religion as a discipline deliberately devised to replace the discipline of war, because such discipline was essential for the maintenance of national cohesion in peacetime. In other words, Livy suggests that a religious revival might provide a remedy for precisely the public disease which Sallust had diagnosed.[3]

Livy, as we have seen, believed that religion strengthened morality. More specifically it was the foundation of the Roman's traditional respect for the inviolability of oaths and contracts,[4] and it induced a state of mind which was willing to imitate a worthy moral example like that set by King Numa.[5] An anecdote later in the History makes a similar point. Flaccus was a young noble of dissolute character, who was elected *flamen dialis* simply through lack of rival candidates, because numerous taboos had made this priesthood extremely unpopular. But when he began to perform his duties, the ritual impressed him so deeply that his way of life was transformed and he became a man of influence on the strength of his moral reputation.[6]

Augustus seems to have shared the belief that religion inculcated morality:[7] he induced each senator before taking his

---

[1] Hor. iii. 24. 25–9. [2] Ps.-Sall. *Ep. ad Caes.* i. 7, ii. 6.
[3] See above, p. 90. [4] i. 21. 1. [5] i. 21. 2.
[6] Liv. xxvii. 8; according to A. D. Nock (1972), 476, such an incident is unique in ancient literature.
[7] Suet. *Aug.* 35. 3: quo . . . religiosius . . . senatoria munera fungerentur.

seat to pour a libation to the god in whose temple the senate was meeting, and in this way hoped to make senators perform their duties more conscientiously.[1] These ideas were not new. We have observed the same rather vague belief in the moralizing function of religion in Cicero. But around 30 B.C., after a long period of extremely unpleasant civil war, they were more likely to have practical consequences.

The civil war is the starting-point of a number of famous poems in Virgil and Horace. The problem facing the poets is why these calamities have befallen the Roman world, and the answer suggested by each is that the disasters of war are a punishment for sin. The original offence may lie far back in time: the failure of Laomedon to fulfil his promises to the gods who had fortified Troy for him,[2] or the fact that Romulus killed his brother at the foundation of Rome,[3] or more vaguely, some inborn wickedness.[4] The appearance of a doctrine of original sin in a pagan Roman context is surprising. One should not be in a hurry to interpret it on the analogy of the Christian doctrine. In the first place the idea performs poetic functions. The civil war generation of Romans is to be pitied all the more because it is being punished for crimes of which it is innocent. In Virgil's 4th Eclogue the idea of transmitted guilt occurs as part of a prophecy of a new age which will eliminate the old sin. The poet offers the hope of a fresh start. The Roman poets' use of the theme is presumably influenced by Greek tragedy, but the Roman belief that the first of a series of events has ominous significance for the rest[5] must also have contributed.

The idea is, however, more than just a literary device. The poets are diagnosing the malady from which Roman society was suffering, and pointing out that civil war, immorality, and the gods were linked in a circle of cause and effect. Civil war is itself an offence against the gods but the poets see it as a punishment for some earlier offence. In accordance with the Greek tragic pattern the gods punish offenders by infecting them with blind rage under whose influence they bring about their own

[1] C. Koch (1954), 85–120.
[2] Verg. *Georg.* i. 511–14.
[3] Hor. *Ep.* vii.
[4] Verg. *Ecl.* iv. 14: sceleris vestigia; 31: prisca fraus.
[5] Ovid, *Fast.* i. 72–3, 165–82.

destruction.[1] Thus Cicero could attack the sacrilegious Clodius: 'When you utter your frenzied phrases at mob meetings, when you drive honest men with stones from the forum, when you hurl blazing torches into your neighbours' roofs, when you set fire to sacred buildings, when you stir up slaves, when you throw sacrifices and games into turmoil, when you know no distinction between wife and sister, when you are indifferent what bed chamber you enter, then it is that you rave in delirium and undergo the only punishment determined by the immortal gods to requite the wickedness of men . . . It is against the mind of the impious that the missiles of the gods are launched.'[2]

But for what sin were the Romans being punished with civil war? Clodius' offence was sacrilege, and in the poem in which Horace is most explicit his diagnosis of the causes of the civil war is similar. 'Though you may be innocent, Roman, you will continue to pay for the sins of your fathers until you rebuild the temples and the collapsing dwellings of the gods and their images foul with black soot. . . . The neglected gods have inflicted many evils on unhappy Italy.'[3] But then he continues the poem:

> A generation fertile in evil first corrupted
> marriages, children and homes;
> fed from this spring a river of ruin
> has flooded our country and nation.[4]

There seems to be a contradiction: neglect of the gods and adultery by married women are successively put forward as the ultimate causes of the sufferings of Italy. But the contradiction can be reconciled. The evils of the Roman world derive from the immorality of her womenfolk. As a result sons are not properly educated, and grow up to be bad soldiers and bad citizens. The process is cumulative. Each successive generation is worse than its predecessor. How can the process be stopped? Only by a return to the worship of the neglected gods. The Roman offence is double, religious neglect and immorality, but these offences are not independent; one sin furthers the other and unless both are reformed, neither can be.

---

[1] Civil war an offence against gods. Hor. i. 35. 85–7: quid intactum nefasti/liquimus? unde manum iuventus/metu deorum continuit? That the gods influence the minds of wrongdoers to choose conduct which will bring punishment was a Greek view. See K. J. Dover (1974), 149–50.

[2] Cic. *Har. Resp.* 18 (39).

[3] Hor. iii. 6. 1–8.   [4] Ibid. 17–20.

Ode iii. 4 has a similar theme. Horace describes the battle between gods and giants ending with the defeat and punishment of the latter. A moral is drawn. The gods hate power that is moved by passion to start every kind of wickedness (*nefas*).[1] What is meant, or at least included in *nefas* is shown by Horace's list of sinners undergoing punishment. Among them is 'the notorious Orion who assaulted the virgin Diana',[2] the 'unrestrained Tityus'[3] who had tried to rape Leto, and Pirithous 'the lover'[4] suffering for his attempt to carry off Persephone. We see that the *nefas* hated by the gods includes a good deal of sex. But not only. After all, the victims of the great sinners were goddesses. The ultimate offence was sacrilege. Again we find that immorality, in this case male immorality, and sacrilege are closely linked. Passionate self-indulgence leads to sacrilege and this incurs a heavy penalty.

Another case of divine punishment is treated in Ode iii. 3. Horace provides a double explanation of the fall of Troy. The ultimate cause was the failure of King Laomedon to keep a promise to the gods, but the immediate responsibility for the Trojan disaster lay with Paris, 'a fatal and immoral arbitrator' and Helen, 'a foreign woman'.[5] In this case sacrilege and perjury were the original offences. But adultery was the instrument through which they were punished.

In a humorous poem, Propertius develops the same idea. 'But now the shrines lie neglected in deserted groves: piety is vanquished and all men worship gold. Gold has banished faith, gold has made judgement to be bought and sold, gold rules the law, and once law has been undermined chastity as well.'[6] The poet goes on to compare himself with Cassandra who prophesied the doom of Troy but was not believed. In this poem the chain of guilt begins with the sin of avarice (as in Sallust). Other sins including sexual immorality and sacrilege follow, and all will be punished.

These passages do not express an unambiguous belief that the gods will uphold conventional morality, but they do treat morality in a supernatural context. Antisocial behaviour, especially sexual immorality, and above all female immorality,

---

[1] Hor. iii. 4. 67.   [2] Ibid. 70–1.   [3] Ibid. 77.
[4] Ibid. 80.   [5] Ibid. 3. 20–1.
[6] Prop. iii. 13. 47–50; M. Hubbard (1974), 88 ff.

is treated with religious horror as something that destroys society. Its existence is a symptom of divine anger against the Roman people, divine anger which is driving the Romans to self-destruction. At the same time it remains uncertain whether the immorality is the cause of the anger, or the means by which the anger is turned into punishment.[1] The poems express an attitude rather than a logically differentiated theology, which can perhaps be summed up as a sense of the unity of the duties of citizenship. If the community is to flourish, the gods must be worshipped and the citizens must exercise self-control, which in the case of women is to apply especially in sexual matters. But none of the duties can be properly performed unless all are, and neglect of any aspect is likely to produce the kind of situation from which Italy has been suffering.

It has been argued that the connection of religion and morality in Augustan literature, especially in the *delicta maiorum* ode of Horace[2] is literary opportunism. In 28 Augustus had rebuilt many temples but failed to gain acceptance for a programme of moral reform. Horace comments on this situation by writing a poem whose theme is that restoration of worship without moral reform is not enough.[3] But this does not account for the fact that Augustus did after all attempt reforms in the two areas at the same time. That he did so suggests that for him religion and morality were linked, if only in that rather vague way in which they were linked by Horace and earlier Roman writers.

This suspicion is strengthened by the fact that each of the two principal phases of moral reform culminated in a religious ceremony of purification. We will look at them in turn. In 29–28 B.C. Augustus was laying the foundation of the new system of government which has often been described as the restoration of the republic. In the course of this he, together with his chief assistant Agrippa, carried out a census of the Roman people on the basis of a special grant of censorial power.[4] At the same time he purged the senate of members he considered

---

[1] One might compare the ambiguity in whether a disastrous event like the outbreak of plague is a portent warning of future danger or punishment for past offence.

[2] Hor. iii. 6.

[3] G. Williams (1968), 610 ff.

[4] Dio, lii. 42; Vell. ii. 89 f.

unworthy. It was probably at this time too that he expelled a number of knights from the equestrian order.[1] He certainly attempted to bring in moral legislation of the kind he eventually introduced in 18 B.C.[2] All this had a good secular purpose. The ground was being cleared for the new political system. The roll of the *comitia centuriata* had to be brought up to date, the senate had to become once more a reasonably sized and responsible assembly.[3] But the whole procedure ended with a celebration of the *lustrum*, the traditional ceremony of purification of the Roman people which like the census itself had not been carried out for forty-one years. The purification solemnly concluded a period of five years. The sacrifice fulfilled the vow taken at the end of the previous period. The censor's prayer asked the gods to renew their support for the five years to come. The ceremony as a whole surely amounts to a religious confirmation of the measures of moral reform that had preceded it.[4]

There was a similar sequence of moral reform and religious purification in the years 18–17 B.C. After the settlement of 23, Augustus departed from Rome and left the city to the management of the senate. The ensuing year saw frightening prodigies, together with a very severe and widespread outbreak of disease. The people of Rome, we are told, believed that these things were happening for no other reason than that Augustus was no longer consul.[5] In other words, the signs and the disease expressed divine anger. Thereupon the people besieged the senate in the senate house to compel it to make Augustus dictator. Subsequently, they also called on him to take charge of the grain supply, as Pompey had done, and to be *censor* for life. For himself, Augustus only accepted charge of the grain supply, but he immediately appointed two censors, the last ever appointed, and himself enforced sumptuary regulations. He abolished some public banquets, restricted others, and made regulations limiting the amount to be spent on entertainments.[6] One might

[1] Suet. *Aug.* 38. 3–40. 1.

[2] P. A. Brunt (1971), 588 ff, with particular reference. to Prop. ii. 7; Liv. praef. 9; Flor. ii. 34; Oros. vi. 22. 3; Tac. *Ann.* iii. 28.

[3] T. P. Wiseman (1969), 70–1.

[4] Lustrum: *fasti Venusini* = *Inscr. Ital* 13, p. 255; *R.G.* 2. 2; R. M. Ogilvie (1961), cf. p. 99 n. 2, below.

[5] Dio, liv. 1. 2: νομίσαντες οἱ Ῥωμαῖοι οὐκ ἄλλως σφίσι ταῦτα συμβεβηκέναι, ἀλλ' ὅτι μὴ καὶ τότε ὑπατεύοντα τὸν Αὔγουστον ἔσχον.

[6] Ibid. 2. 3–5.

conclude that the people felt that the wrath of the gods might be aroused, not only by ritual neglect, but by public acts such as the failure to have Augustus as one of the consuls, and further that the means to appease the gods included measures of moral reform such as were traditionally instituted by censors.

In 19 B.C. Augustus was again absent from Rome. There was rioting and bloodshed. The people insisted on reserving the second consulate for Augustus. Augustus refused the consulate but in October returned to Rome. An altar of Fortuna Redux and an annual holiday were established to celebrate the return. He was then offered the authority of censor but turned it down,[1] and carried through the measures which the senate required by virtue of his tribunician *potestas*. There followed in 18 B.C. Augustus' principal moral reform. He purged the senatorial order,[2] and saw to the passing of the *leges Iuliae de maritandis ordinibus* and *de adulteriis*.[3] Adultery by a woman and condonation of it by her husband was made a crime. Extra-marital intercourse with a woman of high status (*stuprum*) also became a crime.[4] Other regulations included a law against electoral corruption.[5] Presumably he also began preparation for the Secular Games of 17 B.C.[6]

There is considerable uncertainty concerning on what calculation the year 17 B.C. was chosen. But one thing is indisputable, that the Games were held at the end of a period of intensive moral reform, and after Augustus had managed to get acceptance for marriage legislation of the kind which he had failed to introduce in 28. That this was no coincidence is shown by the fact that prayers for the success of the legislation are included in Horace's hymn for the Games: 'Rear up our youth, O goddess [Lucina] and bless the senate's edicts concerning wedlock and the marriage-law, destined, we pray, to be prolific

---

[1] Ibid. 10 *passim*. According to Dio, liv. 5, Augustus accepted censorial power but in the *R.G.* 6, he tells us that he refused it. A. H. M. Jones (1955) argues that Augustus did receive censorial power in 19 B.C. to make easier the forthcoming *lectio senatus*.

[2] Dio, liv. 13–14.

[3] The *lex Iulia de adulteriis*: Suet. *Aug.* 34; Tac. *Ann.* iii. 24; Hor. iv. 5. 21.

[4] P. A. Brunt (1971), 558–66; R. Syme (1939), 443–5.

[5] Dio, liv. 16. 1.

[6] It is not clear on what calculation of *saecula* this year was chosen. H. Mattingly, *C.R.* xlviii (1934), 161 ff. on Verg. *Aen.* vi. 792, suggested that the games were originally planned for 22.

in new offspring. . . Do ye, O gods, make teachable our youth and grant them virtuous ways.'[1]

Horace's hymn was recited as part of the ceremony on the last day of the Games on the Palatine, and on the Capitol. The actual prayers used at these ceremonies have also been preserved, and it is significant that they do not touch the moral themes mentioned in Horace's hymn.[1] One might say that Horace's hymn provides an interpretation in a more modern and philosophical spirit of the traditional, or at least traditionally phrased, prayers of the ceremony.[2]

One can define the moral context of the festival, as interpreted by Horace, more closely. The ritual of the festival marks the succession of one generation of Romans by another. The old generation was ceremoniously buried, the existing Roman people, inevitably tainted by the pollution of the past, were purified ritually, and prayers were said for a new and better race of Romans. Clearly prayers for fertility and the successful propagation of the Roman people belonged to the heart of the institutions. In addition all free inhabitants of Rome had been issued with torches, sulphur, and bitumen, so that the casting out of impurity should be thoroughly done.[3] But ritual means were not enough. Steps had already been taken for a deeper purification through the marriage legislation and related measures.

Like other activities national moral reform required parallel measures in religious and secular areas. It would be possible to argue that they were thought to work quite independently, and that the ritual was expected to maintain the *pax deorum* irrespective of what was done about moral standards in the secular sphere. I would suggest that the evidence does not favour this view. It is difficult to see why the people should react to prodigies and disease by wishing to appoint Augustus precisely to the office of censor. Presumably they thought that the measures to be expected from a censor (i.e. moral regulations) would appease the gods.

The censorship was decidedly a secular magistracy which,

---

[1] *C.I.L.* vi. 32323; Th. Mommsen (1913), 567–626; I. B. Pighi (1965).

[2] Hor. *C.S.* 17–20, 45, trans. C. E. Bennett; contrast Cic. *N.D.* iii. 8: num quis quod bonus vir esset, gratias dis egit umquam.

[3] K. Latte, *R.R.* 48–9: Romans had no single word for ritual impurity.

apart from the concluding ceremony, had no religious duties.[1] There is, however, an anecdote which suggests that the censor's supervision of public morals had religious implication.[2] 'Once Claudius Asellus pointedly reminded Scipio Aemilianus that his censorship had been an unlucky one. Scipio replied: "You need not be surprised, for the censor who performed the concluding ceremony [lustrum condidit] was the one who had restored you from public disgrace." '[3] It is implied in Scipio's remark that the misfortune had been sent by the gods to punish the community for the censor's failure to uphold moral standards.

The anecdote concerned the censors of 143. By the time of the late republic, thoughtful men were certainly conscious that formally correct performance of ritual was not enough. Cicero emphasizes that the gods must be approached with purity of mind.[4] Ovid went as far as to describe the formal view of purification as a primitive error.[5] I suggest that Augustus too insisted that the *pax deorum* could not be renewed by formal purification alone. The gods could be expected to maintain the greatness of the Roman state, or to make the new age happier than the old, only if minds had been purified of the old offences.[6]

We are once again in that undefined region of divine moral concern. We see that it obviously includes behaviour harmful to the family and its continuity, especially the immoral behaviour of womenfolk and failure to have children. But it may also embrace other behaviour of a kind that had traditionally incurred the censor's rebuke, such as conspicuously expensive living, or undignified financial transactions.[7] In other words, the gods were liable to resent behaviour which if it became

[1] R. E. A. Palmer (1965), esp., p. 319.

[2] Cic. *De Or.* ii. 268: Lustrum infelix noli mirari, is enim qui te ex aerariis exemit lustrum condidit.' On the circumstances see A. E. Astin (1967), 175–7. The misfortune may have been the plague of 142 B.C.

[3] Note that the censor blamed (Scipio himself was the other) is the one who performed the concluding ceremony. Failure to uphold standards made him unfit to perform the ceremony and this rendered the whole lustrum *infelix*.

[4] *Leg.* ii. 10 (24–5).

[5] *Fast.* ii. 20–46: 'Ah, nimium faciles qui tristia crimina caedis/fluminea tolli posse putatis aqua . . . sed quae praestanda est et sine teste fide.' Cf. F. Bömer on *Fast.* ii. 35.

[6] Verg. *Ecl.* iv. 13: vestigia sceleris nostra or 31: priscae vestigia fraudis.

[7] Suet. *Aug.* 39; Cic. *Leg.* iii. 3 (7).

widespread was thought to be bad for the community, and their interest was not so much in the eradication of particular sins, as in the maintenance of the *res publica* in a healthy condition. It was felt that the gods could not be piously asked to maintain the state, while the Romans were behaving in a manner that must undermine it.

III

IDEOLOGICAL CONSEQUENCES
OF THE PRINCIPATE

1. *The ambivalent acceptance of the principate*

AUGUSTUS' reforms were successful. The problems that had
nearly wrecked the empire, control of the professional army,
assimilation of the new Italian citizens, and the administration
of Rome itself, were solved. Stable peace was established. Many
had reasons for gratitude. In numerous and important areas
return to the conditions of the late republic was obviously un-
desirable. But peace was bought at the price of a fundamental
change in the nature of the Roman state, the change from
republic to monarchy. This necessitated a radical change of
attitude in the ruling class: they had to adjust to a state which
was no longer their own.

Any monarchical system ran counter to a long-established
and deeply ingrained ideal of freedom. Augustus was aware of
this feeling: indeed, he may well have shared it. Accordingly, he
presented his system as a restoration of ultimate authority to
the senate and people. As the first emperor he was careful to
restrict his authority by means of constitutional rules, with the
result that his position resembled a magistracy, 'outsize' but
still republican. If the constitutional definition of Augustus'
position was incomplete, it was nevertheless important. It
expressed the spirit in which Augustus was going to treat his
leading subjects. The republican ideal of what constituted senatorial dignity would, within limits, remain valid, and the *exempla*
of *libertas*, for instance, the expulsion of Tarquinius the Proud,
would continue to be exemplary. In the same spirit the last
defenders of the republic were added to the canon of Roman
heroes and came to figure in new *exempla*. Augustus had risen
with the support of the veterans and followers of Julius Caesar.
Now as *princeps* he stood above parties and sought the support
also of former republicans. Thus he showed his appreciation of

Cicero: 'a great orator and a great patriot', and of Cato: 'Anyone who does not wish the present status to be changed is a good
citizen.'[1] For most of his reign he tolerated history that represented the opponents of Julius Caesar as the party which had
right on its side in the civil war. Livy was allowed to wonder
whether it would have been better if Caesar had never been
born.[2] Cremutius Cordus described Cassius as the last of the
Romans.[3] Children would continue to learn from history that
republican freedom was the only condition which befitted the
dignity of a Roman noble, and even descendants of men who
owed their position to the favour of an emperor would hold the
republican view of what was due to them as senators.

In this way, the rule of Augustus and his successors was made
acceptable to the men who carried on their administration. It
was nevertheless resented. The emperors could not but fall
short of the ideal Augustus' constitutional settlement had set up
for them. The facts of power forced the *princeps* into monarchical
behaviour, just as it forced the nobility into servility. The result
was disappointment and resentment all round. The senators
constantly felt the loss of liberty, and at least some of the
emperors were equally frustrated. Nothing could be done about
the situation. Emperor and senators co-operated in running
a system of which the benefits were obvious, but which both
partners despised.

The tension at the centre of Roman society is reflected in
much of the literature of the early imperial period, even in the
writings of the most whole-hearted adherents of the Augustan
system. Such a one was the soldier-turned-historian, Velleius
Paterculus.

Velleius came of a leading family of Capua. An ancestor on
the mother's side had raised a legion for Rome in the Social
War and had seen his two sons enter the senate. Velleius'
paternal grandfather had served as an officer in the Roman
army. So had his father. He himself saw military service as
a military tribune in Thrace and Macedonia, and in A.D. 1
accompanied Caius Caesar on a tour of the eastern provinces.

---

[1] Augustus on Cicero, Plut. *Cic.* 49; on Cato, *Macr.* ii. 4. 18. Cf. Hor. i. 12,
35–6; ii. 1. 24: But Augustus also wrote a reply to Brutus' *Cato*: Suet. *Aug.* 85.

[2] Sen. *N.Q.* v. 18. 4.

[3] Tac. *Ann.* iv. 34. 1: laudato M. Bruto C. Cassium Romanorum ultimum
dixisset.

After this he served many years, first as *praefectus equitum* and later as *legatus*, under Tiberius. In civil life he achieved the office of *praetor*. His background and career were typical of a class that contributed greatly to the establishment of the principate, and for whom opportunities of advancement increased under the new system: Velleius' sons both reached the consulate.[1]

The history which Velleius dedicated to one of the consuls of A.D. 30 is, as one might expect, the work of a convinced adherent of the principate. He expresses his satisfaction with the system by praise of Augustus and even more enthusiastic praise for his patron Tiberius, which he couples with denigration of Tiberius' opponents.[2] Accordingly, he finds nothing problematic in the Augustan system. His attitude is summed up by comment on the constitutional settlement of 27 B.C.: 'The Roman world was at peace, the laws were again enforced, the courts were respected, the senate regained its former dignity, and the power of magistrates was brought back to its traditional scope, with the one exception that two praetors were added to the former eight. The famous and traditional state of the republic was restored.'[3] Velleius was simply indifferent to the political realities behind the constitutional façade.

The acceptance of Augustus' claim at its face value was made easier by literary tradition. When Cicero wrote his account of the ideal (Roman) state he concluded it with a sketch of the character and function of the ideal Roman statesman. He calls him *moderator reipublicae* or *princeps civitatis*, and following the examples of Plato's philosopher king, he describes him in the singular. In fact the context shows that he was thinking of a man who would hold a place like Cato or Scipio Africanus among his colleagues in the senate.[4] Obviously a man who has no personal experience of the republican system of government, but profound respect for Roman literature, might see in Cicero's sketch of a *princeps*, the justification of an all but monarchical system.[5]

---

[1] G. V. Sumner (1970); A. Dihle (1955); A. J. Woodman (1973), a fine stylistic analysis, also (1976).

[2] R. Syme (1939), 488. While Velleius praises Sejanus he does not think of him as a possible successor to the empire; see Sumner (1970), 288–97.

[3] ii. 89.   [4] Cic. *Rep.* vi. 9–26 (somnium Scipionis).

[5] V. Pöschl (1936).

While literary traditions, notably but not exclusively the example of Cicero,[1] contributed to the acceptance of the principate as a true restoration of the republic, the essential factor was surely the lack of any contact with the free institution of Rome. For example, Velleius saw Cicero as the great writer he knew, and thought that he had been equally influential as a statesman.[2] He did not know how weak the position of this great *novus homo* had been. More strikingly, he could comment on the transfer of elections from the people to the senate in the reign of Tiberius; rioting was shifted from the forum, soliciting (for votes) from the Campus Martius.[3] Obviously, to this professional soldier from Capua the popular elections at Rome meant nothing at all—in fact, he was one of the first batch of magistrates to hold office after the transfer of elections to the senate.

Accordingly, it was easy for Velleius to present the history of the republic in such a way as to exaggerate the factors making for continuity with the principate. A remarkable feature of Velleius' History are the character sketches of great Romans.[4] Livy too has character sketches, but in his vast work they stand out much less. This is significant. Roman history has been personalized. The institutions and constitutional procedures of Rome have become less significant, the great individuals more so.

This trend is particularly obvious in Velleius' accounts of great political conflicts, for instance, those involving the Gracchi. The tendency is hostile to *populares*, favourable to the senatorial view.[5] Velleius describes Gracchus as an ambitious individual who was properly crushed by the patriot Scipio Nasica. We are told about the agrarian law but there is no discussion of the conditions that did or (according to Tiberius's opponents) did not, justify it. We are told that he deposed a tribune but are told nothing of the constitutional conflict which led to this drastic action.[6] The account stresses personalities and their

---

[1] On Philodemus see O. Murray (1965).
[2] ii. 128. 3.
[3] ii. 126: summoto e foro seditio, ambitio campo.
[4] e.g. ii. 45 (Clodius); 48. 3–4 (Curio); ii. 11. 1 (Marius); ii. 17. 1–3 (Sulla); ii. 29 (Pompey); ii. 41 (Julius Caesar).
[5] J. Hellegouarc'h (1963), esp. 671.
[6] ii. 2–3; cf. ii. 6 on G. Gracchus.

clashes. In general, public figures are estimated by their possession or lack of *virtus* rather than by specific political qualities.[1] The historian is not concerned with constitutional questions.

The writers of the late republic, and Livy, had used the title *princeps* to describe leading men in the state, normally men who had been consul. In the comparatively short history of Velleius this use of the *princeps* title is much more prominent than in Livy.[2]

Outstanding men of earlier Roman history, Metellus Macedonicus,[3] Marius,[4] M. Antonius the orator,[5] Crassus,[6] Pompey[7] the triumvir, are described as *principes*. Caius Gracchus, we are told, had the personal qualities to become *princeps civitatis*, if he had not striven for vengeance or kingship.[8] In the very paragraph in which he summarizes the benefits of the rule of Augustus, he states that Augustus induced the *principes viri* to contribute to the public works of the city.[9] Thus, the position of Augustus appears to be nothing new. He is seen, as he wanted to be seen, as *primus inter pares* of the leading men in the city and only the last in a long succession of *principes*.

As far as the principate is concerned, orthodox views seem to come naturally to Velleius. This applies also to the cults of loyalty. In matter-of-fact language he relates how Tiberius began his reign with the consecration of the dead Augustus. 'When he had restored his father to heaven and honoured his body with human and his soul (*numen*) with divine honours, his first task as emperor was . . .'[10] A little later he refers to the consecration in words which to us, though evidently not to Romans, accentuate the absurdity of the consecration of a dead man. 'Caesar [i.e. Tiberius] deified his father not by a word of command (*imperio*) but by *reverence* (*religione*). He did not call him a god but made him one.'[11] Velleius did not describe the living emperor as a god, but he tells how a German experienced a sense of the supernatural in the presence of Tiberius.[12] Velleius

[1] Evidence, J. Hellegouarc'h (1963), 673–4.
[2] On history of the title see L. Wickert (1954).
[3] i. 11.   [4] ii. 19. 4; 128. 2.   [5] ii. 22. 3.
[6] ii. 20. 6.   [7] ii. 53. 3.   [8] ii. 6. 2.
[9] ii. 89. 4.   [10] ii. 124. 3.   [11] ii. 126. 1.
[12] ii. 107: 'permissu tuo, Caesar, quos ante audiebam, hodie vidi deos'. Does the plural include the image of Augustus carried by the army?

concludes the history with a loyal prayer to 'Jupiter, Mars, Vesta and whatever other divinity has made Rome great' to preserve the emperor Tiberius and the present state of things.[1]

It is all the more remarkable that this whole-hearted admirer of the principate, with his exemplary orthodox political outlook, should nevertheless idealize the men who had died to defend the republic. Velleius' portrait of Pompey is on the whole favourable.[2] In the war against Caesar his was the better cause.[3] Velleius admires Cicero and is indignant at his murder, for which Antony is blamed,[4] But most striking is his sanctification of Cato.[5] He is described as a personification of *virtus*. In all his actions his character was more like a god's than a man's. He never did right in order to be seen doing so, but because he was incapable of acting otherwise. He was free from all human vices and as a result never at the mercy of fortune.[6] Velleius also praises Brutus—except for murder of Caesar.[7] For Velleius there was no inconsistency between admiration for Cato and whole-hearted acceptance of the principate. Cato was simply the embodiment of those Roman virtues which Augustus and Tiberius had restored, as they had brought back everything else that was good in the Roman tradition.

This was a naïve attitude. Cato had stood not only for *virtus* and for conservatism but also for liberty, and liberty was not a matter of being subject to a law-abiding and beneficent master but of being subject to no master whatsoever.[8] From this point of view the *princeps* was undoubtedly a master. Men who by family tradition, or through knowledge of history, had a better understanding of the old republic could not separate the character of Cato from the cause for which he stood.

Livy described the civil war from a Pompeian point of view and his social relations with Augustus did not deteriorate.[9] Asinius Pollio, a friend of Julius Caesar and later a leading supporter of Antony, chose the establishment of the first triumvirate as the starting-point for a history which ended with the defeat of the republican cause at Philippi.[10] The implication is

---

[1] ii. 131: hunc statum, hanc pacem, hunc principem.
[2] ii. 29. 3; 37. 4.   [3] ii. 49. 2.   [4] ii. 66. 2.
[5] ii. 35.   [6] ii. 35; 45.
[7] ii. 69. 3; 72. 1: R. Syme (1958), 140, quoting Jerome *in Hoseam II*, praef., suggests that Livy was Velleius' source.
[8] Cf. Cic. *Rep.* ii. 43.   [9] Tac. *Ann.* iv. 34. 3.   [10] Hor. ii. 1. 1.

that Caesar was at least as responsible for the civil war as Pompey. He also treated Brutus and Cassius sympathetically. No wonder Horace felt that the historian was hazardously walking on ashes covering a fire.[1] Another prominent noble, M. Valerius Messala Corvinus, who had served in turn with the republicans and with Antony before joining Augustus, wrote *Commentaries* on the civil war, one of the sources of Plutarch's *Life of Brutus*.[2] In this work Messala emphasized his own service under Cassius with the republican cause.[3] Neither this frankness about the past, nor his resignation on grounds of principle from the post of prefect of the city, which he felt to be an authoritarian office,[4] harmed him with Augustus. Augustus in turn benefited from the support of so noble and respected a man.

A. Cremutius Cordus, a senator but a much less prominent man than Valerius Corvinus, wrote *Annales* which included the civil war. He praised both Brutus and Cassius[5] and 'proscribed for all eternity the men responsible for the proscriptions':[6] at the same time he was tactful in his treatment of Caesar and Augustus. The work was recited in the presence of Augustus himself, and as long as the founder of the principate was alive the historian came to no harm.[7]

The civil war period simply could not be written from a Caesarian point of view. So, the awkward grandson of Livia, the later emperor Claudius, who could not fittingly glorify republicans, was dissuaded from starting his history with the murder of Caesar. On the urging of his mother and grandmother, he began with the 'civil peace'.[8]

There were limits to imperial tolerance, even to that of Augustus. While a certain amount of freedom was allowed to historians of the civil war, criticism of the Augustan order and of the *princeps* (as opposed to the *triumvir*) was evidently discouraged. Livy did not publish the last books of his history (from 42 to 9 B.C.)

---

[1] Ibid. 7–8.

[2] H. Peter (1897), i. 173; G. R. Hanslip, P.W. 2R. viii. 1. 131–57, s.v. M. Valerius Messala, 261.

[3] Imperatorem suum Cassium praedicabat (Tac. *Ann.* iv. 34. 4).

[4] Incivilem potestatem (Jerome, *Chron.* on year 1991 = 26 B.C.).

[5] See above, p. 102 n. 3 and P.W. iv. 2. 1703–4, s.v. Cremutius.

[6] Sen. *Consol. ad Marc.* 26. 1.

[7] Suet. *Tib.* 61. 3.

[8] Suet. *Claud.* 4: cum sentiret neque libere neque vere sibi de superioribus tradendi potestatem relictam.

during Augustus' lifetime.[1] In A.D. 12 the book of the historian T. Labienus was burnt and the author committed suicide; a critical orator was exiled.[2] Augustus could afford to be more liberal than his successor. Under Tiberius, Cremutius Cordus was prosecuted at the instigation of Sejanus. He committed suicide and his writings were burnt.[3]

Nevertheless, a compromise similar to that allowed by Augustus was maintained under his successors.[4] The ruling emperor must not be criticized. Earlier emperors, with the partial exception of Augustus, were fair game. The republican heroes, Cato, Brutus, and Cassius, might be venerated. Thus history provided a safety-valve through which the discontented could vent their anger harmlessly by attacking the past. It provided means of showing the emperor through criticism of his predecessors what kind of conduct would make him unpopular with prominent subjects. Republican *libertas* was dead. Hardly anybody seriously considered its restoration. But certain practical aspects of it could be presented for general admiration in historiography, and in this way commended to the ruling emperor.

Thus writers of history, though they might have benefited personally from the imperial system, or even played an important role in its administration, wrote with detachment. At one extreme is the unknown author, perhaps M. Servilius Nonianus, who blackened the memory of the emperor Tiberius for ever.[5] But even Seneca, the tutor of Nero, wrote of the empire as a system of government suitable for the Roman people in its old age and second childhood. No longer able to support itself it needed a ruler as a stick to lean on.[6] He also described the civil wars which brought in the principate as 'the time when truth began to depart out of sight'.[7]

[1] *Periocha* of Book cxxi headed: qui editus post excessum Augusti dicitur.

[2] On the suppression of critical literature in the later years of Augustus, see R. Syme (1939), 486 ff. and G. W. Clarke (1972), 77–8.

[3] Tac. *Ann.* iv. 35.

[4] Cf. R. Syme (1939), 488.

[5] F. Klingner (1958). R. Syme, 'The historian Servilius Nonianus', *Hermes*, xcii (1964), 408-24 = *Studies in Tacitus*, 91–109.

[6] Lact. *Div. Inst.* vii. 15. 14. The fragment is usually attributed to the elder Seneca, otherwise M. T. Griffin (1972), 10.

[7] H. Peter, *H.R.R.* ii. 98, referring to the starting-point of his father's historical work. On Seneca's attitude to the end of the republic see M. T. Griffin (1976),

2. *Seneca: the ideology*[1] *of aristocracy under the empire*

The changed political situation gradually transformed the attitude of the Roman upper class to the state. Seneca can be taken as a representative of the tendency. Seneca was no more an average senator than Cicero. Obviously a man of extraordinary ability, he was the outstanding literary figure as well as a leading public figure of his age.[2] As in the case of Cicero, a great many of his writings have survived, but the character of the writings, when compared with those of Cicero, reflects a change in the character of public life. Cicero was active in a free community. For him, as for his fellow senators, public affairs were their own affairs. Seneca served successively as tutor, regent, and adviser to an emperor who could consult whom he pleased and whose decisions were ultimately his own. Senators could no longer feel that they were serving their own state. The alienation which found expression in the historiography of the empire had a far-reaching effect on individual motivation.

Cicero was still moved by the optimistic view of political action that had originated at Athens centuries earlier. Politics is a means for providing a good life for one's fellow citizen and displaying one's own qualities. 'And since we feel a mighty urge to increase the resources of mankind, since we desire to make human life safer and richer by our thought and effort, and we are goaded on to the fulfilment of this desire by nature herself, let us hold to the course which has always been that of excellent men' (i.e. engage in public life).[3]

Politics is the occupation which man owes to the best in himself. 'As the spirit is the only force that moves itself it surely has

---

182–201. On intellectual decline under empire see, for example, Sen. Rhet. *Controv.* 1. praef. 6 ff.; Plin. *N.H.* ii. 117. Other references in A. J. Woodman (1975), 22 nn. 39–40.

[1] By ideology I mean a complex of ideas which assists members of a particular group in living their lives, but is neither as intellectually rigorous and consistent as a philosophy, nor associated with ritual like religion. Many of the ideas discussed in this and the following chapter were derived from Stoic philosophy. But comparatively few literary men and very many fewer non-intellectuals among the aristocracy were Stoics in the full sense. A study of the influence of Stoic philosophy on the Roman nobility is badly needed.

[2] P. Grimal (1948), H. Currie (1972), above all M. T. Griffin (1976). Treating Seneca as a representative figure necessarily involves considerable simplification of the Neronian intellectual scene, cf. E. Cizek (1972) and the review of M. T. Griffin in *J.R.S.* lxvi (1976), 229–30.   [3] Cic. *Rep.* i. 2 (3).

no beginning and is immortal. Use it therefore in the best pursuits. And the best tasks are those undertaken in defence of the native land.'[1] Statesmanship may even be rewarded by immortality: 'No thing of all that is done on earth is more pleasing to that supreme God who rules the whole universe than the assemblies and gatherings of men associated in justice which are called states. Their rulers and preservers come from that place (the stars) and to that place return.[2]

'Man must live for *virtus* but it is not enough to possess *virtus* unless you make use of it . . . The existence of *virtus* depends entirely on its use; and its noblest use is in the government of the state and the realization in facts, not words, of the very things that the philosophers are continually dinning into our ears.'

For Seneca the state has become a much more questionable object of loyalty. This appears, for instance, in criticism of Brutus' part in the murder of Julius Caesar. Brutus, he suggests, was misguided if he still hoped that liberty could exist where the rewards both of supreme power of servitude were too great, or that the earlier constitution of the state could be restored after the ancient manners had all been lost, that equality of civil rights might still exist and laws maintain their rightful place where there had been so many thousands of men fighting to decide not whether, but to which of two masters, they would be slaves.[3]

Seneca hopes for much less from the political process than Cicero did. He anticipates no essential improvement of human condition through political means. Significantly he wrote no 'Republic', no 'Laws'. The most public of his treatises is the *De Clementia* (A.D. 54–5) and its purpose is to advocate qualities of mercy to the young emperor Nero. Seneca distrusted emperors.[4] Like the historians of the Julio-Claudian period he is extremely critical of earlier rulers, with the partial exception of Augustus.

Public life remains the principal field in which the wise man will carry out his duty to his fellows, but the prestige of public life is limited by the exaltation of a rival form of life—contemplation, and a rival citizenship—the fellowship of mankind.

[1] Cic. *Rep.* vi. 26 (29).   [2] Ibid. 13 (13).
[3] Sen. *Ben.* ii. 20. 2. Translations of this and following passages are from J. W. Basore's Loeb edition.
[4] On the relevance of *De Clementia* to problems of contemporary jurisdiction see M. T. Griffin (1976), 160–71.

'Let us grasp the idea that there are two commonwealths—the one vast and truly common state, which embraces alike gods and men, in which we look neither to this corner of earth nor to that, but measure the bounds of our citizenship by the path of the sun, the other, the one to which we have been assigned by the accident of birth . . . The greater commonwealth we are able to serve even in retirement from public life—nay, I am inclined to think even better in retirement—so that we may inquire what virtue is . . . whether it is nature or art that makes men good . . .' —whether all the matter from which everything is formed is continuous or atomic, what God is and whether he interferes actively in his creation.[1]

Both the commonwealth of mankind and the life of retirement figure frequently in the writing of Seneca.[2] Seneca is conscious that he rates the contemplative life more highly than earlier teachers of the Stoic school, but at least in the treatises written before his final departure from Nero's court he continues to stress the opportunities for public service offered by public life to a soldier, magistrate, or advocate. The decision to retire must depend on the circumstance that the character of the state does not allow a self-respecting individual to serve in a public capacity.

Moreover, Seneca does not see retirement in terms of a once-for-all decision, but as a gradual process. 'Let him find something in which he may be useful to the state. If he is not permitted to be a soldier let him seek public office. Must he live in a private station? Let him be an advocate. Is he condemned to silence? Let him help his fellows by silent support. Is it dangerous even to enter the forum? In private houses, at public spectacles, at feasts, let him show himself a good comrade, a faithful friend, a temperate feaster. Has he lost the duties of a citizen? Let him exercise those of a man.'[3]

It might be thought that the greater prominence of these concepts involved a change of ideal and a withdrawal from public life by the aristocracy. This was not so—expect perhaps in the very long term. Seneca and Marcus Aurelius served the state as conscientiously as it had ever been served. The change

---

[1] *Ot.* 4. 1 (31) (contracted).
[2] See the sensitive discussion by M. T. Griffin (1976), 315–66.
[3] *Tranq.* 4. 2–3.

is rather in motivation. Actions are judged less by success or public approval and more by the voice of conscience. 'Nothing shall I ever do for the sake of opinion, everything for the sake of my conscience. Whatever I shall do when I alone am witness, I shall count as done beneath the gaze of the Roman people.[1]

'What guide has man but his own conscience? Crushed though it be, this gives him cheer, this cries out against the mob and hearsay and relies wholly upon itself, and when it sees the vast crowds of those on the other side who think differently it does not take trouble to count votes, but wins the victory by its single vote. . . . Though fire should devour my limbs one by one, though my heart conscious of my rightness should drip with blood, my good intention shall delight in the flame through which its loyalty will shine forth.'[2]

For Seneca life is a never-ending struggle to subject the body to the commands of the conscience. He is enormously conscious of evil in himself and others, and he seeks to overcome this by persistent self-examination and self-criticism. 'We have all sinned—some in serious, some in trivial things, some from deliberate intention, some by chance impulse. . . . Even if there is anyone who has so thoroughly cleansed his mind that nothing can any more confound him . . . yet it is by sinning that he has reached the sinless state.'[3]

The individual turning inward for moral guidance requires assistance. This is provided by literature, ultimately the philosophical literature of Greece, but immediately Latin translations and popularizations like the philosophical writings of Cicero and Seneca's own essays and epistles.[4] In his writings Seneca presents himself as spiritual director of individuals, especially of Serenus in *De Tranquillitate* and Lucilius in the *Moral Epistles*.[5] Philosophers had long been found among the retinue of the great at Rome, but it looks as if under the empire their advice came to fill a deeper need. Philosophy was now more than the interesting game it had once been.[6] Ancestral custom and the code of a ruling class no longer provided an

---

[1] *Vit. Beat.* 20. 4.   [2] *Ben.* iv. 21. 5–6.   [3] *Clem.* i. 6. 3–4.

[4] M. T. Griffin (1976), 346–55, 416–19 shows that the *Moral Epistles* are dialogues in epistolary form rather than genuine letters.

[5] On Annaeus Serenus, *P.I.R.* i. 2, p. 104, no. 618. On Lucilius, *P.W.* xiii. 2, s.v. Lucilius L. Iunior (26).

[6] R. Syme (1958), 552; (1939), 57–9.

adequate guide to living. Philosophy and the philosophical expert had to fill the gaps.[1] It was nothing new that a young Roman noble should model himself on an older figure. Traditionally this was a man well known in public life. The novelty lay in the older man being an intellectual who based his instruction, not on experience of public affairs, but on a systematic philosophical view of the world.[2] There was opposition to the development, and suspicion of philosophy.[3] But this did not prevent Stoic philosophy from steadily deepening its influence.[4]

Stoic philosophy provided an extremely austere guide to living. It proclaimed that striving after virtue was the one thing of value in life, and that success or failure, riches or poverty, in fact all external circumstances were fundamentally insignificant. The Stoic understood that whatever misfortune happened, had to happen, and trained himself to meet it with the emotional indifference that its insignificance in the absolute scale of values merited. In return for the abnegatory life, Stoic philosophy promised little reward other than self-respect and sense of duty done.

Inasmuch as Stoicism involved precepts for life based on a coherent system of belief,[5] it was a religion in the way Judaism and Christianity are religions, and Roman paganism was not. It was, however, in a sense, a religion without a god. Seneca seems to use god, nature, fortune, fate, almost synonymously,[6] and the power so described seems to be as lacking in personality as the laws of modern science. Similarly the Stoic lacked a detailed moral code sanctioned by the authority of a super-human lawgiver. When translated into practice, Stoic morality amounted to something very much like the behaviour that was

[1] The need for a man to serve as a pattern: *Ep.* 11. 8–9; 25. 5. On spiritual guidance by Seneca and other philosophers, see A. Dill (1904), 293–4; 318; C. G. Starr (1954), 222–33. With Seneca cf. Musonius, on whom C. E. Lutz (1947).

[2] L. Hadot (1969), esp. 165–72.

[3] Cf. Tac. *Agr.* 2. 2 and R. Ogilvie's note. Here I am thinking of opposition on educational grounds.

[4] Of this its influence on the so-called 'opposition' to the emperors was only one aspect. See R. MacMullen (1967), 41–58.

[5] The theoretical basis is essential: *Ep.* 94–5.

[6] e.g. *Ben.* iv. 7–8. 3: 'for what else is Nature but God and the Divine Reason that pervades the whole universe . . . it will be right for you to call him Jupiter . . . if likewise you should call him fate it will be no falsehood.' At least the differences can be ignored as far as essentials of Stoicism are concerned: *Ad Helv.* 8. 3.

traditional among the Roman aristocracy, and it was illustrated by *exempla* drawn from the lives of illustrious Romans of the past, like Fabricius,[1] Regulus,[2] and the two Catos.[3] Moreover, the justification of Stoic morality was that it was in accordance with reason.[4] For Stoics human reason was of course part of the divine Reason pervading the universe. But the authority of reason is independent of metaphysics, and a morality based on it can be defended or criticized on a purely human plane.

But this is not the whole story. In a considerable number of passages Seneca employs language which implies the existence of a benevolent, personal god. 'A good man differs from God in the element of time only; he is God's pupil, his imitator, and true offspring, whom his all-glorious parent, being no mild taskmaster of virtues, rears as strict fathers do, with much severity . . . God does not make a spoilt pet of a good man; he tests him, hardens him, and fits him for his own service.'[5]

Man's moral effort provides 'a spectacle worthy of the regard of God as he contemplates his works . . . a brave man matched against ill-fortune. I do not know what nobler sight the Lord of Heaven could find on earth . . . than the spectacle of Cato, after his cause had already been shattered more than once, nevertheless standing erect among the ruins of the commonwealth.'[6]

In the writings of Seneca, God is involved with morality to an extent not found in earlier writings. Moral conduct is an imitation of God.[7] God requires moral conduct on the part of worshippers. He tests man with a view to his moral good. God is just. He punishes sin[8]—but mercifully. God answers prayer. He aids man's efforts towards improvement.[9]

These passages pose a problem of interpretation. The role of a caring, personal god is not consistent with the working of a

[1] *Prov.* 3. 6.

[2] *Prov.* 3. 9; *Ben.* v. 3. 2; *Tranq.* 16. 4; *Ad Helv.* 12. 5.

[3] Cato Maior, *Ep.* 11. 20; 25. 6; 104. 21; 64. 10. Cato Minor, *Ep.* 95. 69–71; *Tranq.* 7. 5; *V. Beat.* 18. 3; *Ad Marc.* 20. 6; *Prov.* 2. 9–10.

[4] e.g. *Ep.* 65. 35; 124. 4. Cf. A. A. Long (1974), 199 ff. on the content of virtue.

[5] *Prov.* 1. 4.

[6] Ibid. 2. 9.

[7] *Ep.* 95. 50: Vis deos propitiare? Bonus esto. Satis illos coluit, quisquis imitatus est. Cf. 124. 23–4 where the imitation is seen as the perfection of reason; see also *Ep.* 31. 9–11.

[8] *Ep.* 95. 50: Hi (dei) nec dant malum nec habent, ceterum castigant quosdam et coercent.

[9] *Ep.* 41. 1–2.

natural order in which every event is predestined by a chain of
cause and effect going back to the beginning of the universe.
Fate cannot show consideration for the individual. Seneca
never faces up to this contradiction. It is not even the case that
in some essays he assumes the existence of a personal deity while
in others he postulates an impersonal one. In the course of the
same work, even in the course of an argument, the benign father
figure turns into the inexorable law of the universe,[1] or into the
faculty of reason situated in the mind of the individual human
being.[2] All this has been described by Sevenster[3] who reached
the conclusion that 'Seneca is in the last resort not serious when
he speaks of the personal god'.[4]

The use to which Seneca puts the concept of a personal god
can be defined more closely. The *De Providentia* which contains
some of the most striking expressions of the idea provides a good
example of Seneca's procedure. The starting-point is a request
from Lucilius that Seneca is to explain how the misfortunes
suffered by good men are compatible with providential government of the world.[5] In other words, Lucilius would like to believe
that the world is governed by a just ruler, but thinks that the
facts contradict this view.

So Seneca proceeds to reassure Lucilius that the sufferings of
the just are indeed consistent with providential government of
the world. Seneca starts the treatise by drawing the picture of
a father- or teacher-like deity who trains and tests mankind with
hardships and takes pleasure in watching how the best rise
above every misfortune, treating it as the external and indifferent thing which it is.[6] Thus Seneca begins by arguing in terms
of a personal God, because this is an idea with which Lucilius is
familiar and, in spite of some intellectual difficulties, at ease.
The argument in terms of a more strictly Stoic concept of Providence comes later.[7] This is, I believe, a characteristic of Seneca's
procedure. He introduces concepts of great familiarity and with

---

[1] Compare *Prov.* 1. 5 and 5. 7–8.

[2] See text cited, p. 116 n. 1, below. Similarly 'obedience to god' is acquiescence
in hardships inflicted by the nature of things, as in *V. Beat.* 15. 6–7.

[3] J. N. Sevenster (1961), 35–49.

[4] Ibid. 37.

[5] *Prov.* 1. 1.

[6] Ibid. 1–3.

[7] See the excellent analysis by J. R. G. Wright (1974), 489.

strong emotional associations like god,[1] prayer,[2] divine justice,[3] or life after death.[4] He seems to be using them in more or less the accepted sense, but then goes on to interpret them in a specialized Stoic way. The effect is to invest with emotions ideas and concepts which in themselves are impersonal and unexciting.

I think the basic difficulty of the teacher of Stoicism was that most men would need some emotionally inspiring motive to face misfortune stoically. Compared with his peers of earlier generations, a noble of the imperial period found it more difficult to stiffen his resolution by thoughts of the tradition of his family, or the applause of his contemporaries.[5] He was alienated from the *res publica*,[6] and even a philosophical director of conscience was likely to be an expert in a particular branch of wisdom rather than a source of inspiration. The feeling that one is part of a vast, if generally beneficent, natural process is cold comfort. It needed to be invested with emotion if the Stoic was not to feel like a prisoner undergoing a life-sentence of solitary confinement. For most people the philosophy could only be helpful if the universe was felt to be in some way capable of noticing and honouring the individual's steadfastly endured suffering.

In a sense the use of 'god' and related terms by Seneca (and other Stoics) is a rhetorical trick. But it is more than that,

[1] e.g. *Ep.* 41. 2: 'bonus vir sine deo nemo potest an potest aliquis supra fortunam nisi ab illo adiutus exsurgere', an eloquent expression of man's moral dependence on God. But god here is the man's own conscience which participates in universal reason. See also *Ep.* 31. 9 ff. or 83. 1.

[2] e.g. *Ben.* iv. 4. 2 seems to accept the universal view that gods intervene beneficiently in answer to prayer. Later the divine benefits reduce to the general bounty of nature. *Ep.* 10. 5: sic vive cum hominibus tamquam deus videat; sic loquere cum deo, tamquam homines audiant. This is a memorable statement of a religious attitude. But in the context it is more concerned with self-discipline than with attitudes to God.

[3] *Clement.* i. 7. 2; *Ep.* 95. 50: gods punish—but not in the sense in which the word is normally used, for prosperity (because it weakens the moral fibre) is treated as a punishment.

[4] Cf. *Ep.* lii. 21; an impressive evocation of the splendour of the life after death; but it is not certain that Seneca ultimately means more than the merging of the individual soul in the Reason that pervades the universe.

[5] For the Stoic only virtue had authority, not rank or birth (*Ep.* 44. 3–6; 66. 3).

[6] Cf. above, pp. 108–10 ff. Public office is indifferent, neither good nor evil (*Ep.* 94. 8); cf. *Ep.* 118. 3, on candidature for office (described in terms of republican elections).

because there had always been a link between Stoicism and religion. Stoics had always been concerned to prove the existence of gods and to maintain religious feeling.[1] As we have seen, they did this by identifying traditional deities with particular parts of the world. In this way they provided intellectual justification for ritual which probably helped the Augustan revival of Roman religion.[2] Seneca was not primarily interested in the revival of traditional ritual.[3] His concern was to enlist religious emotions in support of Stoic morality. His technique was once again a kind of 'double-think'. He assured himself of the existence of God by defining him as an abstract principle, but obtained moral support and consolation in face of life's difficulties by thinking of him as a person. He also strengthened his sense of human dignity and of the value of moral effort by the thought that human reason was a part of the divine substance.

Seneca obviously felt that Stoic philosophy was a solid support in the troubles of life. But it does not follow that he rejected the traditional rites of Roman religion. It is true that his letters tell us little about practice of religious ritual but this is equally true of the letters of Cicero and Pliny, and of the pious fourth-century pagan Libanius, and seems to be a convention of the genre. Seneca certainly was opposed to superstition and even wrote a book attacking it,[4] but then the distinction between legitimate (or restrained) and illegitimate (or excessive) expression of piety had always been part of Roman religion. Seneca was extremely suspicious of religious enthusiasm. For example, he was strongly opposed to the worship of Isis. He was not worried about it as a practical problem. The passages dealing with it are very few. But he objected passionately to a cult whose ritual was designed to stir the emotion of the worshippers.[5] Seneca was very conscious that the 'civil theology' was

---

[1] Cf. A. A. Long (1974), 149. See also *Ep.* 14. 3.   [2] See above, p. 37.

[3] *Fr.* 38 ff., a wise man performs traditional rites: 'tamquam legibus iussa non tamquam dis grata.' He also stresses irrelevance of sacrifice compared with goodness of worshipper: *Ben.* i. 6. 3; iv. 25. 1; *Ep.* 95. 47; 115. 5. He wrote a *De Superstitione* which probably concerned psactices of private worship rather than the state cult. See p. 117 n. 4, below.

[4] See fragments of Seneca's *De Superstitione* in F. Haase, ed., *L. Annaei Senecae opera*, iii. 424–7, mainly derived from Aug. *C.D.* vi. 10. A definition of superstition: Sen. *Ep.* 122. 16.

[5] Cicero on religion and superstition: *N.D.* i. 42 (117); ii. 28 (71). Seneca against emotional religion: F. Haase, ed., fr. 34–5. See also R. Turcan (1967).

less true than philosophy, but he nevertheless taught that the traditional rites ought to be performed.[1] Indeed even when he was writing in the role of natural philosopher he thought it necessary to argue that the disasters foreshadowed by omens or prodigies could be averted by rites of expiation or by prayers and vows (*vota*).[2]

Logic told Seneca that the endless chain of cause and effect which was fate could not be interrupted by ritual, but it remained important for him that the rites of Roman religion should continue to be valid. On a more practical level incidental remarks of Seneca show that he did practise some of the more 'folkloric' components of traditional religion. On New Year's day he deliberately engaged in each of his regular activities (writing, reading, declaiming, and bathing)[3] in accordance with the belief that what happened on the first day would be an omen for the rest of the year.[4] He would also think good thoughts and eat figs.[5] Seneca's behaviour on New Year's day incidentally shows to what extent timeless custom had acquired (if it had not always possessed) a moral significance. It also reminds us that Stoicism was a supplement, not a substitute, for traditional religion.

Seneca's intellectual procedure moved at least one contemporary to passionate opposition. Lucan, nephew of Seneca, wrote a Stoic epic. But unlike his uncle, he refused to display feelings of affection and reverence for an impersonal destiny. The *Pharsalia* are as hostile to religion as Lucretius' *De Rerum Natura*.[6] The dilemma remained real for many generations, but eventually in some mysterious way, men became more certain of the existence of God and therefore felt less need to identify him with a natural principle. Divine intervention, not the endless chain of cause and effect, came to be what men were sure about.[7]

[1] F. Haase, ed., fr. 39; *Ben.* vii. 7. 3: only the world is a temple worthy of God, a temple in the ordinary sense is a mere nook (*angulum*). Still it has been consecrated and should be used accordingly.   [2] Sen. *Nat. Quaest.* ii. 37–8.

[3] *Ep.* 83. 5: qui anno novo quemadmodum legere, scribere dicere aliquid, sic auspicabar in Virginem desilire . . . cf. advice of Col. xi. 2. 98.

[4] Cf. above, p. 26 n. 2.

[5] *Ep.* 87. 3: Cotidie mihi annum novum faciunt (caricae) quem ego faustum et felicem reddo bonis cogitationibus et animi magnitudine.

[6] See below, pp. 147–50.

[7] Augustine, *C.D.* v. 1–11, on predestination shows how natural determinism

Meanwhile Stoic ideas dominated the Roman world. Stoicism was well suited to strengthen a man's stamina for conscientious public service.[1] 'Virtue you will find in the temple, in the forum, in the senate-house—you will find her standing in front of the city walls dirty and stained, and with calloused hands.'[2] It is required of a man that he should benefit his fellow men—many if he can, if not, a few . . .'[3] 'You ask what help in my opinion should be employed to overcome this tedium [of life]? The best course would be to occupy oneself with practical matters, the management of public affairs, and the duties of citizens.'[4]

But the same philosophy could also steel opponents of the regime to resistance. The Stoic was guided by his own judgement of what was right not by external authority and his self-discipline prepared him psychologically for martyrdom. 'If a man can look at flashing swords with eyes unswerving, if he knows that it is of no moment to him whether his soul departs through mouth or throat, call him happy. Call him happy if, when physical torture is decreed for him . . . with mind unperturbed he hears of chains and exile and the empty terrors of mankind' and is ready to say, in the words of Virgil that he has anticipated these hardships in his mind and is prepared to face them.[5] For a time in the reign of the emperor Domitian it looked as if Stoicism would become an ideology of opposition—at any rate this was what the emperor feared.

3. *Astrology in public life*

A feature of life in senatorial and court circles in the early empire was the influence of astrology. Astrology was not new.

---

has shrunk into a mere 'difficulty' in a world picture dominated by a personal god. J.-P. Vernant (1962), 115–29; (1966), 91–143, and 145, distinguishes explanations of the order of the world which involve an external power from those that involve an immanent organization. From its beginning in Ionian philosophy until well into the Imperial period Greek and, following it, Roman thought very much favours the immanent explanation. Vernant suggests that this reflects the organization of a city-state as opposed to a monarchy.

[1] Cf. below, pp. 169 ff.   [2] *Vit. Beat.* 7. 3.
[3] *Ot.* 3. 5, cf. Plin. *N.H.* ii. 5 (18): deus est mortali iuvare mortalem.
[4] *Tranq.* 3. 1.
[5] *Ep.* 76, trans. M. Hadas. Cato, the republican martyr, was a model for all Stoics irrespective of their attitude to empire.

It had been used by many Romans for a long time to help them in private concerns. But the end of the republic and the establishment of the principate gave it a place in public life which it had not had before.

The belief that human destinies can be predicted by observation of the stars originated in Mesopotamia and was known in Greece before the time of Plato. It made great progress in the Hellenistic world.[1] It was in Hellenistic Egypt that a sophisticated science was evolved from Mesopotamian astrology and Greek astronomy and mathematics. The claims of astrology were given plausibility by the fact that the annual rising and setting of constellations had long been associated with the seasonal changes of the weather, and had indeed been held to be the cause of the changes.[2]

Practical exploitation of the theory that the stars which dominated at the time of a man's birth would influence the whole of his life was encouraged by advances in astronomy and mathematics, which made possible accurate observation of the positions of stars and calculation of their positions in the past. Astrology was of course a pseudo-science. The true nature of the forces that operate between different parts of the universe (gravitation, radiation, etc.) remained unknown, and the astrologers' arbitrary procedure of endowing stars with personalities, and postulating the existence of mysterious emanations through which these stellar personalities could exert their influence over huge distances, could in no way fill the gap in knowledge. Nevertheless the prestige of philosophy and mathematics led men to indulge in wishful thinking and believe what they wanted to believe.

Astrologers figure in the earliest-surviving Roman literature.[3] Ennius included them in a scornful account of the underworld of divination along with Marsian augurs, village *haruspices*, diviners who relied on the Egyptian goddess Isis, and interpreters of dreams.[4] The circus was a favourite pitch.[5] But the science was practised at a higher social level too, and there its

---

[1] Early history of astrology, F. Cumont (1912); F. J. Boll (1926).

[2] M. P. Nilsson (1950), 256–67.

[3] F. H. Cramer (1954).

[4] Ennius *ap.* Cic. *Div.* i. 58 (132). Cf. also citation, *Rep.* i. 18 (30). Cato advised that a slave farm-manager should not consult the Chaldaeans, *R. Rustic.* i. 5. 4.

[5] Ennius *ap.* Cic. *Div.* i. 58 (132).

progress was helped by the growing influence of Stoic philosophy. Posidonius (*c.* 135–51 B.C.), the Stoic philosopher who had friends in the highest Roman nobility, and whose writings were one of the main channels through which Stoic thought flowed into Roman education, wrote five books on astrology.[1] He cited the correlation between the phases of the moon and the tides of the sea as an example of the influence a celestial body could exert on earthly phenomena, thus confirming the principle on which the false superstructure of astrology was based.[2] Henceforth astrology was intellectually respectable. The world picture of Stoicism made it a plausible hypothesis. If the future was in fact predetermined by an infinite chain of cause and effect, it was tempting to find means of discovering what the predetermined future would be. If every part of the universe influenced every other part,[3] it would at least in theory be possible to make statements about what would happen in one part by observing others. Observation of the heavenly bodies was obviously of the greatest use in predicting seasonal changes —a point which was eloquently made in Aratus' *Phenomena*[4] and Virgil's *Georgics*,[5] two poems permeated with Stoic ideas. It did not seem unreasonable to infer that the heavenly influence extended to the cycle of human life.[6] In these circumstances one would expect the expansion of astrology to run parallel with that of Stoic philosophy, that is, to develop steadily in the late republic, and dramatically under the early empire. This in fact seems to have happened.

In 86 the consul Octavius let himself be caught and killed by followers of Marius because a horoscope, later found on his body, had encouraged him not to leave Rome.[7] When Sulla was writing his memoirs he began to compose the formal conclusion as he approached the date which (according to astrological computation) was to be the day of his death.[8] Astrologers are said to have showered Pompey, Crassus, and Caesar with, as it

[1] H. Strasburger (1965), 40–53.
[2] Posidonius, fr. 85; Cic. *Div.* ii. 42 (89).
[3] Sympathy: M. Pohlenz (1959), 217; Cic. *Div.* ii. 14 (33). Sen. *Quaest. Nat.* ii. 6, cf. 4. Sex. Emp. *Adv. Math.* ix. 78–80.
[4] Aratus, *Phenomena*, ed. J. Martin (Florence, 1956).
[5] Verg. *Geor.* i. 252 ff.
[6] F. J. Boll (1926); F. Cumont (1912), iv.
[7] Plut. *Mar.* 42. 1–5.
[8] Id. *Sull.* 37.

turned out, false prophecies of long life and natural death.[1]
Varro asked L. Tarutius to complete the horoscope of Romulus.[2] Nevertheless the influence of astrology in the last years of
the republic must not be exaggerated. We have a uniquely rich
source of information about the social life of the period in
Cicero's correspondence. Yet the word *mathematicus* does not
occur in any of Cicero's letters, and it is not to be found in the
speeches either. The word *astrologus* occurs once in the letters
and once in the speeches. Both terms are more frequent in
philosophical writings.[3] This suggests that the interest of
Cicero and his circle in astrology was academic rather than
practical. Indeed, as far as we can tell, of the best-known public
figures, Pompey, Cicero, and Caesar, none had much use for
astrology.

In *De Divinatione* Cicero discusses astrology together with
other techniques of divination. He does not provide any
evidence in its favour.[4] The refutation is substantial.[5] Its arguments have been taken from the Greek philosopher Panaetius,
although Cicero has added a short Roman appendix.[6] One feels
that astrology was still of very little public importance at
Rome.[7] The situation was to be quite different under the
empire.

In the reign of Augustus, belief in astrology was widespread.
Maecenas, the emperor's friend, and patron of the Augustan
poets, believed that his fate was determined by the stars that
had dominated the hour of his birth.[8] The architect Vitruvius
accepted the truth of astrology in a matter-of-fact way. It was
just one of a long series of scientific discoveries.[9] The age saw
the writing of an astrological epic by Manilius, and the poets
occasionally assume knowledge of astrological terms on the
part of their readers.[10] All through the first and second centuries

---

[1] Cic. *Div.* ii. 47 (99).
[2] Plut. *Romul.* 12. 4; Cic. *Div.* ii. 47 (98).
[3] H. Merguet (1877–84); (1877–94).
[4] *Div.* i. 41 (91): one sentence on Syria.
[5] ii. 42 (87)–47 (99).   [6] ii. 47 (98).
[7] The horoscope of Rome and Romulus (Cic. *Div.* ii. 98; Plut. *Romul.* 12. 1)
had no public significance. On this see W. Kroll, P.W. 2 R. iv. 2. 2407–9, s.v.
L. Tarutius.
[8] Hor. *Od.* ii. 12. Horace was more sceptical.
[9] Vitr. 9. 6.
[10] Hor. *Ep.* ii. 2. 187; *Od.* i. 11. 2; Prop. iv. 1. 77 ff.; Ovid, *Ibis*, 207–16.

there was a vast amount of consultation concerning everyday matters of private life or business.[1] But a new and influential development, now that government of Rome revolved round one man, was that the emperor almost invariably used the services of astrologers. Augustus was converted by an astrological forecast of greatness made at the very start of his career.[2] Sometime later he publicized the astral circumstances of his birth, obviously hoping that this would win him supporters.[3] In A.D. 11 when many thought that Augustus' death was imminent, he published a horoscope which suggested that he would live longer.[4] Astrology retained the esteem which it had won under Augustus. Most of his successors consulted one or more astrologers regularly.[5] Thrasyllus, a man of learning in many fields, was a friend as well as the astrologer of the emperor Tiberius. His descendants rose into the senatorial order. Balbillus, the astrologer's son, was influential at the courts of Claudius and Nero and held senior equestrian posts. Thrasyllus' granddaughter married Macro, the praetorian prefect and was mistress of the emperor Gaius Caligula. In 109 a great-grandson of Thrasyllus became consul.[6] These careers were exceptional but some of the later court astrologers too had great influence.[7]

A second development of the principate was that astrology came to be linked with conspiracy. The authorities could assume that an attempt at political innovation would generally be preceded by some inquiry as to whether fate favoured the revolutionaries, and that this would normally involve consultation of an astrologer.[8] Hence astrology was repressed

[1] See Petr. *Sat.* 35–6 (cf. K. F. C. Rose and J. P. Sullivan. *C.Q.* xviii (1968), 180–4) also *Sat.* 39 and 76; Plin. *N.H.* ii. 22–7; Plin. *Ep.* ii. 20. R. MacMullen (1967), 128–33 and notes; id. (1971), 105–16.   [2] Suet. *Aug.* 94. 12.
[3] *Philologus*, lviii, N.S. 12 (1899), 170–204.   [4] *Dio*, lvi. 25. 5.
[5] Tiberius: Suet. *Tib.* 69. Gaius: Suet. *Cal.* 57. Nero: Suet. *Nero*, 36; ibid. 40. Nero's mother: Tac. *Ann.* xiv. 8. Otho: Tac. *Hist.* i. 22. 1. Vitellius: Suet. *Vit.* 3. 2, but Dio, lxiii (lxiv) 4. 3 shows him at odds with astrologers. Vespasian: Tac. *Hist.* ii. 78; Suet. *Vesp.* 14; ibid. 25. Domitian: Suet. *Dom.* 16. 2; Dio, lxvii, 15. 6. Nerva: Dio, lxvii. 15. 6. Hadrian: S.H.A. *Hadr.* 16. 7.
[6] On Thrasyllus and his descendants see F. H. Cramer (1954), 92 ff., and index under Thrasyllus, Balbillus, Ennia Thrasylla.
[7] Cramer, op. cit., index under Ptolemy Seleucos; ibid., p. 143 on astrology under Domitian; ibid. 210–14 under Septimius Severus; ibid. 189 astrology and medicine.
[8] See K. Thomas (1971), 389 ff. on divination and rebellion; ibid. 398: 'prophecies of one kind or another were employed in virtually every rebellion or popular rising which disturbed the Tudor state'.

repeatedly by the government. Astrologers were expelled from Rome in 33 B.C.[1] In A.D. 11 Augustus made it illegal to consult a diviner about the date of the death of any person,[2] a topic on which Balbillus was to write a book.[3] It was also forbidden for a diviner and his client to meet without witnesses.[4] In A.D. 15, following the suppression of the plot of Scribonius Libo,[5] astrologers were expelled from Italy.[6] After this we hear fairly regularly of the prosecution of men who were accused of having consulted an astrologer about the future of the emperor.[7] Ulpian explained the principle: 'those who consult about the health of the emperor are punishable by death or some still heavier sentence; and about their own or relatives' affairs by a lighter sentence.'[8] That such consultation might in fact encourage a man who was in any case eager to attempt a *coup d'état* is shown in Tacitus' account of how Otho overthrew the emperor Galba.[9]

The political importance of astrology was something new. Republican politicians might employ astrologers, but there is no evidence that astrological advice influenced political behaviour. Among the people at large, an astrological prediction might occasionally cause disturbances. Hence astrologers were expelled in 139 B.C.[10] But this single known expulsion of astrologers during the republic must be compared with no less than ten expulsions between 33 B.C. and A.D. 93.[11]

It was certainly no coincidence that the early empire should witness an increase in the public importance of astrology. One factor was the transformation of political action. As long as the

[1] Dio, xlix. 43. 5; Suet. *Aug.* 35.

[2] Dio, lvi. 25. 5; R. A. Bauman (1974), 62 n. 58 argues against Cramer that this was a resolution of the senate and not an edict.

[3] W. and H. G. Gundel (1965), 152–3.

[4] Dio, liv. 31. 2–3; Tiberius made similar regulations, Suet. *Tib.* 63.

[5] See D. C. A. Shotter (1972), 88–98; R. A. Bauman (1974), 60 ff.; Tac. *Ann.* ii. 27 ff.

[6] Dio, lvii. 15. 7; Tac. *Ann.* ii. 32. 5; Suet. *Tib.* 63. 1.

[7] F. H. Cramer (1954), 254 ff. lists fourteen cases from the reign of Tiberius to that of Septimus Severus, ibid. 270 ff. six cases brought against astrologers, ibid. 276 a survey of legal restrictions of divination.

[8] Ulpian, *de officio proconsulis* 7 in *Leg. Mos. et Rom. collatio*, xv. 23. Ulpian died *c.* A.D. 220

[9] Tac. *Hist.* i. 22.

[10] Val. Max. i. 3. 3.

[11] Marquardt, *Stv.* iii. 93. 2. K. Latte (1960), 328 ff.; F. H. Cramer (1954), 233–47.

republic lasted, political change could be brought about by more or less political means, and judgements about the future could be formed on the basis of the facts and rumours of (again more or less) open politics.[1] After Augustus, things were different. Political change required revolution, a daunting task for which the would-be rebel required all possible human and superhuman encouragement. In addition, information about the political situation was much more difficult to obtain, since important decisions were made by the emperor and his advisers in private.[2] No wonder public figures snatched at the information which astrologers offered. The emperor himself had to bear a heavy weight of decision-making, since no matter how many advisers he consulted, he could not avoid the full responsibility. He needed reassurance, and perhaps sometimes obstruction, that was both confidential and independent. Hence the employment of a court astrologer. There was the additional consideration that astrology was thought to be scientific, for it benefited from the prestige of the great names in Greek mathematics and philosophy.[3]

The other factor favouring the progress of astrology under the empire was philosophic. Astrology, whatever its claims, would not have been widely adopted unless people had thought the claims valid. But men in the political classes were predisposed to find astrology true because, as we have seen, Stoic philosophy had in a sense become their religion.[4] In fact astrology, quite apart from its supposed usefulness, reinforced the appeal of Stoic philosophy as a doctrine which asserted the dignified place of rational man in a rational universe. For the Stoic believer in astrology each individual man is a small-scale model of the universe, and the heavens revolve around man in order that he may read his future.[5] This picture of himself gave back to a Roman noble the dignity lost through humiliating submission to an emperor.

The widespread use of astrology had consequences both in politics and in thought. In the first place, astrology could not be

---

[1] Cicero backs his judgement rather than divination: *Ad. Fam.* iii. 6. 3.

[2] Suet. *Aug.* 36: *acta senatus* no longer published. Tac. *Ag.* i. 1; *Hist.* i. 1; Dio, liii. 19. 1–14. J. Crook, *Consilium Principis* (1955), 8.

[3] Older forms of divination became obsolete. See Manil. v. 870; Propert. iv. 10. 3–8.

[4] See above, pp. 112 ff.   [5] Manil. v. 858 ff.

controlled as the traditional Roman divination had been. Dangerous knowledge about the future was available for whoever could pay a prestigious astrologer. Hence, astrology made for political restlessness, encouraging would-be rebels and feeding a sense of insecurity in emperors. Claudius' death was frequently predicted;[1] so was Nero's.[2] Both emperors executed numerous senators. Nero was certainly terrified by the mass of predictions.[3] So was Domitian.[4]

Astrology affected the way men looked at the world because its validity required the existence of unseen connections to transmit the influence of the stars to earth. Once the existence of invincible but powerful forces running through the world was admitted, plausibility was given to techniques that might manipulate such forces: in other words, magic and magicians.

Astrology and magic were not absolutely distinct. The same man might practise both. Thrasyllus, the court astrologer of Tiberius, wrote a lapidary, a text-book on the arcane properties of stones.[5] Divination was a principal object of magic no less than of astrology. The sun, as 'ruler of the universe', played an important role in the theory of both astrology and learned magic.[6]

Astrology could be presented as an empirical science but also as an arcane doctrine ultimately resting on revelation.[7] It is not therefore surprising that magic appears in public life at Rome not much later than astrology.

4. *Magic in public life*

The use of a combination of words and ritual to achieve a result which would otherwise be beyond a person's power to bring about by physical action is as old as Graeco-Roman civilization—perhaps as old as mankind. But the concept of magic was a much less sharply defined one for the ancients than it is

---

[1] Sen. *Apocol.* 3.

[2] Suet. *Nero*, 40. 2.

[3] Tac. *Ann.* xiv. 22; 58. xvi. 14.

[4] Dio, lxvii. 12. 2. 14. Suet. *Domit.* 10. 3. But otherwise secure emperors like Trajan and his immediate successors did not fear astrologers—as they did not fear philosophers either.

[5] W. Vetter, P.W. 2 R vi. (1936), 581–4.

[6] A. J. Festugière (1944), 299–300.

[7] Ibid. 102–31; A. D. Nock (1972), 496–9.

for us. The behaviour of matter was poorly understood, and in many cases, particularly in the field of healing, men would have been hard put to distinguish between a natural and a magical cause.[1] Moreover, since a very large part of everyday life was accompanied by ritual words and actions and the rites were thought essential for the successful accomplishment of one's purpose, it was difficult to maintain on principle that ritual could not achieve physical effect.[2] Nevertheless distinctions were made: some rites were acceptable, others were not. One criterion was provided by the objective. Ritual intended to benefit crops or heal disease was good, but directed to harm individuals or crops it was bad, and from an early time punishable.[3]

In deciding whether a technique was criminal or not the intention with which it was being employed was therefore, within certain limits, more important than the nature of the rite.[4] But the nature of the rite, too, helped to establish a distinction between religion and sorcery.[5] Pliny argues that a tyrant could hope for supernatural support only through secret rites,[6] that is, sorcery. Ritual that took place in an aura of dread or disgust was condemned, or at least disapproved. Readiness to use such rites was itself disgraceful, even if the object was not criminal.[7] It was the kind of thing that might be expected of desperate criminals and which would make the worst charges believable.[8]

It was a characteristic of many rites that they were addressed to the powers of the underworld and sought to enlist the assistance of ghosts. To do this, practitioners made use of

---

[1] C. Bonner, *Studies in Magical Amulets, chiefly Graeco-Egyptian* (Ann Arbor, 1950); id. 'Magical Amulets', *Harv. Theol. Rev.* xxxix (1946), 25–53.

[2] See the very interesting discussion of this point in Plin. *N.H.* xxviii. 3.

[3] On crop magic the law of XII Tables is quoted in Sen. *Quaest. Nat.* iv. 3. 2: 'ne quis alienos fructus excantassit.' Plin. *N.H.* xviii. 4 has an anecdote concerning the enforcement of this law. The word *venefica* (witch or sorceress) is used as a term of abuse in Plautus and Terence. On the distinction between good and bad magic see J. Marquardt, *Prl.* iii. 108–14. Th. Hopfner (1928), cols. 384–6.

[4] See Cic. *Cluent.* 68 (194). Marcian, *Dig.* xlviii. 8. .3

[5] Serv. *in Aen.* iv. 493: qui cum multa sacra Romani susciperent semper magica damnarunt.

[6] *Pan.* 67. 5.

[7] Luc. vi. 420, 589.

[8] e.g. drinking of human blood at swearing of Catiline conspiracy: Sall. *Cat.* 22. 1–2, elaborated in Plut. *Cic.* 10. 3 and Dio, xxxvii. 30. 3.

accessories whose effectiveness appears to have been deduced from their power to arouse strong emotions, especially disgust.[1]

Magic found its way into literature and produced common-places for the description of magical rites which recur in the writings of generation after generation of poets, but nevertheless retain a relationship to practices that were actually carried out.[2] Some poets were closer to reality than others. Theocritus was more realistic than Virgil.[3] But Virgil too described practices which were actually used. 'I bind you with three threads of three different colours, and I take the image three times round the altar. The god takes pleasure in odd numbers. Draw Daphnis home from the city, draw him home, spells of mine! Weave three colours into three knots, weave them Amaryllis, just weave them and say "I am binding chains of love". Draw Daphnis home from the city, draw him home, spells of mine! As this clay grows hard and this wax melts in one and the same fire, so may Daphnis with love of me. Draw Daphnis home from the city, draw him home, spells of mine.'[4]

This is harmless stuff. Horace tells us of the love charm supposed to have been prepared by the witch Canidia whose magic brew included the liver and marrow of a boy who had been buried up to the chin and starved to death in sight of food,[5] Elsewhere we learn how the witch revenged herself on the poet. He has aged, his skin has turned yellow, his hair grown white;[6] Horace also describes how two witches performed love magic in a pauper's cemetery only to be frustrated as a terrified Priapus farted with a deafening explosion.[7]

In writing of this kind we find descriptions of the incredible powers of witches: to call down the stars or the moon,[8] to trans-form themselves into animals,[9] to disperse clouds,[10] and in the case of the powerful Medea, to turn back streams, calm the sea,

---

[1] e.g. Luc. vi. 420.

[2] S. Eitrem (1942), 51 ff.

[3] Ibid. 58–61 on Theocritus, ii, and Verg. *Ecl.* viii, based on it.

[4] *Ecl.* viii. 76 ff. trans. Rieu, cf. *Aen.* iv. 504 ff. a pretended love rite actually intended to harm, and S. Eitrem (1933), 20 ff.

[5] *Epod.* v.   [6] *Epod.* xvii.

[7] *Sat.* i. 8, cf. Eitrem (1942), 63–7 on realism of Horace's poems.

[8] Prop. i. 1. 19; iv. 5. 13; Hor. *Epod.* v. 45; xvii. 78; Tib. i. 8. 21; Verg. *Ecl.* viii. 69.

[9] Prop. iv. 5. 14. Verg. *Ecl.* viii. 97.

[10] Tib. i. 2. 49; Prop. ii. 28. 35; cf. A. F. S. Gow, *J.H.S.* liv (1934), 1–13.

destroy snakes, stop earthquakes, conjure ghosts from tombs.[1] But at the same time the poets allude to techniques which were actually in use. We hear of the 'rhombus' which was turned with the help of threads attached to it,[2] of various kinds of sympathetic magic, such as the placing of a wax doll near the fire,[3] or the piercing of the head of a fish with needles,[4] and we learn about the magical use of the number three.[5] At the same time, we can see that these rites were carried out in pretty sordid circumstances.[6] The typical witch is old, drunken, and a procuress, who in return for pay puts her magic at the disposal of a person wishing to establish or to break an erotic connection. Magic might also be used to restore masculine potency.[7] Witches from the Sabellian and Marsian parts of Italy were thought especially skilled.[8] Marsian charms were believed to be effective remedies against poisonous snakes.[9] The techniques of love magic were sometimes applied to the cure of disease.[10] The poets leave no doubt of the prevalence of witchcraft. At the same time they exploit the black science to make their reader's flesh creep agreeably. The poets make it quite clear that they do not take magic very seriously. The topic lends itself to the production of literary horror, or black humour, but it is not important. It is not linked with any of the activities that really mattered, or were practised by people that mattered.

This was changing. One can see the first traces of the change in the late republic but its effects only become visible in political life under the emperors. One can isolate a number of factors which favoured this development. These include, not necessarily in this order of importance, the emotional needs which induced leading men of Rome to favour Pythagoreanism, the appearance of a magical literature which could benefit from the prestige of learning, the intellectual respectability of astrology, and the political change from republic to monarchy.

[1] Ovid, *Met.* vii. 199–206.
[2] Prop. ii. 28. 35.
[3] Hor. *Epod.* xvii. 76; *Sat.* i. 8. 32 ff.; Verg. *Ecl.* viii. 80.
[4] Ovid, *Fast.* ii. 577–9.
[5] Verg. *Ecl.* viii. 73, 77; Petr. *Sat.* 131.
[6] See esp. Ovid, *Fast.* ii. 571–82. Also Prop. iv. 5. 67 ff.
[7] Petr. *Sat.* 131.
[8] Hor. *Epod.* xvii. 28–9; *Sat.* i. 29.
[9] Ovid, *Ars. Amat.* ii. 202; *Fast.* vi. 142.
[10] Prop. ii. 28. 35 ff; Tib. i. 5. 9 ff.

Although Cicero attributed admiration for the doctrines of Pythagoras to Cato the Elder,[1] the revival of interest in Pythagoreanism was in fact a development of the last years of the republic.[2] The influence of Pythagorean doctrine in the late republic is shown by Cicero's use of it in the myth at the end of *De Republica,* the 'dream of Scipio'.[3] Cicero praises Pythagorean doctrines and institutions elsewhere in his writings too. Roman institutions are said to have been copied from Pythagorean ones.[4] Cicero sometimes reports Pythagorean precepts with approval.[5] The Pythagoreans have discovered the eternity of the soul.[6] Plato was merely a missionary of the Pythagorean gospel.[7] Cicero's contemporary, the antiquarian Varro, wished to be buried according to Pythagorean rites.[8]

The outstanding Pythagorean at Rome was P. Nigidius Figulus,[9] a respected and responsible public figure, with whom Cicero discussed how best to face the threat of Catiline and what to do with the imprisoned conspirators.[10] Later he was elected tribune (60 B.C.), and praetor (58 B.C.), and took Pompey's side in the civil war. This man's house became a meeting-place of men interested in Pythagoreanism.[11] At the meetings he would explain writings attributed to Pythagoras or Orpheus[12] in a difficult and mysterious way.[13]

Nigidius was one of the most learned men of his time and wrote antiquarian books about different branches of divination.[14] These dealt with traditional Roman techniques but also showed influence of eastern practices.[15] Surviving quotations reveal what would today be thought a magical outlook.[16]

---

[1] *De Sen.* 11 (38).
[2] J. Carcopino (1944), 182–206; A. D. Nock (1927), 151–5.
[3] On 'dream of Scipio' see G. Luck (1956).
[4] *Tusc.* iv. 1. 2–4.
[5] *Fin.* v. 2. 4; *Leg.* i. 12 (34); *Off.* i. 17 (56).
[6] *Tusc.* i. 17 (39)   [7] *Rep.* i. 10 (16).
[8] Varro's last wish: Plin. *N.H.* xxxv. 160.
[9] W. Kroll, *P.W.* xvii (1936), 200; O. J. Getty (1941).
[10] Plut. *An Seni,* 27. 8; id. *Cic.* 20.
[11] *Schol. Bob. ad Cic. in Vat.* 318; Ps. Cic. in *Sall.* 5. 14.
[12] Serv. *ad Ecl.* iv. 10.
[13] Gel. xix. 14. 3.
[14] On the interpretation of entrails (Gel. xvi. 6. 12); of dreams (Lydus, *De ostentis,* 45); divination from numbers (ibid. 27); private augury, an almost extinct practice (Gel. loc. cit.).
[15] W. Kroll, op. cit. 200–12.
[16] Pliny, *N.H.* x. 106; xii. 97; xxix. 138; xxx. 84.

From its beginnings Pythagoreanism had included a strong element of the magical. This followed from a belief in kinship between different elements of the world, inanimate, animate, and even human. Hence the treatment of one element might have radical consequences for the condition of another apparently quite separate one. This view lay at the root of certain taboos or 'symbola' which required a Pythagorean to abstain, among other things, from beans, not to stir the fire with a knife, not to wear a narrow ring, and to spit on his nail-parings and hair-trimmings.[1] When Pythagoreanism came to Rome sensational rumours began to circulate about the activities of its adherents. Varro, a contemporary, reported that Nigidius Figulus discovered the whereabouts of lost money by using a boy as a medium.[2] On the birthday of Octavian (later the emperor Augustus) Nigidius is said to have prophesied that the new-born boy would rule the world.[3]

Many years later, Seneca, then a young man, was impressed by the Pythagorean doctrine of the migration of souls and became a vegetarian. He found this was good for his intellectual processes. Later he gave the diet up because his behaviour might have been considered superstitious.[4] Much more sinister rumours were spread. Pythagoreans were accused of raising the dead in their magic rites, and even of sacrificing children for their magic purposes.[5] Nigidius was accused of practising 'forbidden arts',[6] and those who met at his house were described as a fellowship of Nigidian sacrilege.[7] But save for being exiled by Julius Caesar for reasons which might well have been political, Nigidius did not come to any harm. There was at that time at least one other senator seriously interested in occult subjects: Appius Claudius Pulcher, consul of 54, wrote about techniques of divination employing the souls of the dead, and made practical experiments too.[8]

It is probably no coincidence that about this time there took

---

[1] W. K. C. Guthrie (1967), 182–6.   [2] Apul. *Apol.* 42.

[3] Dio, xlv. 1. 3–5; Suet. *Aug.* 94. 5; probably a *post eventum* invention acc. to F. Taeger (1960), 211. At the outbreak of the war between Caesar and the senate Nigidius is said to have forecast an age of civil war which would only end with a tyrant: Luc. i. 639.

[4] Sen. *Ep.* 108. 17–22, cf. M. T. Griffin (1976), 38–47.   [5] Cic. *Vat.* 14.

[6] Dio, xlv. 1. 4: ὡς τινας ἀπορήτους διατριβὰς ποιούμενος.

[7] Ps.-Cic. *in Sall.* 14: in sodalicium sacrilegi Nigidiani.

[8] Cic. *Tusc.* i. 37; *Div.* i. 58 (132).

shape in the eastern half of the empire the new kind of learned magic, documents relating to which have been preserved in numerous magical papyri. This included much traditional practice but also had features not found before, for instance, the magician may threaten one deity with another of greater power; or he may 'introduce' himself to the sun god and thus half pray and half compel the god to become his companion, to inspire him and to help him to achieve his obect.[1]

This magic was learned. The style of the invocations is derived from that of literary hymns.[2] The technique is strongly influenced by astrology. While the magic includes traditional Greek rites addressed to Hecate it combines them with Egyptian and Jewish elements.[3] Much magical literature evidently claimed to be based on the wisdom of Persia. Pliny the Elder who included a history of magic in his *Natural History*[4] seems to have believed this claim. According to him the art was invented by the Persian Zoroaster, and the oldest extant treatise written by one Ostanes who accompanied Xerxes on his Greek expedition. Other works are ascribed to Democritus, and Pliny insists that this was the famous philosopher himself. Pliny considered that some of the techniques were repulsive and utterly lacking in *fas* and *fides*.[5] Nero experimented with magic.[6] An explanation is suggested: Nero asked *magi* to summon the ghost of his murdered mother so that he could ask her forgiveness.[7] But whether this was his motive or not, the experiments ended in failure and Nero dismissed magic as useless. Pliny too was sceptical, but his own *History* shows great influence of magical thought, particularly in chapters concerned with healing remedies whose effectiveness depends on occult sympathies and antipathies.[8]

---

[1] A. D. Nock (1929), 229–31.   [2] Ibid. 223.   [3] Ibid. 228.
[4] Pliny, *N.H.* xxx. 3 ff. On it A. D. Nock (1972). See also F. Münzer (1897).
[5] *N.H.* xxx. 2.
[6] Nero's experiments: ibid. xxx. 5–6.   [7] Suet. *Ner.* 34. 4.
[8] *N.H.* xxviii. 3–4 argues most intelligently that if one accepts the effectiveness of Roman religious ritual it is impossible to deny absolutely that words can heal. Some remedies are said to be effective because of natural sympathies and antipathies, concepts which belong to magic. This is generally stated ibid. xxiv. 1–4 and exemplified in xxix. 17 by the use of a bug (*cimex*) against snakebite. In the case of medicinal herbs it may matter when and how they were picked, e.g. before sunrise, ibid. xx. 14; xxiv. 82; xxv. 92. Healing power is attributed to spittle which was much used in magic (ibid. xxviii. 7).

Pliny was aware of the kinship between traditional healing and magic. He thought this was a result of the fact that magic was an offspring of the healing arts,[1] which had fortified its ambitious and very attractive claims by taking on a religious guise[2] and entering into alliance with astrology.[3] The strength derived from these components accounted, in Pliny's opinion, for the wide extent of this 'most fraudulent of arts'. Astrology was of course only one of numerous techniques employed by *magi* to divine the future. Another and more sinister one was necromancy, the use of spirits of the dead for the same purpose.[4]

We see that learned magic was one of a succession of ideological imports from the Hellenistic world that gradually revolutionized the outlook of the Romans. It belongs together with the rationalist Stoic philosophy and astrology on the one hand, and with mystery religions and, eventually, Christianity on the other; and like astrology and the mystery religions it only began to play a significant part in public life under the empire. We have seen that Cicero used the accusation of abominable magic practices to blacken the character of Vatinius.[5] But what is significant about this attack is that it is unique in the voluminous letters and speeches of Cicero.[6] Under the empire this was different. Early in the reign of Augustus,[7] Anaxilaus of Larissa, a Pythagorean, a natural philosopher[8] and a *magus*, was expelled from Rome. Under Tiberius consultation of *magi*, like the consultation of astrologers, is found among charges against men on trial for conspiring against the emperor. The earliest case was that of M. Scribonius Libo, a rich young man who was directly descended from Pompey and had family links with the imperial house. Libo had had dealings with astrologers, *magi*, and interpreters of dreams. A personal friend, a senator, informed the emperor. Later, accusers of

---

[1] *N.H.* xxx. 1. 2: natam primum e medicina nemo dubitabit ac specie salutari inrepsisse velut altiorem sanctioremque medicinam.

[2] Ibid.: blandissimis desideratissimisque promissis addidisse vires religionis.

[3] Ibid.: miscuisse artes mathematicas, nullo non avido futura de se sciendi.

[4] Ibid. xxx. 1. 1: fraudulentissima artium. On necromancy see T. Hopfner (1935).

[5] See above, p. 131 n. 5.

[6] The trial of Nigidius Figulus (see above, p. 131 n. 6) is the only political magic trial from late republic known to me.

[7] Jer. *Chron.* Ol. 188, Abr. 1989 dates it 29–8 B.C.

[8] Plin. *N.H.* xix. 21–6; 28–37. On Anaxilaus see A. D. Nock (1972), 188, with reference to Wellmann (1928).

lower rank appeared. It was claimed that he had consulted a diviner whether he would ever be rich enough to cover the Appian way with money. But among his papers there was also found a list of names, including the emperor's, with mysterious signs attached to them. Immediately, Tiberius took the affair very seriously. Slaves were tortured and Libo was compelled to commit suicide.[1] A public supplication of thanksgiving was decreed by the senate. Astrologers and magicians were expelled from Italy.

In A.D. 20 the death of the emperor's nephew Germanicus followed soon after a quarrel with the highly aristocratic governor of Syria. Piso was accused of murder and treason. The murder was alleged to have been attempted through magic[2] as well as straightforward poisoning.[3] At any rate the charge of poisoning was refuted.

In the same year the elderly P. Sulpicius Quirinius, a friend of long standing of the emperor, launched a prosecution against his former wife Aemilia Lepida, a descendant of both Sulla and Pompey. Aemilia was accused of having falsely claimed that the rich and childless Quirinius was the father of her son. But the charge was extended to poisoning, adultery, and consultation of astrologers concerning the imperial family. A treason charge was eventually added. The accused was banished.[4]

In 26 or 27 Claudia Pulchra was accused of adultery and of employing incantations against the emperor. The accuser was an ambitious ex-praetor, the occasion the beginning of Tiberius' long vendetta against the widow of Germanicus and her children.[5] The accuser exploited an obvious weakness in the position of Tiberius, the fact that he could not monopolize loyalty to the Julio-Claudian dynasty.

In 34 another noble, again a descendant of a great republican house, Mam. Aemilius Scaurus, fell victim to the hatred of Macro Tiberius' praetorian prefect. Verses of a tragedy which could be interpreted as criticizing Tiberius were brought up

---

[1] Tac. *Ann.* ii. 27–32; Dio, lvii. 15. 4; R. Syme (1958), 399–400; R. Seager (1972), 89.

[2] Tac. *Ann.* ii. 69. 5; iii. 13. 3 (remains of human bodies, spells, lead tablets).

[3] Ibid. iii. 14. 2–3 (tampering with food). But for Romans the distinction between poison and magic was blurred. *Veneficium* meant poisoning as well as sorcery.

[4] Ibid. 22–4, cf. R. A. Bauman (1974), 173–5.

[5] Ibid. iv. 52.

against him, but the effective charges were adultery with the emperor's daughter-in-law, and magic.[1]

In 49 the empress Agrippina, wife of Claudius, found a prosecutor who would help her to remove a possible rival for the affection of the emperor, the beautiful Lollia Paulina, previously married to the emperor Caligula (as his third wife). The charges were association with astrologers and *magi*, and consultation of Apollo of Claros about the marriage of the emperor. Claudius stated that her activities were a public danger. She was banished from Italy, lost her property, and eventually was forced to commit suicide.[2]

In 53 Statilius Taurus was accused of extortion but there was the additional charge—probably the real charge—of magic rites. The motive behind the charge was said to have been that the Empress Agrippina desired the accused's gardens. The informer was expelled from the senate after Taurus had anticipated the verdict with suicide.[3]

In 54 Domitia Lepida, mother of the empress Messalina, grandmother of the soon-to-be-murdered prince Britannicus, was charged with treason in that she had used magic against the life of the empress Agrippina, and because her slaves were disturbing the peace in Calabria.[4]

In A.D. 65 Barea Soranus and his daughter were tried for treason.[5] Servilia was accused of performing magic rites. Tacitus accepts that she had performed such rites, but only to find out whether her father would be acquitted. Both father and daughter were compelled to commit suicide.

The number of magic trials is not great. But there would not have been any at all if the employment of magic had not been a feature of life in the highest class, and one which was considered a public danger. But what precisely was the danger? Magic could be used to harm people. This was a charge against Piso. But the reader of Tacitus does not feel that Roman emperors or Roman nobles of the Julio-Claudian period were afraid of the harm that they might suffer from sympathetic magic. One suspects that the ultimate threat of magic was the

[1] *Ann.* 29; Dio, lviii. 24. 3.
[2] *Ann.* xii. 22.
[3] Ibid. 59. 3 and Koestermann's commentary on the passage.
[4] Ibid. 65; Suet. *Ner.* 35. 1.
[5] Dio, lxii. 26. 1; Tac. *Ann.* xvi. 24; 30.

same as that of astrology; namely, that it was thought to provide reliable information about the future. It would enable a would-be conspirator to estimate whether his scheme had a chance of success. In the case of a discontented noble—and there always were such—the encouragement of the astrologer or *magus* might just be the incentive to remove the last inhibition.

An ambassador of the Holy Roman Empire to Tudor England observed that the English were easily moved to insurrection by prophecies, and historical research has confirmed that diviners frequently were consulted by rebels. There is no evidence that the rebels were ever deterred by an unfavourable prognostication.[1] In a particular case whether a consultation is dangerous depends on the character of the man who consults. The utterances of the three weird sisters were treated with suspicion by Banquo but they struck an answering chord in the heart of Macbeth. The events on the blasted heath would have repaid investigation by Duncan.

The accusation of magic must not be considered in isolation. Together with the *maiestas* charge itself, it was part of the armoury of the prosecution in the treason trials that were so prominent and disagreeable a feature of the early principate.[2] We have seen that magic was often linked with astrology and with the, to modern minds, much more commonplace adultery. The charges could be made on their own or in various combinations.[3] Magic, and to a lesser degree adultery, had the advantage that they could be used for character assassinations as well as to achieve conviction.[4]

One suspects that many of the charges were preferred because ambitious men exploited tensions in the political system, between the emperor and the old noble families, between Tiberius and the house of Germanicus, between Nero and the 'philosophical' opposition, or the tension resulting from public indignation, as after the suspicious death of the popular prince Germanicus,[5] to further their own rise to power and wealth.

---

[1] K. Thomas (1971), 398 ff.
[2] E. Koestermann (1955); R. S. Rogers (1935).
[3] R. A. Bauman (1974), 59 ff.
[4] Bauman, op. cit. 173–6, points out that a charge of adultery provided an opportunity for investigating a person's behaviour generally as under this charge the slaves of the accused might be tortured and evidence for a treason charge uncovered. The legal position: *Dig.* xl. 9. 12. 1.   [5] R. Seager (1972), 108 ff.

Moreover, if recourse to the expertise of magicians was anything like as common as recourse to astrologers, or adultery, are known to have been it will have been fairly easy to get evidence on which to base the charge. Thus accusations of this kind provided an ideal means for bringing down men who were unlikely to risk genuinely treacherous activity.[1] Nero's mother, the empress Agrippina, made free use of such prosecutions to clear the way to power for herself and her son.

Anthropologists have shown that one particular situation is particularly liable to foster magic and accusations of magic. 'This is when two systems of power clash within one society.'[2] This we find was the case under the early emperors. On the one hand, there was the inherited wealth and power of the descendants of the great houses of the republic, sometimes enhanced by links of kinship with the imperial house; on the other hand, there was power based on the favour of the ruling emperor and exercised through public offices awarded by him. The surviving literature of the period shows how deeply this conflict was felt, even if it shows it from one side only, that of the doomed nobles.[3]

The working out of the conflict shows symptoms that have been observed elsewhere. 'In some areas were competition is not easily resolved by normal means we find actual resort to sorcery. Far more important, however, in a situation where articulate and inarticulate power clash, we find greater fear of sorcery and the reprobation and the hunting down of the sorcerer.'[4] This is the situation under the early emperors. Magic was used but the severity with which it was punished was out of proportion to the act and danger.

Witchcraft has in many societies been used as an explanation of misfortune, an explanation that is comforting because it does not involve the frightening possibility of divine anger, nor suggest that the sufferer is himself responsible for his own misfortune.[5] This function magic does not appear to have had in this period, at least at the high social level with which we have

---

[1] No army commander was accused of using magic.

[2] P. Brown (1972), 124.

[3] Title and the analysis are from R. Syme (1939), 490–508.

[4] P. Brown, loc. cit.

[5] Ibid. 131; K. Thomas (1971), 636–9; E. E. Evans-Pritchard (1937), 63–83, 99–106.

been concerned. Prosecution usually precedes any misfortune that might have been expected as a result of the magic.[1]

Of course, we have been dealing with only the tip of an iceberg, the accusations made for political purposes at the highest level of society. But one imagines that the seriousness with which magic was taken by the governing class must have provided great publicity for the techniques and their practitioners, and favoured the diffusion of their use throughout society.[2] Numerous curse tablets inscribed with ritual words have been found, usually in graves where they had been buried in order to make use of the ghost of the dead men. From the texts on these tablets it appears that magic was principally employed to ensure the defeat of a legal adversary, to compel a thief to make restitution to the man from whom he had stolen, to punish rivals in love, or to make the beloved comply with the lover's wishes. Tablets were often used for or against charioteers. Most of the tablets date from the imperial period. It may be significant that the terms *defixio* or *devotio*, used in later literature to describe such spells, are not found in Plautus.[3] Moreover, the curse formulae are derived from the Greek. It looks as if the practice was part of the imported magic.[4]

In the course of the early empire Roman legislation against magic became more severe. The utmost severity spread from charges affecting the safety of the emperor to any kind of magical activity and even to the possession of magic literature.[5] Evidence is lacking to trace the development of the treason trials involving charges of magic after the period covered by Tacitus' *Annals*. It is likely that the history of such accusations was not a continuous one, but that there were long period when they were not made at all.[6] But we have very full evidence for a

---

[1] For a magic charge in a different social situation—or at least reported from a different point of view, see below, pp. 217 ff., on Apuleius' *Apology*

[2] A. Audollent (1904); *R.A.C.* s.v. Fluchtafel.

[3] G. Lodge, *Lexicon Plautinum* (Leipzig, 1924, repr. Hildesheim, 1962).

[4] This might be thought unlikely in the case of a form of attack towards which no one was indifferent in Pliny's time: defigi quisdem diris deprecationibus nemo non metuit (*N.H.* xxviii. 4. 9). But Pliny himself thought that magic was not part of the Italian tradition in spite of *vestigia* in the XII Tables and the fact that human sacrifice had to be prohibited in 97 B.C. (*N.H.* xxx. 3). C. Bonner (1946) notes that a new kind of international amulet related to the magic of the papyri appears from the first century A.D.

[5] P. Garnsey (1970), 107 ff.

[6] Probably none during the Antonine period. In the Severan period the case

comparable series of trials in the third quarter of the fourth century.

of Apronianus, Dio, Epit. lxxvii (lxxvi), 81 ff. There were important cases in the third quarter of the fourth century: Amm. xvi. 8. 1 ff.; xix. 12. 3 ff.; xxviii. 1. 1 ff.; xxix. 1. 5 ff. But at this period there was probably greater fear of the magical rites themselves, with the result that investigations were liable to snowball as they did not in the first century. On the magic trials at Rome under Valentinian I see J. Matthews (1975), 56 ff.

IV

BREAKDOWN AND RECONSTRUCTION

1. *The system rejected: Lucan's* Pharsalia

LUCAN's unfinished epic about the war between Julius Caesar and the republic, the *Pharsalia* or more correctly *De Bello Civili*, was written in the reign of Nero. Lucan, a nephew of Nero's tutor and minister Seneca, was for a time in great favour with the emperor but this did not last; perhaps Nero envied Lucan's gifts as a poet. Lucan participated in the unsuccessful conspiracy of Piso and was compelled to commit suicide (A.D. 65). The poem was left unfinished. Three books were published before the poet's disgrace. The remaining seven appeared post-humously.[1]

The *De Bello Civili* can be said to sum up the intellectual atmosphere of the Julio-Claudian period as Virgil's *Aeneid* sums up the Augustan age. Many attitudes described in previous chapters recur in this poem. The most prominent of all is Stoic philosophy.[2] The historical events of the civil war are shown to be part of an unbroken chain of cause and effect stretching from the beginning of the world to its end. The morality too is Stoic. The pattern of moral excellence set up for imitation is that hero of the Stoics, Cato the Younger.

But if Lucan's poem expresses much of the ideology of the Julio-Claudian period it omits those features which encouraged acquiescence in the *status quo*, and hope. Fate, as represented by Lucan, is not beneficent—quite the reverse. Like Seneca, Lucan introduces the gods without giving them a role distinct from that of all-controlling fate and destiny. They are in a sense a rhetorical device[3] but their function is not that of Seneca's god, which was to humanize fate. It is to accentuate

---

[1] Fondation Hardt (1968); O. A. W. Dilke (1972); W. Rutz (1970); id. (1964); M. P. O. Morford (1967).

[2] On departures from Stoic system, see H.-A. Schotes (1969), 168 ff.

[3] See below, p. 148.

fate's callousness. The principate is anticipated as an unmitigated and degrading disaster. Apart from the preface, Lucan offers no hope that the loss of freedom will be compensated by gains in other areas. Even if we did not know the history of those years, the pessimism of the *De Bello Civili* might suggest that the principate was moving towards a crisis. With hindsight we can see that it reflects the tyranny of Nero and foreshadows the civil war that followed his murder.

The extant books treat the civil war from Caesar's crossing of the Rubicon in 49 B.C. to the Alexandrian war of winter 48/47. The facts are largely historical and Livy seems to have been the principal source.[1] A theme repeated throughout the poem is that the consequences of this war would be irreversible and liberty be lost for good. 'The madness of war is upon us . . . the frenzy will last for many years . . . when peace comes a tyrant will come with it . . . only while civil war lasts shall she henceforth be free.'[2] Or again, as a result of Caesar's victory at Pharsalus, 'We were overthrown for all time to come, all future generations doomed to slavery were conquered by those swords. To us, born after that battle, fortune gave a master.'[3]

Now, regret for the republic was a feature which Julio-Claudian historiography shares with the writings of Seneca. It may well be that when starting his work, Lucan intended to pay no more than conventional respects to the lost freedom. Even though Caesar's cause was going to be treated as a thoroughly bad one from the start, Lucan wrote a highly eulogistic[4] dedication to Nero[5] and seems at this stage to have anticipated no offence. This is remarkable evidence of the extent to which the pessimistic view of Roman society, and resigned acceptance of

[1] R. Pichon (1912); C. Hosius (1893).

[2] i. 666 ff.; the translation here and throughout the chapter is that of J. D. Duff in the Loeb edition.

[3] vii. 640.

[4] Assuming with O. A. W. Dilke (1972), 74–6 and P. Grimal (1960) that this is not ironical but genuinely adulatory. On the problem see papers by L. Herrmann, M. A. Levi, H. Flume, E. Malcovati, E. Griset, G.-B. Conte in W. Rutz (1970), 283–359.

[5] i. 126 f.: quis iustius induit arma / scire *nefas* does not just mean 'Which of the two had better right to start hostilities we *may* not know' (O. A. W. Dilke (1972), 65), but: 'it is *wicked* to know' or perhaps 'it is impious to inquire'. The reason it is impious to know is that knowledge discovers the gods in disreputable company, seeing that they opposed Cato, the pattern of all virtue, and favoured Caesar, of whom Lucan says: gaudensque viam fecisse ruina (i. 150).

the principate as a necessary evil, had become a commonplace to which not even the emperor could object. But it looks as if in the later books, Lucan's dislike of the principate as represented by Nero got out of control, and that these books express the outlook of the man who was about to join the conspiracy of Piso.[1]

Like earlier epic poets Lucan sets his human events in a theological framework. But his theology is not the traditional religion of Rome which Virgil had used to give supernatural sanction to the Roman empire but Stoic philosophy.[2] References to supernatural powers are numerous, varied, and confusing. Sometimes gods are mentioned by name. Far more often we read of *dei, superi, numina, fatum,* or *fortuna*. But although the different names have contradictory implications, a cumulative impression emerges: there is a supernatural power behind events, but it does not resemble the gods as the Romans traditionally imagined them.

The ruling principle of the universe is described sometimes as *fortuna*, sometimes as *fatum*, and sometimes the two terms are used in close succession in such a way that they must be intended as synonyms.[3] For instance, we are told that Pompey prays to *fortuna* (his own *fortuna*)[4] and the request is granted by the fates.[5] The resistance of Marseilles against Caesar's army is said both to have held back fate and to have compelled fortune to waste time.[6] Fortune intended Caesar to be slain at Rome in the senate house but the poet calls on fate to prevent his premature murder in Egypt.[7] Caesar was hard-pressed in the palace at Alexandria but his enemies failed to attack it effectively. 'The fates forbid it and fortune shelters him like a wall.'[8] Fate and fortune are obviously alternative ways of naming the power that controls the world.

As to the precise nature of this supreme power, Lucan expresses himself uncertain 'whether the author of the universe when the fire gave way, and he first took in hand the shapeless

---

[1] O. A. W. Dilke points out v. 385–95; vi. 807–9; vii. 455–9; viii. 835; ix. 601–4; vii. 638 ff.

[2] See H.-A. Schotes (1969).

[3] i. 264: rumpunt *fata* moras; iustos *Fortuna* laborat / esse ducis motus.

[4] On personal Fortune of leaders of the late republic, see S. Weinstock (1971).

[5] Pompey's prayer and its answer: ii. 699–701: Te, *fortuna*, precatur . . . vix *fata* sinunt.

[6] iii. 392–4.   [7] x. 339–41.   [8] x. 485.

realm of raw matter, established the chain of causes for all eternity, and bound himself as well by universal law, or whether nothing is ordained and fortune moving at random, brings round the cycle of events, and chance is master of mankind ...'.[1] Elsewhere he remarks that a great and powerful deity is given utterance by the Delphic oracle 'whether he merely predicts the future, or whether the future is itself determined by his command in the act of prophesying'.[2]

But while Lucan prefers to leave the definition of the working of fortune open, the poem as a whole is planned on the assumption that historical events are the outcome of a long chain of causes. Summing up the causes of the civil war, he writes: 'It was the chain of jealous fate and the speedy fall which no eminence can escape, it was the grievous collapse of excessive weight and Rome unable to support her own greatness.'[3] The Roman disasters were the ultimate consequence of the chain of events that made the Roman empire great.[4]

For Lucan's poem only the most recent links in the chain of causes are relevant. The immediate cause of the civil war was the first triumvirate, the alliance through which Pompey, Crassus, and Caesar subjected Rome to their common rule. The ambition which had inspired the alliance made impossible that it should continue for long: Nulla fides regni sociis, omnisque potestas impatiens consortis erit.[5] The break-up of the triumvirate led to the war between Pompey and Caesar.

But the state of mind that had produced the monstrous alliance was not the result of chance, it was a consequence, an almost unavoidable consequence, of the state of Rome, itself a consequence of the acquisitions of the empire. 'When Rome had conquered the world and fortune showered excessive wealth upon her, good conduct (*mores*) was undermined by prosperity, spoils ... lured man to extravagance, they set no limit to their wealth or their dwellings, greed rejected the food that once sufficed ... poverty the mother of manhood became a bugbear ... The furrows which were once ploughed by the tough plough of Camillus ... grew into vast estates tilled by foreign cultivators. Such a nation could find no pleasure in peace ... hence they were quick to anger, and crime prompted by poverty was lightly regarded, to overawe the state was high distinction which justified recourse to the sword. Might became the standard of right.'

Hence the free institutions became unworkable. 'Laws and decrees of the people were passed by violence . . . Consuls and tribunes alike threw justice into confusion. Hence office was snatched by bribery . . . year by year the venal competition of the Campus destroyed the state.' At the same time there was a financial crisis 'devouring usury and interest that looks greedily to the day of payment. Credit was shattered. To many war became advantageous.'[1]

The analysis is Sallust's but it underlies much of Lucan's account of the war. The Roman *mores* have indeed been subverted. Caesar is, of course, an epitome of what has gone wrong. Invariably putting his own interest before that of Romans as a whole, impious, pursuing violent solutions for their own sake, he is almost the antithesis of a Livian hero. But Pompey, the leader of the opposition to Caesar and of the better cause, is basically fighting for his own power too. Cato, the only exemplary figure in the poem (except perhaps Brutus), was sure of this at the beginning of the civil war,[2] and still expressed serious reservation on the subject of Pompey's aims in the speech he made on Pompey's death: 'the citizen who has fallen, though far inferior to our ancestors in recognising the limits of what is lawful, was yet valuable in our generation which has shown no respect for justice . . .'[3]

Caesar's supporter Curio provides a perfect example of 'Sallustian degeneration'. 'Rome never bore a citizen of such high promise, nor one to whom the laws owed more while his aims were upright. But then . . . ambition and luxury and the formidable power of wealth swept away . . . the unstable principles of Curio and when he had been suborned by the booty of Gaul and Caesar's gold' he played a decisive part in preparing the triumph of Caesar.[4] On the other side the tribune Metellus tried to prevent Caesar from seizing the state treasury. This was a brave deed undertaken on behalf of freedom but Lucan derides his degenerate motivation. 'So true it is that love of money alone is incapable of dreading death by the sword.

---

[1] i. 160–82.   [2] ii. 221–2.
[3] ix. 190–2.   [4] iv. 814–20.

When the constitution was destroyed it made no difference; but money the meanest thing of all stirred up strife.'[1]

The senate as a whole was a shadow of its former self. Its reaction to the approach of Caesar is described in scornful language that must have influenced Tacitus. 'The city-fathers have leapt up from their seats and the dread edicts of war are delegated to the consuls by a senate in flight.'[2] Later we read that 'the magistrates disguised themselves in the dress of the people, no purple accompanied the lictors' rods'.[3] When Caesar entered the city a mob of senators, brought out from their hiding places, filled the temple of the Apollo . . .'. The senators assembled 'ready to vote their agreement no matter whether Caesar should demand kingly power or divine honours for himself, or execution or exile for the senate'.[4]

The people were no better than their leaders. At Rome fear and panic prevailed. 'Men flee to war.'[5] In the army men were prepared to act illegally no less than their leaders. They had scruples,[6] but readily overcame them. So Laelius, the senior centurion, addresses Caesar: 'I swear whoever be the foe whom you triumph over—if you bid me bury my sword in my brother's breast or my father's throat . . . I will perform it all . . . If you bid me plunder the gods and fire their temples, the furnace of the military mint shall melt down the statues of the deities . . . Whatever walls you wish to level these arms shall ply the ram and scatter the stones asunder, even if the city you doom to utter destruction be Rome. To this speech all the cohorts together signified their assent . . .'[7]

The state of mind of the soldiers was a necessary condition for the continuance of civil war. 'Why not confess that you obey the command of crime by your own will? Do you dread so greatly the leader whom you alone made dreadful? If he sound the bugle for war, be deaf to its cruel note; if he advance his standards, stay still. Then in a moment the frenzy of civil war will collapse.'[8] But when it comes to the point they prefer war. In Spain the armies began to fraternize until a Pompeian officer roused the men of his side in the name of freedom and induced them to break the informal truce. 'His words brought back the

[1] iii. 119–21.   [2] i. 487–9.   [3] ii. 18–19.   [4] iii. 104–11.
[5] i. 504: In bellum fugitur.   [6] i. 350–6.
[7] i. 375–8.   [8] iv. 184–7.

love of crime. So when wild beasts have . . . grown tame in a narrow prison they lose their grim aspect and learn to submit to man; but if a drop of blood finds its way to their thirsty mouths, their rage and fury return . . . The soldiers [in this case, of course, Pompey's soldiers] proceed to every crime; and horrors, which fortune might have brought about in the blind obscurity of battle, are wrought by loyal obedience.'[1] The state of mind of another army eventually ruined Pompey. It forced him into a disastrous battle, when by avoiding a decisive clash he might have won the campaign.[2]

Lucan's description of the mutiny of Placentia brings out the essential similarity of military morality in the two camps, although the Caesareans have degenerated further. They mutinied not because they recognized that fighting kinsmen was wrong, but because their greed was disappointed. 'When we drove forth the senate and captured our native city, what men or what gods did you suffer us to rob? As we go in to every crime, though our hands and swords are guilty our poverty absolves us.'[3] The fact that they have agreed to commit crimes on Caesar's behalf takes away Caesar's right to obedience.[4] But a contemptuous speech ended the mutiny and Caesar ordered the surrender and public execution of the leaders. 'Caesar had dreaded that the weapons and hands would be refused him for the performance of this crime, but they put up with more than their cruel commander thought possible, and provided not only executioners but victims also. . . . The men returned to their duty: the execution had settled their grievances.'[5]

We are now in a position to understand the cruelty of providence. Rome is suffering because the character of her people makes civil war inevitable. The character has been shaped by the wealth and luxury provided by empire. The whole sequence is part of a natural process whereby nature brings about the destruction of whatever has reached outstanding size. The process applies to nations as to individuals.[6] This was of course a Greek idea of very long standing which had been incorporated

---

[1] Fraternization: iv. 172 ff., cf. Tac. *Hist.* ii. 37.

[2] vii. 51 ff.   [3] v. 270–3.

[4] v. 290–5 note the epigram, 'facinus quos inquinat aequat'—crime levels those whom it pollutes.

[5] v. 368–74.

[6] Pompey, ii. 72–7; viii. 21 ff.; Caesar, vii. 592 ff.; x. 338 ff.

in Stoic philosophy,[1] and applied to the universe itself. 'Even so when the framework of the world is dissolved, and the final hour, closing so many ages, reverts to primeval chaos, . . . the stars will drop into the sea and the earth . . . will shake off the ocean . . . and the whole distracted fabric of the shattered firmament will overthrow its laws. Great things come crashing down upon themselves—such is the limit of growth ordained by heaven for success.'[2] The collapse of Rome is an example of a process which will eventually bring about the destruction of the world.

It is a feature of Lucan's epic that it is without the 'divine machinery' that directs the action from afar in the manner of the Olympians of Homer or Virgil. There are nevertheless numerous references to gods. But the salient fact about them is that they are almost invariably hostile.[3] The tendency is clear. The Roman world is passing through a period of terrible suffering to which the gods remain perfectly indifferent. Worse, they favour Caesar, the man who is chiefly responsible for the horror. 'O ruthless father of the universe, strike both parties and both parties at once with the same bolt while they are still innocent' is the prayer of the Roman men when civil war is imminent. But of course Jupiter justifies the epithet and lets the war take its course.[4] The gods watch the civil war like a gladiator show.[5] Pompey hopes and prays that the gods will help the right. They do not.[6] If anyone's prayers are answered they are the prayers of Caesar,[7] although he is completely ruthless in his behaviour to men and gods alike.[8] The gods ruin Pompey's side by inspiring his soldiers with a wicked and foolish eagerness for battle—and thus give Caesar the chance to win his decisive victory.[9]

The gods show no gratitude to those that worship them, or are incapable of performing the services expected of them. The Fortune of Praeneste watched her citizens being massacred by Sulla.[10] Jupiter Latiaris had not protected the freedom of the

---

[1] Cleanthes, *Hymn to Zeus*, 18; Sen. Rhet. *Contr.* 1. *praef.* 6; Sen. *Agam.* 57 ff.; *Oed.* 909 ff., cf. H. Le Bonniec (1968), 180–2 including P. Grimal's comment, 198–200.

[2] i. 72–82.

[3] J. Brisset (1964), 64 ff.; Le Bonniec (1968), esp. 168 ff.; H.-A. Schotes (1969), 137 ff.

[4] ii. 59–66.

[5] ii. 6; contrast Seneca.

[6] vii. 349 ff., 445 ff.

[7] vii. 113, 171, 438.

[8] iii. 399–449.

[9] vii. 58–9.

[10] ii. 193–6.

Latins and thus scarcely deserved the annual Latin festival![1]
Most categorical of all is the attack on Jupiter for permitting
the defeat of Pharsalus. 'In very truth there are no gods who
govern mankind, though we say falsely that Jupiter reigns,
blind chance sweeps the world along . . . man's destiny has
never been watched over by any god. Yet for this disaster [the
defeat of freedom in the battle of Pharsalus] we have revenge
. . . civil war shall make dead Ceasars the peers of the gods
above; and Rome shall deck out dead men with thunderbolts
and rays and stars and in the temples of gods she shall swear by
shades.'[2]

I think one can say that in most of these passages the gods are
introduced for a literary purpose. Lucan seeks to transfer the
reader into the middle of the calamitous events and to evoke the
emotions felt by participants. 'I too will incite hope and fear
together and useless prayers, when the story of battle is read,
and all readers will be spell-bound as they read about the
tragedy as if it were imminent and not past.'[3] In pursuit of this
purpose Lucan not only expresses disillusion and despair through
his suffering characters but often himself assumes the role of the
emotionally involved spectator of the calamities, and in his own
person voices indignation over the powers that allow such
things to happen.[4] But there is no more effective way of representing extreme emotion than to give vent to indignation at
the behaviour of the gods, since the reader feels that only the
strongest passion could induce the speaker so to forget fear and
respect of the immortals.

Often 'gods' and 'Fortune' or 'fate' are used in close association in the same passage. When this happens it is usually
the impersonal force that is the effective driving power. For
instance, this is how Lucan anticipates the murder of Pompey:
'the sands of Egypt are doomed to be his grave, not because the
gods (*superi*) chose to deprive him of a grave in his native land,
but to show mercy to Italy. Let Fortune hide that wicked deed
in a remote region far away and let Roman earth be kept
unstained by the blood of Rome's Magnus.'[5] In this passage
Fortune and the gods perform the same action, that is, they

---

[1] v. 400–3. [2] vii. 445–59.
[3] vii. 209–13 and J. Brisset (1964), 69.
[4] Cf. H. Le Bonniec (1968), 168–75. [5] ii. 732 ff.

arrange for the murder of Pompey away in Egypt. The gods are only introduced for the purpose of irony, to contrast their trivial favour with the great injustice of Pompey's miserable death.

When Caesar had cut down a sacred grove his opponents expected him to come to a bad end: 'Who would imagine that the gods might be injured with impunity? But Fortune often protects the guilty and the divinities can only vent their wrath on those wretched already'[1] and so it turned out in this case. Again Fortune determines the course of events and the gods have no independent role. The gods are only introduced to show that in fact the world order does not follow the moral principles men have come to associate with gods—even to the extent that plain sacrilege, the offence that concerns the gods most closely, is rewarded rather than punished.

In Spain Caesar's army suffered from floods but a change of weather improved the situation. 'But now Fortune contented with having frightened her favourite a little came back in full force; and the gods earned pardon by an exceptional exercise of their support.'[2] Again Fortune was already in command and the gods are reduced to her lackeys. In fact, they were earlier introduced into this context with an invocation to worsen the floods and thus, by destroying Caesar's army, to end the civil war.[3] This would have been their duty if they exercised a just and beneficent government of the world. In fact, the reverse happens and Caesar continues to prosper. Once again the gods are only mentioned to accentuate the lack of justice in the world.

In none of these passages are the gods given an independent effective role; as far as the government of human and natural events is concerned, they are redundant. It is reasonable to conclude that as far as Lucan is concerned, they have no separate existence.

This position could have practical consequences. In the world described by Lucan there is very little place for worship. This version of Stoic philosophy could not underpin religion in the way stoicism had done in the age of Augustus.[4] This attitude to the gods was also inconsistent with the Stoic insistence so

---

[1] iii. 447 ff. [2] iv. 121 ff.
[3] iv. 110 ff. H.-A. Schotes (1969), 219 n. 447: passages which show identity of *fatum* and god. [4] See above, p. 37.

strenuously, even tortuously, maintained by Seneca, that that providence is beneficent, and that suffering is a test imposed by something like a supreme father-figure who takes pleasure if the sufferer passes the examination with high marks.[1] For a man who took Lucan's view of the government of the world it would be difficult to persuade himself that the world was one in which all was ultimately for the best. In fact Lucan's brand of Stoicism did not prevail in the long run. It is probably no coincidence that he formulated it on the eve of a major crisis of the imperial system. Significantly Lucan singled out the cult of deified emperors for special scorn.[2]

As we have seen, faith in divination was independent of any particular belief about the nature of the gods. In his poem, Lucan employs various forms of divination traditionally Roman, and modern. The civil war is preceded by terrifying portents and these are duly interpreted in the traditional way by a *haruspex*, in the more up-to-date way by an astrologer (Nigidius Figulus), and in a literary way by a woman in inspired frenzy.[3] Later Sextus Pompeius in his eagerness to learn the outcome of the war ignores traditional agents of divination, like oracles, *haruspices*, and augurs and turns to the sinister but up-to-date technique of witchcraft.[4] The description of the consultation of the witch Erictho follows a literary tradition[5] but includes, nevertheless, allusions to the new learned magic.[6]

Lucan has literary motives for introducing portents. Livy had shown, if it needed showing, how effectively lists of menacing prodigies could be exploited to produce a dramatic setting for a disastrous event. It is also clear that in his descriptions of the consultation of Apollo and of the Thessalian witch, Lucan is trying to achieve some of the effects of Virgil's great descriptions of the underworld in *Aeneid*, vi.[7]

But literary effect is not everything. Lucan leaves the reader in no doubt that he considers the validity of divination a fact of

---

[1] See above, pp.114 ff.

[2] vi. 807–9; vii. 455–9; viii. 835. He rejects the deification of a man because he has been emperor. He does not reject the application of religious terminology to men of *virtus* like Pompey (viii. 841) or Cato (ix. 564–5, 601–4).

[3] i. 522–695.

[4] vi. 413–830.

[5] S. Eitrem (1942), 69–76.

[6] A. D. Nock (1972), 185–7.

[7] E. Fraenkel (1927).

nature.[1] Like Livy, Tacitus, and Claudian, Lucan was aware
that portents can be imagined in situations of stress, or invented
after the event. But his narrative, again like the narrative of
Livy and Tacitus, proves that portents do in fact portend
disasters. He finds the phenomenon puzzling and in his own
person he asks: 'Why didst thou, ruler of Olympia, see fit to lay
on suffering mortals this additional burden, that they should
learn the approach of calamity by awful portents?' He also
wonders how the phenomenon might be explained. He does not
in the least question its reality.[2]

In the case of the oracle of Apollo he provides a Stoic explanation. 'A great and mighty god he is; whether he merely predicts
the future or the future is itself determined by the order of his
prophecy. It may be that a large part of Jupiter is embedded in
the world to rule it and supports the globe poised upon empty
space: and that this portion of the deity emerges through the
cave of Delphi, and there is drawn into the priestess while
remaining linked to the thunderer in heaven.'[3]

Lucan disapproves of witchcraft as a means of learning the
future[4] but he does not deny that witchcraft can forecast and
even, in some cases, change the course of future events. This is
not consistent with the Stoic view that fate or fortune predeter-
mine the outcome of events in this world. So he, or rather his
witch, suggests a distinction between the fates of individuals
which can be altered by witchcraft, and destinies determined
by a chain of causes from the beginning of the world, which
cannot be altered.[5] But elsewhere he admits that he does not
know the explanation. 'Why do the gods trouble to heed these
spells . . .? Is this subservience the reward of some piety unknown to us or is it extorted by unuttered threats? Has witchcraft power over all the gods, or are the . . . spells addressed to
one special deity who can inflict upon the world all the com-
pulsion that he suffers himself?'[6]

Stoic philosophy is able to 'save' the Roman belief in portents and divination. This does not, however, mean that this
important branch of traditional religion remains intact.

---

[1] A consequence of the all-pervading sympathy of nature. See, for instance,
vii. 185–206.
[2] ii. 1–17.   [3] v. 91–6.   [4] vi. 430 ff.
[5] vi. 605–15.   [6] vi. 492–9, cf. A. Bourgery (1928).

Tradiditionally prodigies were a sign that the gods were dis-
satisfied and that the *pax deorum* was in danger. They did not
mean that disaster was inevitable. Experts could draw on the
experience of their science to suggest ritual means by which the
gods might be appeased. Stoic providence, whether thought of
as a person or as an impersonal process, could not be appeased in
this way; fate will take its course. Lucan describes the expiation
of portents before the outbreak of war. It produced a picturesque
ceremony and an occasion for more disturbing signs. The
disaster of war could not be averted.[1]

Like earlier Roman epics and histories Lucan's poem has a
moral lesson. This is taught through the example of the three
main characters, and like the rest of the poem is based on Stoic
philosophy.[2] Caesar is drawn as a warning example of the
destructive characteristics that a Stoic should avoid. Pompey is
shown as a man who from all too human beginnings progresses
to wisdom. Cato has all the qualities of a Stoic hero. In many
ways he is a traditional good Roman. He is moderate. He is
patriotic. He is ready to give his life for his country. He lives
simply. For him sexual love only exists for the begetting of
children to serve the state. He hates tyranny and is the one
altruistic upholder of freedom and of the free functioning of
the traditional senate-controlled institutions of Rome. His moral
principles are largely traditionally Roman.[3]

But he is not traditional in that his conduct is rooted in
a philosophical doctrine. His conscience, assisted by the Stoic
system of value, provides him with all he needs to guide his
life. In a critical hour he refuses to consult an oracle: 'What
questions do you bid me ask Labienus? Whether I would
rather fall in battle a free man than witness tyranny? . . .
Whether violence can ever hurt the good? . . . Whether fortune
threatens in vain when virtue is her antagonist? . . . Whether
virtue becomes more virtuous by success? I can answer these
questions and the oracle will never fix the truth deeper in my
heart.'[4]

---

[1] i. 589 ff. Admittedly one example proves little. It had always been up to the
gods whether they would accept expiation or not. Nevertheless the bulk of divination in Lucan's poem aims at knowledge not at appeasement. For Seneca's view
cf. above, p. 118.

[2] B. M. Marti (1945).

[3] ii. 389: iustitiae cultor, rigidi servator honesti.   [4] ix. 565.

Some moral traits are clearly the expression of philosophical commitment. 'There was no act of Cato's life where pleasure crept in and claimed a share.'[1] Elimination of passion was a Stoic rather than a Roman virtue. So was a sense of kinship with all mankind: 'He alone free from love and free from hate had leisure to wear mourning for mankind.'[2] But in Cato's case Stoic *apatheia* is modified by a powerful involvement with the fate of the Roman people. This will not let him stand aside from the civil war, though he distrusts Pompey almost as much as Caesar.

Cato is presented not as a zealous worshipper of the Roman gods but as a Pantheist: 'Has God any dwelling place save earth, and sea, and air, and fire, and moral conduct (*virtus*)? Why seek gods anywhere else? All that we see is Jupiter; every motion we make is God also.[3] There is no indication that he personalizes the deity or that he is comforted by the thought of divine approval. His is an extremely austere pursuit of *virtus* for its own sake and without the hope of an approving response in the structure of the universe. For practical purposes the concept of a personal god has shrunk to little more than the voice of his own conscience.

Success is, of course, totally irrelevant to the assessment of a man's quality. This is illustrated in the career of Pompey, no less than in the behaviour of Cato. At the beginning, in the opinion of the poet, as in that of Cato,[4] he is little better than Caesar. At the time of his death he is a hero whose soul rises to the heavenly region where heroes dwell.[5] Marti has shown that Lucan uses his career to illustrate progress from human weakness to Stoic wisdom.[6]

Marti is surely right in general terms but the development is presented schematically rather than in convincing psychological terms. Lucan has not taken care to be consistent in the detailed working-out of Pompey's moral growth.[7] One is not convinced that Lucan was interested in the development of character. He

---

[1] ii. 390–1, as in Sophocles' *Oedipus Rex*.   [2] ii. 377–8.
[3] ix. 577–60. *Caelum*, i. li. 179, probably represents fire ($\alpha i\theta\eta\rho$), the fourth element.
[4] ii. 319–23.
[5] ix. 1 ff. and H.-A. Schotes, 92 ff.   [6] B. M. Marti (1945).
[7] e.g. contrast vii. 648–711 and viii. 1–23; in the first passage Pompey leaves the battle in a heroic frame of mind, in the second he is frightened.

is concerned much more with the effect of individual episodes than with the psychological relationship between them. Also Cato's judicious obituary of Pompey seems to look back over the whole of his career without noting any development.[1] The description of the behaviour of the defeated Pompey at Pharsalus is certainly remarkable. By all traditional standards[2] his behaviour was defeatist and discreditable. But Pompey's flight is described as noble. He does not seek death in battle because he fears that this would induce his soldiers to fight unnecessarily to the death. Instead he rode away. 'There was no lamentation nor tears, only a noble sorrow with no loss of dignity, such a sorrow as the calamities of Rome deserved to receive from Magnus. He goes away free from care, having laid down the burden fate put upon him, now he has leisure to look back at past happiness; and hope never to be fulfilled has departed, now he can realise what once he was. Let him flee from the fatal field, and call heaven to witness that those who continue the fight are no longer giving their lives for Pompey but fighting for freedom.'[3] Defeat puts Pompey in a position to take a philosophical view of life, defeat frees him from responsibility for the continuation of a war. Defeat enables him to avoid Caesar's disgrace of rising to power at the cost of fighting his fellow citizens in civil war.[4] In the following book Pompey's behaviour as a Roman commander is questionable,[5] but as an individual and philosopher it is exemplary. Thus his farewell to the Lesbians: 'I am resolved to search the world and find out where goodness is and where crime',[6] and he meets death with admirable control of his thoughts and his feelings. Of course courage is a traditional Roman virtue. What is new and un-Roman is the respect shown by the author for failure.

The Stoicism of Lucan is an ideology of men at odds with the society in which they live. It is eminently suited to steel them for opposition, even hopeless opposition. This was, of course, one of the roles of Stoicism under the early emperors.[7] But in the long

---

[1] ix. 190 ff.

[2] Cf. the *exempla* of the defeated commanders of Cannae: Aemilius Paulus died in the field and Varro was thanked by the senate because he did not 'despair of the republic'.

[3] vii. 680–97.   [4] vii. 705–6.

[5] e.g. viii. 186 ff., 235–8, 262 ff.   [6] viii. 141–2.

[7] R. MacMullen (1967), 46–81.

term opposition to the empire made no sense: monarchy was simply inevitable. As a result the unease which could be given no political expression turned into a more general other-worldliness.[1] Lucan's poem, when compared with Virgil's *Aeneid*, is seen to mark not only the rejection of a political system, but also a growing contempt for all that may be achieved in this world.

2. *Religious anxiety and the fall of Nero*

The Annals of Tacitus describe the reigns of Tiberius, Claudius, and Nero. It is well known that references to divine signs are unequally distributed over the narrative. The account of the reign of Tiberius and of the early years of Claudius has very few *prodigia*. They only become numerous at the beginning of the rise to power of Agrippina and her son Nero. Moreover the few signs in the early books are not recorded for their own sake but are an integral part of the narrative of events that would have found a place in annals without them. Such are the eclipse that frightened soldiers in the course of the mutiny of A.D. 14,[2] a disastrous flood of the Tiber which gave rise to a debate in the senate,[3] and the destruction by fire in A.D. 27 of the Caelian quarter of Rome.[4] Furthermore the oracle of Colophon in A.D. 18 foretold the death of the emperor's nephew Germanicus,[5] and in A.D. 35 remarkable behaviour of the water of the Euphrates gave what at least after the event seemed a clear forecast of the brief principate of Vitellius.[6]

The picture is quite different in Books xi–xvi. Numerous signs are reported and roughly speaking reports become more frequent as time goes on. Moreover, the signs are often reported in the traditional annalistic manner for their own sake, not because they are part of a bigger story. In 47 Tacitus records that Nero received louder applause than Claudius' son Britannicus. This was taken as an omen that Nero would be emperor

---

[1] E. R. Dodds (1965), 7 ff.

[2] Tac. *Ann.* i. 28; cf. bad weather, i. 30.

[3] Ibid. 76 of A.D. 15. The point of the incident is that Tiberius *refused* to treat it as a *prodigium*.   [4] Ibid. iv. 64.

[5] Ibid. ii. 54. *Prodigia* always gathered around the deaths of emperors.

[6] Ibid. vi. 37. Forecasts of this kind invariably gathered around the youth of men who later became emperors.

rather than Britannicus.[1] The first list of *prodigia* comes in the account of the year 51. Birds of ill omen had been seen on the Capitol. An earthquake caused loss of life. There was famine as well.[2] Tacitus has omitted a portent of three suns which Pliny has recorded for the year.[3] Tacitus' list is not linked to any particular event. But it follows an account of how Agrippina decisively consolidated her power by the appointment of Burrus to command the praetorian guard. The literary effect is to hint at coming evils. But these were still in the future. Meanwhile the gods were still benevolent.[4]

The year 54 is introduced by a second list. Military standards had been struck by lightning, a swarm of bees settled on the temple of Jupiter, fantastic misbirths were produced, one member of each magisterial college died in office. This was the year of the murder of Claudius. The narrative links the signs with the murder.[5]

In 55 Britannicus was murdered. There was torrential rain during the funeral. People took this for a sign of divine anger.[6] The account of the year ends with the expiation of a portent. The temples of Jupiter and Minerva were struck by lightning and *haruspices* ordered a purification (*lustratio*) of the city.[7] The historian provides no explicit link with either the murder earlier in the year or with the dissipated and undignified behaviour of Nero which opens the account of the next year.

There follow two years (A.D. 56–7) without *prodigia*. At the end of the account of 58 is a report of a mysteriously virulent fire in the *civitas Ubiorum* (Cologne). Tacitus does not say, perhaps he expects his readers to know, that this city was the *colonia Agrippinensis*.[8] Anyone aware of this would have concluded that the fire portended ill for the empress mother. In fact she was murdered in the following year. The thirteenth Book and the account of the year 58 end together with the notice of a prodigy affecting the fig-tree under which Romulus and Remus had once sheltered. Its branches died and even its trunk began to wither. This was treated as a *prodigium* until the tree brought out

[1] Tac. *Ann.* xi. 19. Again the kind of tale that would be told in an emperor's biography.
[2] Ibid. xii. 43.   [3] Plin. *N.H.* ii. 31 (99).
[4] Tac. *Ann.* xii. 43. 3.
[5] xii. 64; Suet. *Claud.* 46 shows that omens were part of the emperor's biography.
[6] xiii. 7 as in i. 30.   [7] xiii. 25.   [8] xiii. 57.

new shoots.[1] The belief in the *prodigium* may have died away, but the phenomenon was nevertheless according to prevalent Roman ideas a *prodigium*. Pliny[2] tells us that this kind of thing had happened occasionally and was always significant. Syntactically the *prodigium* of the fig-tree is not linked with any event, but its position is significant: the very next sentence begins the account of Nero's mother-murder.

In the year 59 after Agrippina had been murdered hypocritical thanksgivings were proposed in the senate. Thrasea Paetus walked out. Tacitus then tells us that prodigies too joined in the protest.[3] A list follows: a woman gave birth to a snake, the sun was eclipsed, all fourteen districts of the city were struck by lightning. These signs were naturally taken to be a heavenly comment on Agrippina's murder. Tacitus' own interpretation remains ambiguous.[4] But contemporary witnesses, as well as readers of Tacitus' account, must have concluded that Nero's deed had been supernaturally noted. Indignation that the signs were not followed by punishment is also expressed in the tragedy *Octavia*.[5]

In the course of A.D. 60 a comet was seen, and a table at which Nero was dining was struck by lightning.[6] Tacitus condemns as empty superstition the interpretation that a change of ruler was portended, and that Rubellius Plautus was indicated as Nero's successor. In this he was evidently the odd man out. Even so he does not deny that the events had supernatural significance. He only denies a popular interpretation about which there could be disagreement. In Dio the signs are seen to refer to the murder of Agrippina in the previous year.[7] Tacitus himself is willing to recognize an expression of divine anger in an illness that struck Nero after he had bathed in the source of the *aqua Marcia*.[8]

---

[1] xiii. 58: *prodigii loco habitum est* is the technical term for the recognition of a prodigy.

[2] Plin. *N.H.* xv. 18. 20 (72): nec sine praesagio aliquo arescit, *rursusque* cura sacerdotum seritur.

[3] Tac. *Ann.* xiv. 12. 3: prodigia quoque intercessere.

[4] Ibid. 12. 4: quae adeo sine cura deum eveniebant ut multos post annos Nero imperium et scelera continuaverit. I take this to be an example of 'Lucanian' indignation that crime should go unpunished rather than a denial that the manifestations were linked with the murder.

[5] Ps.- Sen. *Octavia*, 229.   [6] *Ann.* xiv. 22.

[7] Dio, lxi. 16. 5.   [8] *Ann.* xiv. 22. 4.

The account of the year 61 has no portents at Rome, though it includes the formidable signs that preceded Boudicca's revolt in Britain.[1]

The account of the events of 62 is long. The year marks a turning-point in Nero's reign. Burrus died, Seneca was dismissed, Octavia divorced and executed. At the end of the account of the year stand two prodigious events: a gymnasium was struck by lightning, and a statue of Nero melted down; Pompeii was demolished by an earthquake. The notice is not linked to any other event.[2]

The year 64 which saw the great fire of Rome is linked with more prodigious events than any other year. First, a theatre collapsed after Nero and the people had left. This to most people seemed a 'bad omen', but to Nero a happy one.[3] Next, Nero had a frightening experience in the temple of Vesta, which induced him to give up a projected tour of Greece. This was certainly an indication of divine displeasure, whether simply at Nero's daring to enter the sanctuary,[4] or because of his more generally disgraceful conduct.[5] Next came the great fire. This was in a sense itself a *prodigium* and as such appeased by Nero.[6] But it could also be seen as a divine punishment. Certainly the conflagration did not end the divine wrath: the year ended with further 'prodigies announcing menacing evils':[7] lightning of unparalleled frequency, a comet, misbirths of men or beasts discarded in the street, monstrosities discovered in the entrails of pregnant sacrificial animals. The *haruspices* interpreted one misbirth as an indication that there would be an abortive usurpation,[8] rightly since the bloody episode of Piso's unsuccessful conspiracy followed straightaway, introduced by the next sentence.

The year saw endless executions following the discovery of the conspiracy. But the gods too were angry; 'The year, made foul by so many crimes, the gods too made conspicuous with bad weather and diseases'. There follows a dramatic descrip-

---

[1] *Ann.* xiv. 32. This belongs to story of that campaign, not to the history of Nero.
[2] *Ann.* xv. 22. It is not described as a *prodigium*.   [3] xv. 34.
[4] Cf. Metellus and the temple of Vesta: Sen. Rhet. *Contr.* iv. 2; cf. Dion. Hal. ii. 16. 3.
[5] *Ann.* xv. 36; cf. Suet. *Nero*, 19.
[6] *Ann.* xv. 44: petita dis piacula.
[7] Ibid. 47.   [8] Ibid. 47. 2.

tion of violent storm and mysterious but deadly pestilence.[1] Executions continued. The repetitive narrative may be monotonous but 'it was a case of anger of the gods striking the Roman world' and this being so, is too significant to be passed over with a single mention.[2]

The end of the Annals is lost. We do not know whether the concluding books, if they were written, continued the pattern of mounting divine anger. But I would argue that it is not chance that the last extant book of the Annals proclaims the theme which is summarized in the preface of the *Histories*: never did more fearful Roman calamities demonstrate that the gods are anxious not for our safety but for our punishment.[3] The civil war of 69 was a punishment which the gods induced the Romans to inflict on themselves, a divinely-sent madness.[4]

It is my contention that the prodigy reports in Tacitus' account of Nero reflect contemporary opinion and that they got into the histories which served as sources for Tacitus because they had impressed people at a time of anxiety. To some extent even republican prodigy lists reflected the tensions of public opinion. But under the empire *prodigia* would not be reported unless they had made a great impression. In republican Rome the expiation of prodigies was a regular procedure which took place in most years at the beginning of the magistrates' term of office. Under the empire, as I have tried to show,[5] this no longer happened and that is why Livy could write that prodigies were now neither reported nor recorded in histories.[6] In fact, expiation of prodigies had not ceased altogether, but the occasions on which it took place were greatly reduced and the institution had come under the control of the emperor. So Nero purified the city on the advice of *haruspices* after temples had been struck by lightning.[7] Later he expiated a comet with

---

[1] Ibid. xvi. 13. 1–3: tot facinoribus foedum annum etiam dii tempestatibus et morbis insignivere.

[2] Ibid. 16: ira illa numinum in res Romanas fuit.

[3] Nec enim umquam atrocioribus populi Romani cladibus . . . adprobatum est non esse curae deis securitatem nostram esse ultionem. (*Hist.* i. 3; cf. Luc. iv. 807 and Plin. *Pan.* 35. 4.)

[4] Cf. Cic. *Leg.* 2. 16 (41–4); *Har. Resp.* 18 (39) for parallel belief at Athens; K. J. Dover (1974), 149–50.

[5] See above, pp. 57 ff.

[6] Liv. xliii. 13, trans. W. A. M. Devitte.

[7] *Ann.* xiii. 24.

executions on the advice of astrologers and *haruspices*.[1] We are
not told who decided on the expiation of the Great Fire.[2] On
the other hand, we hear that Tiberius rejected a request to treat
a disastrous flood as a prodigy.[3] He insisted on setting the
matter right through better flood control. In A.D. 45 the
emporer chose to give a scientific explanation of an eclipse
presumably in place of the expiation that was expected.[4]

As a result of the changed state of affairs there was (probably)
no regular easily available record of reported and expiated
prodigies. Signs would only be remembered and enter the
historical record if they were either sufficiently sensational to
impress a large number of people, or if it was noticed they were
linked in time or place with some striking event. When a man
became emperor a large number of signs foreshadowing his
elevation would be remembered or invented. The same happened after an emperor or an important member of his family
had died.[5]

> When beggars die there are no comets seen;
> The heavens themselves blaze forth the death of princes[6]

was true of the Julio-Claudian period. But this is not the whole
story. Signs would also be remembered if they had been seen at
the time of some outstandingly memorable event or in circumstances of great emotional tension, so that the sign seemed to
provide a supernatural comment on what was happening.
Mutineers under the mental strain of their situation recognized
first an eclipse of the moon, and later unusually wet and stormy
weather as signs of divine disapproval of their actions.[7]

In 27 a conflagration was taken to indicate that the gods censured Tiberius' plan of retiring to Capri.[8] Augustus' departure
from Rome had once been met with a similar reaction.[9] The

---

[1] Suet. *Ner.* 37; *Ann.* xv. 47. [2] Ibid. xv. 44.

[3] Ibid. i. 76. Plin. *N.H.* iii. 5. 9 (55): flood prodigies indicate anger of gods and
imminent danger which can be avoided by expiating rites. Lydus (*De Ostentis*, 8),
flood forecasts invasion. Cic. *Ad. Q. Fratr.* iii. 7. 1: flood is humorously linked with
acquittal of Gabinius. See also Nisbet on Hor. i. 2. 13.

[4] Dio, lx. 26.

[5] See biographies of Suetonius *passim*. The deaths of private individuals were
only recorded with prodigies when they were exceptionally close to the throne
like Agrippa (Dio, liv. 29. 7) or Sejanus (ibid. lviii. 5. 5–7. 1).

[6] W. Shakespeare, *Julius Caesar*, II. ii.

[7] *Ann.* i. 28; 30. [8] Ibid. iv. 64.

[9] See above, p. 96.

people benefited from having the emperor among them[1] and
could convince themselves that this must be the wish of the gods.
It was widely feared that if Claudius married his niece Agrippina, the incest would be punished by some harm to the state.[2]
It is likely that fire seen in heaven soon after the marriage of
uncle and niece, more precisely at the wedding of Agrippina's
son Nero and Claudius' daughter Octavia, reflected popular
worry at the incestuous marriage of the emperor. Later it was
interpreted as having foreshadowed the calamitous end of
Octavia's marriage.[3] Rain at the funeral of Britannicus was
thought to signify divine anger at his murder.[4] The prodigies of
59 were certainly taken to indicate anger of the gods at the
murder of Agrippina.[5]

In all these cases people disturbed by recent events saw
prodigies and interpreted them to mean that the gods too
disapproved of the events that were disturbing them. I would
suggest that the reason why so many more prodigies are reported by Tacitus during the career of Nero is that Nero performed
many actions that might be thought offensive to the gods, and
that awareness of this induced men to see prodigies more
frequently. Tacitus indicates the kind of behaviour of which
gods might disapprove when he describes the dilemma of the
people of Rome forced to choose between two equally unsatisfactory candidates for the empire: 'the two most despicable men
in the whole of the world by reason of their unclean, idle and
pleasure-loving lives, apparently appointed for the task of destroying the empire...now they were to visit the temples and
pray for Otho? or rather for Vitellius? for whom should they
seek heaven's favour? Intercession for either would be equally
impious and vows equally blasphemous.'[6] The thought is that
of the people, but it is clear that the vices which rendered
prayers on behalf of Vitellius and Otho impious were even more
conspicuous in Nero.

Later Tacitus comments on the burning of the temple of
Jupiter: 'This was the most lamentable and appalling disaster
of the whole history of Rome. Though no enemy threatened,
and, but for our immorality, enjoying the favour of the gods

[1] Alan Cameron (1973). [2] *Ann.* xii. 5.
[3] Dio, lx. 33. 2. [4] *Ann.* xiii. 7.
[5] Ibid. xiv. 5; Dio, lxi. 16. [6] *Hist.* i. 50.

(propitiis si per mores liceret deis) the sanctuary of Jupiter Best and Greatest . . . was now thanks to the infatuation of our leaders . . . suffering utter destruction.'[1] This at least implies that if the Roman *mores* had not collapsed, the gods might have been favourable, the leaders clear-sighted, and the temple intact.

In these passages Tacitus expresses the religious concern aroused among Romans by the immoral behaviour of men at the head of their state. Prayers offered by or for such men are blasphemous and unlikely to benefit the supplicant or the community as a whole. Quite the reverse. In such circumstances Jupiter will not even protect his own temple on the Capitol. The belief that a person who approaches a god in prayer should be morally pure we have already found in the republican period.[2] Since then it can only have gained strength under the influence of Stoicism.[3]

A Stoically influenced version of the belief that the gods punish a community for the immoral behaviour of its leading men is found in Statius' epic the *Thebaid*, a tale of endless calamity which *mutatis mutandis* recalls the atmosphere of Tacitus' *Annals*.[4] But in Statius' poem it is made clear that the succession of horrifying episodes is a consequence of a long chain of earlier crimes of which they are the preordained punishment.[5] The sons of Oedipus, conditioned by the offences of earlier generations, commit a sin against *pietas* in spurning their father. Thereupon Jupiter as the executive of fate inflicted on them as a punishment the war of the Seven against Thebes.[6]

The passages of Tacitus and Statius which we have just discussed give an indication of the fears that are likely to have been aroused among Romans by the behaviour of Nero. He was even more impious than the sons of Oedipus. He ascended the throne after the murder of his (adoptive) father. He was thought

[1] *Hist.* iii. 72.

[2] See above, p. 49. At a time when much of state religion centred on the emperor his 'purity' would have been highly relevant to the *pax deorum*.

[3] See above, p. 114, and e.g. Sen. *Mor.* 95. 47–50. Lucan's irony at the expense of the gods implies that gods were supposed to be moral but were not in reality. See also Pers. *Sat.* ii. 15–16, 39–40, 73–5.

[4] F. Burck (1951).

[5] Vesey (1973), 83, 85–6, 90.

[6] *Theb.* i. 213 ff.

to have committed incest with his mother; he certainly murdered her. Incest was an ancient religious offence and one deeply disturbing to ordinary Romans.[1] Eventually Nero supplemented matricide by killing his wife, the popular Octavia. Nero also participated in the vices that disgraced Otho and Vitellius. *Impudicitia* and *luxuria* were certainly conspicuous in his life.[2] Twice he went through ceremonies of homosexual mock-marriage in public.[3] This was an act which Juvenal thought was—or at any rate, ought to be—punished by the gods,[4] and is surely to be included among those which were certain to be punished in the long run, even though the offender seemed to go scot-free at first.[5] Even apart from these sensational crimes and vices, Nero's life was of a kind which would be thought to offend the patron gods of Rome, simply because it was unbecoming and irresponsible in the head of the Roman state. The gods could be expected to take the view of the blunt soldier who told Nero, 'I was as loyal to you as any soldier while you deserved loyalty. I began to hate you when, murderer of your mother and your wife, you became a charioteer, an actor, and an incendiary.'[6]

In these circumstances Romans would have anticipated divine anger, and would have been ready to notice any signs that could be interpreted in that sense. The identification of signs would in turn augment popular religious worry (*religio*), especially if the signs were of a conspicuous and frightening kind, such as the comets of 60 and 64,[7] or plague,[8] or the great fire of Rome[9] and the hardships that followed it. Subsequently, Nero's fall and the civil war confirmed that the signs[10] had

[1] Tac. *Ann.* xiv. 2: nec toleraturos milites profani principis imperium.
[2] Summed up in Ps.-Sen. *Oct.* 432–5.
[3] With Pythagoras: Dio, lxii. 28. 2–3; Tac. *Ann.* xv. 37; Suet. *Ner.* 29 (calling him Doryphorus). With Sporus: Suet. *Ner.* 28; Dio, lxiii. 13. 2.
[4] Juv. ii. 117.
[5] Ibid. xiii. 75 ff., 113 ff.
[6] *Ann.* xv. 67.
[7] A.D. 60: *Ann.* xiv. 22; Ps.-Sen. *Oct.* 230. A.D. 64: Suet. *Ner.* 36. 1; Tac. *Ann.* xv. 47. 1. On the significance of comets see Sen. *Nat. Quaest.* vii. 17. 2; 18. 3; 21. 2. Plin. *N.H.* ii. 94.
[8] Tac. *Ann.* xvi. 13.
[9] Ibid. xv. 44; on hardships see R. F. Newbold (1974).
[10] The bracketing of the murder of Agrippina by portents (*Ann.* xiii. 57–8 and xiv. 12) will have intensified *religio*, as did the bracketing by portents of the defeat of Varus in A.D. 9 (Dio, lvi. 24).

indeed indicated divine anger. It is not therefore surprising that the portents obtained a secure place in the historical record of Nero's reign, when it was written up in the reigns of his Flavian successors.

The atmosphere of *religio* which, if my argument is accepted, produced the prodigy lists can still be sensed in two works of poetic drama. The pseudo-Senecan *Octavia* provides explicit comment on the reign of Nero: 'Look, the very heavens are polluted by the fearful breath of our cruel emperor, the stars threaten unparalleled disaster, to the people ruled by an impious leader'.[1] Seneca's *Oedipus* creates a very similar atmosphere. Admittedly, drama is not history and the *Oedipus* is set at Thebes in Greece, and not at Rome. Nevertheless Seneca has introduced features that belong unmistakably to contemporary Rome. The Thebans are described as the companions of Bacchus in his triumphal procession to the East. They have reached India. They have fixed their banners on the most remote edge of the world. They have seen the Arabs. The Parthians have fled from them. They have even penetrated to the shores of the Indian Ocean.[2] This surely recalls rhetorical descriptions of the extent of the Roman empire.[3] Then Tiresias is not a divinely inspired prophet but a *haruspex* who examines entrails of a sacrificial animal. The procedure is Roman. Plague reveals anger of the gods.[4] A *haruspex* is consulted for a remedy.[5] The entrails reveal a serious situation. The advice given is ritual, a necromantic rite is to be undertaken.[6] The mixing of magic with Roman religion is not traditional, but as we have seen, magic was being used to an increasing extent in highest circles. Another contemporary, as opposed to Sophoclean, feature is the insistence on the Stoic moral that man must willingly yield to fate.[7]

The most sensational contemporary allusion is provided by the words of Jocasta spoken while stabbing herself in the womb: 'strike here right hand, strike at this wide belly which held a

---

[1] Ps.-Sen. *Oct.* 235–7.   [2] Sen. *Oed.* 114–22.

[3] e.g. Verg. *Aen.* vi. 794 ff.

[4] *Oed.* 710–11.

[5] Ibid. 297 ff. Tiresias explains that he uses the technique of the *haruspices* because he is too old to receive the god.

[6] Ibid. 393 ff.

[7] e.g. ibid. 180: 'fatis agimur; cedite fatis . . .'

husband and sons'.[1] Action and words cannot but recall the death of Agrippina:[2] 'Pushing out her womb towards him, she called out "strike at my belly".' Readers were accustomed to look for political allusions—under tyranny people always become very sensitive to this sort of thing.[3] They cannot have missed the allusion to Nero's matricide, unless Agrippina's last words were invented in imitation of those of Seneca's *Jocasta*. One would imagine that Seneca kept the play secret while Nero was alive. But one cannot be sure. Nero seems to have taken pleasure in shocking people.[4]

But whether the *Oedipus* was published in Nero's lifetime or not, the fact remains that it centres on a city polluted by the behaviour of its ruler, and both city and ruler have been drawn in such a way as to provoke comparison with Rome and Nero. If Seneca saw Nero like this, others will have done so too, and the implications of the comparison are disturbing. Could Rome really be safe under such a ruler? Would not the citizens as a whole have to bear the punishment for the sins of Nero? That Nero's behaviour profoundly alienated a great many people was shown by the circumstances of his fall. When the crisis came, Nero was simply without support at Rome. He could rely on none but a few of his own freedmen.[5] The warning which Seneca once passed to Nero through a beautiful slave woman was justified in the end: the soldiers did not put up with the rule of a polluted (*profanus*) emperor.[6]

To sum up: it is likely that the prodigies were an integral part of the account of the fall of Nero in the sources used by Tacitus,[7] and that Tacitus has taken them over in accordance with his usual principle of historiography.[8] Tacitus' prodigy reports

[1] Ibid. 1038–9: hunc dextra, hunc pete uterum capacem qui virum et natos tulit.

[2] protendens uterum ventrum feri exclamavit. (Tac. *Ann.* xiv. 8, cf. Ps.-Sen. *Oct.* 369: hic est, hic est fodendus ferro, monstrum qui tale tulit.)

[3] *Ann.* vi. 29; Dio, lviii. 24. 4–5 on Scaurus' *Atreus*. Tac. *Dial.* 2–3 on the *Cato*, *Thyestes*, and *Domitius* of Curiatius Maternus.

[4] Suet. *Ner.* 21: cantavit Canacen parturientem, Orestem matricidam, Oedipodem excaecatum . . . cf. ibid. 46.

[5] Ibid. 39.

[6] *Ann.* xiv. 2.

[7] It has been suggested that the increasing frequency of prodigy reports in the later books of the Annals is due to Tacitus' use of the *History* of the Elder Pliny (see Koestermann, *Ed.* i. 43).

[8] *Hist.* ii. 50. 2.

include a certain amount of distancing: the historian is un-
willing to be associated automatically with popular belief or
superstition. On the other hand, there is some evidence that
he deliberately sharpened the contrast between the numerous
signs of the reign of Nero and the lack of such manifestations
earlier. Comparison with the fragments of Dio covering the
reign of Tiberius suggest that Tacitus had not exploited such
prodigy reports as were available, and refrained from drawing
attention to supernatural implications of events which might be
thought to have them. In contrast to Dio, Tacitus is seen to have
omitted the admittedly rather silly signs preceding the death of
Germanicus[1] and to have treated as a purely secular phenomena
the sighting of the phoenix in A.D. 34,[2] and the fire at Rome in
A.D. 37,[3] which, according to Dio, foreshadowed the death of
Tiberius. In fact, Tacitus reports no signs anticipating the death
of Tiberius at all, though he must have known of signs that were
generally held to have foreshadowed it. The effect of Tacitus'
treatment is to suggest that the behaviour of Nero was offensive
to the gods in a way that the tyranny of Tiberius had not been.[4]
Incest, matricide, and lack of decorum on the part of a ruler
were more deeply shocking to gods and men than the mere
slaughter of nobles, whether members of the imperial house
or not.

The tradition of the fall of Nero recalls some aspects of early
Augustan literature. The writers have lived through disaster and
express their response to it. One response was to attribute the
calamities to divine anger and by implication to call for
religious and moral revival.[5]

---

[1] Dio, lvii. 18. 3.

[2] *Ann.* vi. 28, cf. Dio, lviii. 27. 1; Plin. *N.H.* x. 2. 5.

[3] *Ann.* vi. 45, cf. Dio, lvi. 26. 5.

[4] *Ann.* iv. 1. 3 is the exception which needs, in my view, to be explained away.
I would suggest that in this passage the *deum ira in rem Romanam* is amoral. It
is brought in as the only possible explanation why the otherwise so suspicious
Tiberius should have fallen under the influence of Sejanus.

[5] Measures of Vespasian that recall Augustus. 1. Temple-building: temple of
Jupiter (Suet. *Vesp.* 8. 5); temple of Peace (ibid. 9. 1); K. Latte, *R.R.* 330 n 3. 2.
2. Censorial activity: censor in A.D. 73 (Suet. *Vesp.* 8. 1; P.W. vi. 2, 2655); census
(Plin. *N.H.* vii. 49 (162)); purged senate and equestrian orders (Suet. *Vesp.*
9. 2; Aur. Vict. *Caes.* 9. 9). 3. Moral legislation: a woman married to another's
slave to be treated as a slave. Creditors of sons '*in potestate*' to have no right to
claim their debt (Suet. *Vesp.* 11; *Dig.* xiv. 6). Perhaps the change in manners
noted by Tacitus (*Ann.* iii. 55) was in part a reaction to the events of 69.

3. *Silius Italicus and the Flavian restoration*

Vespasian,[1] the victor of the civil war of 69, was faced with the task of restoring the Augustan system after it had been shaken to the foundations. He succeeded, and there followed more than a century of stability. This is not the place to go deeply into the causes of Vespasian's success. Men had experienced once more the disaster of civil war and the imperative need of avoiding it. The old republican nobility had been greatly reduced by executions and forced suicides under the Julio-Claudian emperors. Now a large number of new municipal families entered the senate under Flavian patronage;[2] and the surviving old families, like those that had risen under Vespasian, lived less ostentatiously than nobles had done in former times. They were less concerned to acquire empire-wide *clientelae*, and more submissive to the emperor.[3] At the same time the emperor's constitutional rights were defined by law. This weakened the pretence that the emperor was no more than an extraordinary republican magistrate; but avoided frustration since the senators were now precisely informed what the facts of power were; i.e. 'that whatever measure he [Vespasian] shall deem in the interest of the state, whether secular or religious, whether affecting public or private life, he shall have the right and the power to take'.[4]

Some tension remained between emperor and senators (*principatus* and *libertas*), or, to look at the situation from another point of view, between the men favoured by the present emperor and descendants of those favoured by his predecessors and of republican nobility. This was part of the system. Outspoken and provocative assertion of *libertas* continued to receive moral support from Stoic philosophy. Domitian, the third Flavian emperor, struck violently at the opposition. He twice expelled philosophers from Rome and executed a number of the 'radical' senators. Arulenus Rusticus[5] and Senecio[6] were

---

[1] See P.W. vi. 2, s.v. Flavius Vespasianus.
[2] L. Homo (1948), 286–8.
[3] Tac. *Ann.* iii. 55.
[4] *I.L.S.* 244. 17–20.
[5] Tac. *Agr.* 2; Suet. *Dom.* 10; M. Hammond (1963).
[6] Dio, lxvii. 13; Tac. *Agr.* 45.

executed. Artemidorus,[1] Junius Mauricius,[2] Epictetus,[3] and many distinguished ladies[4] were exiled.

But Stoic influence pervaded upper class society and the defence of the principate as well as its criticism was carried out in Stoic terms. This is illustrated by the *Punica*, an epic poem written by Silius Italicus, a senator whose public career reached its climax (the proconsulate of Asia) under Domitian, and who wrote certainly the first six books, but probably most of the poem, in the reign of that emperor.[5]

Like most Latin poetry the *Punica* represents a conscious development of earlier writing in the same genre. In the genre of epic Silius follows in the footsteps of Lucan. Like Lucan's poem the *Punica* is a historical epic whose material is largely derived from Livy. But it is in several respects an *anti-Pharsalia*. Silius Italicus has taken up numerous themes treated by Lucan with a view to improving on the earlier author, or at least hand-ling the subject-matter in an individual way. One doubts whether the oracle of Ammon would have figured in the *Punica*[6] but for a famous scene in the *Pharsalia*. Certainly Silius' Hanni-bal has many characteristics of Lucan's Caesar and a few of Lucan's Pompey. An episode in which Hannibal sends his wife to safety is obviously derived from a similar scene involving Pom-pey and Cornelia.[7]

The *Punica* also represents a reaction against Lucan at a deeper, political level. It is written not in a spirit of opposition but of support for the *status quo*. Lucan had told a tale of the downfall of Rome, to complement Virgil's epic of the founding of Rome. Silius viewed the Roman prospects more optimistic-ally. Accordingly he chose to write about events of the construc-tive period of Roman history, the defeat of Hannibal. Thus he shows Roman virtue in action. Lucan had portrayed Rome in the grip of disgraceful panic at the approach of Caesar.[8] Silius describes how the approach of Hannibal proves a challenge answered with a massive display of Roman virtues.[9]

Silius returns to Virgilian optimism. The Virgilian style and

---

[1] Plin. *Ep.* iii. 11. 7. [2] Tac. *Hist.* iv. 40.
[3] Gel. xv. 11. 5. [4] Plin. *Ep.* iii. 11. 3; Tac. *Agr.* 45.
[5] E. Bickel (1911); E. Wistrand (1956). On the poem as a whole see the ex-cellent book by M. von Albrecht (1964) to which I owe much.
[6] Sil. iii. 10 ff., 647 ff. [7] Ibid. 62 ff.
[8] Luc. i. 467 ff.; ii. 21 ff. [9] Sil. xii. 545 ff., 587 ff.

the innumerable Virgilian reminiscences[1] are merely an expression of the basic purpose. Virgil had sent Aeneas down to the underworld to be informed by the ghost of his father of the historical process it was his mission to initiate, a process which would culminate in the reign of Augustus: 'here, here is the Man, the promised one you know of—Caesar Augustus, son of a god destined to rule where Saturn ruled of old in Latium, and there bring back the age of god . . .'[2] In a derivative episode Silius extended the perspective to include the Flavian dynasty and Domitian the ruling emperor. 'Then, O son of gods and father of gods to be, rule the happy earth with paternal sway. Heaven shall welcome you at last in your old age and Quirinus give up his throne to you.'[3]

But the attitude of the Augustan age could not be recalled so simply. Leaving aside the unpleasant character of Domitian— which Tacitus may have exaggerated—there remained all the nostalgia for the republican past. 'Such was Rome in those days; and if it was fated that the Roman character should change when Carthage fell, would that Carthage was still standing.'[4] In the circumstances it was not easy to create a national epic that was both optimistic and convincing.

Among the means used by Silius to revive Virgilian optimism was a further large infusion of Stoic philosophy. The *Punica* are full of Stoic ideas. *Virtus* is its own reward.[5] The human mind contains a spark of divine intelligence. Heaven is open to those who in life have sought virtue and preserved the divine element within them.[6] Suicide is recommended as a way out of an intolerable political situation.[7] The great heroes of Rome show the traditional Stoically influenced virtues. Fabius Maximus is above all free from passion (like Lucan's Cato), not subject to jealousy, not moved by applause, the opponent of emotional extremism (*furor*) whether encountered in Hannibal or in the temper of his own soldiers.[8] Regulus is artificially introduced into a war that was not his to provide an impressive *exemplum* of *fides* and *patientia*.[9]

---

[1] V. Buchheit (1963).   [2] Verg. *Aen.* vi. 791.
[3] Sil. iii. 607 ff.   [4] Ibid. x. 657–8.   [5] Ibid. xiii. 663.
[6] Ibid. xv. 70 ff. See E. Heck (1970) on relation to Cicero's *De Republica*, vi (somnium Scipionis).
[7] Sil. xi. 57–88.   [8] Ibid. vi. 613; vii. 217.
[9] Ibid. vi. 62 ff.

A Stoic theme which runs through the whole of the *Punica* is the imitation of Hercules. Hercules had long been worshipped at Rome, where—as in Greece—he was a more approachable and popular deity than the great public gods.[1] But it was Stoic philosophy that set him up as a pattern of virtue. The mythical labours were interpreted allegorically, and Hercules was seen as a great benefactor who had made the world safe for man. By slaying monsters and wicked tyrants, he abolished fear and wickedness and established peace. His descent to the underworld for the sake of Cerberus was interpreted as a victory over death. He won his last victory by the magnificent endurance with which he suffered torments on Mount Oeta, and finally received the reward of his virtue by being raised to heaven as a god.[2] Already Livy's *History*[3] and Virgil's *Aeneid*[4] each contained an episode in which the exemplary view of Hercules is exploited. The idea occurs again and again in Silius' poem.

Silius makes a great deal of the siege of Saguntum. This heroic episode is made to take place under the patronage of Hercules. Saguntum is said to have been founded by Hercules who remains the patron god of the city.[5] Murus, the leading warrior of Saguntum, offers a prayer to Hercules.[6] Silius did not invent the Herculean connection of Saguntum which is also found in Statius.[7] But it is not mentioned in Livy. Silius has added it to the Livian narrative in order to strengthen the imitation of Hercules theme.

Fabius Maximus is the Roman hero of the earlier books. Silius relates a legend telling of the descent of the Fabians from Hercules.[8] Again he did not invent the legend. It probably originated in the Augustan age. Livy does not mention it.[9] As in the case of Saguntum Silius has gone out of his way to bring Hercules into the narrative.[10]

Regulus, as was mentioned earlier, is introduced into the

[1] E. R. Dodds (1973), 154. On Hercules as guardian of the house at Delos and Pompeii see M. Bulard (1926), 224–44. Illustrations in *idem, Delos*, ix (1926). Hercules could be treated humorously as well as solemnly, see G. Binder (1974).

[2] On Hercules as a Stoic hero see A. R. Anderson (1928); B. M. Marti (1949); R. Schilling (1942); G. Murray (1946); M. Simon (1955); Sen. *Constant.* 2. 1; Dio Chrys. i. 66.

[3] Liv. i. 7

[4] *Aen.* vii. 185 ff

[5] Sil. i. 273

[6] Ibid. i. 506 ff.; cf. ii. 148.

[7] Stat. *Silv.* iv. 6. 83.

[8] vii. 35. Sil. vii. 35.

[9] F. Münzer, P.W. vi. 2, 1740, s.v. Fabius

[10] E. L. Bassett (1966).

Punica in a lengthy excursus, evidently because of the exemplary character of his conduct.[1] A large part of the excursus is occupied with a battle against a huge snake. Battles with monsters are common in mythological poetry but read rather oddly in a historical context, even though this snake was mentioned by Livy.[2] Silius' epic is full of reminiscences of earlier poems, and the battle against the snake provides opportunity for numerous allusions to earlier descriptions of encounters between a hero and a monster. Regulus' snake is compared with two monsters slain by Hercules,[3] and it is certainly no accident that Hercules was the most celebrated slayer of monsters, and that two of the most striking reminiscences are of Virgil's account of the combat between Hercules and Cacus.[4] Indeed the function of the excursus is comparable to that of the Hercules and Cacus episode in the *Aeneid*.[5] Regulus' victory, like that of Hercules, is symbolic of victory over chaos. Regulus' subsequent suffering too is shown as following the example of Hercules[6]

Regulus made the famous speech with which he opposed the ransoming of prisoners early in the morning. This is how Silius indicates the time of day: 'Scarce was the daylight shining on the famous pyre of Hercules upon Oeta's height.'[7] The choice of this artificial periphrasis for 'just after sun-rise' can have no other purpose than to point out that another act of Herculean suffering was in preparation.[8]

Scipio, the hero of the later books, is the most Herculean figure of all. He was of course the son of a human father and Silius stresses Scipio's filial *pietas*,[9] but like Hercules he has a second divine father in Jupiter. This is asserted by the best-informed source possible, the ghost of Scipio's mother.[10] Later at a critical moment of his life, when the question of the command of the Roman forces in Spain is about to be settled, Scipio has a dream vision of Pleasure and Virtue and thus

---

[1] E. L. Basset (1955); Sil. vi. 140 ff.

[2] Liv. *Per.* 18.   [3] vi. 182.

[4] vi. 159–61 and *Aen.* viii. 296–7; Sil. vi. 194–6 and *Aen.* viii. 237–8.

[5] Cf. Hercules and Antaeus in Lucan, iv. 593 ff.

[6] Von Albrecht (1964), 65–8.

[7] Sil. vi. 452 ff.

[8] With account of torture steadfastly endured by Regulus, vi. 529, cf. endurance of Hercules in *Hercules Oetaeus*, 1715 ff., ascribed to Seneca.

[9] Sil. iv. 454 ff.

[10] Ibid. xiii. 634 ff.; also by Mars: iv. 47 f.

repeats the famous experience of 'Hercules at the cross-roads'.[1] Needless to say, he chooses Virtue and immediately after is elected to the Spanish command and starts on his victorious career. Scipio is a Roman Hercules.[2]

Surprisingly, but historically, the imitation of Hercules was not restricted to the Roman side. Hannibal too is shown worshipping in the temple of Hercules at Gades and looking at the labours of Hercules carved on the doors of the temple.[3] His crossing of the Alps repeats one of Hercules' feats, and Hannibal attempts to improve on his famous predecessor.[4] Hannibal too is a follower of Hercules, but while he is undoubtedly a great phenomenon—like Lucan's Caesar with whom he shares many characteristics—he is obviously not an exemplary figure. He lacks the gentleness which Scipio combines with his formidable war-like qualities.[5] Scipio like a good Stoic is above all anxious not to incur guilt, and readily accepts whatever fate has in store for him.[6] Not so Hannibal, whose whole campaign is against fate and who is ready to fight Jupiter himself.[7] Above all, Hannibal wages an unjust war in breach of a treaty. He is *perfidus*, an enemy of *fides*, and as such doomed to ruin.[8] If Hannibal is also a follower of Hercules, he is a heretical one, and damned.

The honouring of Hercules was not an idiosyncrasy of the poet. There is more evidence of the respect paid to Hercules at the court of Domitian. Several prominent men are known to have been worshippers.[9] The emperor himself built a temple to the god.[10] The cult image represented Hercules with the facial likeness of Domitian. In other words Domitian claimed for

---

[1] Sil. xv. 18 ff. for the corresponding episode in the life of Hercules: Xen., *Mem.* ii. 1 ff.; Dio Chrys. i. 66 ff.

[2] Ibid. xvii. 649–50.

[3] Ibid. iii. 1 ff., cf. Liv. xxi. 21. 9.

[4] Ibid. iii. 356–7, 514.

[5] Ibid. viii. 560: flagrabant lumina *miti* aspectu, *gratusque* inerat visentibus horror.

[6] Ibid. xiii. 517–18: quaecumque datur sors durior aevi / obnitemur, ait, culpa modo pectora cessent.

[7] Ibid. xii. 635.

[8] Ibid. i. 8–11, 56, 296, 303–4, 481.

[9] Vindex (Stat. *Silv.* iv. 6, esp. 89 ff.; Mart. ix. 43 and 44). Pollius Felix (*Silv.* iii. 1 which has humour as well as piety). On the social setting of these poems see P. White (1974).

[10] Mart. ix. 64 and 65.

himself the imitation of Hercules which Silius had ascribed to the Roman leaders in the Hannibalic war.[1]

The imitation of Hercules was not a passing phase. Trajan too had himself compared to the hero[2] and in his reign for the first time Hercules appeared on imperial coins,[3] and among the recipients of vows from the *Fratres Arvales*.[4]

The appeal of Hercules was of course not only due to the fact that philosophers had taken him up. Almost alone of the Roman gods he had a recognizable personality, and his human origin and human failings made him more popular and approachable than other divinities. But in addition he evidently filled the growing need for a god who could serve as a moral pattern[5] and this was only made possible by the way philosophers had allegorized his legendary achievements. Incidentally the cult of Hercules helps to explain why Stoic attitudes pushed to the limit could occasionally seem to threaten the established order. It was because Stoicism was widely admired, that the political attitudes of men known to live by its principles were influential, and that an emperor might have reason to fear even a small group of Stoically motivated opponents.

Compared with Virgil, or Livy, Silius Italicus seems to be less interested in the rich variety of traditional religious and political institutions of Rome.[6] There has been a simplification and concentration of the Roman heritage. But the core of the old religion, the providential care of Jupiter Optimus Maximus for Rome, is proclaimed with greater assurance than ever. Developing a theme from Virgil's *Georgics* Silius presents the Hannibalic war as a test devised by Jupiter to shake the Romans out of sloth and complacency and thus to fit them for their role of governing the world.[7]

[1] See also the comparison of Domitian and Hercules—in Domitian's favour in ibid. 101. This need not mean that the god is not taken seriously. Cf. above p. 21. In Statius' (died A.D. 96) *Thebaid* Hercules is hymned as a moral force, iv. 146 ff.; Tydeus in contrast has many Herculean qualities but uses them immorally like Silius' Hannibal. Cf. D. Vessey (1973), 199 and 225.

[2] Plin. *Pan.* 14. 5; Dio Chrys, *On Kingship*, i. 49 ff., 60 ff., 84; *Or.* iv. 31; xxxi. 17.

[3] *R.I.C.* ii (1962), 293–4.

[4] *Act. fr. Arv.* 7 January A.D. 101.

[5] See above, p.170 nn. 1–2.

[6] Cf. the description of expiation in Sil. x. 74–89 with Liv. xxii. 9–10. Silius' account is simplified and less specifically Roman.

[7] Sil. iii. 571.

It is made clear throughout the poem that Jupiter will not allow Hannibal to win. On three occasions the god prevents an attack on Rome itself. The third is climax of the epic. Two attempts to march on Rome are foiled by thunderstorms. Divine displeasure is manifest. Hannibal knows it. A thunderbolt has struck his shield, the heat has melted his sword and the point of his spear. Nevertheless he remains determined to try again: 'Rome you may thank the winds and stormy weather for a single day's reprieve; but the morrow shall never snatch you from my grasp not if Jupiter descends to earth in person.'[1] On the following day Juno opens Hannibal's eyes and he sees the great gods on guard over the site of Rome. Then at last he admits himself beaten and gives up the attack.

In the whole episode the intervention of Jupiter dominates. Roman faith, Roman determination, Roman piety are briefly indicated. Decision comes from the gods. This is not a narrative in which divine intervention and human action combine equally to achieve a particular result, as they do in Livy's account of the capture of Veii, or Virgil's narrative of the defence of Aeneas' camp,[2] or even Livy's treatment of the saving of Rome from Hannibal.[3] In Silius' poem Rome is saved simply by the miraculous intervention of Jupiter.[4] The introduction of miracles is partly to be explained by epic convention, but not entirely. A few years later, Trajan's attack on the Mesopotamian fortress of Hatra was said to have been defeated by just such divine interference effective through lightning, hail, rains, and thunderbolts,[5] and Septimus Severus underwent the same experience.[6] We would probably be justified in noting a retreat from the 'scientific' aspect of Stoicism. Personalization of the deity had a long tradition in Roman Stoicism. Even 'divinely sent' thunder could be explained by a chain of cause and effect in the same way as Hannibal's attack, or the eventual Roman victory. Nevertheless this is not the obvious interpretation of a narrative such as Silius'. The obvious implication of such a narrative is that the chain of cause and effect is from time to

---

[1] Sil. xii. 633–6.   [2] *Aen.* ix. 788–9, 802–5.
[3] Liv. xxvi. 6.
[4] Other miraculous interventions: iv. 676 ff.: Venus and Vulcan save Scipio from the river Trebia. x. 337: Juno dissuades Hannibal from marching on Rome after Cannae.
[5] Dio, lxviii. 31. 2–4.   [6] Ibid. lxxvi. 12. 4–5.

time broken by the intervention of an angry or a propitious
divinity. Silius' poem shows that the influence of Stoicism was
still gaining ground at Rome at the expense of more specifically
Roman traditions. But the influence of Stoicism is now moral
and theological. There is no attempt to make use of Stoic
explanation of nature. That has been dropped. This is in part a
reaction against Lucan but it also reflects a general tendency to
consider the existence of God and of his moral demands the
essential fact about the world and to pay less attention to the
chain of natural cause and effect.[1]

The action of Silius' poem takes place in a world whose
supernatural government is concerned with moral behaviour.
This is demonstrated most consistently by the treatment of
Fides. Silius has fastened on Livy's theme that the Hannibalic
war was a war of right against wrong, and that the Roman
victory was a victory of right. Skating over historical facts and
ambiguities, it is his essential assumption that the Carthaginians
broke the treaty which had ended the first Carthaginian war
and have therefore broken *Fides* while the Romans maintained
it.[2] The supreme value of *Fides* is asserted throughout the epic
but this theme is most fully developed in the account of the
siege of Saguntum and the excursus on Regulus. The people of
Saguntum were ready to die rather than break their alliance with
the Romans.[3] Regulus chose torture and death rather than
break an agreement, even an agreement with the national
enemy.[4]

Fides comprises the qualities of character which enable a
person or society to honour the obligations which he or it has
undertaken.[5] The virtue of *Fides* had always been held in very
high esteem at Rome. Indeed it was, in a sense, the keystone of

---

[1] The naturalist aspect of Stoicism was too gloomy, insufficiently encouraging,
Statius, in the *Thebaid*, tried to combine determinism of behaviour with insistence
on the justice of punishment. But the result is unbalanced, the horrors of crime
and punishment prevail over the comfort of a moral order. See Vessey (1973),
58, 83–6, 90–1. Tacitus too was impressed by the rigorous Stoic view and strongly
inclined towards fatalism (e.g. *Ann.* iv. 20; vi .22.), but he also felt that it was
incompatible with a moralizing approach to history.

[2] i. 5–6: 'sacri cum perfida pacti/gens Cadmea.' and *passim*.

[3] ii. 480 ff., 332–3, 598 ff.

[4] vi. 131 ff., 466 ff. For history of the *exemplum* see E. R. Mix (1970).

[5] See P. Boyancé (1972), 105–19; (1962), 329–41; (1964), 101–13; Otto in
P.W. vi. 2 (1909), 2281–6, s.v. *fides*.

Roman morality. For a long time already *Fides* had possessed a temple, priests, and a picturesque ritual. Nevertheless the scope of *Fides* as a divinity was limited. *Fides* was thought to exist in the particular agreements she safeguarded, and to reside in the minds,[1] or the right hands[2] of the contracting parties. Breach of faith was not punished by *Fides* herself but by Jupiter.[3] The cult of *Fides* was not widespread.

In Silius' poem *Fides* seems to have considerably wider scope. The people of Saguntum look to *Fides* to protect them, as the Romans look to Jupiter. The relationship between goddess and worshipper is intimate. As described by Silius it recalls descriptions of prophetic possession or passionate love, and is remote from the sober practical spirit of traditional religion. 'Taking possession of their minds and pervading their hearts, her familiar habitation, she instilled her divine power into their spirit. Then piercing even to their marrow she filled them with burning passion for herself. . .'[4] As represented by Silius *Fides* is close to being a goddess of moral conduct; she is the glory of gods and men, the partner of justice. Without her, peaceful life is impossible. There is no place for *Fides* in a world full of extravagance, debauchery, and violence. Passionate love, we are twice reminded, is a particularly dangerous hazard for the sanctity of agreements.[5] *Fides* is sanctioned by rewards and punishment. The household of a man who does not honour agreements will never be free from tears.[6] *Fides* cannot save her faithful Saguntum from destruction, but she will bring its citizens everlasting fame and rest in Elysium.[7]

There is a considerable amount of allegory in Silius' treatment of *Fides*, a device of which Silius makes remarkable use elsewhere in his poem. Here is part of Virtue's address to Pleasure: 'For neither the wrath of heaven nor the attacks of enemies are as destructive as you, Pleasure, are on your own once you have wormed yourself into minds. Drunkenness is your ugly companion, and so is Luxury, and Disgrace always flutters around you with black wings. My attendants are Honour and Praise, Renown and Glory with joyful countenance . . . my household is pure; my dwelling is set on a lofty hill, and it is reached by a

---

[1] Cic. *Leg.* ii. 11 (28). [2] Liv. i. 21. 4. [3] Plaut. *Rud.* 14 ff.
[4] Ibid. ii. 515. [5] Ibid. xv. 274–83; xvii. 69–70.
[6] Ibid. xiii. 284. [7] Ibid. ii. 696–707.

steep path.'[1] Allegory as a means of teaching morals comes into fashion in the early empire.[2] The Stoic doctrine of a world ruled by *fatum* with Jupiter as its executive left little place for other gods. Hence these tended to turn into allegories of various powers and emotions that exist in the universe.

Silius' *Fides* participates in the function of allegory: it is also more than that. It is more than allegory because for Romans *Fides* was after all an object of worship. Cicero explained this feature of Roman religion. Things like wealth, security, concord, freedom, or victory are associated with such power that they must needs be ruled by a god, and it was because of this that they had been given divine status.[3] Whether this is an adequate explanation or not, the fact is that the cult of abstract deities occupied a significant place in Roman religion and continued to do so until the very end of Roman paganism. Early in the fourth century, the Christian Lactantius still felt obliged to insist that *Fides*, Concord, Peace, Chastity, Piety, and Virtue, no matter how desirable these qualities might be, were not themselves divine. Later still, Symmachus, the last defender of the Roman ancestral religion, argued that to end the cult of the goddess Victoria might deprive Roman arms of victory in the field.[4]

The abstract cults were one aspect of the amazing adaptability of Roman religion. The Romans had always worshipped some great gods,[5] but also a large number of minutely specialized deities. In many situations the Romans behaved as if they thought of the divine as a vast force which was infinitely divisible,[6] so that a divine patron could be found for any

---

[1] Ibid. xv. 95 ff.

[2] Vessey (1973), 65, 75–6, 86–7 on Statius' use of allegory. The characters of his epic represent vices or virtues which define each other by antithesis. On allegory in Apuleius see P. G. Walsh (1970), 176 ff. Allegory flourished in the Christian empire, e.g. Prudentius, *Psychomachia*, 26–38 ff., 366, 716, 734, 752, and had a long history in the Middle Ages.

[3] Cic. *N.D.* ii. 23 (61).

[4] Lact. *Div. Inst.* i. 20; Arnobius, iv. 1, and Prudent. *C. Symm.* ii. 45 ff., 57 ff., 236 ff. See also H. Mattingly (1937). Symm. *Rel.* iii. 3.

[5] G. Dumézil (1966), 33–59 shows convincingly that the Romans worshipped gods in the full sense from the beginning. The loss of mythology (ibid. 61 ff.) makes them seem less personal than Greek gods, though even there the deities actually worshipped were not endowed with anything like full personalities (see J.-P. Vernant (1965), 267–8).

[6] Intellectual tendencies favoured this. Plin. *N.H.* ii. 14 shows how the impersonal

conceivable activity. This belief gave Roman cult great flexibility. A new situation could almost invariably be faced with an appropriate religious reponse through the worship of a new divinity, or at least of a not previously defined aspect of the supernatural. A commander campaigning in foreign parts might for instance decide to institute worship of the local prevailing winds.[1] We have seen how abstract cults like the Victory or the Clemency of Caesar, or the Peace of Augustus or very many others were introduced when the state religion was being reshaped to fit a monarchical system.[2] Organization and Romanization of the provinces provided enormous scope for the creation of new cults. Dedications to abstract deities, that is gods described by their function alone, were especially common in the second and early third centuries.[3] They might be described as *Tutela*, or *Fortuna*, or most commonly *Genius* and practically any social unit from the Roman people to a single individual, a province, a city, a street, or a building might be put under the protection of such a spirit. We hear of a *genius* of the meat-market, of the slave market, of a theatre, of a legion, of a cohort even of military discipline itself. This was of course in addition to the deified virtues whose cult went back to the republic, and to the virtues of the emperors.

Silius' treatment of *Fides* must be seen against this background. It too represents the adaptation of Roman religion to a new need. Stoically influenced Romans of the early empire felt that the supernatural government of the world ought to be described as a moral power. The great gods about whom such unedifying stories were told in literature could not easily be made into embodiments of morality—even if Hercules could be allegorized into one. But an abstraction like *Fides* was by its nature pure morality.

all-pervading deity of the philosophers could easily be subdivided into innumerable more or less independent aspects. The world picture of astrology and magic too assumed that the universe was filled with vast numbers of invisible carriers of influences. The individual's *genius*, for instance, transmits the influence of a star to the individual (e.g. Prudent. *C. Symm.* i. 450).

[1] Introduction of the cult of a wind after a naval disaster: Cic. *N.D.* ii. 6; iii. 51; of the Mistral (*circius*) by Augustus while staying in Gaul: Sen. *Quaest. Nat.* v. 17. 5; cf. also the *novum numen* in Ovid, *Fast.* i. 331. See R. M. Ogilvie (1969), 12–13.

[2] See above, p. 76 n. 4. On Hellenistic influence see Cic. *Ad Q. Fr.* i. 1. 31.

[3] See K. Latte, *R.R.* 331–3; M. P. Charlesworth (1937); G. Downey (1975).

But there were limits to the extent to which Roman religion could be made explicitly moral by giving greater emphasis to the cult of a deified virtue. A writer could boost the role of *Fides* in the world. But this was literature. In actual cult *Fides* remained a minor deity of strictly limited authority.[1] When it came to winning the support or appeasing the anger of a supernatural power, in all but highly specialized situations men continued to turn to gods with names, and especially to Jupiter.

It has evidently been very important for Silius that morality should have a place in the divine government of the world. The *Punica* also shows traces of an opposite tendency. If *Fides* comes close to representing a deity of morality the underworld is coming closer to representing deified absolute evil. Hannibal swears his oath of eternal hostility to Rome in a shrine dedicated to the ghost of Dido, where ritual was directed at the ghosts of the underworld, and where the future was foretold by necromancy. Hannibal's oath represents absolute evil. He swears that neither gods nor a valid peace treaty shall stand in his way.[2] In a similar way Juno summons Tisiphone from the underworld for the evil purpose of countering *Fides* who had descended from heaven.[3]

Virtue is rewarded with immortality as in Cicero's *Dream of Scipio*.[4] Wickedness is punished in the underworld; it would hardly be anachronistic to use the word 'hell'. 'But you star-like souls . . . go, glory of the earth . . . and adorn Elysium and the pure abodes of the pious. Whereas he who gained glory by an unjust victory [Hannibal] . . . shall carry down to the waters of Styx a body disfigured and blackened by poison.'[5]

Epic by its nature cannot be quite up to date. The epic of Virgil could give no place to Augustus' personal patron, the Greek Apollo. Far less could Silius' epic recognize the ruling

---

[1] There are few epigraphic dedications; among them thanks for election to office: *I.L.S.* 3776–7; *C.I.L.* ix. 5422. Was this because office involved creditworthiness (cf. *C.I.L.* ix. 60)? A dedication of *fides Augusta I.L.S.* 3775; *C.I.L.* ix. 5422 obviously also proclaims confidence in the trustworthiness of the emperor. That the original of a veteran's *diploma* is displayed on the temple of *Fides* pledges the government to its fulfilment.

[2] Sil. i. 81–140, cf. vi. 703, 713.

[3] Ibid. ii. 526–695, see also iv. 765–823 on human sacrifices. Child sacrifice was of course part of the historical religion of Carthage.

[4] Ibid. xv. 77–8.   [5] Ibid. ii. 696–707.

family's trust in the Egyptian gods Isis and Serapis. After all, these divinities did not even belong to the civilization of classical Greece. Moreover their worship at Rome had long been associated with immigrants and the lower classes.[1]

Vespasian encountered Serapis when he came to Alexandria during the civil war of 69 and two stories were told about this, unlike any other told of Roman emperors. First, a blind and a lame man came to him to be healed at the instigation of Serapis and Vespasian duly healed them. Then Vespasian entered the temple and there saw a man called Basilides (i.e. son of a king). On inquiry it turned out that the real Basilides had at that moment been thirty miles from Alexandria. Vespasian concluded that what he had seen was the god Serapis himself, who had taken on the appearance of Basilides so that Vespasian might receive that name as a favourable omen. This experience greatly strengthened his belief that he was destined to rule the empire.[2] Around the same time the Nile is said to have had an exceptionally beneficial flood.[3]

The accounts of Tacitus and Suetonius show that Vespasian's Alexandrian experiences were used for propaganda purposes and also that the propaganda was exploited at Rome. But one wonders whom precisely Vespasian was trying to impress.[4] The immigrants and freedmen who made up a large part of the worshippers of Isis?[5] One must not underestimate the support for Isis at Rome. After all, her followers had once again established a shrine on the Capitol.[6] Or was Vespasian concerned for the support of the municipal notables of Campania[7] or of his own legions of the Syrian army? Certainly the Egyptian gods had a considerable number of followers, but taking the

---

[1] Isis was worshipped by the mistresses of poets, e.g. Prop. iv. 5. 34; ii. 28. 61–2. Tib. i. 3. 23.

[2] Cf. K. Latte, *R.R.* 283 n. 4; M. Malaise, *Conditions*, 407; Tac. *Hist.* iv. 81; Suet. *Vesp.* 7. 2; Philostrat. *V. Apol.* 5. 27; Serapis had long been known at Rome as a provider of healing oracles: Varro, *Men.* (ed. A. Riese), p. 130, nos. 26, 29. Cic. *Div.* ii. 59 (123).

[3] Dio, lxv. 8. 1. A. Heinrichs (1968), argues that Vespasian on coming to Egypt behaved as a king of Egypt would have done. In that case his first objective was to secure his Egyptian base.

[4] The events are said to have given Vespasian *auctoritas* and *maiestas* which he lacked as a son of a municipal family (Suet. *Vesp.* 7).

[5] Malaise, *Conditions*, 469.

[6] Suet. *Dom.* i. 2; Tac. *Hist.* iii. 74.

[7] Malaise, *Conditions*, 471.

population as a whole their appeal was surely still rather narrow, certainly in the upper classes. One imagines that Vespasian chose to emphasize the favour of the Egyptian gods because he was himself convinced of it rather than because he thought this would help him with the largest number of people. His attitude to Isis and Serapis should be compared with Augustus' to Apollo, or Constantine's to the God of the Christians.

There is certainly evidence that Vespasian and his children continued to honour the Egyptian gods. Vespasian and Titus are said to have spent the night before their triumph in the temple of Isis.[1] Under Vespasian the temple of Isis was for the first time displayed on a Roman coin.[2] Titus visiting Egypt took an active part (wearing a diadem) at the consecration of the Apis bull.[3] He also thought that the fact that he was *pontifex maximus* obliged him to keep his hands unstained (*puras manus*) and disqualified him from pronouncing death sentences.[4]

Domitian had saved himself in the civil war of 69 by dressing up as a worshipper of Isis.[5] Nevertheless the public thanksgiving for this escape was addressed to Jupiter.[6] Domitian rebuilt the temple of Isis on the Campus Martius[7] and put up an obelisk at the Iseum of Beneventum with a representation of himself being crowned by Isis.[8] Domitian was a conspicuous worshipper of Minerva for whom he built two temples.[9] It could be that he thought this goddess a Roman equivalent of Isis by relating her name to the Greek verb 'to know' ($\epsilon i\delta \acute{\epsilon} v a \iota$).[10]

The evidence, such as it is, suggests that the Flavians worshipped the Egyptian gods because they had helped the family to the empire through the Jewish and civil wars.[11] Of the divine couple, Serapis was a powerful supreme god who might be identified with Jupiter.[12] Isis was essentially a goddess of private life but unlike the Roman gods of Rome she was both majestic

---

[1] Jos. *Bell. Jud.* vii. 123. [2] Malaise, *Conditions*, 208 and pl. 19.
[3] Suet. *Tit.* i. 15. 3. [4] Ibid. 9.
[5] Tac. *Hist.* iii. 74. 1; Suet. *Dom.* 1. 4. [6] Tac. *Hist.* iii. 74.
[7] Eutrop. vii. 23. 5; *F.R.A.* 555. 14; Malaise, *Inventaire*, s.v. Roma, 213.
[8] Ibid., p. 203, no. 387. A few years later (88–9) a temple of Isis with two obelisks was put up in honour of Domitian returning from the Dacian war at Beneventum; see ibid. s.v. Beneventum, pp. 296 ff., nos. 10–11 (see also H. W. Müller, 1969). Domitian is reported to have favoured Egyptians (or Egyptian Greeks).
[9] *Chron. Minor.* ed. Th. Mommsen i. 146 and K. Latte, *R.R.* 329.
[10] Cf. Plut. *Is.* 2 and 60.
[11] See Malaise, *Conditions*, 415. [12] Ibid. 195.

and friendly. In addition her worshipper might be initiated. The initiate of Isis was born afresh. This meant that secure under the patronage of Isis, and no longer subject to fate, he became the real master of his life and could make a new start.[1] The initiate might hope for prosperity, the postponement of death, and perhaps, at the discretion of the goddess, immortality.[2] But Apuleius does not suggest that the hope of immortality was the main attraction of the Isis religion. Between them the Egyptian couple provided a combination of assistance in public or private business and psychological support which could not be tapped through any other single Roman cult. The Egyptian cults must be seen in proportion nevertheless. After all, the volume of evidence for their worship by members of the Flavian house is not large. Of the time the Flavians gave to ritual, the Egyptian gods can only have received a relatively small share. They were a supplement to the ancestral gods and not in any sense a replacement. It is probably also true that the Flavians' confidence in the Egyptian gods, if not unique at the highest levels of Roman society,[3] was nevertheless still unusual. It was only towards the end of the second century (in the reign of Commodus) that the example of the Flavian cultivation of the Egyptian gods was equalled and surpassed.[4]

4. *The empire at its high point: the Younger Pliny*[5] *and Tacitus*

The accession of Nerva or, more strictly speaking, Nerva's adoption as his son and successor of the distinguished soldier Trajan, was the beginning of the most harmonious years of the Roman empire.[6] Never before and rarely after did relations between emperor and nobility run so smoothly. The emperors

---

[1] Note that this was also the object of Epicureanism: see A. J. Festugière (1946). See also below, p. 221.

[2] Malaise, *Conditions*, 237 mainly on Apuleius, *Met.* xi. 6, 15, 21.

[3] e.g. the emperor Otho (Suet. *Otho*, 12. 2) and perhaps Nero's empress Poppaea. See Malaise, *Conditions*, 404.

[4] L. Vidman (1965).

[5] See H. P. Bütler (1970); A. N. Sherwin-White (1966); B. Radice, *The Letters of the Younger Pliny*, translated with an introduction (Harmondsworth, Penguin, 1968).

[6] E. Gibbon, *Decline and Fall of the Roman Empire* (ed. J. B. Bury, London, 1896), i. 68.

agreed to safeguard the 'freedom' of the senators. Senators were more concerned with their duties as conscientious administrators or soldiers[1] and less obsessed with their own or their families' dignity. The period ended with the reign of Marcus Aurelius (161–78), an emperor who was also a Stoic philosopher. But throughout the period the moral atmosphere of senatorial life was pervaded by Stoic ideas and the Stoically inspired critics and victims of earlier emperors were universally honoured as heroes and martyrs.

The letters of Pliny illustrate the atmosphere. He belonged to a wealthy[2] family of Como in North Italy. His uncle, the Elder Pliny, had made a career under various emperors but did not reach the senate. This was left to the nephew, in the course of a full life of public service. The Younger Pliny spoke in court as a barrister and held a succession of posts in the legal and financial administration. He reached the peak of his career when he held the consulate for two months in 100. Pliny's active life was almost equally divided between the reigns of the 'bad' emperor Domitian and the 'good' Trajan.

Pliny himself made a selection of his letters, revised and published them. However spontaneous the originals may have been, the collection is undoubtedly a conscious work of literature, intended to give its author a lasting reputation as a writer.[3] The letters paint a picture of the life led by their author and his friends. The picture is idealized, but this only means that it shows the values by which these men sought to live rather than the extent to which they succeeded in doing so. Thus the letters supplement the history of Tacitus and the satire of Juvenal with their gloomy vision of a once proud class demoralized. In fact, the point of view from which Juvenal and Tacitus criticize society does not differ radically from that from which Pliny idealizes.

The letters of Pliny reflect the reign of the 'good' emperor Trajan just as Silius' *Punica* reflected that of the 'tyrant' Domitian, and Pliny certainly did his best to bring out the contrast as sharply as possible. Even though none of the published

---

[1] The Younger Pliny and Agricola the famous governor of Britain are the best-known examples.

[2] R. Duncan Jones (1974), 17–32.

[3] H. W. Traub (1955).

letters was written before A.D. 97[1] (when Trajan was already emperor), the letters have been selected in such a way that the reader is introduced to salient episodes of Pliny's earlier life. As a result there are numerous references to Pliny's experience of the tyranny.[2] Above all, the correspondence emphasizes Pliny's close relations with the so-called Stoic opposition, and efforts he made on their behalf, including his care of the orphans of Arulenus Rusticus, one of the victims of the emperor.[3] Pliny refers with reverence to Thrasea, a famous victim of Nero.[4] To pay one's respects to the dead members of that 'dynasty' of upholders of liberty was now as respectable and creditable as it had been to honour the younger Cato under the earlier emperors.[5]

But while every opportunity is taken to underline the blessings of the Trajanic present by denigratory references to the Domitianic past, at a deeper level a great deal of continuity is manifest. At a dinner party 'the conversation turned on the blind Catullus Messalinus whose loss of sight had increased his cruel disposition . . . and consequently was often used by Domitian to aim at honest men like a weapon . . . Everyone at table was talking freely about his villainy and murderous decisions when the emperor Nerva said, "I wonder what would have happened to him if he were alive today?" "He would be dining with us," said Mauricus.'[6] Another example of continuity is provided by Pliny's own career. He reached the consulate under Trajan but had laid the foundations of his success under the tyrant Domitian.

Continuity also shows itself in the religious atmosphere. This could be described as 'basic Roman', lacking both innovation and antiquarianism. In this it resembles the *Punica*. But when we compare Silius' epic and Pliny's letters we must of course bear in mind the influence of genre. By its nature epic was bound to deal with divine interventions or at least (as in the case of Lucan's *Pharsalia*) to set its action in some sort of philosophical context. A letter writer is not bound to do this, and will only do

[1] A. N. Sherwin-White (1966), 41.
[2] *Ep.* iv. 11; i. 5; vii. 19; iv. 22; vii. 27.
[3] i. 14; ii. 18.
[4] viii. 22.
[5] iii. 11, 16; vii. 19; ix. 13; ix. 21; vii. 30; iv. 21; vi. 29.
[6] iv. 22, trans. B. Radice.

it if he feels personally involved in religion or philosophy. This does not appear to have been the case with the younger Pliny.

Religion whether private or public only occupies a marginal place in the letters. If Pliny has any private religious allegiance, he does not reveal it. Pliny carries out the rites of public religion when it is his duty to do so, but his attachment is perhaps not very profound. Thus he is pleased to have been appointed to the college of Augurs: 'in the first place it is an honour to accept the decision of so wise a ruler as ours . . . secondly, because the priesthood is an old-established religious office, and has particular sanctity in that it is held for life.' Also he has taken the place of Julius Frontinus, 'one of our greatest citizens'.[1] These are not religious reasons. Pliny buys a statue which he hopes will find a place in the temple of Jupiter, but to embellish the town and even more as a personal monument rather than as an act of worship.[2] He is delighted by the combination of natural beauty and religious associations at the source of the Clitumnus. The banks are clothed with ash-trees and poplar whose green reflections can be counted in the clear stream as if they were planted here. 'Close by is a temple of great antiquity in which is a standing image of the God Clitumnus himself . . . Everything in fact will delight you . . . you can study the numerous inscriptions in honour of the spring and the god which many have written on pillar and wall. Most of them you will admire but some will make you laugh—though I know you are really too charitable to laugh at any of them.'[3]

Pliny's allusions take for granted the reality of gods and the effectiveness of prayer: the continued performance of religious ritual goes without saying. Correspondents feel the need to display their public spirit, and their literary culture, their right-mindedness in political matters, their admiration of virtue, particularly when it had been shown in face of death. There is no need to display piety. The round of ritual is the same for all, and well known.

A man ought to remember the gods.[4] This was Pliny's expressed opinion even if the letters do not suggest that he was

---

[1] iv. 8, trans. B. Radice.

[2] iii. 6: 'basim . . . quae nomen meum honoresque capiat'. This was soon after his consulship (Sherwin-White (1966), 225).

[3] viii. i, trans. B. Radice.

[4] vii. 26.

an enthusiastic worshipper. We hear that he put up a temple at
his own expense at Tifernum, a town which had chosen him as
its patron. The temple was to house a collection of statues of
emperors.[1] This act of munificence looks like the performance
of social rather than religious duty. Pliny also rebuilt a temple
of Ceres standing in one of his estates, because it was 'very old
and too small considering how crowded it is on its special
anniversary, when great crowds gather there from the whole
district on 13 September and many ceremonies are performed
and vows made or discharged'.[2] As a provincial governor too,
Pliny was concerned to uphold traditional worship.[3]

The correspondence contains a fair number of expressions of
general piety not related to any named deity. The gods are said
to have heard the prayers of an invalid who wished to outlive, if
only by a single day, the robber Domitian.[4] Pliny prays that the
gods will help a man to find his father who has disappeared
while travelling in Umbria—but he thinks the man has been
murdered.[5] Pliny commends a young man who married 'before
he was twenty-four' and would have been a father had God
willed it so.[6] Pliny felt gratitude to the gods when his wife had
survived a miscarriage.[7] Needless to say Pliny performed the
public vows on behalf of the emperor which were required by
his governorship in Bithyria,[8] but he claims to have prayed for
Trajan in private as well.[9]

Pliny was evidently not a markedly religious man. On the
other hand, the reticence about personal religion is also a
literary convention. The letters observe the same convention of
secularity as was observed in historiography. Literary convention ensured that literary works reflected changing attitudes
only with a considerable time-lag.

Nevertheless changing ideas did find their way into literature.
Pliny's gods are explicitly moral. In the abstract and theoretical
language of a great public speech, he praises Trajan as being
sanctus and *castus* and resembling the gods in every respect.[10] He
prays to Jupiter for help in speaking frankly and truthfully.[11]

---

[1] iii. 4; iv. 1; x. 8.
[2] ix. 39. Pliny consulted *haruspices* before starting the work, cf. Sherwin-White
(1966), ad loc.
[3] x. 96 (Christians).   [4] i. 12.   [5] vi. 25.
[6] vii. 24: si deus adnuisset.   [7] viii. 10.   [8] x. 35–6.
[9] x. 13.   [10] *Pan.* 1. 3.   [11] Ibid. 1. 6.

The gods love emperors if they make themselves loved by their subjects.[1] They avenge crime.[2] In worship, the gods require uprightness and purity, rather than carefully prepared formulae[3]

In the letters in which Pliny refers to the principles governing his own life, the gods are not mentioned. He and his friends act as they do because such conduct is fitting.[4] In other words, he must perform the duties which a Roman man of standing is and always has been expected to perform. These he sums up: to help his friends—understood in the wide and political sense in which the word was used in Roman public life—and to help his country.[5]

Traditionally the reward for a public man was fame: fame in his lifetime and if possible after his death, fame for himself and for the continuation of a family tradition. Pliny accepts fame as a proper incentive,[6] and is eager to assist the lasting fame of great public men with his writing.[7] At the same time he is convinced that the scope for glory in public life has been reduced by the facts of the principate. 'I have told you this primarily to give you some genuine news and then to be able to talk a little about political matters; a subject which gives us fewer opportunities these days, so none must be missed . . . Everything today depends on the will of one man who has taken upon himself for the general good all our care and responsibilities.' Elsewhere he complains that for the historian 'there is much more to censure than to praise in the serious vices of the present day'. Pliny would like to do something by which he will be remembered 'not perhaps by action since here the opportunity no longer rests with us, but at any rate by literary words'.[8] Pliny's contemporary Tacitus felt similarly.[9] It was easier for Roman senators to accept the facts of the

---

[1] Ibid. 72. 4.
[2] Ibid. 49. 1.
[3] Ibid. 3. 5: deos ipsos non tam accuratis adorantium precibus quam innocentia el sanctitate laetari, gratioremque existimari qui delubris eorum puram castamque mentem quam qui meditatum carmen intulerit. Cf also, 63. 7–8.
[4] *Ep.* iv. 23: decebat; iii. 1: honestum.
[5] Ibid. ii. 14. 14; iv. 23; vi. 29. 1; vii. 9; vii. 15. 1; viii. 21.
[6] Ibid. 3. 1; ii. 1. 2; iii. 21. 6.
[7] v. 8. 1.
[8] iii. 20. 10; v. 8. 13; iii. 7. 14.
[9] W. Liebeschuetz (1966), 132–4.

principate—Pliny certainly did that—than to find a new system of values. We have seen what was the historical background to this detachment from the institutions of even a well-ruled principate. Viewed in a different perspective, the attitudes can be recognized as a faint reflection of the sense of the vanity of all human actions which was spreading in the second century, and induced the emperor Marcus Aurelius to compare the elation he felt at his victories to the satisfaction of a spider that has caught a fly.[1]

Pliny's culture was that of an orator not a philosopher. He expresses admiration for a philosopher who realized in his life the philosophical ideal of character.[2] He also suggests that philosophers teach only what a conscientious public figure would do by instinct.[3] Nevertheless he shows the influence of Stoic doctrine. Virtue is to be practised for its own sake. Right or wrong intention should be judged for what they are, not by results.[4] A man shows greatness of mind in that he cares nothing for show but refers everything to his knowledge that he has done the right thing,[5] and a noble character will seek the reward of an action in his own consciousness of it rather than popular opinion.[6] For himself, Pliny endeavours to prove that under the tyranny of Domitian he had been ready to do his duty as friend regardless of danger.[7]

The theme of death frequently occurs in Pliny's letters. Ability to meet death fearlessly, whether in a political context or in private life, is the supreme test of character in Pliny, as it had been in Seneca, Lucan, Silius, and Tacitus. Correllius Rufus at the age of sixty-eight committed suicide because he decided that the sufferings of gout outweighed the pleasures of continued life. Pliny is sad, but he obviously takes pride in this display of character by his old patron. 'Correllius was led to make his decision by the supremacy of reason which takes the place of inevitability for the philosophers. He had many reasons fos living but he had suffered so long from a painful affliction that his reasons for dying outweighed everything that life could

---

[1] Marcus, *Med.* x. 10.   [2] *Ep.* iii. 11 (Artemidorus).
[3] vii. 9; i. 10.   [4] v. 9.
[5] i. 22. 5. A. Sherwin-White (1966), on i. 12. 3, notes that Pliny uses *conscientia* for his own awareness of his past deeds. It is contrasted with *fama* in i. 8. 14; v. 1. 10; iii. 20. 8.
[6] i. 8. 14.   [7] iii. 11.

give him.'[1] What matters is the supremacy of reason over fear of death, not the actual fact of suicide. Another friend announced that he would commit suicide if the doctors thought that his disease would prove fatal, otherwise no matter how great his suffering he would go on living. 'This was a particularly difficult decision, which merits the highest praise. Many people have his impulse and urge to forestall death but the ability to examine critically the arguments for dying, and to accept or reject the idea of living, is the mark of a truly great mind.'[2]

We must note that the motive is self-control based on self-respect, a refusal to live a life which because of physical pain, or bereavement, or disgrace, is no longer worth living. The decision is not aided by any religious belief, certainly not by a hope of immortality. Pliny comments on the death of his patron Virginius Rufus: 'if it is right to grieve, or even to give the name of death to what has ended the mortal existence rather than the life of so great a man, for he lives, and will live for ever and in a wider sense in our memories and on our lips now that he has left our sight.'[3] Elsewhere he writes: 'Since we are denied a long life let us leave something to bear witness that at least we have lived ... "Rivalry is good" when friends stimulate each other by mutual encouragement to derive immortal fame.'[4] Pliny wrote to Tacitus 'I know that immortal fame awaits him (the elder Pliny) if his death is rewarded by you'.[5]

Friends are not supported by the hope of any life after death, nor is their steadfastness in death supported by religious thoughts. Men of Pliny's circle fought the pain of bereavement by taking comfort from the courage with which death has been faced rather than by hoping that death would not be final.[6]

Pliny's morality is gentle,[7] and far from the cult of vigour which one might expect in the governing class of a ruling people. His attitude is marked by humanity and understanding. 'My own idea of the truly good and faultless man is one who forgives the faults of others as if he was daily committing them himself,

---

[1] i. 12 (abbreviated).
[2] i. 22, cf. 8. 9: tantoque laudabilior munificentia nostra fore videbatur, quod ad illam non impetu quodam sed consilio trahebamur.
[3] *Ep.* ii. 1.
[4] iii. 7: on death of Silius Italicus.   [5] vi. 16.
[6] iv. 11. 7–9; v. 16; vi. 24.
[7] Cf. A. Sherwin-White (1966), on v. 16. 10.

and who keeps himself free from faults as if he could never forgive them . . . Let us always remember what was so often said by Thrasea whose gift of sympathy made him the great man he was: "Anyone who hates faults hates mankind".[1]

'We are never so virtuous as when we are ill. Has a sick man ever been tempted by greed or lust? He is neither a slave to his passion nor ambitious for office . . . It is then that he remembers the gods and realises that he is mortal; he feels neither envy, admiration, nor contempt for any man . . . So here for our guidance is the rule put shortly which the philosophers seek to express in endless words and volumes: in health we should continue to be the men we would become when sickness prompted our words.'[2]

Pliny and his circle were idealists. Although they lived extremely comfortably they directed their lives to the performance of duty rather than to success or pleasure.[3] But their ideal of life was not provided by religion. Service of the gods was part of the good life, but only part. The way of life as a whole is best defined as the slowly evolving custom of the class to which they belong.

The world of Pliny and his friends appears eminently reasonable, governed by the same material sequence of material cause and effect as the world of today. But there is evidence that this reasonable world is the possession of only a small circle and that it is extremely vulnerable since it is not fortified by a securely founded view of the world. Suetonius the historian and author of the *Twelve Caesars* has had an alarming dream which makes him fear that he will lose a lawsuit on which he is engaged. He asks Pliny to obtain an adjournment. Pliny is sympathetic though he can cite a dream of his own which did not affect a lawsuit adversely.[4]

Marcus Regulus, a noble who had rebuilt his family's fortune by notorious prosecutions under Nero, and who had continued as a prominent member of the Roman Bar under Nero's 'good' successors, evidently had a far less rational view of the world than Pliny. When about to appear in court he used 'to paint round one of his eyes (the right if he was appearing for the plaintiff and the left for the defendant), change a patch over from one eyebrow to the other, and he would never fail to

[1] viii. 22. 3.   [2] vii. 26.   [3] iv. 23.   [4] i. 18.

consult the *haruspices* on the result of his case. This may have been gross superstition on his part but it did show respect for his profession.'[1] The same man is said to have so impressed a wealthy widow with what purported to be a horoscope confirmed by the reports of a *haruspex* and an astrologer, that she left him a legacy. His own fortune Regulus divined in the entrails of a sacrificial animal.[2] That Regulus and his clients should believe in the forecasts of astrologers and *haruspices* is not surprising. After all most of the authors we have studied were more or less truly convinced of the efficacy of divination.

Pliny too believed in portents. Larcius Macedo a senator, was visiting the baths accompanied by a retinue of slaves. One of the slaves touched a Roman knight to indicate that he should make way for his senatorial master. The knight was offended and struck a heavy blow not at the slave, but at the master. Some time later Macedo was killed by his slaves while bathing at home. The Roman incident turned out to have been a portent.[3] Gaius Fannius was writing a history of the victims of Nero which he was eager to make a long one. When he had completed only three books Fannius dreamt that Nero entered his study, sat down beside him and proceeded to read one book after the other. When he had finished the third book he got up and left. Fannius recognized a portent of his own death. He would not live to write more than the books Nero had read. So it proved.[4]

Pliny himself was inclined to believe that the normal rules of causation might occasionally be set aside by ghosts. He consulted one of Trajan's principal advisers, Licinius Sura[5] who was evidently interested in the borderland of natural and supernatural,[6] on the subject of three ghost stories. Two of them were probably well-known tales. According to the first one Curtius Rufus saw a woman of superhuman size and beauty who correctly foretold his eventual governorship of Africa, and his death in the province.[7] Another concerned the experience of the philosopher Athenodorus in a haunted house; a ghost pointed out the place where the remains of its body had not received proper burial. In the third incident some slaves of

---

[1] vi. 2. 3.   [2] ii. 20.   [3] iii. 14.

[4] v. 15; a dream appearance had induced Pliny the Elder to write his *German Wars* (iii. 5. 4).

[5] C. P. Jones (1970); A. Sherwin-White (1966), 309–10.

[6] *Ep.* iv. 30.   [7] Cf. Tac. *Ann.* xi. 21.

Pliny himself had their hair miraculously cut while sleeping. Pliny was inclined to understand this as a super-natural intimation that he would not have to face the trial with which Domitian was threatening him.[1]

Pliny wonders whether ghosts really exist and have some sort of supernatural power or whether they take shape only from our fears. But he is 'personally encouraged to believe in their existence by the experience of Curtius Rufus',[2] and his telling of the other stories is certainly slanted in favour of a supernatural explanation.

These things occurred in private life. For attitudes to public portents held in the time of Trajan we must turn to Tacitus. In his writings Tacitus included a good many references to portents and prodigies but often accompanied them by sceptical comments. Hence there is room for discussion of what the notices meant to the historian. One alternative is proposed by R. Syme: 'In the *Historiae* Tacitus is openly sceptical about signs and wonders: common enough in unsophisticated ages they now occur only in a season of crisis or panic. The secret ordinances of fate, the voice of oracles and all the omens—these found credit, but after the event.'[3]

But Tacitus' account of the career of Vespasian shows that the historian was not simply sceptical; for he has pointed out that Vespasian's greatness had in fact been foretold. The first promising signs were seen by him long before the start of his public career.[4] In A.D. 69 these old prophecies were confirmed by oracles, of Venus at Paphos,[5] and of the god of Mount Carmel in Judaea.[6] Finally, when his rivals had already been defeated he received marvellous confirmation of his title to the empire from Serapis at Alexandria.[7]

Tacitus is often concerned with the subjective effect of prophecy. He points out that portents induced people to think of Vespasian or of his son Titus in connection with the empire.[8] He tells us that Vespasian was excessively influenced by this kind of

---

[1] *Ep.* vii. 27.

[2] Ibid. 27. 2.

[3] R. Syme (1958), 522.

[4] *Hist.* ii. 78. See R. T. Scott (1968). I am now closer to Scott's general position than I was in my review, *J.R.S.* lix (1969), 312–13.

[5] *Hist.* ii. 4.   [6] Ibid. 78.

[7] Ibid. iv. 8; cf. Suet. *Vesp.* 6.   [8] *Hist.* ii. 1.

thing, and that the supernatural forecasts greatly assisted his decision to allow himself to be proclaimed emperor.[1] True, Tacitus tells us that 'for us' belief in the imperial destiny of Vespasian was only established after the event,[2] but it is made abundantly clear that the signs of this destiny had been seen much earlier. Tacitus shows that the signs had been to some extent self-fulfilling, but not entirely so. The fact of essential agreement of different oracular instruments widely separated by geography strongly suggests genuine foreknowledge. Even the ancient books of the priests of the Jews had foretold that the present was a time when the Orient would triumph. The Jews took this to apply to themselves, when in reality (according to Tacitus) it referred to Vespasian.[3]

Tacitus criticizes reliance on supernatural forecasts[4] and on astrology,[5] but not because they are meaningless. While some phenomena taken for signs by the unsophisticated may be insignificant,[6] and some astrologers may be charlatans,[7] most signs are eventually fulfilled.[8] Thus we read that when Galba was about to go to the Praetorian camp to adopt Piso a thunderstorm broke out. In earlier times an electoral assembly would have been abandoned in these circumstances. But Galba ignored the storm. The adoption took place and proved disastrous.[9] The warning of thunder and lightning was confirmed by events. So was the advice of the *haruspex* who interpreted what proved to be Galba's last sacrifice.[10] The trouble with the signs is that they usually cannot be interpreted exactly. From early youth Vespasian knew that a great career lay ahead of him. He did not know how high it would take him. Each successive stage might have represented the final fulfilment of

---

[1] Ibid. 78.

[2] Ibid. i. 10. 3; cf. Suet. *Vesp.* 7: inopinato principi.

[3] *Hist.* v. 13.

[4] Ibid. ii. 78: responsa vatum . . . siderum motus referre nec erat intactus tali superstitione [Vespasianus].

[5] Ibid. i. 22: astrologers are *genus hominum potentibus infidum, sperantibus fallax*.

[6] Ibid. iv. 26.

[7] Ibid. 22: Ptolemaeus persuaded Otho not by genuine knowledge but by 'coniectura et rumore senium Galbae et iuventam Othonis, computantium'. Astrologers might be dangerous charlatans, e.g. *Ann.* ii. 27, but were often right (ibid. vi. 20, 21–2; iv. 58).

[8] See also *Ann.* v. 13: a commander ignores signs and comes to grief; *Hist.* v. 13: Jewish practice of not expiating prodigies is criticized.

[9] Ibid. i. 18.   [10] Ibid. i. 74.

the prophecy. The priest on mount Carmel told Vespasian 'you will have a great residence, far flung boundaries and a multitude of people.'[1] The reply was widely thought to refer to the empire. It was essentially ambiguous all the same. In the temple of Serapis Vespasian saw a phantom in the likeness of a well-known man called Basilides, 'son of a King'. Vespasian, whose armies had just defeated a rival for the empire, and who was hoping to found a dynasty, took the name to be the god's answer to his problem. Maybe it was, but it could have meant something quite different or nothing.[2]

Scepticism or rationalism there is in Tacitus but it is a mistake to equate it with the rationalism of the modern unbeliever. Tacitus' scepticism is rather that of a man who believes in the science in which he is an expert, but is also aware that not all interpretation proposed in its name are true. He is interested in the way errors arise and concerned to refute them. Thus he notes that Otho was deceived by an astrologer as a result of a general tendency of men to believe what they cannot understand,[3] that forecasts of Vespasian's rule were believed after the event;[4] that men are more credulous in war;[5] that wishful thinking leads to disastrous interpretations of signs.[6] He suggests, perhaps ironically, that the Roman people were naïve to conclude that the gods must be angry at the murder by Nero of his stepbrother and rival for the empire.[7] He remarks that the *prodigia* seen after the murder of Agrippina were meaningless and happened without divine concern (*cura deum*), since Nero continued his criminal reign for many years.[8]

For Tacitus prodigies are interesting not only because they are evidence of divine government, or at least of the universal sympathy of the world, but also because they reveal fascinating aspects of human psychology. An example is the account of the emperor Otho's departure from Rome to meet the army of

---

[1] *Hist.* ii. 78.   [2] Ibid. iv. 82.   [3] Ibid. i. 22. 3.
[4] Ibid. i. 10. 3; but they had already influenced men before the event: *Hist.* ii. 1, 78.
[5] Ibid. iv. 26.   [6] *Ann.* xiv. 22.
[7] Ibid. xiii. 17: ut vulgus iram deum portendi crediderit adversus facinus, cui plerique tamen hominum ignoscebant.
[8] Ibid. xiv. 12, cf. B. Walker (1952), 250. I would suggest that the sentence is rhetorical. Tacitus is not denying that the phenomena were prodigies. He is using irony to express indignation. Like Silius (vi. 84) and Lucan (frequently) he attacks the gods for not intervening. Only in Tacitus the attack is not explicit but implied.

Vitellius.[1] The departure of the army was preceded by prodigies 'and numerous signs and wonders of the kind that in
primitive centuries were observed even in peace time but are
now only heard when people are afraid'.[2] There was also a
flood which caused great damage and blocked the road the
army was to take, and 'though the obstruction sprang from
chance or natural causes,[3] the mere fact of its occurrence was
interpreted as a sign from heaven and an omen of imminent
disaster'.

Now this incident could easily have been composed into an
exemplum of neglected religion like Livy's account of the setting
out of C. Flaminius on his disastrous campaign against Hannibal. Tacitus has not done this. He expressly mentions that
Otho took religious precautions before leaving the city[4] and he
gives a military justification for hastening the departure even
though the Sacred Shields had not yet been laid up.[5] Tacitus is
rather concerned to illustrate the psychology of *prodigia* reports.
He shows that in times of stress, people become credulous.
Various signs were seen 'that in primitive times were observed

---

[1] *Hist.* i. 86.

[2] rudibus saeculis: *rudis* is basically inexperienced or untrained, uneducated; so
Dial. 19. 19; *Agr.* 3. 17 (with false modesty). It can be a good quality, e.g. *Agr.* 21. 2:
'homines dispersi ac rudes eoque in bello faciles.' Here I think it signifies neither
approval nor disapproval. It is factual. In the old days such signs *were* noted and
expiated regularly, now they are unnoticed except in times of fear.

[3] 'A fortuitis vel naturalibus causis in prodigium vertebatur.' The translation is
by K. Wellesley. I do not think that Tacitus implies that seeming chance or natural
causation is incompatible with a phenomenon being a *prodigium*. A *prodigium* was an
unusual event but did not necessarily involve suspension of the normal laws of
nature (see, for instance, Seneca's theory of divination, *N.Q.* ii. 32). A *prodigium*
might well seem to be produced *fortuitis vel naturalibus causis* but of course the
vast majority of happenings so produced were not true *prodigia*. What interests
Tacitus is that in certain circumstances men would interpret as a *prodigium* a happening which they would normally ignore as commonplace and insignificant. This
is the point of other passages that seem to differentiate between *prodigia* and *fortuita*
or *natura*. *Hist.* ii. 1: 'inclinatis ad credendum animis loco ominum etiam fortuita.'
Hst. iv. 26: 'apud imperitos prodigii loco accipiebatur ipsa aquarum penuria; . . .
quod in pace fors seu natura tunc fata et ira deorum vocabatur.' *Ann.* iv. 64:' qui
mos vulgo, fortuita ad culpam trahentes . . . (by interpreting a fire as an omen,
something which in Tacitus' expert view it was not, or at least need not be). In the
lists of *Ann.* xii. 43 and 64 Tacitus seems to distinguish between undoubted prodigies
and others which were merely taken as such, e.g. famine and the deaths of
magistrates.   [4] *Hist.* i. 87.

[5] Ibid. 89; Suet. (*Oth.* 8) censures Otho. Tacitus' justification: *Hist.* i. 89:
aspernatus omnem cunctationem ut Neroni quoque exitiosam et Caecina iam
Alpes transgressus exstimulabat.

even in peace time but are now only heard when men are afraid'. He goes on to point out that the most frightening signs were those, such as a severe flood, which were dangerous in themselves. Lastly, he notes that what appears the most obviously relevant sign, the blocking of the road to the front,[1] was only noted when danger from the flood had receded.

Tacitus intended to illustrate human credulity. People believed with insufficient reason.[2] But I do not think this should be taken to mean that Tacitus himself believed that omens as such were meaningless. His accounts of the rise of Vespasian and of the fall Galba clearly show that omens were significant. It is a mistake to set isolated generalizing statements against the tendency of a whole narrative. It would be going too far to claim that Tacitus simply denies that the phenomena accompanying Otho's departure were signs. After all, Otho did come to a bad end.

The language of this passage and others like it is uniquely Tacitean, but the attitude is already found in Livy and republican writers. It is a traditional attitude developed by priests who were also public men and senators and for whom the decision as to what signs were to be accepted as genuine was part of the routine of public life, which required the calming of worries caused by popular interpretation of unusual occurrences. The traditional Roman procedure for dealing with prodigies was, among other things, a device for maintaining public morale.[3] But it could only do this if genuine signs and genuine interpretations could be distinguished from false and superstitious ones.

The rational discrimination with which Tacitus views divination is a survival of the political religion of the republic. It was never lost completely[4] but for the future the element of belief was more significant than the discrimination. It was this

---

[1] *Hist.* i. 86: iter belli esse obstructum.

[2] The originators of the reports were various: i. 86 (*diversis auctoribus*). The signs (other than the flood) are given in *oratio obliqua* as if Tacitus dissociated himself from the truth of the report. Elsewhere there are reports of signs in *oratio recta*: *Hist.* v. 13; *Ann.* xii. 43. 1; xiv. 12. 8; xv. 47. 1. In ibid. xii. 43 and 64 he seems to distinguish between authentic *prodigia* and others merely taken as such. Plutarch's list of prodigies at Otho's departure shows that some had better authentification than others. Tacitus treats all with equal distrust.

[3] See above, p. 9.

[4] C. Gnilka (1973), esp. 147–55.

belief that kept the door open for a much wider range of supernatural communication than was traditionally received by Romans. The fact that supernatural interventions and even divine commands on the whole only occupy a very small place in the world of Pliny and Tacitus—as earlier—was more a consequence of tradition and a sense of fitness than of conviction about the nature of the world. The gods did communicate with the Roman state through portents, but the signals should not be taken to be more than vague warnings. Precise popular interpretations should usually be rejected as superstition. Detailed guidance other than in matters of ritual was not to be sought from supernatural signs.

Late in life Pliny encountered Christians who believed that their God gave detailed commands which lay altogether outside the range of Roman religion. When members of this sect refused to do homage to the gods of the empire, Pliny had no hesitation about having them executed. He did not discover any criminal acitivity among them, but their attitude represented perverse and extravagant superstition,[1] which was dangerous and not to be tolerated. Tacitus, Pliny's colleagues at the Roman Bar, in the senate, and in the world of literature would certainly have agreed. After describing the horrible sufferings Nero inflicted on Christians, burning some, throwing others to be eaten by dogs, all for the entertainment of the public, he comments that the Christians were pitied even though they were guilty and deserving of the most extreme penalties.[2] But Pliny and Tacitus stand at the end of an epoch. Even Romans were coming to accept far more detailed guidance from oracles and other sources of supernatural wisdom.

5. *Public religion and political change in the early empire: a summing up*

The outstanding impression produced by the study of public religion from the late republic through the early empire is one of continuity. Throughout the period it remained axiomatic that the state could not flourish without the successful appeasement

---

[1] Plin. *Ep.* x. 96.   [2] Tac. *Ann.* xv. 44.

of the gods. Moreover, the gods who have to be appeased remain the traditional gods, with Jupiter as much as ever the supreme patron of the Roman state.

But there has been evolution and this was closely bound up with the establishment of a monarchical form of government. Most important of all, public religion has changed direction. Since public welfare had come to depend so much on the well-being of the ruler, it was now the principal object of public religion to ensure divine support for him and his family.

Under the republic public religion had added the prestige of ceremony and divine sanction to the decisions reached by the constitutional process. Under the empire religion employed new ceremonies that expressed and developed loyalty to the ruler. Cults of loyalty included the worship of dead emperors, and various approximations to the worship of the reigning one. But worship of the living ruler was much less important than the offering of worship to gods on the ruler's behalf. The Roman emperor was not thought to have supernatural powers. Ruler worship involved a transfer of impressive ceremonies and formulae from their original religious purpose to the essentially secular one of honouring a mortal.

It would be a mistake to deduce from this redeployment of religious ceremonial that religion itself had lost its significance. What made the diversion of religious ceremonies non-sacrilegious was the nature of the Roman gods, the fact that they were not jealous. The gods of Rome insisted that they must be offered punctiliously all honours due to them but they did not worry about what honours were paid to other gods or to men.

Under the empire Greek philosophy, above all Stoic philosophy, assumed a much greater role in the lives of the upper classes. This was a development of private rather than public religion but among its causes perhaps the most important was the new form of government. The principate was accepted, but only with reservations. It was very widely agreed that the monarchical system was morally inferior to the republic that it had replaced. Submission to the authority of one man was felt to be inevitably degrading and demoralizing. This alienation from the government of the community undermined the civic values and ambitions which had for generations provided the governing class with its motivation and self-respect. What was needed was a new source of value which lay outside the area ruled by the emperor, and reference to which would enable a man to live his life with dignity and self-respect. It was this which many found in Stoic philosophy.

The influence of Stoicism can be observed to a greater or lesser degree in all the writers of the early empire. Seneca shows how this philosophy could help a man to face the strains of life at the imperial court. Lucan illustrates Stoicism in a different role, that of an ideology of resistance to tyranny. The *Punica* of Silius Italicus show that Stoic ideas were used to fortify the imperial system after it had been shaken by the civil wars of A.D. 69. It is likely that only a small proportion of the Roman upper class were fully committed Stoics. But the influence of Stoic ideas was inescapable. Tacitus would not have been troubled by problems of free will and predestination if he had not lived in an age dominated by Stoic ideas.

Stoicism provided new motivation; it did not provide new values. Manners and morals evolved slowly. Meanwhile the ancestral religion continued to perform its traditional role of maintaining good relations with the gods. It was marginally assisted by new cults such as the worship of Isis and Serapis or of Mithras. But on the whole the appeal of these cults belongs to the area of personal religion. The normal response to a breakdown of the imperial system was a revival of ancestral religion and morals.

The imperial period saw new developments in the area of divination. Belief in the significance of signs and portents was a permanent feature of Roman religion. But when free government came to an end the techniques that had been part of republican politics lost credit and prominence. Instead there was a great increase in the use of astrology and magic for gaining information about the future. Both techniques offered far more detailed replies than had been provided by traditional divination. Recourse to astrology and magic was at least in part a response to the secrecy that now shrouded public affairs.

The new techniques of divination were sophisticated and, in the case of astrology at least, made use of Hellenistic advances in astronomy and mathematics. But they did more than anything to undermine the rationalist atmosphere, since they suggested that men could achieve knowledge and power by other than physical means. The supernatural world was brought nearer, and men became more ready to accept statements on the authority of revelation or divine inspiration. This readiness may well represent the deepest change in intellectual attitude between the early and the later empire.

V

TOWARDS THE LATER EMPIRE

1. *The end of an epoch*

TACITUS stands at the end of the tradition of Latin historio-graphy. With all the eloquence of a master of language he described the two contrasting aspects of the principate, demonstrating at the same time why it was inevitable and why it was insupportable. Tacitus was able to do this impressively: he, like all his generation, was steeped in Stoic ideas and particularly the teaching that virtue requires behaviour to be consistent and sincere.[1] He can therefore bring out the degrading character of a political system which put a premium on conduct that was inconsistent and insincere. Such was the behaviour of the senate at the accession of Tiberius. 'Meanwhile at Rome, consuls, senate, knights, ran headlong into slavery. The greater a man was, the greater the insincerity and the haste, with expression carefully composed so as to show neither happiness at the death of one emperor nor too much grief at the succession of the next, they combined tears with joy, mourning with flattery.'[2] He also gives some memorable descriptions of false religion. 'Executions now abounded in the city, and thanks-offerings on the Capitol. Men who had lost their sons or brothers, or other kinsmen or friends, thanked the gods and decorated their houses with laurel and fell before Nero kissing his hand incessantly.'[3]

Tacitus was the last historian to draw this picture of the empire. Indeed he was probably the last writer of full-scale history to write in Latin for 150 years.[4] History was about to

---

[1] Consistency: ὁμολογία, *convenientia*. See Stob. ii. 7. 6a; Cic. *Fin.* iii. 6. 27; Sen. *Ep.* xxxi. 8; xxiv. 5; lxxiv. 36. See E. V. Arnold (1911), 282–3. Sincerity is a special case of consistency, namely, between principles and behaviour, cf. Marcus, *Med.* xi. 14–15, also iii. 2.

[2] Tac. *Ann.* i. 7. 1.   [3] Ibid. xv. 71, trans. M. Grant.

[4] None other has survived and none is known to have existed. See T. D. Barnes (1968).

give way to imperial biography and, as far as we can know, writers of imperial biography were not numerous. If one looks for them, one can find portents of the development. Tacitus wrote an acute analysis of the decline of rhetoric. 'In consequence of the long period of peace and the unbroken spell of inactivity on the part of the commons, and of peaceableness on the part of the senate, by reason also of the working of the great imperial system, a hush has fallen upon eloquence, as indeed it has upon the world at large . . .[1] What is the use of long arguments of the senate, when good citizens agree so quickly? What is the use of one harangue after another on public platforms, when it is not the ignorant multitude that decides a political issue, but a monarch who is the incarnation of wisdom?'[2]

The empire was bad for public debate and thus for rhetoric. But history too was part of the political debate, and conditions which harmed rhetoric also harmed history. In addition, it had always been a principal role of Roman history to provide moral *exempla*. But life under the emperors gave few opportunities for exemplary behaviour of the traditional kind. Hence the historian's task had become narrow and inglorious 'to record a succession of cruel edicts, of prosecution heaped upon prosecution, to tell of friends betrayed, of innocent men brought to ruin, of trials all ending in one way, with a uniformity as monotonous as it is revolting'.[3] Tacitus treated the conflict of *princeps* and liberty in such a way as to make its commentary on human society of lasting relevance. This does not alter the fact that the theme was exhausted. As a practical political issue the matter had been decided more than a hundred years before. As a moral issue it had remained actual much longer, but even there Trajan and his immediate successors seemed to have found a compromise acceptable to most men. It was time to write about new issues, which would have meant widening the perspective to make the empire rather than Roman society the centre of the picture. There is no indication that Tacitus or any Roman was ready to do this.

But the collapse of Latin historiography after the reign of Trajan must not be studied in isolation. It was accompanied by

---

[1] Tac. *Dial*. 38.
[2] Ibid. 41, trans. C. G. Starr (1965), 258–9.
[3] *Ann*. iv. 32–3, trans. M. Grant.

the collapse of epic and satire. This catastrophe of Latin literature is an extraordinary phenomenon.[1] It certainly was not
brought about by a decline in literary culture, an unbroken
succession of highly literary Christian writers is proof of this.
So are the panegyrics which were written in Gaul in the fourth
century and whose elaborate artificiality is obviously based on
a continuous tradition in the rhetorical schools. What happened
to Latin literature must be the result of a profound cultural
transformation.

A feature of the cultural scene at Rome in the age of the
Antonines is the great influence of Greek literature and Greeks.
The court was thronged by Greek exponents of rhetoric, or
sophists.[2] Their presence was not a purely literary phenomenon.
The Greek sophists were usually members of leading families
of their city. Their visits to Rome were the means by which the
great cities of the eastern provinces brought their requests to
the notice of the emperor. The personal relationship that grew
up between sophists and emperor was part of the network of
relationships that kept the empire together. The sophists were
not alone. Other men from the same level of Greek-speaking
provincial society were finding their way into imperial posts,
the senate, and the consulate.[3]

The eastern provinces were at last beginning to supply
administrators for the empire.[4] The Greek world was at the time
going through a literary revival known as the Second Sophistic.
It originated in the intense literary life of the upper classes of
the Greek cities of Asia Minor, and in the public orations and
literary competitions of the great inter-city festivals which
flourished in the area as never before. The interest of writers
and orators concentrated itself on literary effect, and especially
the re-creation and preservation of the literary Attic of the
classical period. Literature tended to separate, both in language and subject-matter, from the society that produced it.
History that mattered was the history of classical Athens. Later
periods, especially the imperial period of Rome, were despised.

[1] On catastrophe of Latin literature: H. Bardon (1956), 299–315; J. Bayet
(1965), 412–16.
[2] P. L. Brown (1971), 64; G. Bowersock (1969). E. L. Bowie (1970) summarizes
the Greek authors writing at the time.
[3] G. Bowersock, op. cit. 50 ff. On senate see G. Barbieri (1952), 433–42.
[4] On ambiguity of 'Greek' origin see F. Millar (1964), 9 ff. and 186–90.

Genuine originality was shown by this literature only in philosophy and in the expression of religious experiences.[1]

This movement came to Rome. Not only did Latin authors of the Antonine period have the same preoccupations as the Greeks, but Rome and Italy became centres of creativity in Greek. Galen wrote his voluminous medical work while practising at Rome.[2] Plotinus and his pupil Porphyry taught and wrote in Italy.[3] The emperor Marcus Aurelius himself wrote his *Meditations* (to use their usual title) in Greek.

The effect of this movement (or perhaps of more obscure developments of which the influence of this movement was a symptom) on Latin literature was a disastrous narrowing of scope. All the genres with contemporary social relevance ceased. The effect was far more drastic than it had been in the Greek world. After all, the Greeks continued to write contemporary history,[4] and the Greek world produced a great satirist in Lucian. Latin contemporary history was reduced to imperial biography, whose interest centred on character rather than social organization.[5] Interest and admiration for the past found expression in antiquarianism rather than history.[6] The one branch of secular thought that continued to be productive in Latin was jurisprudence, which was of course technical and closely linked to administration. General literary comment on Roman society ceased.

At the same time Rome lost its monopoly as a creative centre of Latin literature. The classical Latin authors had diverse origins in Italy or the Roman municipalities of the western provinces. But Latin literature remained to an astonishing extent a Roman phenomenon. Writing, literary themes, and audience were closely bound up with life in the capital itself, and especially with life of the highest social class.[7] In the

---

[1] On Second Sophistic see A. Boulanger (1923); E. L. Bowie (1970).

[2] Galen at Rome: A.D. 162–6 and 169–99.

[3] Plotinus at Rome: 245–69. Porphyry at Rome: 263–8; at an unknown later date he returned to take over Plotinus' school.

[4] F. Millar (1969), esp. 14–16.   [5] T. D. Barnes (1968).

[6] See the surviving *Attic Nights* of Gellius.

[7] The literature of the early empire was dominated by Spaniards, e.g. Seneca, Lucan, Quintilian, Martial; but all wrote for Roman audiences and almost all their writing took place at or near Rome. Martial's preface to Book xii (written in Spain for dispatch to Italy) explains why. Cf. the extent to which French literature of the seventeenth and eighteenth centuries was a Parisian phenomenon.

second century there is a change. The first non-Roman centre was North Africa. Cornelius Fronto (*c.* 100–*c.* 166), the earliest of the North African writers, probably did most of his writing in the traditional way at Rome where he was, among other things, tutor of the young Marcus Aurelius.[1] But Apuleius (*c.* 125–*c.* 190) wrote in Africa,[2] and he was followed by a long succession of African authors: Tertullian (*c.* 160–225), Cyprian (d. 258), Arnobius (*fl.* 300), Lactantius (d. 325?).[3] The last four were Christian publicists. This is not a coincidence. It is likely that it was precisely the rapid expansion of Christianity towards the end of the second century[4] that produced literary discussion in provincial centres that had not known it before. Most of the literature (or at least of that which survives) was Christian apologetic. But it is likely that Apuleius was moved to write his masterpiece, the *Metamorphoses*, by desire to defend the worship of Isis from Christian charges and claims.[5]

The second half of the second century was evidently a period of profound intellectual reorientation. At the same time a superficial observer of Roman society will have noticed little change. Polite literature, in this study represented by the correspondence of Fronto and the *Meditations* of Marcus Aurelius, reflects the conservatism of the society that produced it. Special attention, perhaps hindsight, is needed to discover signs that the classical conventions of balance, self-control, confidence in human values, and separation of sacred and profane, were breaking up. On the other hand, the writings of Apuleius, although still permeated by the literary tradition, reveal something of the ideas that were becoming important.

The correspondence of Cornelius Fronto (*c.* 100–67)[6] takes us into the world of the Second Sophistic at Rome. Fronto was the leading exponent of the archaizing movement and his letters expound, among other things, the stylistic ideals of the archaizers. We find ourselves once again in the world of

---

[1] On Fronto: M. D. Brock (1911); F. Portalupi (1961); P. V. Cova (1970); cf. background of Seneca discussed by M. Griffin (1972).

[2] P. Walsh (1970), 248–51.

[3] J. Fontaine (1968).

[4] W. H. C. Frend (1952); T. Barnes (1971), 60–84.

[5] P. Walsh, op. cit. 188. Fronto too attacked the Christians—viciously: see Minucius Felix, *Oct.* 9. 6; T. Barnes, op. cit. 149 n. 6.

[6] E. Champlin (1974) against G. Bowersock (1969), 124–6. M. P. J. Van den Hout (1954).

senatorial society. We return to the manners and conventions of
Pliny and his friends, modified but in no way revolutionized by
the passage of two generations. The atmosphere is still rational.
Emotion is still kept at a distance. Stoic philosophy still sets the
intellectual background. The atmosphere has become rather
more religious. But then many letters in the collection were
either written to or by Fronto's pupil, the future emperor
Marcus Aurelius, who was a deeply religious man, and the
religious atmosphere is largely created by letters of Marcus
Aurelius himself.

If the correspondence has a more strongly religious tone than
that of Pliny, the religious statements are of the same kind.
Many are exclamations implying that life is governed by gods,
who are not, however, named: 'if the gods allow it, we have some
hope of recovery.'[1] 'I am much relieved by the news of my little
lady telling me that thanks to the gods (*dis iuvantibus*) she is
getting better.'[2] 'A happy New Year . . . to you and our lord
your father and your mother . . . that is my prayer.'[3] 'All the
blessings you have prayed for me are bound up with your
welfare.'[4] 'I purpose—with divine agreement—to take a drive
tomorrow.'[5] 'The lying-in of Faustina is approaching, we must
have confidence in the gods.'[6] 'I have prayed to the gods to
give you many happy returns of the day.'[7]

Such phrases are not very informative. They do not provide
evidence that Marcus Aurelius was attached to the cult of any
particular deity or deities, or indeed that he derives satisfaction
from religious ritual. One letter suggests that the emperor took
an interest in religious antiquities.[8] What is conveyed by the
letters is a strong sense of dependence, the feeling that the health
of one's nearest and dearest is at the mercy of supernatural
beings. Moreover, in this particular context supernatural

---

[1] iv. 11, from M. Aurelius = ed. C. R. Haines, i. 202; cf. ibid. v. 55, M. Aurelius
to Fronto = Haines, i. 252.

[2] *Ad M. Caes.* v. 24 (M. Aurelius to Fronto) = Haines, i. 212.

[3] Ibid. 30 (Fronto to M. Aurelius) = Haines, i. 228. Cf. reply, ibid. 31 =
Haines, i. 230, and the birthday greeting from M. Aurelius to Fronto, ibid. 32 =
Haines, i. 230.

[4] Ibid. 33 (Fronto to M. Aurelius) = Haines, i. 232.

[5] Ibid. 40 (Fronto to M. Aurelius) = Haines, i. 242.

[6] Ibid. 45 (M. Aurelius to Fronto) = Haines, i. 246.

[7] Ibid. 54 (Fronto to M. Aurelius) = Haines, i. 250.

[8] Ibid. iv. 4 = Haines, i. 174, suggests an antiquarian interest in ceremonies.

power is not thought of as an impersonal process, but as the will of personalities who can be influenced by prayer.[1] One letter contains a very artificial prayer to Aesculapius,[2] but usually the gods that look after health are not named.[3] It is not easy to say whether this is literary convention or a reflection of Marcus Aurelius' personal attitude. The religious language of the letters is concentrated in the limited area of health, but since concern about illness can be very disturbing indeed, the belief that gods will answer prayers for the sick is likely to have a strong influence on the whole of a man's outlook.

Marcus Aurelius kept a book of jottings—Brunt calls it a kind of spiritual diary—to record his views on the order of the universe and man's place in it.[4] This book, the famous *Meditations*, allows us to see the letters to Fronto in a much wider context. Many passages in the *Meditations* give a deeply religious impression. God or gods (nameless) are mentioned frequently. Marcus Aurelius is convinced that his life is ruled by the gods, that all advantages and benefits he has received are a gift from them.[5] He asserts, argues, and seems to have more or less convinced himself that divine providence is good and wishes all men well. It enables men to avoid all evils.[6] Of course, he can only maintain this position by holding—like all Stoics—that the conditions which ordinary men consider evils, such as death, dishonour, pain, or poverty, are not evils at all. The only absolute evil is wilful wrong-doing and for this the gods cannot be blamed but only the wrong-doer.[7] Nevertheless Marcus Aurelius gives the impression of having the attitudes of a thoroughly pious man. He accepts whatever the gods have sent. He reveres and praises them. He tries to live with them and he

---

[1] e.g. *De Fer. Als.* 4 = Haines, ii. 18: Illatenus dolueris, mi magister, si me compotem voti di boni faciunt. *Ad Ant. Imp.* i. 1 = Haines, i. 30: 'bonam salutem . . . peto a deis die mihi sollemni natali tuo.' Cf. also ibid. ii. 4 = Haines, ii. 156; *Ad M. Caes.* i. 2 = Haines, i. 82: qui ubique estis di boni valeat oro meus Fronto; ibid. v. 8 = Haines, i. 196; ibid. 16 = Haines, i. 220; ibid. iv. 11 = Haines, i. 202; almost all written by Marcus Aurelius.

[2] Ibid. iii. 9 = Haines, i. 50.

[3] So also in the *Meditations*. K. Latte, *R.R.* 334–5 gives epigraphic evidence that men were less ready to identify the divine with particular deities.

[4] P. Brunt (1974).   [5] *Med.* i. 17. 1.

[6] The only evils recognized as genuine are of course moral evils (e.g. viii. 1) such as insolence, anger, weakness in the face of pleasure or pain. These a man can avoid (viii. 8).

[7] ii. 1.

feels that the rational part of his soul that controls his life is a part of the divine substance.[1]

But the reader of the *Meditations* must always remember that Marcus Aurelius uses the word god and related terms in the specialized sense of the Stoics. God is the first cause[2] of the endless chain of cause and effect[3] which produced and is the universe and all that is in it. But he is not thought of as existing outside the matter of the universe and can be identified with the reason that pervades and co-ordinates the universe. Thus he does not necessarily have any qualities of personality, and the divine gifts and benefits are simply the world as it is, and as it has been shaped by natural causation. The divine element in man's soul is simply his share of the reason that pervades everything.[4] While Marcus Aurelius often describes relations with the gods in the vocabulary of personal relationships,[5] when the gods' fundamental nature is in question they are described impersonally, and the term God (or gods), Nature, the Whole, the Kosmos, fate, or 'What befalls' are used synonymously.[6]

Once again we are reminded that while keeping within orthodox Stoic philosophy, it was possible to describe the world deistically, or materialistically, or in terms of a combination of the two. The relative strength of the two elements depends on the character of the individual Stoic, or even on the situation in which the philosophy was invoked. Marcus Aurelius was not, at least in my opinion, an agnostic[7] but he composed some memorable sentences to affirm that the moral teachings of Stoicism remained valid, no matter what was the truth about the gods.[8]

---

[1] v. 33; vi. 30: reverence and praise for god; v. 27: tries to live with gods.

[2] ii. 12. 4–13; v. 27. 1.   [3] M. Pohlenz (1964), 95.

[4] Ibid. 101; *Med.* ii. 12. 4–13. 1; v. 27.   [5] P. Brunt (1974).

[6] Ibid. 15, nn. 92–4. When Marcus Aurelius thought about a rational explanation of the universe he still found immanent organization more plausible than external power, cf. p. 217 n. 3 below, on J. P. Vernant (1962), 115–29 and (1966) 97–143.

[7] e.g. *Med.* iii. 16: those who do not believe in gods (τῶν θεοὺς μὴ νομιζόντων) are classed with those who fail their country. Marcus was initiated at Eleusis like earlier emperors (Brunt, op. cit. 16 n. 104) but his motive was 'ut se innocentem probaret' (S.H.A. *Marcus*, 27. 1) or to fulfil a vow made at a crisis in war (Philost. *V. Soph.* ii. 1. 2). Marcus sacrificed at home even on *dies nefasti* (Dio, lxxii (lxxi) 34. 2).

[8] *Med.* vi. 44; viii. 17; ii. 11 are memorably agnostic—but for a particular rhetorical purpose.

I would suggest that one factor which moved Marcus Aurelius towards the deistic side of Stoicism was a need for reassurance that there was a purpose in life. Again and again, he reminded himself that all that happened in the world was just, and for the good of the whole.[1] But since goodness and justice are qualities of man, to think of the universe as good and just is close to thinking of it as governed by a just being. One passage expresses Marcus Aurelius' belief in the gods with memorable confidence. 'If any ask: "Where have you seen the gods or how have you satisfied yourself of their existence that you are so pious a man?" I answer, "In the first place they are even visible to the eye. In the next, I have not seen my own soul either, yet I know it. So from continual proof of their power I am assured that gods also exist and I reverence them." '[2] This might, of course, mean no more than that the nature of the world (i.e. 'proof of their power') has assured him that gods exist in the ambiguous way in which they are defined by Stoic philosophy. But the paragraph seems to be written in a direct and straightforward style, and taken like this, it is a statement of belief in the existence of gods as ordinary people think of them.[3]

When Marcus Aurelius described gods as 'visible to the eye' he probably meant the heavenly bodies, which many Stoics, following Plato, held to be gods. But there is evidence that Marcus Aurelius thought that he received communications from the gods. In what seems to be the climax of the first book, Marcus Aurelius thanks the gods 'that I had clear and frequent conceptions (τὸ φαντασθῆναι) as to the true meaning of a life according to Nature, and that as far as the gods were concerned and their influence (διαδόσεσι) and assistance (συλλήψεσι) and intentions (ἐπινοίαις), there was nothing to prevent me from beginning to live in accordance with Nature'. He also refers to 'reminders (ὑπομνήσεις) and almost-instructions (μονονουχὶ διδασκαλίας).'[4] It is not quite clear what form the gods' assistance

---

[1] iv. 10; iii. 2, 11. 2. What seems bad for the part is good for the whole: ii. 3; v. 22; Brunt, op. cit. 15 n. 99.

[2] *Med.* xii. 28.

[3] Stoic view on star gods: Cic. *N.D.* ii. 15 (39). Divine sun: Sen. *Ben.* vi. 31. 3; Cic. *Ac.* ii. 41 (126); Diog. Laert. vii. 139. The reference to the visible gods, i.e. the heavenly bodies, shows that M. Aur. is thinking of individual divine beings not simply of the whole.   [4] i. 17. 5.

and reminders took. It is possible to argue that they amounted to no more than the application of Marcus' own reason to the working of the universe. But the emperor's choice of words suggests that the communication was discontinuous and broken up into separate messages.[1] I would conclude that the emperor believed that from time to time he received communications from the god. He says very little about this in the rest of the *Meditations*[2] but he asserts as if it was a fact that the gods help men through dreams and oracles,[3] and he expresses his gratitude for medical remedies revealed to him in dreams.[4] As we have seen earlier, illness among the family or friends was a situation in which Marcus Aurelius felt very much in the power of the gods.[5] There was, however, another situation in which he thought the gods might help. 'Who told you that the gods do not co-operate with us even in the things that are in our power? Begin with prayers for such things and you will see. A common prayer is: how may I sleep with that woman? You pray: how can I stop lusting to sleep with her. Another prays: how can I get rid of that man? You pray: how can I make myself to put up with him.'[6] It may well be that in such situations the Stoic emperor had found prayer helpful. Certainly such little evidence as there is suggests that he was pious in private life.[7]

We also know that as emperor Marcus Aurelius placed great hopes on religious ritual. A catastrophic visitation of plague induced Marcus to bring about a thorough renewal of religious rites.[8] When the Marcomanni threatened to invade Italy, he performed a great mass of ritual at Rome. This included non-Italian rites performed by local priests specially summoned to Rome for that purpose.[9] He thus revived the policy, followed by the senate to the end of the Hannibalic war but not much afterwards, of calling in divine supporters from abroad to assist the state in a crisis.[10]

---

[1] So also in xii. 28: ἐξ ὧν τῆς δυνάμεως αὐτῶν ἑκάστοτε πειρῶμαι, ἐκ τούτων ὅτι τε εἰσὶ καταλαμβάνω καὶ αἰδοῦμαι

[2] The Romans were traditionally distrustful of all kinds of personal mysticism. Scipio, the conqueror of Hannibal, was the exception that proves the rule.

[3] ix. 27.　　　　　　　[4] i. 17. 8.　　　　　　　[5] See above, p. 206.

[6] ix. 40. See Farquharson's translation and note with a ref. to Pers. ii. 9.

[7] See p. 208 n. 7 above.

[8] S.H.A. *Marcus*, 21.　　　　　　　[9] Ibid. 13.

[10] W. Warde Fowler (1922), 314–34; J. North (1968).

The gods responded to Marcus' piety. In his wars against the Germans he was assisted by two separate miracles. In 172 during the campaign against the Marcomanni a siege engine of the enemy was miraculously destroyed by a thunderbolt, which it was thought had been sent in answer to the emperor's prayers.[1] The incident was officially celebrated on the coins of the year and later by a carved representation on Marcus' Column.

In our two literary sources an account of a rain miracle is combined with the lightning miracle. But the fact that the rain miracle is depicted quite separately on the Marcus Column and the evidence of coins show that this was in fact a separate manifestation.[2] Dio relates that in the course of a battle against the Quadi fought probably in 173,[3] the Roman army was thoroughly demoralized by heat and thirst. It was surrounded by the enemy and there was danger of a general surrender. At that point, the situation was saved—not without divine inter-position as Dio says—by a sudden gathering of cloud followed by rain. One version stated that an Egyptian *magus* named Arnuphis serving in the entourage of the emperor had invoked various gods, especially Mercury of the Air, and thus attracted the rain.[4] When the barbarians attacked the soldiers felt re-freshed and, drinking and fighting at the same time, they won a great victory.[5] Inscriptions on coins of 173 show that Mercury was given credit officially. The fact that on some coins there is represented a temple with Egyptian columns suggests that this Mercury stands for the Graeco-Egyptian Hermes Trismegistus.[6]

The incident was thought extraordinary at the time. Dio seems to have been sceptical, at least as far as the Egyptian *magus*'s role in the miracle was concerned.[7] Moreover, the Christians thought it worthwhile to claim the credit for so remarkable an example of divine intervention.[8] But perhaps the

[1] S.H.A. *Marcus*, 24. 4.
[2] A. R. Birley (1966), 234 and 237; J. Guey (1948), 16.
[3] A. R. Birley (1966), 237, 336–7. [4] Dio, lxxii. 8. 3.
[5] At this point Dio mistakenly inserted the lightning miracle (ibid. 10) as did S.H.A. (*Marcus*, 24. 4).
[6] K. Latte, *R.R.* 330 n. 2; Malaise, *Conditions*, 428–32.
[7] Dio, lxxii. 8. 4 introduces account with λόγος ἔχει.
[8] Xiphilus, who has preserved Dio's account, also includes the Christian version (ibid. 9) which is mentioned in Tert. *Apol.* 5. 6, cf. *ad Scap.* 4 and the (faked) letter of Marcus Aurelius transmitted at end of Justin, *Apol.* i. Credit was also claimed for Julian, part-author of the Chaldaic Oracles (*Suda* s.v. Ἰουλιανός, ed. Adler, 434).

most significant aspect of all is that the Roman state should have officially proclaimed that a miracle had happened on its behalf.

The existence of the *Meditations* is in itself evidence of Marcus Aurelius' unceasing striving for moral self-improvement. He wrote to Fronto: 'When the writings of Stoic philosophers show me how far short my character comes of this better way time and again your pupil blushes and is angry with himself . . . Therefore I do penance (poenas do) am angry with myself, am sad, compare myself with others, do without food . . .'[1] But man cannot live the good life according to nature unless he has the right 'beliefs' (δόγματα) 'on the nature of good and evil, showing that nothing is for a man's good save what makes him just, temperate, brave and free,'[2] and from the nature of a man's beliefs in this area it will be possible to predict his behaviour.[3]

Like all Romans of his class Marcus admired the ability to face death fearlessly. 'How admirable is the soul which is ready and resolved, if it must be this moment released from the body, to be either extinguished or scattered or to persist. This resolve, too, must arise from a personal and deliberate decision; not out of sheer opposition [like the Christians] but after reflection and with dignity and in such a way as to persuade even an outsider without theatrical display.'[4]

Whether the explicit reference to the Christians is a gloss or not, the fact remains that Marcus Aurelius and men of similar outlook could not admire the behaviour of Christian martyrs. To the outsider Christians appeared to provoke their own execution by publicly defying the order of a Roman magistrate to sacrifice for the good of the community. That men should court death like this would seem not so much courage as dangerous folly. Marcus admired a heroic death but it should be the result of a personal decision and not of mass hysteria or group fanaticism.[5] Willingness to face death should be justifiable by rational arguments which would appeal to an ordinary rational man. The Christian argument that God forbids the

---

[1] Fronto *Ad M. Caes.* iv. 13 = Haines, i. 216.
[2] *Med.* viii. 1–2.
[3] viii. 14: Whatever man you meet say to yourself at once 'what are the principles this man entertains about human goods and ills'.
[4] xi. 3. P. Brunt believes that the explicit reference to the Christians is a gloss.
[5] Cf. Livy on the mass suicide at Astapa (xxviii. 22. 5–11) and Abydos (xxxi. 17), and F. Walbank in *J.R.S.* lv (1965), 11.

worship of any other deity did not have this appeal.[1] The Roman gods were not jealous in this way. Moreover, to a man like Marcus Aurelius who had little hope of personal immortality, the martyrs' certainty of heavenly reward would appear completely baseless. So to him their behaviour appeared irrational, deluded, and in no way admirable.

But the weakness of Marcus' attitude are apparent too. Paganism can offer no reward after death for virtue in this life. Individualism can only resist a collective movement as long as the movement has not too many members. The theatrical elements in martyrdom might prove sufficiently impressive to establish the validity in public opinion of the beliefs which were previously thought crankish.

Marcus Aurelius' Stoicism had behind it a very long history in the Graeco-Roman world since Hellenistic times. The principal ideas were expressed and upheld by generation after generation of outstanding men. From the Roman world it is only necessary to mention Cicero, Seneca, Epictetus, and Musonius. But the Stoicism of none of his predecessors seems as joyless, austere, and arduous as that of Marcus Aurelius. It had been one of the principal contributions of Stoicism that it enabled men to keep their self-respect by making them independent of socially-held values. A Stoic would not be upset by being poor, or a failure, as long as he was conscious of having pursued virtue, of having lived his life 'according to nature'.

In the case of Marcus the process of debunking collective values has cut him off from almost all ordinary satisfaction. First of all, like many predecessors, though more finally than they, he destroys the power of deriving pleasure from the senses. 'How useful when roasted meats and other foods are before you to see them in your mind as here the dead body of a fish, there the dead body of a bird or pig. Or again to think of Falernian wine as the juice of a cluster of grapes, of a purple robe as sheep's wool dyed with the blood of a shellfish and of sexual intercourse as internal rubbing accompanied by spasmodic ejection of mucus . . . you must do this throughout life; when things appear too enticing, strip them naked, destroy the myth which makes them proud.'[2]

---

[1] Accounts of trials: H. Musurillo (1972).
[2] *Med.* vi. 13. On this see T. W. Africa (1965), 201 whose translation is quoted.

Marcus Aurelius appears frequently to have despaired of the significance of all human activity. 'Consider, for the sake of argument, the times of Vespasian; you will see all the same things: men marrying, begetting children, being ill, dying, fighting wars, feasting, trading, farming, flattering, asserting themselves, suspecting, praying for the death of others, grumbling at their present lot . . . coveting a consulate, coveting a kingdom. Then turn to the times of Trajan; again everything is the same; and that life too is dead . . .'[1] Man must help other men, but there is little satisfaction in it since all human activities and creations are so insignificant *sub specie aeternitatis* and man is so insignificant himself. Marcus can compare life to dirty bathwater: oil, sweat, and scum.[2]

Earlier Roman Stoics could derive satisfaction from the achievements of the Roman statesmen of the republic or the heroism of the fighters for freedom or from the greatness of the Roman state. The *exempla* of the past and the grandeur of Rome provided an incentive for effort, perhaps not Stoic but nevertheless human. Seen in the perspective of Marcus Aurelius, the fame of great men lasts only marginally longer than that of little men, while the Roman empire is just one of a succession of kingdoms that rises, falls, and is forgotten. 'The very names of the celebrated heroes of olden times are now, as it were, obsolete.[3] Camillus, Caeso, Volesus, Dentatus and a little later Scipio and Cato, then also Augustus, and then Hadrianus and Antoninus. For all things quickly fade away and become legendary, and soon absolute oblivion encases them.'

If Marcus Aurelius was in any sense typical of the Roman senatorial class of his time it would seem that Stoicism had come near the end of its usefulness to the Roman nobility.

It is difficult to decide how far Marcus Aurelius was a characteristic representative of the senatorial class of his time. But he seems to have been typical in the concern he showed for his health.[4] In the correspondence between Marcus Aurelius and Fronto there passed a quantity of information about the writers' health which is without parallel in earlier Latin letter

[1] iv. 32.
[2] viii. 24.
[3] iv. 32. γλωσσήματα: words fallen out of use. Cf. Quint. i. 8. 15 and Farquharson (1944) on the passage.
[4] J. Beaujeu (1964), 54–75.

collections. It looks as if a new genre of literary letter has come into existence.[1] Many contemporaries appear to have shared the interest in illness. This was the age of the famous doctor Galen who had a higher social position than any doctor had previously enjoyed at Rome. Men of the highest society attended his lectures on anatomy. At the same time in the Greek East the sanctuary of Aesculapius at Pergamum was flourishing and attracting huge numbers of patients.[2] Aristides, one of the stars of the Second Sophistic, wrote a kind of autobiography to record the way his life was directed by the medical advice of Aesculapius.[3] Many Romans travelled to Pergamum to submit to remedies which the god suggested to his worshippers in dreams while they were sleeping in his sanctuary.[4] There were prominent Romans also among the men who fell victim to the false prophet Alexander of Abonuteichus and the oracle of his invented snake god.[5]

Interest in illness and its cure was linked with interest in philosophy and religion. Scientific healing was based on general theories of the nature of man provided by philosophers, and the most highly qualified doctors had studied philosophy before they began their specialist medical studies. For the general public, medicine threw a light on philosophy, and vice versa. In addition, the valetudinarianism of a man like Aristides included a desire for the religious experience which could be obtained through a course of temple healing. A visit to Pergamum was an alternative to initiation of the kind undergone by Lucius in Apuleius' *Golden Ass*.[6] No doubt many underwent both kinds of experience. But one suspects that initiates of mystery religion were still rather few in the senatorial aristocracy.[7] It is not an accident that the great family which dominated a society devoted to the mysteries of Bacchus in Campania was of Greek origin, and that the great majority of the members were

---

[1] The letters were assembled in Book v of the 'Letters to Marcus Caesar', presumably to be show-pieces of their kind. See G. Bowersock (1969), 73 n. 1.

[2] See ibid. 55–75.

[3] On Asclepius see E. J. and L. Edelstein (1943–5). On Aristides' *Sacred speeches*, C. A. Behr (1968).

[4] J. Beaujeu, op. cit. 60 ff.

[5] Lucian, *Alexander, The False Prophet*.

[6] See below, pp. 220 ff.

[7] Malaise, *Conditions*, 77–9 on senatorial membership of Egyptian cults.

Greeks from Greece or Asia Minor.[1] Imperial patronage of the cult of Egyptian gods was continuous only in the first half of the third century.[2] It may well be that initiation became common in the most exclusive circles only when it was dying out in the lower classes.[3]

We are given literary insight into the motives which led men to initiation in the writings of Apuleius. Socially he was of course much closer to authors of senatorial society than to the mass of, for instance, Isis worshippers.[4] He was a very rich man and no doubt among the leaders of society in proconsular Africa.[5] He had received a very thorough Latin literary education,[6] and he almost certainly spent some time in Rome itself, perhaps as a barrister.[7] But his outlook was evidently much less traditional than that of his Roman senatorial contemporaries—at least as far as this is mirrored in literature. Various explanations can be suggested. Apuleius certainly had a very original mind: his prose style provides vivid evidence of this.[8] Then he had received a very thorough Greek education in Greece itself.[9] As a result he was not a follower of Stoicism but of Neoplatonism, the philosophy which was to dominate philosophic thought in the coming centuries.[10] Finally, he was

[1] A. Vogliano and F. Cumont (1933); A. Bruhl (1953); J. Beaujeu, op. cit. 63 ff.

[2] Malaise, *Conditions*, 437 ff. There is a parallel between the new dynasty of Septimius Severus and of the Flavians earlier (cf. above, pp. 180–2). One must always distinguish worship of Egyptian gods for public reasons, e.g. victory, or the corn supply, or the discovery of a conspiracy from worship for personal reasons.

[3] Malaise, *Conditions*, 451 ff.; cf. the cult of Cybele which at Rome was a public cult introduced to gain the goddess's support for the hard-pressed community (Latte, *R.R.* 258). The earliest evidence for initiation by means of the *taurobolium* is of A.D. 295 (*C.I.L.* vi. 505). See J. F. Matthews (1973), 178–9; J. Rutter (1968).

[4] On social background of worshippers of Egyptian gods see Malaise, *Conditions*, 71 ff.; 43 per cent. have Greek names. They include a high proportion of freedmen or even slaves (ibid. 75 ff.). They were found among municipal magistrates especially in Campania (ibid. 81 ff.) and in very much smaller numbers in the equestrian order (ibid. 79) and there were fewer still in the senatorial class or the army. The typical Isis worshipper was a townsman of modest wealth—by inference a craftsman or shopkeeper, ibid. 101 ff.

[5] This follows from the fact that he was provincial high priest (*Florida*, 16. 38). (This is surely the priesthood which could be described as the highest honour of Carthage.)

[6] M. Bernhard (1927), 364.

[7] P. G. Walsh (1970), 249 and M. Hicter (1944), 15 ff.; (1945), 61 ff.

[8] M. Bernhard (1927).

[9] *Florida*, 18. 5; *Apol.* 23. 2.

[10] Neoplatonism: T. Whittaker (1928); R. T. Wallis (1972); F. Regen (1971).

neither by birth nor by settlement a Roman of the city of Rome.
The greater part of his adult life was spent in North Africa. As
a great landowner his life was very different from the freedmen, shopkeepers, and craftsmen who made up the bulk of the
followers of Isis in Italy.[1] But he shared two characteristics
with them. He experienced the rootlessness of not living in his
native community of Madaura, and for much of his life lacked
the moral support of living in the community in which he had
grown up.[2] Secondly, his philosophy was concerned with deity
as a source of power,[3] and with establishing a relationship
between it and the individual by many means including
magical ones.[4] Platonist philosophy might be said to provide
a mystery religion for use by an individual, as opposed to a
community. The outcome of all this is that Apuleius' writings
provide a good deal of insight into the background of the
religious transformation which was coming over the Empire.

Apuleius' *Apology*[5] is the first-surviving literary work in Latin
to reflect the atmosphere of life in a provincial town. Apuleius
delivered this speech in his own defence when he was on trial
for magic at Sabrata in 158–9. It is incidentally the only
complete Latin court speech to have completely survived from
antiquity apart from the speeches of Cicero. In the course of his
defence, Apuleius gives a vivid description of the social context
in which the charges originated. We are in the society of the
small town of Oea (Tripoli) and its large rural territory. It is a
religious society. Men are expected from time to time to enter
a temple for prayer.[6] Estates have sacred places, shrines, dedicated groves, sacred stones.[7] On passing a holy place one moves
one's hands to the lips in a gesture of prayer. First fruits are
offered to the gods of agriculture.[8] Apuleius carries an image of

---

[1] See p. 216 n. 4 above.

[2] This is a major theme of the *Metamorphoses*, cf. below, p. 220.

[3] One might say that while Stoicism had been concerned predominantly with
the immanent order and regularity of the universe, the Neoplatonists were in the
first place concerned with a source of creative power behind the universe. For the
distinction (first suggested by J.-P. Vernant), see S. C. Humphreys, *Daedalus* (1975),
91–2.

[4] *Apol.* 26: 'Magic is a science acceptable to the gods, well versed in the cult and
respect to be rendered to them, pious and knowledgeable in things divine.' Good
magic which brings men close to the divine is distinguished from bad magic which
uses spells for manipulative purposes (ibid. 27. 5 ff.).

[5] Cf. A. Abt (1908) and P. Brown (1972), 119–46, on sorcery.

[6] *Ap.* 56. 4.   [7] 56. 6.   [8] 56. 5.

a god with him to which he makes offerings.[1] The image happens to be of Mercury because the sculptor made it that way[2] but in fact it represents the first cause, God.[3] Apuleius has been frequently initiated into mystery cults.[4] Many of his fellow citizens are initiates of Bacchus.[5]

The world is full of ominous events. A woman whose husband has died is a woman of ill omen.[6] Fertile fields and growing corn are an auspicious background for a wedding.[7] Applause after a lecture is taken to be a good omen in the case where the visiting lecturer should choose to get married in that place.[8]

There is universal belief in the possibility of magic. Men are afraid of spells, and in this connection the uneducated are especially suspicious of philosophers—not surprisingly if we bear in mind the stories which Philostratus wrote about the amazing powers of his philosophical hero Apollonius of Tyana. Philosophers in general and Apuleius in particular are agreed that magic is possible,[9] and propose 'scientific' theories to explain it.[10] According to Apuleius magic is carried out with the aid of demons intermediate between God and men. Apuleius also allows the possibility of divination through a medium in a trance state, the divine soul being temporarily dissociated from the body.[11]

Magic and medicine are widely separated in estimation but not in technique or materials. Apuleius was a student of fish, examining different specimens and even dissecting them.[12] Enemies claimed that his interest was magical[13]—he, that it was philosophical and medical.[14] Magic aroused violent emotions. The mere fact that Apuleius recited the names of famous writers on magic was enough to create an uproar in court.[15] The hostility to magic did not operate indiscriminately but in an easily definable social context. The accusation brought against Apuleius arose in circumstances in which such charges

---

[1] 63. 4. [2] 61. [3] 64.
[4] 55. 8; 56. 7 (in Greece). [5] 55. 8 (Liber in Africa).
[6] 92. 8. [7] 88. 4. [8] 73. 3.
[9] 25 ff.; 42 ff. [10] 43.
[11] 43. 3; E. R. Dodds (1973), 156–210: 'Supernormal phenomena in Classical Antiquity', esp. 199 ff.
[12] 41. 1.
[13] 33. 4.
[14] 27. 6; 40. 1 ff.
[15] 91. 1, and the accusation of magic aroused popular feeling against Apuleius, 82.

have been brought, indeed are occasionally still brought, in many societies widely separated by place and time.

The heart of the matter was tension in the family. Apuleius had married a rich widow. The brother of her deceased husband and the father-in-law of the elder son of her first marriage feared that Apuleius would get the widow's property.[1] So when the elder son died, Apuleius faced a formal accusation of having used criminal magic to entice the widow into marriage.[2] At the same time he had to reply to insinuations that he had caused the death of his stepson.[3]

The indignation of the accusers would have been increased and given wider sympathy by the previous behaviour of Apuleius and his wife. The woman had long been contracted to marry a brother of her deceased husband.[4] Her marriage to Apuleius broke the contract. Moreover, the marriage feast had been held in the country and not, as was expected, in the city.[5] The change of venue saved heavy expenditure in gifts to the general public who would have called to offer their congratulations in the city.[6] No doubt the stinginess was resented. Many would have looked forward to the wedding largesse at the great house as a right. Finally, the deceased stepson had insulted his widow and her relatives by bequeathing her nothing but dress material, and that of a kind worn by prostitutes.[7] One might add that Apuleius belonged to a leading family. He was not only rich but highly educated and widely travelled. He felt, and no doubt from time to time showed, contempt for more rustic members of the landowning class of his town.[8] A good deal of social jealousy would have operated. In these circumstances what would seem to be extremely weak evidence (of course we have only Apuleius' account) could be taken seriously. Possession of a mirror,[9] purchase of particular kinds of fish,[10] an order for a pocket statue of a god,[11] ostensibly harmless references to boys[12] or to toothpowder[13] in Apuleius' poetry, were made the basis of a capital charge before the proconsul of Africa. In the

---

[1] 90 ff. Property is at the root of the affair. Apuleius' defence is that he received only a small dowry, and in no way diverted his wife's property from his stepsons—quite the contrary (99 ff.).

[2] 27. 7; 41. 5.   [3] 1. 5; 2. 1.   [4] 68. 5.
[5] 87. 9 ff.   [6] 87. 10.   [7] 97. 5.
[8] 16. 10–11; 98. 2.   [9] 13. 5.   [10] 31.
[11] 61.   [12] 9–12.   [13] 6. 5.

event Apuleius was acquitted.[1] But the unwritten custom of the little town of Oea had been asserted.

As informative as Apuleius' *Apology* are his *Metamorphoses*. As the former enables us to place in a social context much evidence about the progress of magic, so the latter gives us a unique worshipper's point of view of conversion to one of the mystery cults, in this case, the cult of Isis.[2]

Unlike Apuleius in the *Apology*, Lucius in the *Metamorphoses* is not in his homeland. In fact it is precisely his absence from home in search of experience that has got him into trouble.[3] Eager for experience of magic and of sex[4] he finds both, and is changed into an ass. It is from this transformation that Isis saves him, and he finds in the worship of Isis the ability to deal with the desires that have ruined him. Thus one can see the starting points of his conversion: the loneliness of life without the support of family or local society, intellectual restlessness, and the feeling that he was being dominated by his sexual urges. It may even be that we are intended to see the intellectual and sexual restlessness as the factors which prevent men from staying quietly at home.

The goddess appears to Lucius and her other worshippers in dreams. She appears frequently and even guides the progress of Lucius' initiation by co-ordinated dreams sent to Lucius and to the priest in charge of his case.[5] Worship of the goddess produced great happiness.[6] Contemplation of her statue became the greatest pleasure in life.

Isis is the supreme goddess of the world, the sole sovereign of mankind, the queen of heaven. Worship of all the other goddesses of the pagan pantheon is in reality directed to her as the names of the other goddesses are really her names. But the cult and name of Isis are the ones which are truly her own.[7]

The worship of Isis is of course strongly institutionalized. She has a temple with a hierarchy of priests, impressive processions and symbols. Visually the cult stresses its Egyptian origin. It obviously does not belong to the everyday Greek or Roman

---

[1] The plausible conjecture of A. Abt (1908), 88.
[2] P. G. Walsh (1970), 176 ff.
[3] Ibid. 177 on *Met.* xi. 15.
[4] ii. 6. 1; iii. 19. 4; cf. the warnings, i. 7. 8; 8. 1.
[5] xi. 19. 2; 24. 4; 29. 1. 3. She guides Lucius step by step.
[6] xi. 19. 1; 24. 5.   [7] xi. 2–3; 5.

world.[1] The institution is entered by a process of initiation. At the heart of this was some kind of dramatic performance, in the course of which the initiate was shown the universe and the realms of the gods of the underworld and of the upper world.[2] It is likely that for this purpose the initiate was in some way identified with the sun, and allowed to see what the sun sees in the course of its voyage above and below the earth.

The visit to the underworld was a kind of death, and initiation a kind of rebirth. As such one would expect life after death to be a consequence of initiation. Up to a point, it is. Lucius will be a worshipper of Isis for life and after death also.[3] But life after death[4] is given much less emphasis than it is in Christianity. In fact the hope of eternal life is not offered explicitly. The immediate effect of initiation is a restructuring of this life. The goddess will look after the initiate's professional interests.[5] She prolongs his life.[6] In any case, she will free him from the tyranny of Fortune.[7] It is difficult for us to feel the full significance of this. Perhaps it helps to envisage the depressing effect of the view that everything that happens in the world is predestined, and that no human effort can make any difference to this and that while no divine grace will grant alleviation, there is a possibility that fate might be deflected by hostile magic. If Isis was able to liberate men from this constraint she restored purpose to human effort.

Isis required purity from her worshippers.[8] Before initiation Lucius had to be ritually washed and to go ten days without meat or wine.[9] It was a repeated complaint of Latin poets that their girl friends stayed away before festivals of Isis.[10] Initiates

---

[1] Malaise, *Conditions*, 217 ff.; *Met.* xi. 8–12.

[2] xi. 24. 7; cf. R. E. Witt (1971), 158–64.

[3] xi. 6: in ipso subterraneo semirotundo me quam vides Acherontis tenebris interlucentem . . . campos Elysios incolens ipse . . . adorabis.

[4] Physical death and life after it receives less attention because initiation is described as a death and in a sense life after death starts with that. See A. D. Nock (1932), 344–57; (1972), 296–305, on mystery religions and the after-life.

[5] xi. 20. 4; 28. 6; 30. 3.

[6] ii. 6. 7; this may only mean the metaphorical prolongation of life at initiation described in 21. 7.

[7] xi. 15. 2–5: . . . pristinis aerumnis absolutus Isidis magnae providentia gaudens Lucius de sua Fortuna triumphat. Nam cum coeperis deae servire tunc . . . senties fructum tuae libertatis.

[8] 19. 3; 6. 7.   [9] 23. 1–2.

[10] Ovid, *Amor.* ii. 13. 7–18; iii. 9. 33; Tibullus, i. 3. 23–34; Prop. ii. 33. 2.

shaved their hair[1] and wore special clothes.[2] These regulations could be dismissed as requirements of an exclusively ritual purity, but this interpretation does not do justice to the spirit of Apuleius' fable. Isis is a moral goddess. She has pity on Lucius because of his original innocence,[3] and her help means not only that he is saved from an unpleasant physical predicament, but that he is freed from the moral failings of which that predicament was the punishment.

Isis worship as illustrated by Apuleius has many features in common with Christianity. Her worship involved the whole personality. It offered hope of a new start in life. The religion of Isis set standards of ritual but also of moral purity. The priest acted to some extent as a moral director.[4] Isis worship was outside the public worship of the city. It was a religion which was chosen and not acquired by birth. The nucleus of her communities was provided by immigrants from the Greek East.[5] The foreignness was in no way hidden but turned to advantage, as an advertisement of exotic but very ancient wisdom.

But there were significant differences. A man became a worshipper of Isis for life, but Isis worship was not exclusive. Men joined a fellowship of Isis worshippers to satisfy their individual religious needs. Worship of the goddess would then dominate their lives in a way which traditional Roman worship never had done. But there is no reason to suppose that Isis dispensed her worshippers from existing obligations to the gods of their home or of the community. Above all, Isis worshippers formed private religious organizations. They in no way sought to supersede the ancient cults carried out by the community for the community. Isis and Jupiter could coexist indefinitely. It would also seem that, apart from ritual, the procedure of communities of Isis was less governed by fixed rules of precedent and custom than were Christian communities. Decisions as to who were to be initiated were left to the goddess, and her instructions sent through dreams.[6] Evidently the process of formal organization, as opposed to dependence on *ad hoc*

---

[1] *Met.* xi. 30. 5.

[2] During initiation, xi. 24. 1–4 and after.

[3] xi. 6. 7; 16. 9.

[4] Is it an accident that Lucius visited his home town after initiation (xi. 26. 1)?

[5] See above, p. 216 n. 4.

[6] xi. 21. 4; 22. 5; 27. 8.

inspiration, had gone much less far than in Christian communities. There is also little evidence of formal arrangements between Isiac communities of different towns. Inscriptions suggest that Isis worshippers thought of themselves as belonging to a particular community and a particular temple.[1] When Lucius left Corinth he made a formal leave-taking from the goddess of Isis there. On arriving at Rome he was accepted as an Isis worshipper on the ground of his initiation at Corinth,[2] but he did in fact undergo two further initiations at Rome. The garment with which he had been invested after initiation at Corinth remained at Corinth, and in any case it would not have been valid at Rome.[3] Lucius did not expect the second and the third initiations. Evidently there was no formal rule as to what was done when an Isis worshipper moved from one community to another. Again there clearly was nothing like the sense of belonging to a single Church which united scattered Christian communities.

2. *Collapse and transformation in the third century*

The reign of Marcus Aurelius was the last of the 'golden age' of the Roman empire. After his death men became aware that the circumstances of the empire were changing and, as they thought, for the worse.[4] There was no sudden calamity. First there was the reign of Marcus Aurelius' son Commodus (A.D. 180–92), whom one might compare with Nero in that he was by character unsuited to be emperor.[5] After the assassination of Commodus, as after the suicide of Nero, there was a succession of short-lived rulers and a strong emperor emerged only after civil war. This was Septimius Severus (A.D. 193–211) who reorganized the empire and established a new dynasty.[6] In this he might be compared with Vespasian. But the stresses in the structure of society had become greater since 69. The innovations instituted (or only accepted and confirmed) by Severus were more far-reaching and his treatment of senatorial opponents

---

[1] Malaise, *Conditions*, 147; *Met.* xi. 29.
[2] xi. 26. 3.   [3] xi. 29.
[4] G. Alföldy (1974).   [5] A. R. Birley (1969).
[6] A. R. Birley (1971) soberly corrects M. Rostovtzeff (1926) who, in a stimulating way, exaggerated the element of revolutionary military despotism in the reign of Septimius Severus.

very much more ruthless.[1] The remaining emperors of the Severan dynasty, Caracalla (A.D. 211–17), Elagabalus (A.D. 218–22), and Alexander Severus (A.D. 222–35) all died by assassination after short reigns. Meanwhile the empire continued to prosper. But the murder of Alexander Severus in A.D. 235 ended the dynasty and deprived the empire of the great stabilizing factor of dynastic loyalty, with the result that, as in A.D. 69 and in A.D. 192, various armies felt free to proclaim their own commander emperor. The empire now entered a dark age which lasted about fifty years.

The history up to A.D. 229 was written by a contemporary, Cassius Dio (A.D. 163 to beyond 229), who described his own times, to conclude a vast history of Rome from its foundation.[2] Dio was a senator, an adviser of several emperors, and twice consul. He stands at the end of a long line of senatorial historians of Rome. But Dio was a Greek. He came from an old and wealthy family of Nicaea. It is likely that he was a descendant of Cassius Asclepiodotus whose property had been confiscated by Nero on account of his friendship with Barea Soranus, a famous member of the Stoic opposition group and a victim of that emperor. Dio's family, education, and culture were Greek, but politically he felt a Roman. 'His identification with Rome is complete and unquestioned, and just as hostility is unthought of, so praise is superfluous.'[3]

As a senatorial historian, Dio had many Latin predecessors. But he had no contemporaries.[4] It was a mark of the disastrous narrowing that had befallen Latin literary civilization that the last senatorial historian was a Greek, writing in Greek, just as Marcus Aurelius, the last Roman Stoic, used Greek to record his philosophical thoughts.

In the Greek world the tradition of Herodotus and—particularly relevant in Dio's case—of Thucydides was still alive. There were numerous histories of events in the eastern provinces,[5] while Appian had not long ago applied the tradition to Roman

---

[1] G. Alföldy (1968).   [2] F. Millar (1964).   [3] Ibid. 190.
[4] There were no Latin writers of continuous histories. Septimius Severus wrote an autobiography and there was Marius Maixmus, the writer of imperial biographies and—perhaps—his double, R. Syme's 'Ignotus'. See R. Syme (1971); Alan Cameron (1971). T. Barnes (1970) shows that the so-called *Kaisergeschichte* was written in the fourth century.
[5] F. Millar (1969).

history by writing an extensive narrative of the wars of the republic. It may be true to say that by studying Roman history and identifying with it, Greek senators or equestrian officials assimilated themselves to the imperial people whose citizenship they had received, and whose administrative duties they had begun to share. Allowing for the fact that these Greeks retained their own literary civilization, one might compare them with the earlier historians of Italian origin, men like Livy or Velleius, who wrote Roman history under Augustus and Tiberius.

Dio has made a real effort to understand the constitutional and institutional background of Roman history. This is particularly evident in his account of the reign of Augustus.[1] The establishment of the principate, the settlement of 27 B.C., and its successive modifications are systematically recorded. Like earlier senatorial historians, Dio is concerned to show that Augustus established a monarchy, and that the restoration of the republic was a pretence. Nevertheless he evidently took the constitutional arrangements laid down under Augustus seriously, considering that they provided the rules by which the Roman empire had been governed ever since.[2]

Dio was not happy about the condition of the empire. He thought that since the death of Marcus Aurelius it had passed from a golden age to one of iron and rust.[3] His account shows that Septimius Severus had undoubtedly been a highly effective emperor, but also that he was very much more ruthless than Marcus and his 'good' predecessor. Moreover, the three most recent emperors, Caracalla, Elagabalus, and Alexander Severus, had all in their different ways been unsatisfactory.

Dio's narrative reveals a more disturbing, because more fundamental, development. This was in the position of the army. The fact that the empire was in the gift of the army had again been demonstrated in A.D. 192, and after that people were not allowed to forget it. The army could never again be taken for granted as it had been for long periods in the recent past. Dio did not like this. His feelings are like those which many have about the progress of trade union power today. The new atmosphere is summed up in Septimius Severus' dying advice to his sons: 'Remain united, enrich the soldiers and despise all others.'[1] One disturbing consequence was the upsetting of social rank. Men who had risen through the army would reach for the highest positions, even the empire itself, in a way which had been unthinkable earlier.[2] Dio was also worried about military discipline,[3] and had reason to be. As provincial governor, he had tried to discipline the troops in Pannonia, and incurred their enduring resentment. The Praetorian Guard displayed solidarity with the Pannonian troops and put pressure on the emperor, with the result that Dio was not allowed to reside in Rome during his second consulate.[4] Toward the end of his life there took place the revival of the Persian empire which was to be a threat to the eastern provinces for centuries to come. Dio thought it dangerous only because of the indiscipline of the army.[5]

Dio was critical of the condition of the empire. But he has not built his criticism into the structure of his narrative. Instead he has adopted the Thucydidean technique of using speeches as a vehicle for general reflections.

The account of the settlement of 27 B.C. is preceded by a discussion between Agrippa and Maecenas about the best way of governing the empire. Maecenas suggests numerous reforms, reforms relevant not to the age of Augustus but to that of Dio. The list is comprehensive: the place of the senate in the empire, the government of cities, the recruitment of the army, the employment of *equites*, the administration of Italy, the role of the emperor's council.[6] Dio had thought about these matters. But this thought scarcely shows in the history which is a purely factual year-by-year account of the events of each reign.

As regards religious developments, Dio shows the same reticence as earlier writers of senatorial literature. If the apostasy from ancestral gods to Christianity disturbed him, the surviving parts of his history show few signs of it. Dio lets Maecenas advocate the prosecution of religious innovators, and of practitioners of black magic and divination—also of philosophers.[7] It is likely that he had the Christians in mind when he

---

[1] Dio, lxxvii (lxxvi), 15. 2.
[2] lxxix (lxxviii), 41. 1–4; lxxx (lxxix), 7. 2.
[3] lxxix (lxxviii), 1. 3; 3. 4.
[4] lxxx. 5.   [5] lxxx. 4.
[6] Maecenas' speech: Dio, lii. 14–40.   [7] lii. 36.

warned of religious innovators, but of course regulations of this kind had been known at Rome for a long time.

With very few exceptions, such as the Roman failure to capture Hatra,[1] and the rain miracle of Marcus Aurelius,[2] Dio's account is entirely, and traditionally, secular. The new religiosity appears only marginally in the history. Prodigies had always figured in Roman historiography and even educated men had by and large never ceased to believe in their validity. But the reader of Dio receives the impression that the senators, and even the emperors, of Dio's own time were more sensitive to signs, and likely to recognize them far more frequently than their predecessors had been. Supernatural messages have become more commonplace. This is illustrated a number of times in what Dio says about his own life.

Dio's first book was a pamphlet on dreams and portents that foretold the accession of the emperor Septimius Severus.[3] This was only diplomatic. The emperor thanked him and in the following night Dio dreamt that the divine spirit of Fortune (τὸ δαιμόνιον) ordered him to write a history of the civil wars of Severus. This too won imperial approval and Dio decided to expand it into a full-scale history of the Romans. This was an enormous task. It took him twenty-two years to reach A.D. 192. He received encouragement from the goddess Fortune who repeatedly appeared to him in dreams. Some time after the death of Septimius Severus he dreamt that the late emperor was ordering him to write also the history of Septimius' son and successor, Caracalla.[4] No doubt the dreams told Dio what he wished to do in any case. Earlier in life he had been puzzled by a drawing which represented a response sent by the oracle of Amphilochus at Mallus in Cilicia: a boy was shown strangling two serpents, and a lion pursuing a fawn. Later he learnt that the man to whom the oracle had been addressed, together with his brother, had been strangled on the orders of the emperor Commodus. He concluded that this was what the oracle had meant. One supposes that if the man had performed heroic deeds, he would have been identified with the boy (Hercules) rather than the snakes, and the oracle would have been equally

---

[1] Dio, lxviii. 31.   [2] See above, pp. 211–12.
[3] Dio, lxxiii (lxxii), 23. 1.
[4] lxxix (lxxviii), 10. 1–2.

well fulfilled.[1] Dio tested the prophetic power of the river Aoüs
at Apollonia in Illyria. To consult the oracle one uttered a
prayer and then threw incense into the water. If the river
accepted it the prayer was granted. The river might not be
questioned about death or marriage—presumably to prevent
politically motivated inquiries. Dio found that the claims made
for the oracle were valid.[2]

Dio relates several incidents witnessed by himself which
illustrate how men of all classes were ready to recognize a
divine message. When the emperor Commodus was going to
fight in the arena as a gladiator he ordered the senate to attend
in cavalry gear and woollen cloaks. The senators recalled that
this was the dress worn at imperial funerals. After the performance the emperor's helmet was taken out of the arena by
the gates through which the dead were normally removed.
Every one of the senators, Dio assures us, was convinced that
this was an omen foreshadowing the early death of Commodus.[3]

The usurper Didius Julianus, who was hated and feared by
senators generally, and by Dio in particular, was sacrificing
outside the senate-house in the presence of the senate and of a
military escort. Suddenly three stars came into view around the
sun. The soldiers, pointing them out to each other, remarked
that they portended disaster for the emperor. The senators also
saw the stars, and while they dared not keep their eyes on them,
hoped and prayed that they might indeed be an *evil* omen.
Events proved that they were.[4]

Septimius Severus had prophetic dreams at various stages
of his career. As emperor he published the predictions of his
rise to power.[5] Severus' victory over his rival Niger was assisted
by signs which encouraged his own side and discouraged the
opposition. The most important was a storm, accompanied by
thunder and lightning, which blew directly into the faces of
Niger's men during the decisive battle. As a result both sides
felt that the gods favoured Severus, and Niger's army was
demoralized.[6] Earlier a Pannonian priest of Jupiter had raised
the morale of Severus' supporters when he dreamt that a black

---

[1] Dio, lxxiii (lxxii), 7. 1–2. [2] xli. 45.
[3] lxxiii (lxxii), 21. Cf. lxxiv. 4. [4] lxxiv (lxxiii), 14. 4.
[5] lxxv (lxxiv), 3. Cf. above, p. 180 on similar behaviour of Vespasian.
[6] lxxv (lxxiv), 7. 7.

man (niger) entered and was killed in Severus' camp.[1] At the beginning of the civil war between Severus and Albinus the people watching the horse-races at Rome suddenly and, as it seemed, spontaneously burst into prayers for the state. The senators present, Dio among them, took this for a divine sign of some kind or other and worried what the meaning might be. Their apprehensions were increased by a fire in the northern sky and a fine rain of silver. Dio records that he used the silver to plate some coins which retained their plating for three days.[2]

A dream touching on the succession to the empire was taken extremely seriously. In 205 a senator was accused of treason in his absence. It was said that his old nurse had dreamt that he would be emperor, and that this had induced him to use magic. The matter was investigated, and it transpired that a second senator, a bald man, had been present while the nurse was telling her dream. This discovery meant that bald senators were in grave danger, and when the report was read in the senate it produced general alarm. All heads turned towards hairless senators murmuring: 'Is it so and so?' Dio involuntarily felt his head to make sure his hair was still there! An individual was identified as the bald senator in question and immediately executed.[3]

The value of Dio's *History* as a source for the study of religious trends is limited. We learn that senators and emperors were sensitive to signs. They also made use of astrologers and, particularly the 'bad' emperors, magic.[4] In the later books of Dio the signs are always linked with specific events. They are not reported at the beginning of the year and there is no reference to appeasement of prodigies. But otherwise relationships between gods and state are traditional. History remains essentially secular, and *exempla* which point a religious moral are practically absent. The relations of god and men are not a problem on which history is intended to throw light.

Soon after the end point of Dio's *History* came the murder of Alexander Severus, and the long drawn out third-century crisis of the empire followed. 'In the fifty years between the death of

---

[1] Dio, lxxv (lxxiv), 8. 1–2.
[2] lxxvi (lxxv), 4. 7.
[3] lxxvi (lxxv), 9. 2–4.
[4] Use of magic was a commonplace of abuse of 'bad' emperors: J. Ziegler (1970), 18–25, cites examples Dio, lxxviii (lxxvii), 18. 4; lxxx. 11; lxxiii. 16. 5.

Alexander Severus (235) and the accession of Diocletian (284) there were about twenty emperors who may be styled legitimate without counting the nominal co-regents that some of them created, still less the host of usurpers who from time to time ruled parts of the Empire usually for brief periods only, but sometimes like Postumus in Gaul for nearly a decade.' This is A. H. M. Jones's characteristically concise summary of the 'third-century anarchy'.[1] There was in addition a chronic military emergency. For the first time the Roman empire had to sustain heavy pressure simultaneously on many frontiers; the invasions of the armies of a revived Persian empire in the East coincided with massive migratory movements of Germans in the West. The plague which had been introduced into the empire in the reign of Marcus Aurelius burst out in successive epidemics that swept through many provinces. The frontier defences gave way. The western and Balkan provinces were repeatedly devastated by Germans, and Syria by Persians. At times it must have seemed that the empire could not survive.[2]

We are very badly informed about the political and military history of this period. As has been mentioned there were no Latin historians at all. The Greek Herodian takes the history of the empire a little beyond Dio, that is, to the accession of Gordian III in A.D. 238.[3] The fact that he wrote when the crisis was further advanced enables him to analyse some of its causes a little more sharply than Dio, to whom he is immensely inferior as a recorder of reliable fact.[4] After him there is silence.[5] The Greek histories that were written in the second half of the third century have not survived. The third century did produce a considerable volume of Christian literature, particularly in North Africa and Egypt.[6] From it we learn about the expansion of Christianity and its progress among the literary classes. We have contemporary information on the general persecutions launched against the church by the emperors Decius and

---

[1] A. H. M. Jones (1964), 23.
[2] On third-century anarchy, see *C.A.H.* xii (1939), esp. 165–231, by A. Alföldi; M. Rostovtzeff, *S.E.H.R.E.* (Oxford, 1926), ix–xii. On the crisis as seen by contemporaries, see G. Alföldi (1974). Other papers cited in the bibliography. See also bibliographies of chapters on the third century in H. Temporini, *A.N.R.W.* ii. 2. 551 ff.
[3] E. C. Echols (1961).
[4] G. Alföldi (1971), 427–49.
[5] See above, p. 224 n. 4.
[6] J. Fontaine (1968).

Valerian. We are particularly well informed about events at Carthage, thanks to the writings of Cyprian.[1] We can trace the progress of Cyprian's thought about the crisis of the empire: for some time around 350 he concluded that the end of the world must be near but later he seems to have decided that the empire and the world would continue after all.[2]

The fact that we have a considerable amount of Christian literature shows that the lack of secular writing, and consequently of information about war and government, is not simply due to the anarchy of civil and external wars. There was a change in the character of the evidence because society was being transformed. The world of the late empire was coming into existence, or at least new patterns of life that had been evolving gradually over centuries now broke through ancient conventions and became manifest everywhere. The nature of the literary evidence reflects the new strength of Christianity in some provinces of the empire, as well as a loss of interest in the contemporary world by authors and readers of secular literature especially in the Latin-speaking parts of the empire.

The reduction in the epigraphic evidence confirms the impression of profound cultural transformation. The historian of the early empire gains a great deal of information from the inscriptions of tombstones, monuments, public buildings, dedications to gods, and so on. In the second half of the third century these almost cease. Again this cannot simply be a result of war. The phenomenon was universal, and independent of the extent to which particular areas were affected by military operations.[3] Moreover, the recovery of the empire was not followed by a return to the old abundance of epigraphic commemoration.[4]

Inscriptions had been a means of publicizing the decisions of public assemblies and local senates. They had also expressed the competition of the wealthy citizens for public esteem. In the

---

[1] See W. Frend (1965).   [2] G. Alföldy (1973), 479.

[3] Africa suffered very little in the mid third century, yet public buildings and inscriptions cease almost completely. See B. H. Warmington (1954), 28–9.

[4] This is not to deny that there was recovery in both building and inscriptions especially in the reign of Diocletian. For Africa, see the table in ibid. 33. On the rise and fall of inscriptional commemoration in Pannonia, see the detailed analysis of A. Mòcsy (1970), 199–212. On Syria, see W. Liebeschuetz (1978).

third century civic institutions over large parts of the empire were in decline. Civic office came to be something which men were compelled to hold, and which consequently they would not wish to commemorate with monuments.[1]

But this cannot be the whole explanation. The decline of municipal institutions was much more marked in the West than in the East.[2] But the reduction in the number of long commemorative inscriptions affected the East no less than the West. Inscriptions ensured that a man's achievements should be remembered after death. It looks as if men had become less concerned to be remembered in this way. It may be an indication of other-worldliness that more men were indifferent whether their careers and civic or imperial services lived on in the minds of their fellow citizens.[3] It would be tempting to conclude—but difficult to prove—that a decline in the striving for posthumous fame was paralleled by deepening belief in personal immortality.[4] However, that may be, it is hard to avoid the impression that the dramatic decline in competitive display was causally linked with a lowering of esteem for the achievement which had previously been advertised with most pride, that is, public service whether performed for the city or for the empire.[5]

Great religious changes were certainly taking place. It is comparatively easy to trace the advance of Christianity in areas such as North Africa, Egypt, Asia Minor, and Italy.[6] But in the case of pagan cults our knowledge of earlier periods depends to a considerable extent on inscriptions, and the shrinking of inscriptional evidence in the later third century makes it difficult to assess what was happening. As a result, the change-

---

[1] A. H. M. Jones (1940), 180–91 is clear and sober; R. Ganghoffer (1963).

[2] See W. Liebeschuetz (1972) and P. Petit (1955) on relatively flourishing condition of eastern cities. J. Wacher has reminded me that Britain *never* had many municipal inscriptions, and that the decline in the use of inscriptions is nevertheless as great there as elsewhere. It is possible that there was a shift in the material of commemoration from inscribed stone to paint or mosaic. But this would not explain all the facts.

[3] This does not, of course, mean that indifference was total. What is significant is the change compared with the earlier period. The traditional concern for commemoration remained stronger at court and among governors than in municipal society. See P. Brown (1972), 65 n. 4; 66 n. 3.

[4] E. R. Dodds (1965).

[5] W. Liebeschuetz (1978).

[6] W. Frend (1965); A. von Harnack (1906).

over from paganism to Christianity is difficult to study on a local scale.

There certainly is a striking reduction in the number of surviving religious dedications, and this applies to all cults,[1] including the mystery religions. These eastern cults had reached a climax of popularity in the Severan period,[2] and then began to decline.[3] It is true that they had a considerable following among the nobility at Rome almost to the end of the fourth century[4] but this was probably exceptional. By that time the cults seem to have lost most of their followers elsewhere.[5] The cult of Mithras alone appears to have enjoyed widespread popularity into the fourth century,[6] and its adherents mostly belonged to a limited social group of officers and officials.[7] It may well be that among the empire-wide cults those of the principal Roman deities, Jupiter, Mars, and Hercules, were still the most important.[8] This is also the message of the imperial coinage.[9] In a period of incessant civil war it is perhaps not surprising that most of the surviving manifestations of religion aimed at obtaining divine protection for the emperor.[10] There is evidence from the Balkans and the western provinces

[1] The most studied case is the displacement in N. Africa of Saturn worship by Christianity. Frend has argued that in Numidia this change was sudden and followed the Romanization of the old Berber worship (Frend (1952), 83–6). This conclusion depends largely on the ending of dated dedications to Saturn in the mid third century. But the ending of inscriptions is a universal phenomenon which need not have religious causes. In fact, it seems that Saturn worship continued through the fourth century alongside flourishing Christianity. See M. Leglay (1966), 96–105, 437–92.

[2] Malaise, *Conditions*, 437–43.

[3] See E. Schwertheim (1974), 321, G. Grimm (1969) on Eastern cults in Germany; R. Meiggs (1960), 370 on Ostia, G. Alföldy (1961), 122 on Aquincum.

[4] J. Matthews (1973); H. Bloch (1945); D. N. Robinson (1915), whose distinction between traditional pagans and worshippers of oriental cults has been disproved by Matthews.

[5] Malaise, *Conditions*, 480.

[6] Survival of Mithras worship at least to the end of the third century or the first quarter of the fourth: G. Alföldy (1961), 121 ff. on Aquincum; M. J. T. Lewis (1966), 106 and tables, pp. 140–2 on Britain; V. J. Walters (1974), 9, 14, 21, 27 on Gaul; R. Meiggs (1960), 389 on Ostia. There is no fourth-century evidence from Cologne: G. Ristow (1971), 5. G. Alföldy (1974), 195–7, 209–10 on Noricum. A. Mòcsy (1974), 324 on Pannonia.

[7] C. M. Daniels (1975).

[8] G. Alföldy (1961), 141, 121; R. Meiggs (1960), 381, 385; A. Mòcsy (1974), 324.

[9] See *R.I.C.* v. 2 (1962), index iv. Of the originally non-Roman gods, Sol is by far the commonest. [10] G. Alföldy, op. cit. 121, 123.

that native cults continued to attract the devotion of their worshippers, particularly in the countryside.[1] In most of the empire the peasantry remained pagan. So did most of the soldiers and officers on whom the security of the empire depended.[2] But this was an inarticulate and non-proselytizing religion. Pagan cults remained what they had always been, simply part of the routine of life. People normally performed the rites as members of a group such as the family, the city, the senate, or the regiment; but pagans as such were not a group, and no collective emotions were aroused by the need to defend pagan religion. It seems as if towards the end of the third century the Christian efforts to draw men away from the cults of their fathers ceased to arouse the popular indignation which they had once aroused in times of stress and hardship.[3]

A more articulate and sophisticated form of paganism survived among the highly educated in the cities of the East, and presumably among the senatorial nobility in the Latin West. This was the heir of the intellectual paganism of the authors examined earlier in this book. It was reinforced by Neoplatonism. Some older Neoplatonists had taught that the individual must establish a relationship between himself and God by an effort of his intellect.[4] Ritual was largely irrelevant.[5] Others, as we have already learnt from Apuleius, claimed that ritual drew the divine into the presence of the worshipper.[6] For this purpose they gave particular importance to theurgy, the use of certain magical techniques, supposedly received by divine revelation for religious purposes; to provide contact with the divine, to enable the worshipper to avoid his predestined fate, and to achieve immortality.[7] The movement became self-consciously

[1] Very strongly in Britain, see W. H. C. Frend (1955), (1968). On the area around Trier, see E. Wightman (1970), 238 ff. Slow progress of Christianity in rural Syria: Liebeschuetz (1978).

[2] A. H. M. Jones, *L.R.E.* (1964), 96. G. R. Watson (1968); H. von Schoenebeck (1939), 66–9, and especially E. Gabba (1974), 75–109.

[3] See W. Frend (1965), 455.   [4] See R. T. Wallis (1972), 3.

[5] On Porphyry, see J. Bidez (1913), also *Ad Marcellam*, 14, 16, 17, 18–19.

[6] Jamblichus' *De Mysteriis*, ii. 11 argues in reply to Porphyry that theurgy rather than philosophical thought produces union with the gods.

[7] On theurgy, see E. R. Dodds (1947) and (1973), 200–10. This was a fusion of magic and religion, employing rites of the kind used to consecrate amulets to animate images, that is to induce the deity to enter into his statue. See L. Bonner (1946), 44; G. Hock, *Griechische Weihgebräuche* (Munich, 1905), 49 ff.; T. Hopfner, *Griechischer Offenbahrungszauber*, i (1921), 806–12.

pagan and hostile to Christianity. Porphyry wrote that there was no reason to wonder that plague had ravaged Rome for so long, since neither Asclepius nor any other god could now take up their abode in the city. Ever since Jesus had received honours, no one had experienced benefits from the gods.[1] Porphyry went on to compose a great refutation of Christianity.[2] At the same time, or a little later, Porphyry's pupil Iamblichus, laid theoretical foundation for pagan fundamentalism by constructing an elaborate system which combined Neoplatonist spiritual religion and theurgy with the whole body of religious practices of the Greek world.[3] In this way he provided new philosophical justification for primeval customs like the worship of images and sacrifices.

There were times when Neoplatonism was influential at court.[4] It was a 'religion of professors',[5] and literary education was highly valued in Roman society. But various factors limited its impact. One was the fact that philosophical paganism had no contact with the mass of the population; another that by the year 300 senators had been virtually excluded from all positions of power, whether in the army or in the administration.[6] Finally, the fact of their literacy made the educated vulnerable to Christian apologetic literature, and by this time there were Christian writers who could compose a plausible case for their religion, and argue it in admirable Latin or Greek.[7]

3. *The Diocletianic revival*

The restoration of the empire after the anarchy of the third century was a massive task. It is significant that Diocletian eventually called on one senior (Augustus) and two junior (Caesares) colleagues to assist him.[8] The conditions in which

[1] Quoted by Theodoret, *De Cur. Graec. Affect.* 12 = *P.G.* lxxxiii. 1150–1.
[2] See J. Geffcken (1920), 63–7.
[3] Ibid. 103–14. R. T. Wallis (1972), 130.
[4] Both Plotinus and Porphyry spent much time at Rome. On the Neoplatonism at court, see J. Gagé, *A.N.R.W.* ii. 2. 828–52. A. Alföldi (1967), 228–81.
[5] The expression was coined by A. Piganiol for the paganism of fourth-century sophists (1972), 263.
[6] M. T. W. Arnheim (1972), 34–48. B. Malcus, *Opuscula Romana*, vii (1969), 213–37; G. Alföldy (1969), 233–45.
[7] See below, pp. 252 ff.
[8] On Diocletian and the creation of the tetrarchy, see W. Ensslin (1948), 1; A. H. M. Jones (1964), 737–76; W. Seston (1946); P. Petit (1974), 527–56.

government had to be carried on were transformed. The empire no longer had a permanent capital. The emperors travelled with their court and the main residences were not at Rome but nearer the frontiers.[1] A great part of the administration of the empire, particularly in the eastern provinces, was performed by men whose civilization was not Latin but Greek.[2] In the West, officials were of course Latin in speech and civilization, but they no longer had the cohesion derived from a common origin in Rome or Italy. The Roman senatorial class was—for the time being at least—almost excluded from the government of the empire.[3]

This is not the place to describe the administrative measures by which Diocletian and his colleagues enabled the empire to survive.[4] But we have seen that as far as the Romans were concerned, administrative and military measures of reform were never sufficient unless they were paralleled by religious and moral ones. This remained as true in the age of Diocletian as it had been in the times of Augustus and Vespasian.[5]

Religious revival in the past had meant in the first place rebuilding of temples, and revival of old rites at Rome itself. This was not so under Diocletian.[6] He was a great builder in all the principal cities of the empire, and he instigated a building programme at Rome also. He rebuilt the Julian Basilica which had been damaged by fire, and presented the city with its greatest complex of baths, the famous Baths of Diocletian. But principally his buildings at Rome, as elsewhere, seem to have been secular.[7]

The comparative neglect of temple building by the emperors[8]

---

[1] A. H. M. Jones (1964), 49, 366.

[2] G. Barbieri (1952), 459. But it seems that the proportion of senators from Greek provinces remained constant, ibid. 193–283. On equestrian officials: H. G. Pflaum (1950), 193–4.

[3] See above, p. 235 n. 6.

[4] Clearly summarized by A. H. M. Jones (1964), 42–70.

[5] See above, pp. 90 ff. and p. 166 n. 5.

[6] See the comparatively short list of dedications: W. Ensslin (1948), 2479.

[7] On Diocletian's building schemes at Rome, Nicomedia, Antioch, and Carthage, see Lact. *Mort. Pers.* 7. 8; Aur. Vict. 39. 45; Malalas, 306. 12. Summarized by W. Ensslin (1948), 2475.

[8] There was some revival of temple building on local initiative in municipalities. For evidence from Africa see B. H. Warmington (1954), 30–2 mentioning *C.I.L.* viii. 26472, 5333, 11326, *Inscr. Alg.* 1241. From elsewhere: J. Geffcken (1929), 30–1.

can be explained by the fact that the empire for the moment no longer had a single fixed centre where the state ritual could be carried out. The centre was wherever the emperors happened to be and the aim of public worship was not so much the preservation of Rome, or of any other city, as of the emperors. It is likely that there was a great deal of religious ritual at court. Certainly the emperors publicized their piety. Fragments have survived of a monument commemorating Diocletian's *Vicennalia* which once stood in the Forum at Rome.[1] It consisted of five columns. The highest supported a statue of Jupiter while a pair of columns on the left and the right of the Jupiter column each carried an image of one of the Augusti together with one of his respective Caesars. Another Jupiter column was erected at Nicomedia, and it was in front of this that in 305 Diocletian and his fellow Augustus formally abdicated.[2] The emperors' piety towards Jupiter, as towards Hercules, Mars, and Sol, was also displayed on coinage.[3] It may be significant that the gods appeared mainly on gold coins, while silver and bronze coins bore abstractions like the *Genius Populi Romani*. Since gold coins were produced for the payment of higher salaries, it seems that the emperors were particularly keen to display their worship of the great gods of the state to officers and high officials.[4]

We are informed about the imperial religion of the tetrarchy by a number of festival speeches usually known by their rhetorical classification as panegyrics. These orations were spoken to a large audience at some imperial occasion by a man who had been chosen because of his reputation as an orator,[5] and whose task it was to bring the festival to a rousing climax by uniting everyone in strong emotional approval of the emperor.[6] The emperor was usually, but not always, in the audience, but it was not part of the speaker's function to express the views of his subjects to the ruler. The *panegyrici Latini* represent the point of view from which the ruler wanted his actions to be

[1] H. P. L'Orange (1938); H. Kähler (1964).
[2] Lact. *Mort. Pers.* xx. 2.
[3] *R.I.C.* v. 2: up to 294 the coinage is dominated by Jupiter with Hercules in second place. Sol is rare. There has been a retreat from Sol and a return to Roman worship relative to the coinage of Probus, for instance. From 294 to 305 the frequency of Mars and Sol increases but Jupiter and Hercules continue to dominate.
[4] Ibid. vi. 110.
[5] E. Galletier (Paris, 1949–55). The orations are cited in Galletier's numbering.
[6] J. Straub (1939), 146–59; F. Burdeau (1964), 1–9.

seen.[1] They are designed to set the tone of an assembly, but the tone was chosen by the prince.

When one tries to evaluate the religion of the panegyrics, it is necessary to make allowance for conventions of the genre and of court ceremony. One of these is the application of religious language to the emperor. In the panegyrics the ruler, his family, his edicts, his palace, and in fact everything associated with him is described with epithets strictly appropriate only to a divinity.[2] This practice had a long history going back to Augustus; and in the course of time, and as the actual position of the emperor became less secure, the use of religious vocabulary[3] and ritual in court ceremony had become more extravagant.[4] But this still did not mean that the emperor actually claimed to be a supernatural being, or that in his case the dividing line between man and god was abolished.

In fact the orations do make a distinction between the immortal gods and the emperor.[5] They also continue to praise emperors for their *felicitas*. Now 'luck' and 'success' are highly desirable and even mysterious qualities, but also purely human ones.[6] A god does not need them. Moreover the tetrarchs never described themselves as gods on coins.[7] In this respect their

[1] Alan Cameron (1970), demonstrated that the panegyrical poems of Claudian reflect the views that Stilicho, who commissioned them, wanted to propagate. It may be that eastern panegyrics, e.g. *Ors.* xii and xiii of Libanius, the panegyrics of Themistius (cf. G. Dagron (1968)), and the *On Kingship* of Syresius (cf. C. Lacombrade (1951)), were more advisory.

[2] From orations addressed to Constantine: ix. 4. 5: divino consilio hoc est tuo; ibid. 16. 5: sacris aedibus (the palace); ibid. 25. 4: debebitur et divinitati simulacrum aureum; ibid. 26. 5: divina suboles tua; x. 2. 6: qui semper divina meditantur; ibid. 3. 3: divina virtus; ibid. 35. 3: divini principis monitis. Addressed to the Christian Theodosius I, xii. 3. 6: cui forma divina; ibid. 4. 5: deum dedit Hispania quem videmus; ibid. 8. 3: divino patre.

[3] The arrival of Diocletian and Maximian at Milan in 291 is treated as a divine event. As the emperors approach *tota Italia clarior lux diffusa* (*Pan.* iii. 10. 4), and the emperors are manifest gods: *conspicuus et praesens Juppiter . . . non advena sed imperator Hercules* (ibid. 10. 5) and in the palace *velut interioribus sacrariis* the emperors received the *adoratio* of dignitaries (ibid. 11. 3). On this, S. MacCormack (1972). Quite apart from adapting itself to real changes in the constitutional position of the emperor such language had to become more extreme in order to compensate for the devaluation of the phraseology over centuries of use.

[4] A. Alföldi (1970), 25–79. On the slow evolution of *adoratio* culminating in the 'adoration of the sacred purple' in the later empire, ibid. 62–3; also H. Stern (1954); W. T. Avery (1940).

[5] Gods and emperor distinguished: ii. 6. 4.   [6] *Felicitas*, iii. 19. 3.

[7] *R.I.C.* v. 1, p. 397, ibid. v. 2, p. 656 lists a few coin legends under *deo . . . Augusto*, ibid. vi (A.D. 294–313) has no coins with this legend.

practice even marked a retreat from that of some of their predecessors.

The fundamentally secular position of the rulers of the tetrarchy is confirmed by Christian writers of the time. The worship of a human being was—as it still is—extremely offensive to Christians. But the topic of ruler worship is largely absent from Christian writing in the age of the Great Persecution. In his pamphlet *On the deaths of the persecutors* Lactantius did his best to blacken the memory of the persecuting rulers. Any claim to divine status going beyond accepted ceremony would have laid the emperors open to charges of delusion, arrogance, and sacrilege. Lactantius made no such charges. In earlier persecutions the refusal of Christians to worship the emperor had been an issue. At any rate Tertullian included a long justification of the Christian attitude in his *Apology*.[1] But Arnobius and Lactantius, the principal Latin apologists of the age of Diocletian, did not think it necessary to refute this accusation.[2] In fact, the events of the Great Persecution do not suggest that the divinity of the emperor was an issue.[3] The religious language and ritual of court etiquette was largely maintained by Christian emperors.[4] This could not have happened unless the ceremonies had lost all religious associations.

It has been suggested earlier that the Romans had always been aware that the religious language of imperial ceremonies was being used to make statements of secular loyalty and gratitude. This was still the situation around A.D. 300. The only change lay in the fact that monarchy had been accepted together with all its consequences, and there was no longer need to pretend that the ruler was merely the first citizen. When the principate gradually changed into full monarchy, encouragement was given to all ceremonies that expressed the monarch's superiority over his subjects.

To insist that notwithstanding the fact that they were addressed and honoured like gods, the tetrarchs were not believed to be gods, is to make more than a verbal point. The heart of the matter is that the imperial office remained a

[1] *Apol.* 34–5.
[2] Lact. *Div. Inst.* ii. 16 criticizes worship of *dead* emperors.
[3] *C.A.H.* iii. 659 (N. Baynes); cf. id. (1955), 345.
[4] E. Ch. Babut (1916); F. Martroye (1928); H. Kruse (1934); L. Warren Bonfante (1964).

perfectly secular one. Since the late second century, men had become much more willing to accept that supernatural powers might be reached through the medium of a living or a dead human being. Living martyrs, their bones and other relics, Pythagorean or Neoplatonist philosophers, and Christian 'holy men', might all be thought capable of performing miracles of one kind or another. Not so the emperors. Even the healing kings of the Christian Middle Ages possessed a power which the emperors lacked.[1] In practice much less was expected of a Roman emperor in the way of supernatural capability than of a significant number of his subjects.

The use of religious language to describe the emperor and objects closely associated with him is not peculiar to the panegyric of the tetrarchic periods. But these speeches nevertheless have a religious character of their own. This is particularly marked in the orations of 289 and 291 which expound a consistent imperial theology. The Jovius title adopted by Diocletian and the Herculius title of Maximian imply—and the orator confirms the implication—that the senior emperor was descended from Jupiter and the junior from Hercules. When in due course each Augustus selected a Caesar, the latter, by virtue of his new rank, joined the divine dynasty of his Augustus.[2] There is a close parallel between the government of heaven and earth. Jovius and Herculius are the earthly representatives of the heavenly Jupiter and Hercules. As Hercules once rendered Jupiter the service of defeating the giants, so Maximian aided Diocletian by defeating barbarians.[3] All benefits enjoyed by men are owed to Jupiter, the ruler of heaven, and to Hercules, the pacifier of earth. The relationship between the Augusti is the same. Diocletian initiates action. Maximian carries it out.[4]

The speech of 291 celebrates one of the joint birthdays of the Augusti.[5] It points out parallels between emperors and gods.

[1] On holy men of late antiquity, see P. Brown (1971); on healing kings of medieval Europe, M. Bloch (1923).

[2] W. Seston (1946), 215 ff.

[3] ii. 4. 2.

[4] Ibid. 11. 5–6.

[5] Differing from Seston, op. cit. 222–3, I take the *geminus natalis* to be the true birthday of Maximian, not the day on which he took the title Herculius. iii. 2. 2 and ibid. 19. 2 should refer to days of actual birth. It could be that by coincidence Maximian and Diocletian were born on same day of the year (in different years). More likely they were born on different days but shared the celebration of each

The emperors' tireless benevolence resembles that of the gods Jupiter and Hercules,[1] and so does their division of duties.[2] Like the gods, the emperors watch over territories from which they are physically absent.[3] The emperors' ability to meet in spite of all obstacles of geography and season implies a divine independence of the rule of Fate.[4] The radiance of the imperial presence is such as to inspire their subjects to spontaneous worship.[5]

The speech of 297 is addressed not to Maximian but to the Caesar Constantius. In it one can already note a certain detachment from the 'Diocletianic' view of monarchy. Nevertheless it begins with a striking statement of the parallel organization of the divine and the human orders. The speech was delivered on 1 March, on the anniversary of Constantius' accession to the rank of Caesar which is shown as part of the great natural process. As the world began in spring,[6] and each spring brings about its renewal, so the accession of Constantius has now assured the future of the world.[7] Moreover, the creation of Caesars has raised the number of emperors to four, a number which has a basic function in the construction of the universe: there are four elements, four seasons, four continents, etc.[8] The orator then points out how the activity of Constantius confers benefits on mankind more continuously than the sun.[9]

There is evidence for this theology apart from the panegyrics: for instance, coins which combine portraits of Jupiter and Hercules, each bearing significant symbols, seem to represent the heavenly counterpart of the imperial government of Diocletian and Maximian.[10] A sequence of mosaics in the villa of Armerina shows the deeds of Hercules culminating in his defeat

birthday as they are said to have shared each other's different ages, ibid. 7. 7, and each other's honours, ibid. 11. 2. I imagine that the birthday of each emperor was celebrated with *vota* for both.

[1] ii. 3. 1–8.　　　　　　　　　　　　　　　　　　[2] Ibid. 4–6.
[3] Ibid. 13. 5–14, *passim.*
[4] Ibid. 13, cf. W. Ensslin (1923), 78.　　　　　　[5] Ibid. 10. 4–5.
[6] A reminiscence of Verg. *Georg.* ii. 336 ff.　　　[7] iv. 2–3.
[8] Ibid. 4. H. Castritius (1969), 26–9 argues that patron gods were now increased to four, Sol being assigned to Constantius and Mars to Galerius.

[9] iv. 4. 3, cf. ibid. 2. 2–3; this may be an allusion to Constantius' worship of Sol but the orator does not describe the sun as a divinity. This suggests that Sol was not part of the official theology of the tetrarchy but rather an object of personal piety of Constantius.

[10] *R.I.C.* v. 2, index, p. 631.

of the giants and the crowning of Hercules by Jupiter. If, as is possible, the villa belonged to Maximian, the prominently placed illustration of the Hercules myth illustrated the owner's constitutional position and function.[1]

What is the significance of this peculiar theology of tetrarchy? I have already argued that it cannot signify that the emperors were thought to be actual gods.[2] It does imply that they enjoyed close co-operation of the gods. The orators produce evidence of this. Fine weather aided the shipwrights who were building a fleet for Maximian but when water was needed for the launching, Jupiter sent rain.[3] The *felicitas* of the emperors was manifest in good travelling weather,[4] good crops, absence of disease,[5] and not least, numerous wars among the barbarian enemies of the empire.[6]

Close support is also proclaimed by the epithet *conservator* which is the one most frequently given to Jupiter on coins.[7] A rather less unequal patron–client relationship is suggested by the predicate *comes augusti* which is frequently applied to Hercules.[8] Divine support is not limited to protection: the god may endow the emperor with some of his peculiar powers. Thus coin-legends recalling the *virtus* of the emperor or emperors are very frequently illustrated by engravings of Hercules. Finally, the theology implies that Jupiter and Hercules feel responsibility and concern for the actions of the Augusti, who are their delegates, and, in a special sense, their children.[9]

It would have been quite possible for Diocletian to claim divine support for his system without calling into existence a new theology.[10] A possible explanation is that the imperial

---

[1] H. P. L'Orange (1965), 76 ff.; H. Kähler (1973), on *Pan*. ii. 4. 2–3; iii. 6–7. Admittedly the certain identification of the owner awaits the full publication of the material.

[2] I follow N. Baynes (1935), 83–4; also see above, pp. 238 ff.

[3] ii. 12. 5–8.   [4] iii. 9. 2.   [5] iii. 15. 3–4.   [6] Ibid. 16. 2.

[7] *R.I.C.* vi. 701–2; vii. 741–2.   [8] Ibid. vi. 698–9. A. D. Nock (1947).

[9] *R.I.C.* vi. 163, 165, 173, 351, 366, etc. The obvious *virtus* of Hercules, and one which would be appreciated by the soldiers paid with the coins, was that of a warrior, but we have already met a tradition of long standing which honoured Hercules for a much wider range of qualities, including the ability to bestow immortality. See above, pp. 170–3. On divine parentage of emperors see references in Seston, op. cit. 215–16. See also A. Wlosok (1960), 232–46.

[10] Roman emperors had always claimed the patronage of a particular god. Constantius and Constantine claimed the protection of Sol, Licinius of Jupiter, both supreme gods; Galerius claimed a special relationship with Mars.

theology was intended to explain to the subjects of an empire an exceptionally complex form of monarchy, and one that involved two Augusti who were of equal rank but of whom one, Diocletian, nevertheless had superior authority. The theology also shows in what spirit the tetrarchs, in particular the two Augusti, had to work the system if it was to survive. It is significant that the imperial virtue which the orator of 291 considered fundamental to the success of his god-descended emperors was *pietas*. In the context of the speech, this means essentially the emperors' ability to get on with one another.[1] But theology claims to do more than teach by parable. The theology of the tetrarchy attempts to support a potentially unstable system by showing that it is closely integrated into the government of the world. Whether or to what extent it achieved this aim we lack the evidence to judge.

The 'imperial theology' of the tetrarchy is without parallel in the history of imperial Rome. Jupiter and Hercules had of course always been part of Roman religion, and the emphasis given to these two divinities marks a revival of Roman religion, and a retreat from the Greek and Near Eastern worship of Sol that had been favoured by Aurelian. Nevertheless the mythological construction of the theology as a whole is un-Roman. It is obviously derived from Hellenistic theories of kingship,[2] and related to the theological framework in which Eusebius was to place the Christian monarchy of Constantine.[3] One can go further. The imperial theology of the greatest of the persecutors had important features in common with the religion which they persecuted. Jupiter is the supreme god. His son, Hercules, acts as his executive representative, and as a benefactor of man.[4] The resemblance to Christian theology is obvious. Of course, imperial theology makes use of this pattern a second time: Jupiter and Hercules are each represented on earth by a 'Son'. The pagan state religion and Christianity were never closer in theology than at the time of the Great Persecution.[5]

[1] iii. 6. 3–7; 18. 5; 19. 3.

[2] Cf. Dio Chrys. i. 84. Dio's orations *On Kingship* have the closest approximation to an imperial theology in the early empire. But they were not official.

[3] N. Baynes (1934), 13–18; F. Dvornik (1966), 611–30.

[4] H. Mattingly (1952), 131 sees a deliberate reshaping of paganism to make it acceptable to Christians. This goes too far.

[5] The religions were also brought closer by the fact that Christianity was not yet so rigidly defined, cf. below, pp. 258 and 265.

Related to the adoption of Hellenistic theories of kingship is a certain simplification of the Roman state religion. For earlier Romans like Trajan, Jupiter Optimus Maximus—or at any rate precisely the Jupiter whose temple stood on the Capitol—was the supreme god of Rome.[1] In the panegyrics of the tetrarchy, the supreme god is simply Jupiter. He is not given his ancient title and he is qualified as *capitolinus* only in contexts involving the temple on the Capitol.[2] A parallel development is the gradual disappearance of all the traditional Roman gods except Jupiter, Hercules, and Mars, from the coinage.[3] It may well be that simplification and standardization contributed to loss of commitment, and so to the ending of the old cults not many years later. But for the moment the theology of the tetrarchy affirmed in a new way the importance of the traditional religion of the state.

It was, as we have seen, in accordance with tradition that a religious revival should be accompanied by a moral one. Diocletian was responsible for a good deal of marriage legislation.[4] One edict survives in unabbreviated form and this expicitly states that 'there is no doubt that the immortal gods will be favourable and gracious to the Roman name—as they always have been—if we will ensure that all people dwelling in our empire live in every respect fully good, religious, and chaste lives'.[5] Encouraged by this conviction, Diocletian proceeded to enforce everywhere the traditional Roman rules defining what marriages among kin were incestuous. Especially he suppressed the brother-and-sister marriages which survived in Egypt.[6]

The revival of ancient Roman manners[7] now also included

---

[1] Plin. *Pan.* 1. 6; 8. 1; 52. 6; 94. 1.

[2] *Pan.* vi. 8. 7; vii. 15. 6; xii. 9. 5.

[3] Compare *R.I.C.* ii (Vespasian to Hadrian) index 3 s.v. Apollo, Ceres, Diana, Fortuna, Janus, Minerva, Neptune, Venus, Vesta with *R.I.C.* vi (Diocletian to Maximinus), index 3. The old gods have become very rare or disappeared altogether.

[4] *C.J.* ii. 48. 2; v. 4. 17; 5. 2; vi. 35. 6; ix. 9. 19; 21–7.

[5] *F.I.R.* ii. 558–61 = *Mos. et Rom. Leg. Coll.* vi. 4. 1: Ita enim et ipsos immortales deos Romano nomini, ut semper fuerunt, faventes atque placatos futuros esse non dubium est, si cunctos sub imperio nostro agentes piam religiosamque et quietam et castam in omnibus mere colere perspexerimus vitam.

[6] A. H. M. Jones (1964), 972.

[7] *Mos. et Rom. Leg. Coll.* vi. 4. 1: quoniam piis religiosisque mentibus nostris ea quae Romanis legibus caste sancteque sunt constituta venerabilia maxime videntur et aeterna religione servanda.

the forced return to ancestral religion of men who had forsaken it for other practices. A law addressed to the proconsul of Africa orders him to suppress Manichaeism from fear that this religion, introducing 'the savage and abominable customs of the Persians', might poison the peaceful and disciplined Roman people.[1] The leaders of the movement are to be burned alive together with their scriptures. Followers are merely to be beheaded unless men of rank—in which case their property must be confiscated and they themselves sent to work in the mines.[2]

In the circumstances it is surprising that for many years Diocletian and his colleagues took no steps to check Christianity. In the course of the third century Christianity had become a power to be reckoned with. Since 260 it had been tolerated in practice. In important parts of the empire, especially Asia Minor and North Africa, it had become the majority religion. In many areas there were large urban communities. The Christians of a city were subject to a bishop, and the bishops of each province met regularly, and to varying extents subordinated themselves to the bishop of the provincial capital. There was no formal organization beyond this, but Christians everywhere had a sense of belonging to a single community and letters between bishops preserved uniformity of belief and ritual.[3] The existence of so large an organization within the empire must have offended the sense of propriety of Roman administrators whose predecessors had hesitated to organize a fire-brigade lest it should become the source of subversive activities.[4] Nevertheless for a long time Christians were fully tolerated in the empire of Diocletian. We hear of friction between authorities and the Christians only in the army, and there it seems to have been on a small scale, caused by individual Christian conscientious objectors, who either refused to serve at all, or refused to attend ceremonies of the state religion.[5]

---

[1] Ibid. xv. 3. 4 (probably of A.D. 297).
[2] Ibid. 6–7.
[3] W. H. C. Frend (1965), 440–76. Christians at court: Euseb. *H.E.* viii. 1. 3–4.
[4] Plin. *Ep.* x. 33–4.
[5] *Acts of Maximilian*, a conscript who refused to serve in 295 (Knopf–Krüger, 86–7); of the centurion Marcellus who flung down his belt of rank during a parade service in 298 (ibid. 87–8); as did Fabius the standard bearer in 299 (ibid. 89–90); also perhaps Achilles and Nereus at Rome (*I.L.C.V.* 1981).

The turning-point came around 299–300. Diocletian and his court were sacrificing at Antioch, and after repeated sacrifices the desired signs did not appear. The *haruspex* explained this through the presence of profane persons. Among the officials attending the ceremony were certain Christians who had protected themselves from demons by making the sign of the cross. Because of the presence of these Christians the gods had refused to communicate with the emperor. Diocletian promptly ordered that all Christian civil servants or soldiers should either sacrifice, or lose their positions. But the order was not enforced systematically. After some time the affair died down.[1]

But the question of whether the Christians should be tolerated or not continued to worry court circles, and particularly the Caesar Galerius. The matter was debated in the imperial consistory and it was decided to put the question to the gods.[2]

The use of oracles to establish theological truth was a feature of the time. Porphyry in his treatise *The philosophy of oracles* cites a number of responses of anti-Christian tendency.[3] Apollo was asked what god should be approached by a husband to detach his wife from Christianity. He replied in effect that the case was regrettable but hopeless.[4] Someone inquired of Hecate whether Christ was indeed God. She replied that his soul survived death but as that of an outstandingly good man, not of a god.[5] Lactantius reports the response of Apollo of Colophon to the question: who or what is God? It begins: 'self-produced, untaught, without a mother, unshaken, a name not to be encompassed in a word, dwelling in fire; this is God.'[6] Apollo of Claros was asked the question: who is Iao? He replied that Iao, Hades, Zeus, and Helius all were descriptions of the one supreme God, but applicable at different seasons of the year.[7]

---

[1] Euseb. *Chron.* ad ann. 301: *paulatim ex illo iam tempore persecutione adversus nos incipiente* probably refers to the consequences of the incident. But perhaps Eusebius was aware of a longer and more gradual development towards persecution in the army than suggested by Lactantius. Lact. *Mort. Pers.* 10; Euseb. *H.E.* viii. 4; G. E. M. de Ste Croix (1954); for date, J. Moreau (1954), 266 on *Mort. Pers.* 10. 19.

[2] Ibid. 11.

[3] See J. J. O'Meara (1959) and (1969); P. de Labriolle (1934), 233–7.

[4] Augustine, *C.D.* xix. 23. 1; J. J. O'Meara (1959), 49–61.

[5] *C.D.* xix. 23. 2; J. J. O'Meara, op. cit. 52.

[6] Lact. *Div. Inst.* i. 7.

[7] Macr. *Sat.* i. 18. On theological oracles see A. D. Nock (1928), 280–90 = (1972), 160–9, also (1934), 54–104 = (1972), 357–400.

The outcome of Diocletian's recourse to oracles was unfavourable to Christianity. According to a letter of the emperor Constantine, Apollo of Didyma replied that he could not answer truthfully because of the 'just upon the earth'.[1] Whether Apollo actually used this phrase or not the oracle induced Diocletian to consent to persecution or at least to suppression of Christianity at court. In 303 he published the First Edict, on 23 February, the festival of the god Terminus. No doubt that god was to assist the emperor's attempt to put a limit to the progress of Christianity.[2]

The decision needs explanation. One suspects that the unanimity of the oracles reflects a view which had become predominant in the emperor's entourage. The question is why the decision was so long delayed. If Diocletian believed that the calamities suffered by the Roman empire were a punishment sent by the gods for the abandonment of pagan worship by Christian converts, one would expect him to have launched his attack much earlier. In fact, the persecution was launched a generation after the calamities of the empire in the third quarter of the third century, and at a time when the Roman world must have seemed well on the way to recovery. This suggests that the persecution was instigated not by acute religious anxiety but by reflection; in other words, the motives were doctrinal and ideological.

One can imagine that the question whether to persecute or not was a dispute between pragmatic and ideological politics. For pagans who took their traditional attitudes only half as seriously as Christians took theirs, the behaviour of the Christians in condemning absolutely every form of honour to the gods of society must have seemed dangerous and intolerable. But in practice it had long been found politic to tolerate them. Diocletian's mother and wife were Christians. The interest of his own domestic peace counselled toleration,[3] and he must have been aware that apart from their arrogant attitude to his gods Christians were not as a body anti-social. Above all, during the first fifteen years or so of his reign, Diocletian was preoccupied by

---

[1] Euseb. *V.C.* ii. 50.

[2] *Mort. Pers.* 11. 7; 13. 2. P. de Labriolle (1934), 320–3; H. Grégoire (1913), 81 ff. and *Byzantion*, xiv (1939), 321 on *C.I.G.* 2883d; also A. Rehm (1938); A. Wilhelm (1943).

[3] *Mort. Pers.* 15. 2; J. Moreau notes that this is not corroborated elsewhere.

an endless succession of dangers that were vastly more urgent than that of the Christian.

But when the other problems had been mastered,[1] and time for reflection was available, the Christian question was still there. There could be no doubt that the behaviour of Christians endangered the peace of the gods. Whatever views Diocletian himself may have held, there would certainly have been plenty of people to urge this point to him. On the one hand, the last fifty years or so had produced a philosophical movement which sought to give a new intellectual basis for the whole range of traditional religious practice, and which was definitely hostile to Christianity.[2] On the other hand, it is likely that some of the old hostility to Christianity survived among the less sophisticated, particularly because of Christian pacifism,[3] in the army.[4] It is difficult to estimate the relative importance of the two points of view. According to Christian sources, the Caesar Galerius was the principal advocate of persecution.[5] The same sources point out that he was an uncivilized boor. Such a man one would not expect to be influenced by Neoplatonism. But then the charge of lack of education was a commonplace of rhetorical abuse.[6] In any case it was precisely one of the objectives of the philosophical writing to revive age-old and unsophisticated rites by giving them intellectual respectability. Of the younger generation of emperors Maximinus Daia was surely an intellectual.[7] Of Diocletian's advisers favouring persecution we know of one, Hierocles, who wrote an attack on Christianity based on the writings of Celsus and possibly Porphyry, and who proved an enthusiastic persecuting official.[8]

---

[1] Approximate chronology according to table at end of *C.A.H.* xii: 296 Britain recovered. 196-7 revolt in Egypt suppressed. 297-8 suppression of revolt in N. Africa; Persian war. 301 Price Edict. 303 persecution of Christians begun at Nicomedia. 305 abdication of Diocletian.   [2] See above, p. 235.

[3] J.-M. Hornus (1960); A. von Harnack (1905).

[4] Perhaps most strongly among the inhabitants of the Balkans (G. Alföldy (1961), 123-4), the most valuable recruiting area in the empire, which produced the most effective emperors and the most determined opponents of Christianity, e.g. Decius (Wittig (1932), 1250). Galerius (*Mort. Pers.* 9. 1) and Maximinus Daia (son-in-law of Galerius).   [5] *Mort. Pers.* 9 and J. Moreau's commentary.

[6] P. Brown (1972), 83; R. Syme (1971), 179-93.

[7] See Euseb. *H.E.* ix. 2-5 for an account of his extremely sophisticated attack on Christianity. Lact. *Mort. Pers.* 18. 13 calls him semi-barbarous, cf. 19. 6 and J. Moreau's commentary on Maximinus' extraordinarily rapid career.

[8] Lact. *Inst.* v. 2. 12. Porphyry's attack may be later than Hierocles'. See T. D. Barnes, *J. Theol. S.*, N.S., xxxiv (1973), 424-42.

Such as it is, the evidence suggests that the decisive impulse came from military considerations.[1] It was in the army that there had actually been friction between the authorities and individual Christians. It was precisely against Christianity in the army that the first measures of persecution were taken.[2] The two most determined opponents of Christianity, Galerius and his son-in-law Maximinus Daia were both military men, and Galerius had recently led an army to victory over the Persians.[3] At the time of the First Edict, his prestige and influence must have been very great.

It looks therefore as if it was the influence of a victorious army and its commander[4] which, not for the first time in Roman history, produced a decisive change in the policy of the empire, with the result that toleration of Christianity was abandoned, and the so-called First Edict of the Great Persecution published. This started a train of events whose outcome was precisely the opposite of what the opponents of Christianity were aiming at, namely, the rule of a Christian emperor and the complete eclipse of the traditional religion.

When Diocletian published the First Edict he hoped to avoid bloodshed. He ordered that all over the empire copies of Christian scriptures should be collected and destroyed, churches demolished, and Christians prohibited from meeting for worship. Soon after, fires broke out in the palace at Nicomedia, and there were revolts in several districts of Asia Minor. Christians were held responsible and Diocletian's Second Edict ordered the arrest of all bishops and priests. The prisons of the Roman empire were not designed for the long-term detention of large numbers of prisoners, so Diocletian published the Third Edict ordering the release of the prisoners on condition that they sacrificed. Finally, in spring 304 the Fourth Edict ordered everyone to sacrifice. In 305 Diocletian resigned. It is doubtful whether the Fourth Edict was ever promulgated in the western half of the empire. At any rate the resignation of Diocletian

---

[1] J. Moreau (1961), 100–1.   [2] See p. 245 n. 5.

[3] See W. Seston (1946), 180 ff.

[4] Many of Galerius' troops came from the still largely pagan Illyricum: Festus, *Brev.* 25; Eutrop. x. 4. But in estimating the influence of the religion of the mass of the soldiers, it is important to remember that the army of Gaul, which was presumably just as pagan as Galerius' Balkan army, was not alienated by Constantine's Christianity. Cf. p. 253 n. 4, below. See E. Gabba (1974), 104–7.

meant the end of persecution in most of the western provinces. In the East, in the areas controlled by Galerius and Maximinus, persecution was resumed with greater vigour and thoroughness than before, and in the Asiatic provinces continued until 313.[1]

The great attack on the church was unambiguously a failure.[2] Galerius and Maximinus Daia, the most fanatical of the persecutors, were compelled to call off the measures they had begun in 311. Each of the original persecutors seemed to have met with retribution. Diocletian fell gravely ill soon after the Second Edict.[3] Galerius died of a slow, agonizing, and disgusting disease.[4] Maximian committed suicide in disgraceful circumstances. His statues were overthrown and his inscriptions erased.[5] Of the tetrarchs only Constantius, who had shown sympathy for the Christians in his part of the empire, and had limited persecution to the destruction of churches, died in power.

The experiences of the emperors of the younger generation only served to enforce the moral that Heaven had decided the conflict of religions in favour of Christianity. Not much more than half a year after the edict of Galerius, Maximinus Daia resumed the persecutions, he combined physical pressure with propaganda, and at the same time tried to revive paganism by organizing a pagan Church. He proclaimed the benefits that were gained from the traditional worship with a precision and confidence which was new to the style of the imperial government. 'Who could be found so stupid or devoid of all sense as not to see that it is thanks to the beneficent activities of the gods that the soil does not refuse the seeds committed to it . . . and that the form of impious war does not rise consistently upon the earth . . . and that typhoons do not burst without warning bringing destruction in their wake . . . and the earth does not sink down from her deepest hollows . . . And all of these things happened at once as a result of the fatal error implicit in the

---

[1] On the events of the Great Persecution, see N. Baynes, *C.A.H.* xii. 647–77 modified by G. E. M. de Ste Croix (1954). A wealth of source material and modern research is worked into W. H. C. Frend (1965), 477–535, reviewed by G. E. M. de Ste Croix, *J. Theol. St.* xviii (1967), 217–21.

[2] W. H. C. Frend (1959).

[3] *Mort. Pers.* 16; Diocletian's death, ibid. 42 (exaggerating the pain of it); execution of wife and daughter, ibid. 51.

[4] Ibid. 33; Euseb. *H.E.* viii. 16. 2–5.

[5] Ibid. 13. 16.

empty folly of these immoral people when it enslaved their minds, and . . . came near to making the entire world suffer.'[1] While Maximinus was making the most intelligent attempt to restore the old religion in the East, Constantine in the distant western province of Gaul was following the opposite policy. Faced with a difficult war with Maxentius, the ruler of Italy and North Africa, he decided to seek the support of the god of the Christians. Again events proved the Christian case. On 28 October 312 Constantine's army, the soldiers bearing shields painted with a Christian symbol, completely defeated the forces of his rival. Maxentius was killed. Constantine was supreme in the West. Meanwhile Maximinus Daia was fighting an unsuccessful war with the Christian King of Armenia. Famine and plague laid waste his own territory. He began to relax the persecution.[2] But it was too late. On 30 April 313 he was decisively defeated by Licinius fighting with the support of the Highest God. Maximinus was given no time to regroup his forces. In headlong retreat he granted full tolerance and restoration of their churches to the Christians.[3] When Licinius was about to enter Syria he committed suicide. So ended the last of the persecuters. Christian publicists, especially Lactantius and Eusebius, were not slow to write up the history of these years as a resounding demonstration of the truth of Christianity.

These events made a deep impression. This was not so much a result of a very large number of martyrs. In fact, the martyrs can only have formed a very small proportion of the Christian population. Thanks to Eusebius' *Martyrs of Palestine* we are exceptionally well informed about the persecution in the two Palestinian provinces.[4] It seems that between 303 and 311, eighty-six Christian inhabitants of the provinces died either by execution or after deportation. Only one bishop was martyred. The Christian population is likely to have amounted to tens if not hundreds of thousands.[5] In Egypt persecution may well have been more intense but elsewhere in the East less so. In the western provinces persecution was of much shorter duration.

---

[1] Ibid. ix. 7. 8.   [2] Ibid. 9. 13–23.

[3] Ibid. 10. 7–11.

[4] *De Martyris Palaestinae*, ed. E. Schwartz, Kleine Ausgabe (Leipzig, 1955), 401–42.

[5] A. von Harnack (1904–5).

Frend estimates that the total number of victims spread over the huge empire was between 3,000 and 3,500.[1]

But it is in the nature of martyrdom that it does not require a large number of victims to make a profound impact on their sympathizers and on society at large. Moreover, martyrs were not the only ones to suffer. Many others had experienced torture or forced labour, or imprisonment, and very many more still had faced the agonizing alternative of betraying their religion or facing the threat of torture and death. The demolition of churches, and the collection and destruction of Scriptures must have looked to many believers like an attempt on God himself. Then the defeat of the persecution and the fall of the persecutors came as a divine judgement. The final result of the Great Persecution provided a testimonial to the truth of Christianity which it could have won in no other way.

4. *Latin apologists of the age of the Great Persecution: Arnobius and Lactantius*

Whether the deepest causes of the Great Persecution were intellectual or not, the Persecution certainly took place in circumstances of intellectual debate. Less than twenty years earlier, Porphyry had written a systematic refutation of Christianity.[2] This itself seems not to have been widely known since the learned Eusebius of Caesarea did not know it in 311–13,[3] and Lactantius does not appear to have known it either.[4] But Porphyry's book had furnished material for other writers who were more widely read. One of them was Hierocles, the persecuting official, and others were described by Arnobius as the *viri novi*.[5] Of the Christian replies to pagan attack, the writings of Eusebius of Caesarea were easily the most distinguished, and in the long run the most influential.[6] But for a

[1] W. H. C. Frend (1965), 536–7. This estimate errs if anything on the generous side: cf. G. E. M. de Ste Croix (1954), esp. 100–5.

[2] See J. Bidez (1913), 64–79; A. Cameron (1967). But cf. above, p. 248 n. 8.

[3] Hierocles accused of plagiarizing Celsus (*P.G.* xxii. 796).

[4] P. de Labriolle (1934), 310.

[5] P. Courcelle (1953), 261 ff., 'Anti-Christian arguments and Christian Platonism', in A. D. Momigliano (1963), 151–92. See also A. J. Festugière (1940).

[6] For the works of Eusebius written during the persecution, see D. S. Wallace-Hadrill (1860), 17–18 and details of editions, ibid. 206–9. A. D. Momigliano (1963), 89–94; J. Quasten (1960), 328–34.

study of the evolving attitudes of the Roman governing class, Arnobius and Lactantius, the Latin apologists, are more significant.

Arnobius and Lactantius help to explain the failure of the Persecution, and the astonishing progress of Christianity immediately afterwards, because they have succeeded in showing convincingly and without blatant distortion that the Christian world view was not very different from that of educated pagans, in fact that the differences did not justify a confrontation. It is true that the apologists, like most of their kind, are concerned more with rational choice by the individual than with the motives of collective behaviour.[1] They do not analyse the factors that enabled Christianity to acquire a mass following in many cities of the empire, and to maintain its unity in spite of the vast expansion in numbers. The apologists do, however, help to explain the response to Christianity of an important group, the educated Roman upper class, the intellectual heirs of the men whose attitudes we have studied earlier. These men still mattered, and it was a fact of very great consequence that some of them—the most important was the emperor Constantine—became converted,[2] while others were not unduly disturbed by the progress of Christianity,[3] so that, when the time came, they were quite willing to serve a Christian emperor, who was employing the enormous prestige of the imperial office to further the interest of his religion. In A.D. 300, no group could have prevented Christianity from being a massive fact within the Roman empire, but without at least the passive connivance of the educated and the soldiers,[4] it could not have become the state religion.

[1] Cf. P. Brown (1972), 90, on the inability of Late Ancient authors to appreciate the irrational in any social function, even in the pantomime.

[2] P. Brown (1972), 161–82 = (1961), 1–11.

[3] In contrast to M. T. W. Arnheim (1972), I would insist on the surprisingly small amount of opposition aroused by the religious policy of Constantine and his Christian successors. The ending of animal sacrifice in public ritual, for instance, seems to have provoked little active protest, not enough to enter the historical record. Religion briefly became a political issue under Julian, and again at the time of the final Christian triumph under Theodosius I.

[4] The army, with its many recently Romanized barbarian officers, and peasant or barbarian other ranks, seems to have been basically indifferent to which gods their emperor addressed himself for victory. Trust in the ruler seems to have included confidence in his god. See A. H. M. Jones in A. D. Momigliano (ed.) (1963), 23–5, and above, p. 249 n. 4.

Arnobius,[1] like Apuleius, Tertullian, and Cyprian, wrote in Africa. There is evidence in his book that it was composed near the beginning of the Great Persecution.[2] In fact the argument is remarkably academic. One might think that the essential design even precedes the Persecution.[3]

The case Arnobius answered was a very general one. It was that since Christianity had come into the world the gods had deserted mankind, with the result that pestilence, drought, war, famine, locusts, mice, and hailstones[4] had troubled humanity. Of these inflictions, only famine seems to be treated as a contemporary problem.[5] It might be concluded that in Africa the Great Persecution took place against a background of food shortage.

Arnobius' book is addressed to pagans rather than Christians. He makes little or no use of the Bible, but a great deal of Roman secular literature. Within this too, he is selective. His approach is philosophical rather than historical in that he argues in terms of the government of the world, and not of the success or failure of Roman institutions. Arnobius cites an enormous amount of antiquarian information, but comparatively few historical *exempla*. This is in marked contrast to the procedure of Augustine,[6] and Orosius,[7] who resumed the defence of Christianity about a hundred years later, when Romans were again more conscious of their early history.[8]

But if Arnobius is little concerned with the *res publica*, his

---

[1] Arnobius, *Adversus Nationes*, ed. Aug. Reifferscheid (1875) = *C.S.E.L.* iv. Arnobius is cited in the translation of H. Bryce and H. Campbell in the Ante-Nicene Fathers Library, xix. On Arnobius, see Bardy in *R.A. Chr.* i. 709 ff.; H. Kraft (1966).

[2] *Adv. Nat.* i. 13: Christianity about 300 years old. This suggests a date, after A.D. 300; ibid. ii. 71: Rome is 1,500 years old. According to the Varronian era this would be 297. Destruction of scriptures and breaking up of Christian meetings: iv. 36. This should be after the First Edict of the Great Persecution in 303. i. 26–7: the oracles which preceded the Persecution. i. 16: the defeat of the Persians in 298. It looks as if the work was written soon after 303.

[3] According to a note in Jerome's *Chronicle*, imprecise in other respects, the recently converted Arnobius wrote to convince his bishop that the conversion was genuine (*Chron.* 2342).

[4] *Adv. Nat.* i. 3.

[5] i. 3; 13. The wars and plague seem to be more remote. Similar charges had been refuted by Cyprian's *Ad Demetrianum, P.L.* iv. 564 ff.

[6] *C.D.*, esp. iii.

[7] *Historiae contra Paganos passim* in edn. of C. Zangemeister (Teubner, 1889).

[8] See A. D. Momigliano (1963), 95–9.

approach is nevertheless very Roman. In the manner of a line of defenders of ancestral religion which stretches from Cicero to Symmachus,[1] Arnobius' defence of Christianity is based on scepticism. He frankly admits that he does not know the causes of the calamities that were being laid to the charge of Christianity.[2] But he can put forward convincing arguments to show that natural phenomena which already happened long before the arrival of Christianity were very unlikely to be the gods' retaliation for the spread of Christian worship.[3]

Leaving unanswered the problem as to why natural calamities happen, Arnobius proceeds to argue that, even when judged by the criteria of the best secular thought, Christianity was much more likely to be true than traditional religion.[4] At the very least Christianity was a worthwhile gamble. It offered its adherents immortality. If the claim was justified, the benefit would be infinite; if not, no harm was done.[5] On the other hand, Arnobius had no difficulty in showing that traditional religion had implications about the nature of the gods and their demands which were not reconcilable with philosophical ideas either of deity or of morality. This is the basis of the refutation of paganism which occupies by far the longest part of Arnobius' work.[6]

Much of this material had a long history in Roman literature. Some is derived directly or indirectly from Varro.[7] But already Cicero's *De Natura Deorum* (not to mention *De Divinatione*, and even earlier Ennius' *Euhemerus*) contained many arguments that could be used to demolish traditional religion. Indeed, Arnobius tells us that pagan contemporaries of his were advocating the destruction of copies of Cicero's subversive work.[8] Of course, Cicero and Varro had written without subversive intentions. Quite the contrary. In their days, Roman religion was securely buttressed by the prestige of the Roman institutions of which it formed part. Around A.D. 300, pagans as well

---

[1] e.g. Cotta in Cic. *N.D.* iii. 2 (5–6); the pagan speaker in Minucius Felix, *Oct.* 6. 1 and on this G. Lieberg. *Rh.M.* cvi (1963), 62–79. Symmachus, *Rel.* iii. 8.

[2] *Adv. Nat.* ii. 60; i. 7–12.   [3] i. 3; 4; 5; 6.

[4] i. 25 to end of ii. P. Courcelle (1963) argues that Book ii is composed of a succession of answers to objections to Christianity, especially its doctrine of immortality, raised by Hermeticists, Platonists, and the sect of the *viri novi*, on whom see Festugière (1840), 99.

[5] ii. 4.   [6] iii–vii.   [7] v. 8; vii. 1.   [8] iii. 6–7.

as Christians were less inclined to think of religion as simply part of the social organizations, but as something bigger existing outside and above secular institutions. As a result the consideration which had once neutralized rational criticism of traditional religion dropped away, while the prestige which the arguments received from the literary status of Cicero and Varro was as great as ever.[1]

Arnobius' defence of Christianity is scattered with reminiscences of Lucretius' *On the Nature of Things*.[2] For instance, he praises Jesus in words that strongly recall Lucretius' praise of Epicurus.[3] The literary reminiscences are to some extent Arnobius' tribute to a classical author's mastery of language. But there is a deeper sympathy. Arnobius was seeking to prove that public misfortunes, whether war, famine, or disease, were not sent by angry gods to punish the Romans for the existence of Christianity, and that it was therefore pointless to persecute the Christians.[4] Now Lucretius' famous book sought to prove that the processes of the world cannot be subject to divine intervention,[5] and that divine anger was therefore not the correct explanation of misfortune.[6] Lucretius had further produced arguments that the world could not have come into existence for the sake of man.[7] It followed that man had no reason to expect that nature would always favour him, and that there was no justification for seeking scapegoats if conditions became hostile. Lucretius had also found memorable words to describe the nature of the gods, and precisely the fact that they were inaccessible to anger,[8] so that mankind had no reason to

---

[1] Diocletian and his colleagues still saw Roman paganism as part of the institutions 'quae semel ab antiquis statuta et definita suum statum et cursum tenent ac possident' (*Mos. et Rom. Leg. Coll.* xv. 3. 2), but their belief no longer gained the active support of an important part of the population. In the battle of ideas Christians especially Eusebius, made effective use of arguments from history creating a new genre, ecclesiastical history, for the purpose. The defenders of traditional religion at this decisive period neglected history as if it were irrelevant.

[2] H. Hagendahl (1958), 12–47.

[3] i. 38, cf. Lucretius, v. 1–12.

[4] See the programmatical sentence in i. 2 ending with the title of Lucretius' poem.

[5] Lucr. v. 81 ff.

[6] Ibid. 1204–40 explains how the illusion that storms, etc., were sent by angry gods originated.

[7] Ibid. 198 ff.

[8] Ibid. i. 44–9 = ii. 646–51, cf. Arnobius, vi. 2

fear their wrath. Much of this was incompatible with Christianity, but it did at least constitute an irrefutably Graeco-
Roman demolition of the arguments for persecution. Moreover,
On the Nature of Things includes an eloquent denunciation of the
folly of worshipping idols. It is not surprising that Arnobius felt
great admiration for the work.

Arnobius was also greatly impressed by Lucretius' proof of
the mortality of the human soul, and of its essential likeness to
the souls of animals.[1] Evidently the idea harmonized well with
Arnobius' sense of the worthlessness of human existence. This
conviction Arnobius shared with many contemporary pagans,[2]
no less than Christians,[3] but unlike Porphyry he had no hope
that man could rise to God by the power of a rational and
divine soul. Something as frail as the human soul cannot have
been created by God[4] and cannot be immortal by its nature.[5]
Immortality is a miracle offered by God through Jesus.[6] This
view is far from orthodox Christianity, or at least from what
was to be defined as orthodox Christianity, but Arnobius has
expounded it at such length that it must have formed an important part of his personal faith.

Arnobius' departures from what was to become standard
Christian doctrine are just what makes his book a significant
historical document. It views Christianity to some extent from
the outside, and displays features that would have attracted an
educated pagan. In fact, Arnobius himself was a fairly recent
convert. It is even said that he wrote the book to convince his
bishop that the conversion was sincere. He had begun life as
a pious pagan. 'But lately . . . I worshipped images produced
from the furnace . . . bones of elephants, paintings, hangings
on ancient trees; whenever I espied an anointed stone and
one bedaubed with olive oil, as if some power resided in it, I
worshipped it . . . and begged benefits from a senseless block.'[7]
His had been the North African religiosity we know from
Apuleius.

As so often in the religious history of the later second and
third centuries, the decisive experience is said to have come to

---

[1] Lucr. iii, *passim.*
[2] Cf. Porphyry, *Ad Marcellam,* 32–4. E. R. Dodds (1965), 1–36.
[3] A. Wlosok (1960).   [4] *Adv. Nat.* ii. 37–47.
[5] ii. 14–30.   [6] iii. 60.   [7] i. 39.

him in a dream.[1] His belief in the truth of Christianity was confirmed by the healing miracles of Jesus. True, miraculous cures
could have been performed by a magician (*magus*), but Jesus
did not work like a *magus*. He achieved cures without aids such
as juices of herbs, without incantations, or sacrifices, and he was
even able to delegate his power.[2] Moreover Jesus' miracles
could be distinguished from those of magicians by the test of
purpose. Jesus used his powers not for divination, not to cause
disease, not to produce quarrels among relatives, not to open
locked doors without a key, not to influence chariot races, not
to induce illicit love. Those were the objectives of magicians.
Jesus performed miracles to help suffering mankind. That was
divine.[3]

Arnobius admits that faith in the miracles requires belief in
the truth of the Scriptures. But this belief is facilitated by
knowledge of the rapid growth of the Church and of the great
number of widely separated men who accept the truth of these
books.[4]

Arnobius' writings reflect his recent conversion. He seems to
have little knowledge of the Bible; at any rate, he scarcely ever
quotes from it. He hardly deals with the Christian community,
its discipline, its festivals, and its organization. Christianity is
essentially a system of belief and worship which the individual
chooses because it is true, and because it offers the hope of a life
after death. The essence of Christianity is monotheism. Christians worship the supreme God. The way in which Jesus participates in the divinity is left obscure. In one passage he compares
him to the Sibyl filled with Apollo's oracular power.[5] Arnobius
—at least for argument's sake—refrains from denying the
existence of the pagan gods but of course insists that Christians
do not worship them. 'For as we are in communication with the
very source of divinity from which the divine nature of all divine
beings whatsoever is derived, we think it superfluous to approach
each one individually; since we neither know who they are, or
what names they have, nor are able to see or understand, or find
out their number . . . In the Kingdom of earth we are in no way
obliged to do reverence to members of the royal family as well
as the rulers themselves but whatever is due to them is . . .

[1] *Jer. Chron.* 2342.   [2] i. 43–53.   [3] i. 43.
[4] i. 55 ff.; ii. 5; ibid. 8: defence of faith.   [5] i. 62.

implied in the worship paid to the Kings themselves.'[1] This argument would have been found thoroughly unsatisfactory by Christian writers before or after Arnobius' time.[2] Even for Arnobius' younger contemporary Lactantius the pagan gods were demons and absolutely evil. But the fact that early in the fourth century a Christian could write like this obviously made conversion to Christianity a less violent break with Roman tradition than it would otherwise have been.

Christianity was different not only in the object of worship but also the manner. Christians did not build temples. Their community centres were mere places of assembly, not houses of God.[3] Worship was imageless and Christians practised no sacrifices. Not only did the Christians lack these essentials of traditional worship but they abhorred them when used by their neighbours. Arnobius defends the Christian attitude and explains the absurdity of thinking of god as a being confined to an image or a temple, and in need of sacrifices and capable of being appeased by gifts.[4] His arguments are unfair in that they attribute a very naïve attitude to pagans.[5] But they gain strength from having long been part of the Roman philosophical tradition. Varro had taught that Roman worship had originally been imageless,[6] and also that gods did not demand sacrifices.[7] The Stoics, Seneca, for instance, had insisted that true worship consisted of moral conduct.[8] Admittedly the Neoplatonists since the later second century A.D. had tried to rehabilitate images and sacrifices by using them in theurgy.[9] But even these opponents of Christianity were not unanimous. Porphyry attacked Christianity and defended images, but he was against animal sacrifice.[10] Indeed it would seem that the tide of even

---

[1] iii. 2–3.

[2] J. M. P. B. van der Putten (1971) argues that Arnobius admits the existence of pagan gods for arguments sake but does not believe in it. On tolerance and lack of it in apologetic literature, see J. Vogt (1968).

[3] Monumental church architecture was by and large a consequence of the conversion of Constantine. See below, p. 299 n. 6 f.

[4] vi and vii.

[5] For what an educated pagan said in defence of images, read Dio Chrys. *Or.* xii. 25 ff., 40 ff. J. Bidez (1913), 143 ff.: le traité περὶ ἀγαλμάτων. N. H. Baynes (1955), 128–33.

[6] Tert. *Apol.* 25. 11; Plut. *Numa*, 8. Augustine, *C.D.* iv. 31.

[7] Arn., *Adv. Nat.* vii. 1.   [8] See above, p. 117 n. 3.

[9] See above, p. 234; also H. Lewy (1956); S. Eitrem (1942).

[10] See J. Bidez (1913), cited, n. 5, above.

unsophisticated opinion had turned against sacrifice. At any rate, the end of the practice under the Christian emperors seems to have caused remarkably little comment.

The Christian religion as presented by Arnobius is in many ways a sombre one in this respect too recalling Lucretius' Epicureanism. It offers immortality and provides an incentive for moral conduct, but promises few benefits in this world. No doubt the prospect of contact through prayer with the supreme power in the world offers psychological support, but believers are given no reason for supposing that prayers will improve their earthly condition. With one exception, the characteristic post-Antonine readiness to accept the authority of sacred books,[1] a great deal of classical rationalism survives in Arnobius. Christianity as described by Arnobius could not claim to perform the role of the traditional public religion of Rome. In fact, as far as Arnobius is concerned, there is an element of paradox in the triumph of Christianity. He had argued that the calamities which persecutors explained as the gods' punishment for Christianity were in fact due to natural causes and that divine wrath had nothing to do with them. Indeed belief in gods subject to wrath was unworthy of educated thought. But with the triumph of Christianity, belief in the wrath of God and the possibility of arousing it by religious error came back with a vengeance, and as a result it became a regular part of imperial policy to suppress religious dissent.

The *Divine Institutes* (*Institutiones Divinae*) of Lactantius[2] are certainly later than the *Adversus Nationes*, even though it is not easy to decide when precisely they were written. The dedications to Constantine suggest the persecutions are over[3] and that the persecutors have been punished. But Book v treats the persecutions as still continuing.[4] It would seem that when the work was being written it was already clear that the attack on Christianity had failed. Not only does Lactantius repeat the ancient Christian challenge that the number of the faithful is

---

[1] The Chaldaean Oracles: *Edition* by E. Des Places (1971), monograph H. Lewy (1956). The Hermetic Corpus: A. J. Festugière (1944–5). Popularity of Oracles: S. Eitrem (1947).

[2] On Lactantius, see J. Stevenson (1957). The *Divine Institutes* are cited in the translation of W. Fletcher in the Ante-Nicene Christian Library, xxi.

[3] i. 1. 13 ff.; vii. 26. 11 ff.

[4] So also vi. 17. 6. See T. D. Barnes (1973), 39–41.

growing as a direct result of persecution,[1] but also, in contrast to earlier apologists, Lactantius is indifferent to the charges that were made against the Christians. By and large he passes them over with contempt, and concentrates on proving the truth and even the 'Romanism' of Christianity. He can even afford to treat the persecution as something that discredits the cause it professes to maintain. Gods that order atrocities so that they may receive the sacrifices of compelled worshippers only bring disrepute upon themselves.[2] Lactantius was writing at a time when a Christian no longer needed to write a defensive apology, and when the sufferings of the martyrs had begun to shock public opinion. The Christians had practically won. By the time *Divine Institutes* were completed they had won. It remained for Lactantius to write further books: on *The Anger of God* and on *The Deaths of the Persecutors*.[3] These, as it were, complete his case. In the first he defends the doctrine that God is angered by sin. This contradicted the deeply held philosophical view maintained even by Lactantius' teacher, Arnobius, that the divine nature must be passionless.[4] Lactantius overcame the difficulty by describing the Christian God in terms of the Roman father of the family.[5] In the *Deaths of the Persecutors* Lactantius provided practical proof of the truth of his earlier writings. Divine judgement had been passed unambiguously in favour of Christianity.

Lactantius' *Divine Institutes* is a work of propaganda. His aim is not so much to obtain tolerance for Christianity as to win it adherents, moreover adherents among the governing classes, men well educated in the Latin literary classics. Literary education was, and would continue to be for many years, an obstacle to the acceptance of Christianity. 'Philosophers and orators and poets are pernicious, because they are easily able to ensnare unwary souls by the sweetness of their discourse.' Lactantius felt that of his distinguished predecessors Tertullian had been too obscure, and Cyprian convincing only to those converted already. Accordingly, he planned a work in the Roman literary tradition.[6] The title *Institutiones Divinae* recalls the text-books from which students of law acquired the elements

---

[1] v. 13.   [2] v. 21.
[3] J. Moreau (1954), and the convincing paper of T. D. Barnes (1973).
[4] Arnobius i. 23; 25; vii. 36.
[5] A. Wlosok (1960).
[6] *Div. Inst.* i. 1.

of legal science.[1] The author is also consciously following the tradition of Cicero's philosophical works.[2] The treatise systematically answers the problems discussed in *De Natura Deorum, De Finibus,* and *De Officiis* from a Christian point of view. The treatise ends with some apocalyptic chapters about the end of the world. These appear to be thoroughly un-Roman but in fact perform the role of the myth at the end of several Platonic dialogues, and more specifically of the *Dream of Scipio* in Cicero's *De Republica.*

From beginning to end of his treatise Lactantius supports Christian teaching with references to the Roman classics which it had been, and probably still was, his professional duty to teach to the young.[3] Cicero is quoted again and again.[4] Essential arguments are supported with quotations from Virgil or Seneca. From Arnobius, Lactantius has learnt to appreciate Lucretius, who furnishes classical formulations of a passionate rejection of idolatry.[5] In contrast biblical citations are conspicuous only in one of the seven books: the one concerned with the life of Jesus and its significance.[6]

Lactantius' earliest work *De Opificio Dei* includes hardly any specifically Christian passages, doctrines, or concepts. Christians are 'the philosophers of our sect',[7] Christianity is 'the true philosophic doctrine'. God is described in universally acceptable deistic terms. Lactantius concludes with an apology for writing with more obscurity than was befitting on account of the 'necessity of circumstances and time'. When, God being willing, times become favourable he will write more explicitly.[8] This neutral terminology would be of great use in the post-Constantinian empire when Christianity and paganism had to coexist; and in many circumstances of life, especially public

---

[1] *Div. Inst.* i. 1: 'and if some skilful men . . . published Institutions of civil law . . .'.

[2] Lactantius alludes to the example of Cicero—without naming him. 'If some of the greatest orators . . . having completed the works of their pleadings, at last gave themselves up to philosophy and regarded that as . . . rest from their labours, if they tortured their minds in the investigation of those things which could not be found out . . .' (i. 1).

[3] Born and educated in North Africa, he was called to Nicomedia by Diocletian to teach Latin rhetoric—no doubt to the boys of court society, and to sons of local families who hoped to enter the imperial service.

[4] References in R. Pichon (1901).

[5] H. Hagendahl (1958).   [6] iv.

[7] *De Opificio Dei,* i. 2.   [8] Ibid. 20. 1.

life, Christians and pagans had perforce to emphasize what united rather than what divided them.[1]

The essence of Christianity as presented by Lactantius, is monotheism, worship of the one supreme God. The argument for Christian monotheism was aided by the fact that from the earliest times a kind of monotheism had coexisted with the worship of innumerable deities. Pagans dealing with phenomena which could not be assigned to a particular specialized deity would invoke an undifferentiated and nameless divine nature which they described anonymously by terms like the gods or simply god.[2] We find this already in Herodotus,[3] who wrote in the mid fifth century B.C., and it appears with increasing frequency in writings of the early empire, especially in wishes and exclamations.[4] Such remarks spontaneously uttered in conversation, Tertullian had urged, betrayed an unconscious recognition of divine truth.[5] Lactantius too argues: 'If any weighty necessity should press upon men, they remember God. If terror of war has resounded, if the pestilential force of disease has overhung them, if long continued drought has denied nourishment to the crops . . . they betake themselves to God, aid is implored from God, God is exhorted to succour them.'[6]

Lactantius had no difficulty in showing that the orderly and harmonious universe must be governed by a single authority. Like an army composed of many regiments, the world could only achieve the harmonious co-ordination of its different components through the control of a supreme commander.[7] Moreover, Lactantius could demonstrate that a monotheistic view of the world is implied in numerous passages of Greek and Latin classics.[8]

[1] Ibid. i. 20, cf. i. 1.

[2] See above, p. 177 n. 6. In works other than *De Mortibus Persecutorum* Lactantius avoids using words in their technical Christian meaning, e.g. *oratio* in the sense of prayer (rather than speech). See T. D. Barnes (1973), 41 n. 137, and J. W. Borleffs, *Mnemosyne*, N.S. lviii (1930).

[3] Linforth (1928), 204–39.   [4] See above, pp. 186 n. 6 and 207.

[5] H. Chadwick (1966), 93, Tert. *Apol.* 17. 5.

[6] *Div. Inst.* ii. 1.

[7] Ibid. i. 3. *P.L.* vi. 124B. Also 'to say that the universe is governed by the will of many, is equivalent to the declaration that there are many minds in one body'.

[8] i. 5, e.g. Verg. *Aen.* vi. 724–7; *Georg.* iv. 221–2; ibid. ii. 325–7. Ovid, *Met.* i. 21 ff.; also of course numerous philosophers and the oracular or semi-oracular literature represented in the writings of Orpheus, the Sibylline Oracles, and certain theological oracles of Apollo (i. 5–6).

The divinity of Jesus had to be reconciled with monotheism, but this was not difficult to do convincingly. After all, philosophers had managed to reconcile the infinite variety of gods of traditional religion with a monotheist picture of the world. Certainly Lactantius insists on the divinity of the Son. 'He who worships the Father only does not worship him at all, since he does not worship the Son. But he who receives the Son and bears his name, he together with the Son worships the Father also, since the Son is the ambassador and messenger and priest of the Father.'[1] In other words, worship of the supreme God includes recognition and adoption of the name of the Son. The role of the Son is further expounded, 'for, since there was no righteousness on earth, God sent a teacher, as it were a living law, to found a new name and temple, that by his words and example he might spread throughout the earth a true and holy worship'.[2] And worship for Lactantius is essentially a matter of moral life.[3] Thus the role of Jesus is essentially that of a moral teacher. Of course, Lactantius insists that in both precept and practice Jesus was far superior to all other teachers of mankind, and he also gives due emphasis to the powers with which Jesus is invested by virtue of being the Son of God. Nevertheless, the claim made for Jesus was basically a familiar one. Seen in this way, he could take his place naturally in the long line of moral philosophers whose memory was held in high honour by educated Greeks and Romans. In fact this 'theology' would have been more acceptable to a pagan than to a well-informed Christian. Moreover, Lactantius' God consists of two persons, not three. There is no mention of the Holy Ghost.[4] The relationship of Father and Son is explained by an analogy which is thoroughly Roman but would surely have been found unsatisfactory by theologians of the Greek world. 'When someone has a specially beloved son, who however is still at home under parental authority, the father may grant to his son the name and power of "master" but in civil law it is one household and has one master. In the same way, the world is one house of God; and Father and Son who dwell in concord in the world are one

[1] *Div. Inst.* iv. 29.

[2] iv. 25.

[3] vi. 24.

[4] Contrast definitions of Tertullian in *Adversus Praxeam, P.L.* ii. 154–96 and Novatius in *De Trinitate, P.L.* iii. 911–82. J. Moingt (1966–9).

God; for the one is as two and the two are as one.'[1] This nevertheless involves subordination of Jesus and would not be tolerable to those who thought that in becoming followers of Jesus they had placed themselves under the protection of the supreme God and no other. The difference between those who accepted Christianity more or less as interpreted by Lactantius or Arnobius and those who did not was fundamental. It would lead to the Arian controversy.

Worship of God according to the exposition of Lactantius is largely identical with moral conduct. 'God's offering is innocence of soul; his sacrifice, praise and a hymn.'[2] Earlier he had written: 'Therefore upon the altar of God ... which is placed in the heart of man and cannot be defiled with blood, there is placed righteousness, patience, faith, innocence, chastity and abstinence.'[3] Lactantius can cite Seneca in support of this view: 'Will you think of God as great and placid ... not be worshipped with the immolation of victims and with much blood ... but with a pure mind and with a good and honourable purpose.'[4] It is evident that (as preached by Lactantius) Christian worship would appeal to an educated, philosophically-minded Roman.

Lactantius rams home the superiority of Christianity. 'What is the religion of the gods? ... I see nothing else in it than a rite pertaining to the fingers only. But our religion teaches justice ... has its existence altogether in the soul of the worshipper ... has the mind itself for sacrifice.'[5] The comparison is tendentious. The fact that Christian religion linked worship and moral conduct so explicitly and emphatically must have worked in its favour with educated Romans. The nature of traditional paganism made it difficult to give ethics an explicit and central part in it. Christianity indisputably did so.

Naturally Lactantius made the most of this. He points out that Christianity combines two activities which were traditionally separate, philosophy and worship. 'Since [in paganism] philosophy and the religious system of the gods are separated and far removed from each other, seeing that some are professors of wisdom [philosophy] through whom it is manifest that there is

---

[1] *Div. Inst.* iv. 29, cf. the household analogy in iv. 3. The translation is from R. MacMullen (1969), 121.

[2] vi. 25.   [3] vi. 24.   [4] vi. 25 and Seneca, *Ep.* 25. 2.   [5] v. 20.

no approach to the gods, and that others are priests of religion, through whom wisdom is not learnt, it is manifest that the one is not true wisdom and that the other is not true religion . . . but when [in Christianity] wisdom is joined by an inseparable connection to religion both must necessarily be true, because in worship we ought to be wise (philosophical), that is to know the proper object and manner of worship, and in our wisdom to worship, that is to complement our knowledge by action.'[1]

Lactantius' approach is eminently rational. But the rationalism has limits. There is, for instance, the rejection of geometrical astronomy and of logical deductions based on it. 'How is it with those who imagine that there are antipodes opposite to our footsteps . . . Is there anyone so senseless as to believe that there are men whose footsteps are higher than their heads? . . . that the crops and trees grow downwards?' He then goes on to show how this absurd conclusion is derived logically from the folly of explaining the daily rising and setting of sun and stars by circular motions of the heavens.[2]

This scientifically absurd passage has a rhetorical function. It is intended as a demonstration that philosophy can lead to dangerously misleading conclusions. It is part of the argument of Book iii, the whole of which is devoted to one theme: the inability of philosophy to discover the most important truths.[3] Only religion can do that; but religion is based on revelation and authority. Of course, the basic authority is found in the Bible:[4] the narrative of the New Testament supported by the extremely ancient prophecies of the Old. But wherever possible Lactantius makes use of pagan authorities. A presupposition of the whole is readiness of the reader to accept the authority of oracles.

We have seen that attitudes had changed considerably since the early empire.[5] The authority of oracles was called into question by Cicero, who could conceive the possibility that the whole of divination was an illusion. Since then not only had scepticism as to the possibility of divine revelation through oracles declined, but educated men had grown ready to accept detailed and explicit communications from the gods. Notably

---

[1] iv. 3.   [2] iii. 24, cf. Lucret. i. 1051 ff.
[3] Cf. Wlosok (1960), 201–4.   [4] iv. 5.
[5] See above, p. 260 n. 1.

there was in circulation oracular literature, of indefinite age and obscure origin, which combined the prestige of divine inspiration with that of the mysterious wisdom of the East.[1] Among these writings were the so-called Sibylline oracles, a large collection of Greek oracular poems which had been composed, at least in some cases, by Jewish writers without becoming part of the Jewish canon, and then had been adapted to Christian use.[2] Their authority was no doubt increased by the fact that quite different oracles bearing the same name had long been part of Roman public religion. Thus they could provide support for Christian doctrines that might otherwise have seemed incredible. Teachings confirmed in this way were the historicity of the life and passion of Jesus, and the coming of a Last Judgement and of the Kingom of God.[3]

To the same class of literature belonged the Hermetic treatises, a large class of writings purporting to be dictated by the Egyptian god, Thut, in the Greek guise of Hermes Trismegistus. The writings expound a religion whose aim is the achievement of immortality, and which prescribes repentance, ascetism, and religious enlightenment as means of gaining its object.[4] Lactantius quotes Hermetic writing as evidence for the immortality of the soul,[5] to forecast an age of flood, fire, war, and pestilence,[6] and to support the doctrines of the unity and namelessness of God.[7] In the same way, Lactantius quotes oracles of Apollo[8] and the Oracles of Hystaspes[9] when it serves his purpose. Lactantius was the first Christian apologist to do this. His action is understandable in an age when there were many fringe Christians, and when the persecutors had exploited oracles against the Christians. But citation of pagan oracles implies that they possess genuine inspiration. This Lactantius can afford to do

[1] One might compare the 'ancient prophecies' that were current in late medieval England (K. Thomas (1971), 389 ff.).

[2] A. Rzach (1923); J. Geffcken, *Oracula Sibyllina* (1902, repr. 1967), also *idem*, *Komposition der Orakula Sibyllina* (Leipzig, 1902, repr. 1967); V. Nikiprowetzky (1970).

[3] Especially *Orac.* vii and viii in A. Kurfess (1951). Sibyl cited as foretelling sufferings of Jesus: *Div. Inst.* iv. 18; Last Judgement: ibid. vii. 20, 23–4; Kingdom of God; vii. 24.

[4] Festugière (1953), esp. 97–118; id. (1950), 81–4 argues that there were no Hermetic communities. The writings are literary, not ritual.

[5] *Div. Inst.* vii. 13.   [6] vii. 18.

[7] i. 6; also forecasts of the miracles of Jesus, iv. 15.

[8] i. 7.   [9] H. Windisch (1929).

because of the traditional Christian identification of pagan gods with evil spirits.

The oracles work through the inspiration of demons, corrupted angels, who misuse knowledge acquired in the divine service to gain the confidence of mankind before leading it to destruction. The demons 'wander over the whole earth and contrive a solace for their own perdition by the destruction of man. They fill every place with snares, deceits and errors. They cling to individuals, occupy whole houses, assume the name of genii. They are worshipped as averters of the very evils which they themselves cause.'[1]

Demons are rendered helpless by Christian prayer and Christian symbols. In the presence of Christians or of Christian symbols they cannot communicate with their pagan worshippers through sacrifices.[2] Christianity provides effective protection from their attack. 'They injure only those by whom they are feared. Those whom God protects, they cannot injure.' The name of God has power to drive demons out of the bodies of men of whom they have gained possession. Often—so Lactantius claims—the demons emerge howling a confession of their defeat, that they have been conquered, that they are burning, that they are eager to depart.[3]

The identification of the pagan gods with demons performs an essential function in the *Divine Institutes*, as in earlier apologies of Christianity. For the advocates of Christianity had not only to show that their religion was true, but also that paganism was false and utterly to be rejected.

This was a bold claim to make concerning the ancient religion of an imperial people. The Christian attack on the gods was, of course, helped by the rationalism of earlier Romans, the sceptical spokesmen in Cicero's dialogues, the poem of Lucretius, and rationalist passages in Livy.[4] The morality of the gods as portrayed in Greek and Roman mythology was discreditable.[5] Apologists needed only to repeat and develop the old criticism.

---

[1] *Div. Inst.* ii. 15 (abridged).   [2] iv. 28.   [3] ii. 16.

[4] On Roman rationalism, see above, pp. 29 ff.

[5] On the original social and ritual context of the myths, see W. Burkert (1972), 39–45, 122 ff.; J.-P. Vernant (1965); H. Hommel (1972), esp. 413 ff. The trouble with the myths was that they had since time immemorial broken loose from the precise circumstances in which they had had religious meaning. They had become part of the raw material of literature to be interpreted and used by authors according to their own literary purpose.

The Romans of earlier times could maintain that certain gods had once been human rulers, without implying that they were no longer to be treated in every way as immortal gods.[1] It was easy in the changed atmosphere to point out the inconsistency of this attitude and to generalize that the supposed gods were simply dead men. Nevertheless, polytheism, apart from the 'sentimental' value of traditional cults, had two very powerful arguments in its favour, that divination seemed to work, and that the belief in gods was universal. The Christians, since the first Apology of Justin and probably before that, refuted these two arguments by asserting that both phenomena were the work of demons who, for their own purposes, had tricked mankind into honouring them as gods.

The transformation of the gods into demons has a significant psychological consequence. The gods had sometimes been cruel or arbitrary, but they could be placated by offerings in quite the same way as arbitrary and tyrannous humans. They were not essentially hostile or spiteful. Christianity offered man enormously powerful assistance, but it also proclaimed the existence of powerful and totally evil adversaries. Life became a battle in which men must fight for God against 'the enemy'. 'For God who created men for this warfare, desired that they should stand prepared in battle array, and with minds keenly intent should watch against the stratagems and open attacks of our single enemy who as is the practice of skilful and experienced generals, endeavours to ensnare us by various arts . . . for he infuses into some insatiable avarice . . .' He infects others with anger, or lust, or envy, or ambition, or philosophic curiosity, and all the while he has only one aim: to separate men from God and to lead them to utter destruction.[2] Lactantius can adapt the old allegory of Hercules at the crossroads. No longer is the choice between virtue and pleasure, but between God and the devil, with heaven as the destination of those who choose the former, and eternal punishment as the end of the others.[3]

For the Christian life was a never-ending state of emergency,

---

[1] e.g. Liv. i. 16: apotheosis of Romulus. Saturn and Faunus are said to have been kings. Many emperors were deified after their death, cf. above, pp. 66 ff.

[2] *Div. Inst.* vi. 4 = *P.L.* vi. 648. There had been a tendency to believe in supernatural personifications of absolute evil, especially in connection with magic, in later Greek or Roman paganism. Cf. above, p. 179. But it was left to Christianity to fill the world with evil spirits.   [3] *Div. Inst.* vi. 3 = *P.L.* vi. 643.

in confrontation with an army of treacherous, cunning, and infinitely malicious spirits. 'We must be on the watch, we must post guards, must undertake military expeditions, must shed our blood. . . .'[1] Henceforth, the emotions that arise in men in time of crisis could be aroused in new contexts. They were brought into play in the first place in religious disputes, particularly sectarian divisions within the Christian community itself, but also in other circumstances where the actions or opinions of individuals could be represented as instigated by demons and absolutely evil.[2]

Personal devotion was, of course, given a much greater place in a Christian's life than in that of a traditional Roman. For Cicero, religion was essentially the correct performance of the prescribed rite. To exceed this and to pray outside the prescribed occasions was superstition. The Christian precept was quite different: 'If it is an excellent thing to pray once, how much more so to do it more frequently. If it is well to do it at the first hour, then it is well to do it all day.'[3] Or again: 'Worship of God . . . requires the greatest devotion and fidelity, for how will God either love the worshipper, if he is not himself loved by him, or grant to the petitioner whatever he shall ask, when he draws nigh to offer his prayer without sincerity or reverence? But these men [the pagans] when they come to offer their sacrifice present to their gods nothing from within, nothing of their own . . . Therefore when the worthless sacrifices are completed, they leave their religion altogether in the temple.'[4] It would probably be a mistake to treat Lactantius' comparison as if it was an objective statement. No doubt feelings of reverence and sincerity were present in the minds of praying pagans too. But there is no disputing that Christianity took a much more positive view of religious emotion. While the traditional Roman reaction was to damp down religious fervour, the Christian

---

[1] vi. 4 = *P.L.* vi. 647.

[2] Metaphors of war, v. 20 (*P.L.* vi. 616); v. 22. 17; vi. 4. 15 ff.; vii. 27. 15. Heresy (i.e. sectarianism) instigated by demons: iv. 30.

[3] iv. 28 contrast Cic. *Leg.* ii. 28 (72). Cicero would have agreed with eighteenth-century suspicion of enthusiasm exemplified by a saying of Henry More: 'If ever Christianity is exterminated it will be by enthusiasm'—cited by K. Clark, *The Gothic Revival* (London, 1928), 134. See also R. Knox, *Enthusiasm* (Oxford, 1950). Lactantius deliberately defends Christian zeal against the traditional Roman attitude that zeal or enthusiasm is not religious but superstitious, cf. S. Calderone (1972).   [4] *Div. Inst.* v. 20.

tendency was to encourage it, but also to confine it within the bounds of communal and ecclesiastical discipline, and to ensure that it flowed in approved channels of tradition and orthodoxy.[1]

Lactantius presents his message in as traditionally Roman a form as possible. We hear much of moral conduct while Christian ritual is only mentioned allusively. But in the descriptions of ethics the old form covers a considerable shift in emphasis.

In republican Rome, notably in Cicero's *De Officiis*, moral duties were discussed in a social context. The problem was how a man should behave in each of the great variety of relationships that comprise life in society.[2] But this was not the problem as seen by Lactantius. For him, virtue is to worship God[3] and 'whoever strives to hold the right course of life ought not to look to the earth, but to heaven: and to speak more plainly, he ought not to follow man, but God; not to serve these earthly images, but the heavenly God.'[4] The distinction is theoretical, but it is nevertheless fundamental. In traditional Roman society, religious community, and secular society were one, to such an extent that there was very little formulation of rules of conduct in religious terms. It was taken for granted that the gods would enforce the customs of the Roman people.

But a Christian was a member of two societies, each with its own rules, and while in practice a great deal of harmonization was possible, the possibility of conflict was always there.

In Lactantius' detailed classification of duties, the influence of Cicero is recognizable. Following the Stoic Panaetius, Cicero had divided the rules of conduct into four classes of duties according to whether they are related respectively to the search for truth (*sapientia*), or the preservation of society (*justitia*), or to the achievement of greatness of character (*animi magnitudo*) or self-control (*modestia, temperantia*).[5] Lactantius follows this classification, more or less[6]—as Ambrose was to do after him.[7]

---

[1] On discipline, see O. D. Watkins (1920).

[2] v. 19, 34, cf. A. Wlosok (1960), 184–90.

[3] Various relationships listed *Offic.* i. 17 (53).

[4] *Div. Inst.* vi. 5; vii. 5, cf. Wlosok (1960), 192.

[5] Four classes of conduct: *Offic.* i. 5 (15).

[6] Book iv: wisdom; v–vi. 13: justice; vi. 14–19: greatness of character interpreted as the use of affections; vi. 20–3: self-control interpreted as control of the senses. I am not suggesting that Lactantius has imitated the structure of *De Officiis*, only that he had Cicero's, i.e. Panaetius' classification of virtue in mind.

[7] H. Hagendahl (1958), 347–72.

The search for truth is, of course, represented by the Christian religion. The other three classes are recognizable, but modified in a significant way. As in *De Officiis*,[1] justice is considered the basic virtue.[2] But the concept of justice has changed. Lactantius analyses it into two components: piety and equity, and piety is the essential pre-condition of equity.[3] Lactantius insists that justice cannot be achieved without the worship of the true God. He proves this with reference to the classical myth of the ages of the world. The injustice and strife which characterized the iron age in Greek and Latin poetry was, according to Lactantius, due to abandonment of the worship of the true God, whom primitive man had worshipped, for the false gods who have been worshipped ever since. The worship of Jupiter and injustice entered the world together.[4] Justice can only be restored if people return to the worship of God, i.e. become Christians.[5] The argument turns into an effective reply to the persecution: the atrocities committed on behalf of the gods in the course of the persecution are proof that justice is incompatible with the worship of pagan gods.[6]

The other component of justice, equity, is defined in social and indeed revolutionary terms: 'Therefore neither the Greeks nor the Romans could possess justice, because they had men differing from one another by many degrees, from the poor to the rich, from the humble to the powerful . . . for where all are not equally matched there is no equity; and inequality itself excludes justice.'[7] This is not a political programme in Lactantius any more than was the Stoic doctrine of natural equality on which it is based.[8] Lactantius was concerned to show that the worship of the gods had resulted in injustice, not to advise how a new society could be built.

The social action which Lactantius proposes at greatest length is charity. Lactantius is aware that the behaviour advocated by him is related to that which Cicero had classified

---

[1] Justice has the greatest scope: 'latissime patet ea ratio qua societas hominum inter ipsos et vitae quasi communitas continetur . . .' (*Offic.* i. 7 (20)). See also i. 43 (155). Justice in a wider sense, i.e. the virtue that holds together society, is further subdivided into justice in a narrower sense and 'well-doing' (*benificentia, benignitas, liberalitas*) (i. 7 (20)).

[2] *Div. Inst.* v. 5.   [3] Ibid. 15.   [4] Ibid. 5–6.
[5] Ibid. 8.   [6] Ibid. 9.   [7] Ibid. 15.
[8] Cf. *Offic.* 17 (21): sunt autem privata nulla natura.

as *benevolentia* and *liberalitas*, but he also insists that Christian giving is different in one fundamental respect. Aid is to be given freely, in consideration not of the social ties that exist between donor and recipient, but simply of need.[1] Captives are to be ransomed, but the poor rather than relatives and friends. Widows and orphans should be protected, the sick attended to, the dead buried. For Cicero the moral duties are part of the nexus of benefits, received and given, which link a man to his society.[2] For the Christian they are to be performed strictly for their own or rather for God's sake.

The two remaining classes of Cicero's analysis of duty can also be recognized in the *Divine Institutes*. Lactantius' chapters on the use of the emotions overlaps with the aspects of behaviour treated by Cicero under greatness of mind, while Lactantius' treatment of the disciplining of the senses corresponds to some extent to Cicero's discussion of self-control (*patientia* and *temperantia*).

For Cicero, greatness of mind required the emotional detachment traditionally advocated by Stoicism. 'One must be free of all disturbance of the mind, desire and fear, no less than excessive grief and pleasure and anger, so that the mind can enjoy calm and freedom from care, a condition which is conducive to consistency and dignity.'[3] But Lactantius criticizes the Stoic teaching on the emotions.[4] For Lactantius the passions are not in themselves evil.[5] Lactantius starts from the treatment of Cicero in the *Tusculan Disputations* but he modifies the philosophical opinions he finds there to bring them into accord with Christianity, as he sees it. Fear is neither to be eradicated nor relieved, but to be redirected towards God, who can bring about that nothing else at all need be feared. Desire of temporal joys is a vice but of heavenly things virtue. Only desire for heavenly things can guarantee the endurance necessary to overcome the suffering through which they are gained. Thus Lactantius teaches that self-control is not to be achieved by the

---

[1] *Div. Inst.* vi. 10–12, cf. H. Hagendahl (1958), 353–8. *Div. Inst.* vi. 12 criticizes *Offic.* ii. 18 (64). *Div. Inst.* vi. 11 criticizes *Offic.* ii. 15 (54).

[2] *Offic.* i. 45–60 considers the different relationships involved in benefits and discusses priorities.

[3] Ibid. 20 (69).   [4] *Div. Inst.* vi. 14–19.

[5] vi. 19; H. Hagendahl (1958), 338–41 points out derivation from Cic. *Tusc.* iv. 6 (11–14).

suppression of passions, but by their redirection, or sublimation. An unfashionable example: 'we should not be angry with those who revile and injure us, but should always be ready to use our hands on the young, that is, when they err we should correct them with continued stripes, lest by useless love and excessive indulgence they should be trained to evil and nourished in vice.'[1]

Lactantius' insistence that the passions have a potential for good is clearly related to his struggle to make the angry and punishing God of the Bible philosophically acceptable. This necessarily also involved rejection of the ideal of the passionless sage which had had so long a history in ancient thought and society, and which had led Lactantius' own teacher Arnobius into opinions which were highly dubious from a Christian point of view. No doubt too the view of life as a campaign against demons inevitably involved mobilization of the passions.

After dealing with the passions, Lactantius proceeds to the related topic of the five senses and their proper use.[2] This topic occupies the place of Cicero's discussion of the duties of the fourth virtue.[3] But compared with Cicero, Lactantius shows a narrowing of point of view both in the range of conduct covered and in flexibility. Cicero is concerned to discuss conduct over the whole range from the morality of public men to matters of manners and etiquette. The factors determining the rightness of conduct are complex too. The nature of the individual, his social status, the particular situation, generally held standards of right and wrong, as well as aesthetics, are taken into account. Lactantius is concerned with one object, to fit man for worship of God and to discipline his senses for that purpose. The approach is essentially restrictive though it does involve some moral advance too. The eyes should not be allowed to see the cruelty of gladiator shows or the demoralizing spectacles of the theatre,[4] the ears are to hear sacred literature rather than the superficial harmony of profane literature,[5] the sense of smell is not to enjoy perfumes.[6] Homosexual love is pernicious. Heterosexual love must be restricted to the marriage partner. Con-

---

[1] *Div. Inst.* vi. 19.   [2] vi. 20–3.
[3] Cic. *Offic.* i. 27 (93). Cicero is not consistent in naming the fourth virtue, *Tusc.* iii. 16: 'temperantia, moderatio, modestia'. *Offic.* i. 27 (93): 'verecundia, temperantia, modestia, sedatio perturbationum animi, rerum modus', also included is 'id quod dici Latine decorum potest, Graece enim πρέπον dicitur'.
[4] *Div. Inst.* vi. 20.   [5] Ibid. 21.   [6] Ibid. 22.

trary to the usage of Roman law a sexual relation outside marriage is condemned as adultery, even when it is maintained by the husband and does not infringe the conjugal rights of another man.[1]

The ethics expounded in Lactantius' treatise differ in several important respects from the traditional ethics of Rome. Capital punishment and war are prohibited:[2] '. . . it will neither be lawful for a just man to engage in warfare, nor to accuse anyone of a capital charge since it makes no difference whether you put a man to death by word or by the sword, since it is the act of putting to death itself which is prohibited . . . With regard to this precept of God there ought to be no exception at all . . .' The absolute prohibition of killing also extended to the ancient practice, prevalent in all classes of society, of killing or exposing unwanted children.[3]

Lactantius is explicitly opposed to certain traditional public virtues. He advocates munificence, but it is not to be displayed in the public entertainments traditional in the cities of the Roman empire such as wild beast shows, gladiatorial combats, or theatricals.[4] He also opposes generosity displayed in the financing of public building schemes. Buildings are destroyed sooner or later, the rewards of charity last for ever.[5] Justice does not include patriotism, 'for what are the interests of our country but the inconveniences of another state or nation?—this is to extend the boundaries which are violently taken from others, to increase the power of the state, to improve the revenues—all which things are not virtues but the overthrowing of virtues.'[6] He deprecates political ambition. It originates with the devil who incites men to devote their lives to the holding of magistracies, to reaching the consulship, and even the throne itself.[7] In contrast, 'the righteous man, since he has entered upon a hard and rugged way, must be an object of contempt, derision and hatred . . . He will be poor, humble, ignoble, subject to injury and yet enduring all things which are grievous; and if he shall continue his patience unceasingly to that last step and end, the crown of virtue will be given him and he will be rewarded with immortality.'[8]

---

[1] Ibid. 23.   [2] Ibid. 20. 16.   [3] Ibid. 20.
[4] Ibid. 19.   [5] Ibid. 11.   [6] Ibid. 6.
[7] Ibid. 4.   [8] Ibid.

Obviously the application of such teachings must have social consequences. Lactantius' can claim that the golden age would be brought back. 'If God only were worshipped there would be no dissension and wars; since men would know that they are the sons of God . . . they would know what kind of punishment God prepared for the destroyers of souls . . . There would be no frauds or plunderings if they had learned, through the instruction of God, to be content with that which was their own . . . There would be no adulteries or debaucheries . . . if it were known that whatever is sought beyond the desire of procreation is condemned by God. Nor would necessity drive women to prostitution; males would restrain their lust and the pious and religious contributions of the rich would succour the destitute.'[1]

This may or may not be realistic. The significant fact is that both the advice and the hoped-for consequences are drawn up without any regard for the realities of the Roman state, its institutions, and traditional customs. Throughout his treatise Lactantius shows the greatest respect for the Latin literary tradition. The classical language and the classical writings are treated with veneration, expressed through adaptation or citation. The philosophical thought of Greece, at least as popularized by Roman authors, is paid the tribute of being allowed to furnish the basic structure of Lactantius' apology for Christianity. The element which contributes least is the *respublica*, the social and political custom of Rome. The sense of the unity of Roman institutions, religious, military, and political, which is so strong in Cicero, Livy, or Virgil, is missing. At any rate, Lactantius, eager as he is to point out the Roman aspects of Christianity, sees no need to bring Roman social and political traditions into his argument.

Lactantius and Arnobius say little about the Church as a community, even though the cohesion of the churches, cemented by the regular communal services and the penitentiary discipline, was historically one of its most striking features. Their silence is partly tactical. The fact that Christians were in a sense a separate nation contradicted the tendency of the apologists to stress the common elements. On the other hand, it is likely that the rapidly growing churches of the late third century included many converts, especially in the higher social

[1] *Div. Inst.* v. 8.

classes, who remained on the fringe of Christian community life. The Christianity of such men will have resembled the picture drawn by the two apologists. It was nevertheless not typical. A pagan who knew only Christians of this kind would form a mistaken idea of Christianity. He would think it to be much closer to the traditional individualist philosophies than it in fact was. This made conversion easier, even if it meant that the convert was incompletely aware of the consequence of conversion.

Both Arnobius and Lactantius present a personal religion which promises to help the individual to live morally, and to receive a heavenly reward after death. It was not like the paganism which it was so soon to replace, a religion designed to secure divine support for the community. But this limitation was not important if Christianity was true. If the supreme God was the God of the Christians, then he was the deity on whom the well-being of the state depended, and his religion must become the public religion. And the truth of the Christian claim seemed to have been sensationally vindicated by the failure of persecution and persecutors—especially when read in Christian histories.

5. *The conversion of Constantine*

The precise circumstances of the conversion of Constantine have been much debated.[1] The reason is that the three accounts nearest to the event contain important discrepancies.[2] Evidently Constantine did not publish an official version of his conversion at the time it happened. After he had defeated Maxentius with the aid, as he believed, of the Christian God, Constantine behaved like a Christian. He gave the Church not only toleration and restitution, but rich subsidies and privileges.[3] But he did not publicly declare himself a Christian, or provide any official definition of his religious position. There is nothing

---

[1] N. H. Baynes (1929) and (1939); E. Schwartz (1913); J. Burckhardt (1949, first edn. 1852).

[2] Euseb. *Ecclesiastical History*, Greek text ed. E. Schwartz, in Gr. Christ. Schrift. 9. *Life of Constantine*, Greek text ed. I. H. Heikel, in Gr. Christ. Schrift. 7. Lactantius, *The Deaths of the Persecutors*, Latin text, *C.S.E.L.* xxvii. 171–238.

[3] A. H. M. Jones (1964), 80–2; 93 ff.; grants to church: Euseb. *H.E.* x. 5. 15–17; immunity of clergy, *H.E.* x. 7; *C.T.* xvi. 2. 1 (315), 2 (313).

surprising in such behaviour on the part of a ruler of a state in which Christians were still a minority. It is a commonplace of politics that a new policy is followed for a long time before its adoption is acknowledged. But the result was that accounts of the conversion had to be based on rumour, and it is not surprising that the nearly contemporary accounts of Lactantius in, *De Mortibus Persecutorum*, and of Eusebius, in *The Ecclesiastical History*, differ from one another, and from the version which Constantine himself near the end of his life told Eusebius, and which is found in *The Life of Constantine*.[1] Eusebius wrote his history at Caesarea in Palestine a long way from Italy and he was at least as interested in the defeat of the local persecutor Maximinus Daia by Licinius as in that of the remote and tolerant[2] Maxentius by Constantine.[3] Lactantius may well have been writing in the West and with Constantine in mind as a reader.[4] He is likely to have been better informed than Eusebius, but in view of Constantine's politic reticence he too was not in a position to tell the whole story. As A. H. M. Jones has pointed out, the falsity of the later third version cannot be deduced from the existence of two earlier accounts, which differ from each other and can by the nature of things not be exhaustive.[5]

The version told by Constantine in his old age inspires confidence because it is so unlike any other publicized case of conversion to Christianity that one cannot imagine it to have been invented by a fully informed Christian such as Constantine was in his later years. Constantine claimed that he was converted in a period of stress. The stress was not caused by any of the usual motives for conversion, fear of death, longing for moral regeneration, seeking after truth, but by the need for powerful supernatural assistance to counter that which his rival Maxentius was thought to be tapping, and with whose aid he had already disposed of two powerful opponents.[6] The traditional gods had not helped earlier enemies of Maxentius. Constantine

[1] *V.C.* i. 28.

[2] T. D. Barnes (1973), 44.

[3] Euseb. *H.E.* ix. 9 (Maxentius), 10 (Maximinus).

[4] J. Stevenson (1957); J. Moreau (1954), 13–22 on life of Lactantius; T. D. Barnes (1973).

[5] A. H. M. Jones (1949), 98.

[6] Euseb. *V.C.* i. 27; Maxentius had already defeated Galerius and Severus and was thought to have been helped by divination or magic. Zos. ii. 16. 1; Euseb. *H.E.* ix. 9. 3.

needed something else. In this situation Constantine recalled that of all the tetrarchs only Constantius, his father, had died as emperor and been succeeded by a son. So Constantius' god seemed to meet his own requirements. But there was a difficulty not easily understood today, and perhaps not easily invented after the event: Constantine did not know who his father's god was.[1]

Thus Constantine prayed to the unknown god to reveal who he was. The prayer was answered. First in a vision,[2] then in a dream,[3] Constantine saw the sign of the cross which would give him victory. He accepted it joyfully, and only then began to learn[4] what was involved in the worship of the god to whom the sign belonged. He became a worshipper, and confidently set out on his campaign. Victory proved him right. Henceforth the placating of the Christian God became a corner-stone of his policy, and gradually over the years he acquired knowledge of the doctrines and requirements of Christianity.

Constantine's account gains plausibility[5] from the very oddness of its starting-point: belief in a supreme God, together with ignorance of who the supreme God was; more surprisingly still, belief in his father's God with ignorance of who his father's god was. This ignorance cannot have been merely a result of Constantine's long absence from his father's court—after all, he saw Constantius shortly before his death, and in any case took over his court. The obscurity of Constantius' god must have been a result of his habits of worship. Eusebius tells us that he 'knew' only the supreme God.[6] He was a reluctant persecutor. He had churches destroyed and temporarily exiled Christians from his court.[7] He did not compel surrender of scriptures.[8] He was evidently not a Christian. He seems to have been particularly attached to the worship of Sol: perhaps that god had been worshipped by his family in their Balkan home.[9] Unlike Constantine after his conversion, Constantius had not banned all

---

[1] *V.C.* i. 27. [2] Ibid. 28. [3] Ibid. 29. [4] Ibid. 32.

[5] Eusebius' authorship of *V.C.* is demonstrated by F. Winkelmann (1962), and F. Vittinghoff (1953).

[6] Θεὸν τὸν ἐπὶ πάντων εἰδώς (*V.C.* i. 27).

[7] Lact. *Mort. Pers.* 15. 7 with J. Moreau's note. Euseb. *H.E.* viii. 13. 14 is probably mistaken in denying that Constantine destroyed church buildings. Euseb. *V.C.* i. 16 suggests that he temporarily exiled Christians.

[8] N. H. Baynes (1939), 679.

[9] H. Castritius (1969), 29 n. 30.

reference to the polytheist gods from official panegyrics.[1] His gold coins[2] bore Jupiter and Hercules, the gods of Diocletian and Maximian respectively,[3] as well as Mars, perhaps the patron of Galerius.[4] He cannot have worshipped any god, not even Sol, exclusively, otherwise Constantine would not have found himself in his dilemma. Presumably Constantius had been a syncretist who considered that the various gods of paganism should be worshipped as aspects of the supreme God;[5] alternatively, he might have held the view that the many gods were subordinates of the supreme God.[6] But whatever the nature of Constantius' religious beliefs and practices, it was not self-evident what precisely had made them so effective. As a result Constantine found himself in the position not uncommon towards the end of the third century and the beginning of the fourth of requiring a theological oracle.[7] He was in the position of the client of the oracle at Colophon who asked Apollo who he was, or alternatively what God was.[8] Perhaps his position was even closer to that of the Egyptian worshipper who asked his god Mandulis whether he was the sun god, evidently suspecting that he was.[9] Constantine too is likely to have started his inquiry with the feeling that the Christians had the right answer.

A significant aspect of the conversion of Constantine is that it took place in the area of religious overlap at which the persuasive writings of Arnobius and Lactantius had been directed. Constantine was not converted from polytheism to monotheism. He started from a belief in a supreme God. His conversion meant that he discovered that the supreme God had to be worshipped in a particular way. He realized that if he worshipped the Christian God he could not personally worship any other, but he did not realize, as perhaps Arnobius had not done either, how exclusive and intolerant Christianity actually was. Like the religion of Arnobius and Lactantius, the religion of Constantine

[1] See esp. *Pan.* v. 8–16.
[2] On the relation between the inscription of a coin and its metal, see *R.I.C.* vii. 47.
[3] *R.I.C.* vi. 163 ff. on gold coins of Trier. Sol became prominent after A.D. 305–6, ibid. 204.
[4] H. Castritius, op. cit. 28–30.
[5] Cf. Celsus in Origen, *contra Celsum*, viii. 66; Maximus of Madauras in Augustine, *Ep.* 16 = *P.L.* xxxiii. 81–3.   [6] Arn. *Adv. Nat.* iii. 2.
[7] A. D. Nock (1934), 53–74 = (1972), 357–74; P. de Labriolle (1934), 234 ff.
[8] *Div. Inst.* i. 7: quis esset omnino deus.   [9] A. D. Nock, op. cit.

was based on philosophy (acceptance of a supreme God) and
revelation (the vision). The Christian scriptures, dogma, and
ritual were initially unimportant. A letter which Constantine
addressed to the people of the eastern provinces in 324, after the
defeat of Licinius, illustrates his point of view. Christianity is
represented as ethical worship. Persecution is the cruel opposite
of worship, very much as in Lactantius. Constantine claims that
ethical worship had been known since the beginning of the
world but largely abandoned. He describes Christianity as 'the
Law' and uses other terms which imply that he thinks of it
primarily as a regulated way of life.[1]

Belief in a supreme God was common ground to Christians
and many pagans. Licinius, the man who opposed Constantine
in the last of his civil wars, shared this belief. When going into
battle against Maximinus Daia he ordered his soldiers to recite
a prayer to the supreme God.[2] Indeed, Lactantius and Eusebius
treat his victory over Maximinus as parallel in significance to
that of Constantine over Maxentius. But Licinius did not go on
to identify the supreme God with the God of the Christians. To
judge by the coins, he equated him with Jupiter Optimus
Maximus, the traditional protector of the Roman state.[3] We
also have the base of a statue dedicated by Licinius to Sol.[4] But
the prayer of Licinius such as it was, was acceptable to Christians: Constantine ordered his pagan soldiers to use it.[5]

The existence of common ground between educated pagans
and educated 'fringe' Christians like Arnobius and Lactantius
is illustrated by Constantius' attitude to Sol Invictus, 'the
Invincible Sun God'. Sun worship may well have been traditional in Constantine's family.[6] Sol figured on coins of
Constantine's father and became extremely prominent on the
bronze coinage of Constantine himself after 310,[7] that is, after he

[1] Euseb. *V.C.* ii. 48–60 and the important remarks of H. Kraft (1955), 74–86.
[2] Lact. *Mort. Pers.* 46; Euseb. *H.E.* ix. 9; cf. 11. 9.
[3] *R.I.C.* vii. 591–608 on coins of Nicomedia A.D. 313–24.
[4] *I.L.S.* 8940, and L. Homo (1931), 230, on statue of Sol dedicated by Licinius
with ritual regulations. *C.I.L.* viii. 8712: a small sanctuary of Sol in honour of
Licinius and Constantine.
[5] Euseb. *V.C.* iv. 19–20.
[6] Cf. Himerius, *Ecl.* xii. 6; Jul. *Or.* iv. 131; also H. Dörries (1954), 343 n. 4; H.
Castritius (1964), 29–30.
[7] See *R.I.C.* vii. 111 for Constantine's coinage. Particularly striking is the regular
appearance of Sol on bronze coins. Mars still appears after 310.

had defeated Maximian's attempt to regain power, and had finally broken with the tetrarchic system. The speaker of the panegyric of that year (310) makes much of a visit of Constantine to a temple of Apollo, and of religious experience he had there.[1] The surprising thing is that Sol continued to be prominent on Constantine's coins for six or seven years after his conversion in 312.[2] The god even appeared, occasionally, on coins issued after the war against Licinius,[3] which Constantine had waged as the Christian leader of a kind of holy war.[4]

The explanation of such paradoxical behaviour is likely to be that the divinity of the sun was an intellectual concept as well as an object of worship. Plato had used the sun in a famous simile to illustrate the role of the good in the world.[5] Elsewhere he ascribed divinity to it, as to other heavenly bodies.[6] Neoplatonists had described the sun as a hypostasis emanating from God.[7] Astronomers noted that there was a correlation between the position of the sun and that of other stars. Since it was widely believed that stars influenced human life, the fact that the sun seemed to control the movement of the stars suggested that it was the supreme deity. The sun god was also given a key role in magic. To believers in magic, and there were many in the fourth century, this confirmed the sun's supernatural power by the most practical proof imaginable.[8]

Consideration of these facts naturally led to the intellectual conclusion that the sun was closely linked with divinity, whether it was itself the supreme divinity, or an assistant of the deity, or only an image of it. But this train of thought did not provide the sun with temples, images, or regular worshippers. True, there were cults of particular sun gods,[9] including the god whose great temple and college of priests had been established at Rome by the Emperor Aurelian. Finally, there was Mithras,

---

[1] *Pan.* vii (Galletier), 21; P. Orgels (1948).
[2] *R.I.C.* vii. 48.
[3] See M. I. Alföldi (1964).
[4] Euseb. *V.C.* ii. 1–18.
[5] Plato, *Rep.* vi. 19.   [6] Plato, *Tim.* 40B.
[7] Jul. *Or.* iv (Hymn to Helios), 132–3.
[8] Macr. *Sat.* i. 17–23; on sun in magic, see above, p. 132 n. 1.
[9] H. Seyrig (1971) draws a necessary distinction between monuments expressing devotion to the sun and those implying the existence of a formal cult. Sun worship in the strict sense was not widespread and should be described as an 'Arab' rather than an 'Eastern' practice.

the most widely worshipped invincible sun god of them all.[1] But the worshippers of particular sun gods formed only a small proportion of the persons who associated the sun in some way with the supreme God because philosophy or astrology or magic suggested that it should be so associated or even identified.

To the outsider it would seem that the sun had a privileged place even in Christianity.[2] He could read that Jesus had risen from the dead on Easter Sunday, that is, on a day consecrated to the sun. The weekly Sunday service too would seem to be honouring the day of the sun. During worship Christians faced east, the direction of the rising sun. It is likely that in the minds of many fringe-Christians, Jesus and the sun were closely associated.[3] For the informed Christian this was of course absurd, but the facts of Christian worship called for explanation. The one most commonly given was that the movements of the sun provided a visible model of the surpeme truths of theology. Lactantius, for instance, makes it quite clear that the sun is an insensible created object like earth and stars and the universe as a whole.[4] But he also suggests that the structure of the world is a model of the supernatural order: 'God established two parts of the earth itself opposite to one another and of a different character—namely, the east and the west, and of these the east is assigned to God, because he himself is the fountain of light . . . and because he makes us rise to eternal life. But the west is ascribed to that disturbed and depraved mind [the devil], because it conceals the light, because it always brings on darkness, and because it makes men to die, and perish in their sins.'[5]

---

[1] Zos. i. 61. 2; other refs., K. Latte (1960), 340–50; F. Cumont (1923); G. H. Halsberghe (1972). Sol still needs a book. On the problem of the identification of Mithras and Sol see remarks of M. Simon at the Second International Congress of Mithraic Studies, summarized in *Journal of Mithraic Studies* (1976), 91. For evidence see *C.I.M.R.M.*, epigraphical indices, s.v. Sol.

[2] See especially F. J. Dölger (1918), (1925), (1940); E. Kirschbaum (1948/9), 400–6; J. Carcopino (1953), 150 ff.; J. Moreau (1953); H. Rahner (1963), 89–176.

[3] On Sunday worship see F. H. Coulson (1926). Justin, *Ap.* i. 67 explains that the day of Helios is celebrated as first day of creation because on this day Christ rose from the dead. Tertullian (*Ad. Nat.* i. 13) remarks that people take Sol to be the Christian God because Christians pray facing the direction of the rising sun and rejoice on the day of the sun. Already in the second century Melito of Sardes compared the death, visit to Hell, and resurrection of Jesus to the rising and setting of the sun.

[4] *Div. Inst.* ii. 10, cf. 10. 6.   [5] Loc. cit.

The allegory also gives a special role to the sun itself: 'for as the sun, which rises daily although it is but one—from which Cicero would deduce its name Sol, because the stars are obscured and it alone is seen—yet since it is a true light and of perfect fulness, and of most powerful heat, and enlightens all things with the brightest splendour, so God, although he is one only, is possessed of perfect majesty and might and splendour.'[1]

Lactantius comes very near to presenting the sun as a visible equivalent of God; the symbol nearly becomes identical with the object symbolized. 'Therefore, if you always direct your eyes towards heaven, and observe the sun where it rises, and take this as the guide of your life, as in the case of a voyage, your feet will spontaneously be directed into the way; and that heavenly light, which is a much brighter sun to sound minds than this which we behold in mortal flesh, will so rule and govern you as to lead you without any error to the most excellent harbour of wisdom and virtue.'[2]

It is likely that the Invincible Sun that appears on the coins of Constantine and his predecessors represents this wider concept of the sun, an image of the supreme deity, rather than a God of Worship. The coins inform the population of the empire that the emperor considers himself under the special protection of the supreme God; they do not make a statement about the particular God worshipped by the emperor. We have seen that Sol Invictus as such was not normally worshipped at all but that the title covered a variety of more closely defined traditional sun gods each of whom had his own specific cult.[3]

It was a feature of imperial art that the images of the emperor and Sol were assimilated one to the other. The emperor was represented with a radial crown and his right hand lifted in a gesture of blessing in the manner of Sol,[4] while the Invincible Sun could be represented with captives or driving his chariot over crushed enemies like an emperor.[5] Such images do not express an emperor's personal creed. They are rhetorical statements of the greatness of the emperor. The parallel of Sol and

---

[1] Loc. cit.   [2] vi. 8.

[3] H. Kraft (1955), 10–11.

[4] See H. P. L'Orange (1934), esp. 95 ff. *R.I.C.* vii. 767, s.v. Imperatorial gesture.

[5] *R.I.C.* vi. 714; iv. 643–4; cf. Firmicus Maternus, *Math.* i. 14: *Sol* given epithet *princeps*.

emperor suggests that the imperial office is part of the world order, and that the role of the emperor on earth corresponds to that of the sun in heaven. In accordance with the same convention the solemn arrival (or *adventus*) of the emperor was regularly compared to the rising of the sun, or at least to the return of light.[1] Constantine allowed this particular comparison to be made on the famous arch which the senate put up to commemorate the victory over Maxentius just outside the gates of Rome. The victorious entry of Constantine was like the return of the sun after a night of tyranny. The new ruler was lord of the earth as the sun ruled over the universe. The point is made by a medallion of Sol in his chariot placed above a relief representing the *adventus* of Constantine.[2] This way of representing the imperial position had the additional advantage of being unambiguously monarchical, after all, Constantine was in the process of destroying a tetrarchic system.

Sol Invictus answered a need. Constantine required a symbol which would demonstrate the nature of the power which he wielded. He also wished to proclaim his confidence in the supreme God. At this stage, he did not feel free to employ controversial Christian imagery.[3] Sol Invictus provided an image acceptable to many Christians and many pagans. In the later years of his reign Sol faded from the coinage, but elsewhere the use of the image to describe the function of the emperor in the world continued. It was still found under Constantine's successors.[4]

The same striving for a religiously neutral description of the divine foundations of Constantine's imperial position is found in the panegyric[5] which an anonymous orator delivered in the presence of the emperor at Trier in autumn 313,[6] to celebrate, among other things, the liberation of Rome from Maxentius. Constantine is represented as a man of great and justified faith in the support of the supreme deity. It was this faith that gave

[1] S. MacCormack (1972), esp. 727–33.

[2] H. P. L'Orange and A. von Gerkan (1939).

[3] Cf. P. Bruin, *R.I.C.* vii. 61–4.

[4] e.g. in Constantinian poems of Optatianus Porphyrius, nos. 11, 12, 14, 15, 17–19. For medallion of Constantius II in a chariot with right hand raised like Sol, see H. P. L'Orange (1934), 99, cf. 105. Also A. Alföldi (1948), 58.

[5] On panegyrics as instruments of publicity, see Alan Cameron (1970), 37, 377 ff.

[6] *Pan.* ix, ed. Galletier = xii in Baehrens's Teubner text.

him the courage to set out against Maxentius when his advisers were against the operation, and to face a powerful enemy with only a quarter of the forces at his disposal.[1] The orator begins his speech by insisting that Constantine must be in direct communication with the supreme divinity.[2] His peroration is a prayer in which the supreme divinity is asked to let Constantine reign for ever.[3] In the body of the speech God is shown to have been on Constantine's side. Before the decisive battle at *pons Mulvius* the 'divine mind'[4] drew Maxentius out from the shelter of the powerful walls of Rome. Maxentius' army, with the exception of the praetorian guard, took flight at the mere sight of Constantine's majesty.[5] The insistence on the ease of the victory is quite in the traditional manner of Roman writers composing an *exemplum* of divine aid to Roman arms.[6] The audience heard next that providence (represented by negative final clauses)[7] deprived Maxentius of a hero's death by drowning him in the Tiber, and as a further benefit prevented inconvenient rumours by letting his body be found.[8]

The orator defines the supreme God with studied ambiguity in such a way as to satisfy the widest possible range of religious opinion. He suggests that the supreme deity is in direct communication with Constantine but has delegated concern for ordinary people to lesser gods.[9] Thus not even polytheism is altogether excluded. On the other hand, there are passages in which the divine guidance seems to have been identified with the emperor's own reason.[10] This recalls the internalized deity of the Stoics. That the emperor's moral and intellectual qualities, such as *virtus* and *mens*, are repeatedly qualified by adjectives like 'divine'[11] is of course the standard application of religious vocabulary to court ceremony. The oration ends with a prayer for the emperor in which the supreme deity is addressed in

---

[1] *Pan.* ix. 2. 2.

[2] Ibid. 2. 5: 'cum illa mente divina . . . quae . . . uni se tibi dignatur ostendere.' Is there here a reference to the dream and/or vision of Constantine?

[3] Ibid. 26.   [4] Ibid. 16. 2.

[5] Ibid. 17. 1.   [6] e.g. Liv. v. 49. 5. 6.

[7] G. P. Walsh (1961), 51–2.   [8] *Pan.* ix. 17. 2–3.

[9] Ibid. 2. 3: delegata nostri diis minoribus cura. Cf. above, pp. 258 f. on Arnobius' (perhaps tactical) admission of subordinate gods.

[10] Ibid. 4. 2: sua enim cuique prudentia deus est.

[11] Ibid. 1. 1: sacratissime imperator . . . numine tuo; 4. 5: divino consilio hoc est tuo; 10. 3: divina virtus tua.

a formula of words that recall epic invocations of Jupiter as the 'supreme creator of all things'.[1] The prayer itself has the traditional structure of a Roman prayer. The deity is first addressed by name, then defined more closely in a relative clause; there is a statement of the claims which the supplicant can make on the benevolence of the deity, and finally there comes the request.[2] But in this prayer, the definition is unusual in being philosophical and syncretistical:[3] 'whose names are as many as you have willed that there should be tongues of men[4]— for by what name you yourself wish to be called we cannot know[5]—and whether you are some divine power and intelligence which pervading the whole universe is mingled with all the elements[6] . . . or whether you be some power above all the heaven which looks down on this work of yours from an even loftier citadel of nature . . .' This invocation is consistent with the traditional religion of the state and with that of its greatest epic poet with pure monotheism, as well as with alternative philosophical ideas of God. Such comprehensiveness is the rhetorical equivalent of the symbol of Sol Invictus.

There is nothing specifically Christian either in the prayer or elsewhere in the speech. Nevertheless, the orator shows that he is aware that Constantine is a worshipper of the supreme God, as worshipped by Christians. Thus he argues that because God is both powerful and good he will preserve Constantine. Not to do so would detract from either his goodness or his omnipotence.[7] This argument seems to be tailored to fit the Christian rather than the Roman concept of God. The speech also contains a polemic against divination. The orator recalls that Constantine had undertaken the campaign against the advice of the *haruspices*[8] while his opponent was given to the use of all forms of divination.[9] The outcome of the war had clearly discredited the

---

[1] 26. 1: summe rerum sator. Cf. Verg. *Aen.* i. 254; xi. 725.

[2] e.g. the prayer, *Aen.* vi. 56 ff. G. Appel (1909).

[3] Contrast the relative clauses in *Aen.* vi. 57–8 or Hor. i. 30.

[4] Cf. Apuleius, *Met.* xi. 5 of Isis.

[5] Cf. the Unknown God of Acts, 17: 23.

[6] For the Stoic doctrine, see above, p. 36.

[7] *Pan.* x. 26. 3: et certe summa in te bonitas est et potestas: et ideo quae iusta sunt velle debes, nec abnuendi est causa cum possis. Nam si est aliquid quod a te bene meritis denegetur, aut potestas cessavit aut bonitas.

[8] Ibid. 2. 4.

[9] Ibid. 14. 3: 'prodigiis aut metus sui praesagiis monebatur'; cf. 4. 4.

pagan science. Most significantly of all, the orator has evidently
taken pains to avoid naming the old gods in any context which
gave them an active role.[1] Not even Apollo is mentioned.[2] In
this respect the speech is very different from earlier panegyrics.
The contrast would tell us, even if we did not know, that this
speech was addressed to an emperor who had personally dissociated himself from the traditional gods, though he remained
anxious to consider the susceptibilities of pagan officials and
soldiers.[3]

The same neutral monotheistic style was used for the inscription of the arch of Constantine at Rome.[4] The arch was in a
sense a voluntary offering of the Roman senate, but the religious
formulation evidently reflects the policy of Constantine in the
same way as that of the panegyrics.

Since Constantine's conversion had been a private act, not
involving the Roman state, it did not automatically make
Christian symbols the appropriate religious emblems for public
monuments. It was sufficient, for the time being, that public
religious symbols were no longer of a kind to offend believing
Christians. And so when Constantine, around 318–19, decided
that the display of Sol on coinage was not consistent with
Christianity, he replaced it not with Christian symbols, but
with representations of imperial anniversaries, or slogans such
as Victoria, Pax Perpetua, or Saeculi Felicitas.[5] While the
Christian standard, the Labarum, appeared on coins in 327,
this was exceptional. Constantine evidently never came to hold
the view that the coins, monuments, or ceremonies of the Roman
state were appropriate media for displaying his adherence to
Christianity.[6]

This is also apparent from the panegyric delivered in 321 on
the fifth anniversary of the accession of Constantine's sons to the

---

[1] Two passages have polytheistic implications. ix. 13. 2: Constantine is compared
with the god who uses the same lightning to send now favourable, now unfavourable messages. This should be Jupiter but he is described as *ille mundi creator et
dominus* and could be the God of the Bible. Ibid. 18. 1: 'sancte Thybri quondam
hospitis monitor Aeneae.' Both are patently rhetorical.

[2] Contrast viii. 6; 13. 1 (A.D. 312); vii. 21. 4: Apollinem tuum . . . teque in illius
specie recognivisti (A.D. 310).

[3] On paganism among soldiers and officials see H. von Schoenebeck (1939).

[4] *C.I.L.* vi. 1139: 'quod instinctu divinitatis mentis magnitudine . . . rempublicam
ultus est.' On the neutrality of the sculpture see above, p. 285.

[5] *R.I.C.* vii. 48.   [6] Ibid. 62.

rank of Caesar. Essentially, the oration is a speech in praise of Constantine. It covers largely the same ground as the speech of 313, and centres on the defeat of Maxentius.[1] The theme of divine support for Constantine, which was prominent in the earlier speech, is given even greater emphasis. The audience is left in no doubt that Constantine has been backed to the hilt by the divinity. The speech is, of course, from beginning to end monotheistic. Names of traditional pagan gods occur a few times but obviously as nothing but rhetorical ornament;[2] they are given no influence whatsoever over events.

Constantine's victory is shown to have been a divine gift. As in the speech of 313 emphasis is placed on the ease of victory.[3] The orator even records that heavenly armies had been seen to move to Constantine's support.[4] A similar sighting of heavenly armies is found in Eusebius' account of Constantine's war against Licinius in 323–4.[5] But the heavenly armies of 312 are said to have been led, not by an angel or a martyr, but by Constantine's deified father. This detail is not orthodox Christianity. It is nevertheless a deliberate allusion to imperial policy. Constantine had consecrated his father in the traditional way, evidently thinking that the consecration would strengthen his own position.[6] If Constantius Chlorus was indeed in heaven, he would surely wish to lead the heavenly forces in his son's support.

The theology has also moved further from traditional religion than that of the earlier panegyric. In this speech, there are no reminiscences of traditional pagan formulae or of classical rationalism. There is nothing definitely Christian either, but a number of hints suggest that the point of view is Christian. To take them in inverse order of importance: 'the orator praises the

---

[1] *Pan.* x (Galletier).

[2] Ibid. 7. 1: 'per varios casus . . . Mars dubius erravit', figuratively states that fighting was indecisive. 16. 6: Constantine early in his reign capturing two German Kings is compared to Hercules strangling two snakes in his cradle, cf. also below, pp. 290–1, on the Dioscuri. Such phrases were to be acceptable even at the deeply Christian courts of Theodosius I and Honorius.

[3] Ibid. 30. 2.   [4] Ibid. 14.

[5] *V.C.* ii. 16. In both cases the manifestation is a portent of divine support.

[6] Constantine evidently stressed the consecration of his father and the fact that he was 'divi Constantii filius', e.g. *C.I.L.* vi. 1140; x. 1483; xi. 9. He encouraged praise of his father provided it was less than his own, e.g. *Pan.* ix. 3 and x. 14. 6. Consecration continued under early Christian emperors. The father of Theodosius I, though never emperor, was the last of the *divi*: *I.L.S.* 1277.

chastity of Constantine while denigrating that of philosophers.
This is a theme derived from Christian apologetics.[1] He suggests
that the emperor has been exalted by the act of humbling himself to perform public service. The sentiment is surely a Christian one.[2] Most significantly, the divinity who rules the world is
seen as a moral power that sees into the hearts of men and
favours the good and breaks the bad.[3] Constantine prevailed
over Maxentius because he was a good man, while his opponent
was bad. Their conflict was fundamentally one between vices
and virtues.[4] I think we can conclude that the orator while not
explicitly defining the supreme deity, did in fact have the
Christian God in mind when he wrote these passages. Certainly
they agree very well with the characterization of God, which
Constantine was to publicize a few years later, in the letter
addressed to the inhabitants of the Oriental provinces after the
defeat of Licinius.[5]

One passage might seem to contradict the theory that the
orator was propagating a toned-down Christian point of view.
Referring to the heavenly army under the leadership of Constantius, which had come to the aid of Constantine, he suggests
that this experience would enable men to believe the old story
that the Dioscuri had helped the Romans to win the battle of
Lake Regillus. Here the orator seems to be going out of his way
to confirm a pagan *exemplum*. But in fact, the *exemplum* has been
given a new twist. The orator insists that the divine intervention
at Lake Regillus was a reward for moral virtue because the
ancient Romans had lived 'with their desires reined back,
sparingly and strenuously'. He also stresses that only two youths
came to their aid while a whole army had been seen to aid
Constantine.[6] In other words, the pagans of old had shown the

[1] x. 34. 2.

[2] x. 18. 3: numquam est excelsior principatus quam cum se publico submittit
officio.

[3] x. 7. 3–4.

[4] See x. 9: Maxentius displayed 'flagrantissimae cupiditates, libido, ignavia,
petulantia'; Constantine has 'prudentia, temperantia, virtus, gravitas, modestia,
decus', cf. ibid. 31, 'subacta vitiorum agmina quae urbem graviter obsederant,
scelus domitum victa perfidia, diffidens sibi audacia et importunitas catenata, furor
vinctus et cruenta crudelitas . . . frendebant; superbia atque arrogantia debellatae,
luxuries coercita et libido constricta nexu ferreo tenebantur'. For Roman ante-
cedents of this kind of thought see above, p. 176.

[5] Euseb. *V.C.* ii. 16.

[6] *Pan.* x. 15.

same virtues as Constantine but they had received much less help because Constantine's merit had been so much greater. The old *exemplum* is confirmed but also superseded.

The panegyrics of 313 and 321, like the inscription on the Arch of Constantine, express an important aspect of Constantine's religious policy: he was a Christian himself, but Christianity was not the official cult of the state. Constantine made no attempt to hide his personal allegiance; it suffices to recall the great basilicas founded in Rome itself, and the new capital unsullied by pagan rites established at the old Byzantium.[1] He ruthlessly stripped temples of their treasures and ornaments,[2] and personally refused to take part in traditional pagan ritual.[3] On the other hand, he remained *pontifex maximus* and head of the traditional state cult, and the ancestral rites of the city of Rome continued, with the possible exception of bloody sacrifices. Moreover, in public ceremonies which necessarily involved both pagan and Christian participants a linguistic convention was employed which emphasized the common ground between the religions and avoided expressions which would offend some of those present.

This convention was evidently extremely effective. Although the West was still predominantly pagan, and Rome itself the centre of a largely pagan nobility, the conversion of Constantine produced remarkably little political reaction. One reason may well have been that the pagan nobles did not feel that they were being coerced to follow Constantine's example as far as their personal religion was concerned, or even to admit Christian rites or Christian terminology into the public ceremony of Rome. The Constantinian compromise held for a long time because the common ground implied by the neutral monotheism of public ceremonies was genuine.

6. *Moral and religious consequences of the conversion of Constantine*

In one important respect the Christianity of Constantine at the time of his conversion in 312 was something new. It differed

---

[1] A. Alföldi (1948), 110. On 'secularized' shrines of Fortuna of Rome, of Rhea (Fortuna of Constantinople), and of Dioscuri, see Zos. ii. 31; cf. below, p. 299 n. 9.
[2] Euseb. *V.C.* iii. 54; Libanius, *Or.* xxx. 6. 37; lxii. 8; Jul. *Or.* vii. 228b; Anon. *de reb. bell.* 2. 1.   [3] Zos. ii. 29. 5.

from the religion of early Christians, and even from that of 'Roman' Christians such as Arnobius and Lactantius in that Constantine[1] was not, in the first place, concerned[2] to save his soul or the souls of others. His object was to obtain the support of the supreme ruler of the universe[3] for himself in his struggles with a rival for power, and more generally in the defence and administration of his realm. The prayers of the Church, especially of its professional element, were to ensure that the most powerful source of supernatural assistance was always enlisted on his side.[4] The basic conception was Roman rather than Christian. Constantine wished to maintain the *pax deorum* as his predecessors had done, but he looked to a new divinity and for new procedures to maintain it.

Constantine certainly did not realize the full significance of his change of religious allegiance. The fact is, the Church could never be simply the religious department of the *respublica*, as the old religion had been. The Church had its own officers, the clergy, who were absolutely distinct from the officers of the state.[5] It accepted the authority of sacred writings and of traditions which were not part of Graeco-Roman civilization. Its objectives were spiritual and other-worldly and not necessarily compatible with those of the secular administration.[6] The weekly services, sermons, the discipline of penance,[7] and religious instruction offered the clergy means of indoctrination

[1] A small selection of vast and excellent literature on Constantine: E. Schwartz (1936); N. H. Baynes (1931) and (1939); A. H. M. Jones (1948); R. MacMullen (1969). H. Dörries (1954) is a comprehensive survey of the source material; H. Kraft (1955) contains German translations of Constantine's letters as well as a convincing account of his theological development.

[2] If he was not aware from the start he soon became aware that the church was concerned with the salvation (*salus*) of its members, e.g. in letter to bishop Chrestus of Syracuse in 314, Euseb. *H.E.* x. 5. 21–4. But salvation never plays a prominent part in the surviving letters of Constantine. Of course they are all public letters.

[3] Significantly his letters are more concerned with divine *power* than any other attribute. See H. Kraft (1955), 74–7 on Euseb. *V.C.* ii. 24–42, 48–60.

[4] H. Kraft, op. cit. 46–9 on Euseb. *H.E.* x. 5. 15–17; 6. 1–5; 7. 1–2. Of course this was only the starting-point of a long religious development.

[5] They came to be drawn from the same social class: see A. H. M. Jones (1964), 920–9; but they formed part of a separate and parallel organization. The possibility of state–church conflict was always a possibility; it had been literally unthinkable in the pagan state.

[6] Clerical immunities and the coercion of religious dissent were areas where the interest of clergy and administration potentially and actually diverged.

[7] On penance, see O. D. Watkins (1920).

which had no precedent. At the same time the wish to be saved provided the strongest possible incentive for the believer, whether emperor or humble citizen, to receive ecclesiastical teaching. The incorporation of the Church involved a fundamental transformation of Roman institutions, with consequences that were bound to be very great indeed.

In the event, the most revolutionary aspects of Christianity proved to be Christian asceticism[1] and religious intolerance.[2] Each made a large contribution to the transformation of Graeco-Roman civilization into something else.[3] But this was in the long term. The immediate effects were much less dramatic. Constantine knew that the God of the Christians was less easily placated than traditional gods. It was not only that Christianity was more expensive, since it required a much larger paid staff than the worship of the old gods.[4] The Christian God took an active interest in the whole lives of his worshippers, as the pagan divinities had not done. A ruler who hoped to benefit from Christian prayer would feel obliged to do his utmost to foster the kind of behaviour which the God of the Christians prescribed. Constantine was aware that his new religion had implications for government, and tried to realize them,[5] even if the over-all effect of his measures was modest. For instance, as Lactantius had pointed out, Christian justice involved equality between man and man.[6] But Lactantius had not suggested how this ideal could be realized, and neither Constantine nor his successors made any attempt to achieve equality. On the contrary, their society was characterized at the top by hierarchy and subtle graduations of official rank, and lower down the social scale by the distinctions between *honestiores* and *humiliores*,[7] and between free men and slaves. As far as social equality was concerned, the fact that the emperor was a Christian made no difference whatsoever. But in the area of social welfare Christian teachings were in accordance with the tendency of the time. Christianity

---

[1] I am thinking of the impact of monasticism and of the relative devaluation of secular literary education. See P. Lemerle, *Le Premier humanisme byzantin* (Paris, 1971), 43–73.

[2] The most far-reaching effects were the inability to absorb Arian barbarians and, later, the alienation of monophysites in the eastern provinces.

[3] See the essays edited by L. White (1966).

[4] A. H. M. Jones (1964), 904 ff.

[5] A. Ehrhardt (1955); J. Vogt (1944).

[6] See above, p. 272.　　　　　　　　　　[7] P. Garnsey (1970), 221–71.

rejected the motivation that had induced generations of civic politicians to contribute munificently to the civic services in return for glory and popularity.[1] Christianity advocated charity to the needy, not for glory but for God's sake;[2] it encouraged the establishment of large-scale charitable organizations within the local churches.[3] Constantine immediately after his conversion responded to the Christian appeal to help the needy,[4] and it may be that one long-term effect of his conversion, and the subsequent accelerated expansion of Christianity, was that better provision was made for the urban poor. On the other hand, Christian denigration of 'vain glory' sapped the motivation of traditional munificence, and so contributed to the decline of self-governing urban institutions.

Christianity forbade killing.[5] The largest-scale killing of all, killing in war, continued of course.[6] Judicial executions continued too, although later in the century we hear of Christian officials reluctant to order executions.[7] Neither Constantine[8] nor any other emperor tried to abolish capital punishment. Constantine made an attempt to replace penal crucifixion by strangulation.[9] He also forbade the branding in the face of men condemned to the mines.[10] But on the whole, the stresses under which the empire laboured were more effective in sharpening penalties than Christianity was at softening them. The fourth century saw a widening use of torture, and freer use of savage punishments.[11] Constantine prohibited gladiatorial combats, but it was about a century before gladiator fighting was finally ended at Rome.[12] Christianity condemned infanticide.[13] Con-

---

[1] A. R. Hands (1968).

[2] Cf. above, p. 273.

[3] See J. Gaudemet (1958), 303; W. Liebeschuetz (1972), 241–2.

[4] See Euseb. *H.E.* x. 5. 15–17; 6.

[5] A. von Harnack (1905); A. H. M. Jones (1969).

[6] Eventually the Church justified bloodshed in defence of one's country, see J. Gaudemet, op. cit. 706; P. Courcelle (1948), 12–13.

[7] Libanius, *Or.* xlv. 27; iv. 36, cf. A. H. M. Jones (1969), 983 on the uncertainty of the Church's teaching in this field.

[8] See J. Vogt (1944).

[9] Sozomen, i. 8; Aur. Vict. *Caes.* 41; but *C.T.* ix. 5. 1 of 320? still orders crucifixion.

[10] *C.T.* ix. 40. 2.

[11] On the development towards more severe penalties starting in second century, see P. Garnsey (1970), 122–52; J. Vergote (1939).

[12] *C.T.* ix. 40. 2. A. Chastagnol (1966), 21–2.

[13] e.g. Tert. *Apol.* 9. 6–8.

stantine included it within the term of the murder law.[1]
Infanticide had been an important means of family limitation.[2]
We are not yet in a position to estimate how far infanticide was
reduced and with what effects—perhaps we never will be. If
there was a decline in infanticide, it must have increased the
unwanted population. Perhaps this was one of the factors that
made monastic celibacy popular over large areas of the empire
later in the century.

Christianity had teachings about sexual relations and
marriage which differed from the traditional customs of the
Roman world. Marriage should be indissoluble and strictly
monogamous. Celibacy was a higher state than marriage, and
fornication was a sin. Constantine legislated to bring the Roman
law nearer the Christian ideal.[3] He limited the valid grounds for
divorce to stated offences.[4] Adultery was to be punished by
death.[5] Married men were prohibited from having concubines.[6]
The civil disabilities of the childless were abolished.[7] Particularly severe penalties were laid down for abduction whether or
not the girl was willing,[8] and for affairs between free women
and their slaves.[9] It is likely that the stern moral legislation was
linked in some way with the catastrophical events in Constantine's own family which culminated in the execution of
Crispus, his bastard son, and a little later of his wife, Fausta.[10]
The long-term effects of this legislation are difficult to estimate.
A succession of divorce laws by later emperors show that divorce
by consent, which had been permitted by Roman law, was not
easily abolished.[11]

It is clear that Constantine did try to make Roman manners
correspond more closely to Christian prescription. It is also
clear that his efforts were not systematic. They were the outcome
of special situations rather than of planning. At best they merely

[1] *C.T.* ix. 15. 1 (318).
[2] On abortion and contraception, see K. Hopkins (1965).
[3] A. H. M. Jones (1964), 972–4.   [4] *C.T.* iii. 16. 1 (331).
[5] *C.J.* ix. 9. 9; 29. 4; hostesses of inns are included among those liable under the
law, but not barmaids: *C.T.* ix. 7. 1.
[6] *C.J.* v. 26. 1 (326).
[7] *C.T.* viii. 16. 1 (320), cf. Euseb. *V.C.* iv. 26.
[8] *C.T.* ix. 24. 1 (320).
[9] Ibid. 9. 1 (326): the woman to be executed, the slave burnt alive.
[10] A. Piganiol (1972), 35–6; Zos. ii. 29.
[11] A. H. M. Jones (1964), 974–5.

started trends whose progress was slow. The truth is that it is very hard to change long-established patterns of behaviour by legislation. Romans had long been aware of this.[1] No doubt Constantine and his advisers were aware of the difficulties too.

The most important effect of the conversion of Constantine was the boost it gave to the expansion of Christianity. In large areas of the western provinces of the empire, especially in the Balkans, it was only now that Christians came to form a significant part of the population.[2] And even in areas where Christianity was well established, it was only in the Constantinian period and after that it won large numbers of converts beyond the urban artisan-shopkeeper class, and that the urban aristocracy began to become Christians. While there may have been a few Christian members of senatorial families (almost exclusively among women) in earlier times, the story of the conversion of the senatorial nobility begins with the conversion of Constantine.[3] Of course the strength of Christianity was not created by Constantine; after all it had grown despite the opposition of generations of his predecessors in the imperial office. Nevertheless, it was the conversion of Constantine which in many areas decisively damaged the traditional religion.[4]

The great expansion of Christianity owed little or nothing to force. Imperial patronage and the prestige of the imperial example were sufficient.[5] But there was one field which imperial coercive power was at least intermittently employed by Constantine. This was the suppression of discord within the Christian Church itself. For Christian activists at any rate, unity of doctrine had always been a matter of the very greatest importance. Constantine, in the early years after his conversion, was not very well acquainted with doctrine but was convinced that unity and the ending of discord were essential. He believed that

---

[1] Tac. *Ann.* iii. 53–5.

[2] On the middle Danube area see A. Mòcsy (1974), 322–4; on cities but not countryside of N.W. and N. Gaul see E. Griffe (1964), 179 ff.; on Noricum see G. Alföldy (1964), 210.

[3] P. Brown (1961).

[4] G. Alföldy (1963), 12–14 on the rapid progress of Christianity in the Danube region and the disappearance of traditional cults.

[5] Constantine's preference was made obvious to all by the language of his edicts, the magnificence of his churches at Rome and Constantinople, and even by a mosaic on the outside of his palace: Euseb. *V.C.* iii. 49.

the God who had defended him, and defeated his enemies, now required him to maintain unity in the Church.[1]

Holding this view, he became very rapidly involved in the disputes that rent the Christian churches.[2] The first of such disputes, the Donatist controversy, claimed his attention immediately after the defeat of Maxentius, the Arian controversy later. The ensuing activity was complicated, and the consequence for the Church and the empire enormous. They have been described elsewhere.[3] Here it is sufficient to underline the importance of the precedent. Henceforth it was accepted by Church and ruler that it was the emperor's duty to use the secular power to enforce religious unity. The principle was only challenged by the victims of intervention, and as a rule only as long as the authorities were intervening against them.[4] The idea that God was prone to anger because of division in his Church provided Romans of the later empire with an explanation of public disaster that was usually available, and for which there was a self-evident remedy in the suppression of dissent.[5] Unfortunately this procedure for maintaining the *pax dei* was in the long run disastrously divisive.

Constantine himself was subject to conflicting emotions about religious coercion. He believed that God held him responsible for the unity of the Church, and he felt passionate hostility towards those who divided it. To judge by his writings, it was mainly in the area of Christian dissent that he recognized the machinations of the devil.[6] But Constantine was never eager to force his own views on others. His object was to bring about the

[1] Constantine disturbed by divisions in the Church: Euseb. *H.E.* x. 18–19; ibid. 21–4; ibid. 22, he states that those who cause faction endanger their salvation. According to Euseb. *V.C.* ii. 54–5 the achievement of uniformity of belief concerning the Deity and the establishment of peace in the world were Constantine's principal aims. According to Euseb *V.C.* iii. 17 he saw the establishment of church unity as a duty he owed to God in return for so many favours.

[2] He did not feel similarly obliged to put pressure on pagans to bring them into the Church although he made it clear that he favoured their conversion. See his letter to the inhabitants of the eastern provinces in ibid. ii. 48–60. On the subject of tolerance in this period see J. Vogt (1968).

[3] On the Donatist controversy see W. Frend (1952), 141–68. E. Tengström, (1964).

[4] See A. H. M. Jones (1964), 934–7.

[5] See comments on disaster at Adrianople in 378: Sozomen, vi. 40; Ambrose, *D.F.* i. 3; ii. 140; *Ep.* 27–9.

[6] The devil cause of heresy: H. von Soden (1950), 18. 18; ibid. 44; 36. 9; Euseb. *V.C.* ii. 71; Opt. *Appendix*, x; Athanasius, *de decr. Nic. synod.* 38; ibid. 40. 1, 12, 35.

widest possible agreement among the bishops, but once an agreed formula had been found, he was ready to enforce it.[1]

Constantine was impressed by the argument that religion cannot be forced, the argument which has been put forward so frequently on behalf of Christians at the time of persecution.[2] His policy was no doubt also restrained by the Roman administrative tradition of religious neutrality.[3] The Roman government had only very rarely tried to suppress religious practices and the history of the persecutions of the Christians, even of the Great Persecution, shows how incapable it was of doing so effectively. The result of these restraining factors was that under Constantine the occasions on which the force of the state was used to enforce unity among the Christians were few, and of short duration. It was, of course, a paradox of Constantine's position that while he considered it his duty to put pressure on dissenting Christians he did not feel the same about non-Christian pagans and Jews. But here again there is some evidence of internal conflict. Constantine did talk contemptuously of both pagans and Jews.[4] Moreover, he clearly thought some pagan practices, for example, ritual prostitution and, probably, bloody sacrifices, were objectionable to the Deity and he strongly wished the non-Christians to be converted.[5]

Constantine, in various ways, some more successful than others, tried to Christianize the Roman empire. At the same time Christianity, as a result of being the religion of the emperor, was being Romanized and the Church became something like an image of the empire. As more members of the

[1] The summons to synod at Rome (Euseb. *H.E.* x. 5. 18–20); letter to Chrestus of Syracuse (ibid. 21–4); the letter to Alexander and Arius. Euseb. (*V.C.* ii. 64–72, esp. 68–70) shows that Constantine considered the doctrinal points insignificant, but unity all-important; cf. also his address to bishops at Nicaea, ibid. 12–13.

[2] Ibid. 56. 60. On this, H. Dörries (1960), 329 ff. Religious tolerance advocated in time of persecution: Tert. *Apol.* 24. 6; 28. 1; *Ad Scap.* 2. 2; Lact. *Inst.* v. 20. See also A. Alföldi (1948), 53.

[3] See R. Klein (1971), 89–90.

[4] Constantine and the Jews: *C.T.* xvi. 8. 1. 3, but ibid. 4 restores the immunity withdrawn in 3. Euseb. *V.C.* iii. 17–19 abuse of Jews in letter recommending the Easter dating agreed at Nicaea. The letter to eastern provinces after the defeat of Licinius proclaims toleration of paganism as well as rejection (Euseb. *V.C.* iii. 48–60, esp. 56 and 60). In 326 Constantine refused to take part in public ritual at Rome (Zos. ii. 29. 5). He was responsible for destruction of temple at Mamre (Euseb. *V.C.* iii. 53), of a temple of Aphrodite at Aphaca (ibid. 55), of a temple of Asclepius at Aegae (ibid. 56). He confiscated temple treasures (ibid. 54).

[5] N. H. Baynes (1931), 27–9.

ruling classes were converted the social status of bishops and that of secular dignitaries began to converge.[1] The ecclesiastical administration based on city, province,[2] and patriarchate[3] began to mirror the imperial administration based on cities, provinces, and dioceses. The great prestige of the bishops of the capital cities of Rome[4] and Constantinople[5] became comparable—if only remotely—to that of the emperor himself. More significantly, in the matter of unity of belief the emperor sought to exercise leadership in the Church scarcely less authoritatively than he was accustomed to exercise it in secular affairs.

The architecture of the great churches constructed at the expense of Constantine was based on that of imperial audience halls.[6] The size and rich decoration of these buildings proclaimed far and wide that Christianity was the religion of the emperor. The ceremonies that took place in these imposing structures would also be seen to have borrowed elements from imperial art and ceremonial.[7]

Christianity was becoming an imperial religion. It was not yet the religion of the state. The empire of Constantine continued to be a multi-religious society. The emperor was a Christian. His subjects were Christians, pagans, or Jews. In Rome and the West the rites of the old state religion continued to be carried out.[8]

In the East the situation was rather different. Constantinople, the capital, had never had Roman state cults and so Christianity as the religion of the emperor was in a sense the state religion already.[9] Many of the eastern cities had large Christian communities and bishops who played an important role in urban

[1] A. H. M. Jones (1964), 923 ff.   [2] Ibid. 874–83.
[3] Ibid. 483–94.   [4] Ibid. 887 ff.
[5] 890 ff. Of course, this position was that of powerful patriarchs, not of rulers of the whole Church. Moreover in the East the patriarch of Constantinople had rivals at Antioch and Alexandria.
[6] On the buildings see R. Krautheimer (1967); A. Grabar (1967), 170, suggests influence of synagogue buildings.
[7] On the influence of imperial art on Christian iconography see A. Grabar (1936), 188 ff.
[8] A full study of fourth-century rites at Rome is lacking, but see D. N. Robinson (1915); H. Bloch (1945); J. Matthews (1971). On some surviving ritual see H. Stern (1953), 98 ff.
[9] G. Dagron (1968), 198. Constantinople did have some civic temples. They (or some of them) remained but sacrifices and worship of images were prohibited (Euseb. *V.C.* iii. 48) and on it H. Kraft (1955), 117.

life. In these circumstances Constantius, Constantine's son and successor in the East since 337, attacked paganism directly. Many temples were destroyed, and the emperor legislated to prohibited sacrifices. In practice the suppression of pagan practices depended on local initiatives which were only forth-coming in cities with a Christian majority among the decurions.[1] Moreover the pressure seems to have been relaxed in the last few years of Constantius' reign, and ended with his death in 362. Continuous and systematic government-supported[2] sup-pression of paganism only came in the last decade of the fourth century. Until then, the imperial administration was, most of the time, over most of the empire, neutral between the old and the new religion. The situation is reflected in the later Latin panegyrics. After the oration of 321, divine support recedes from the foreground. There is a return to the tradition of treating government as an essentially secular activity. Even the deistic version of Hellenistic-Eusebian theory of monarchy expounded by Themistius at Constantinople scarcely appears in our Latin collection.[3]

But if there is very little political theology, the speeches written after 321, including the speech addressed to Julian the Apostate,[4] are written in terms of a neutral monotheism which would be acceptable to Christians and pagans alike. This is also found in Ausonius' *Gratiarum actio ad Gratianum*, a speech of precisely the same type as our panegyrics.[5]

It was of course the essence of the religion of the panegyrics to be capable of being understood in either a pagan or a Christian sense. The convention even allowed a Christian emperor to be associated with pagan institutions. Ausonius praises the purity

[1] Constantius' laws, *C.T.* xvi. 10. 2. 3. 4. 6 did lead to prohibition of sacrifices at least in some areas: Julian (ed. Wright), *Ep.* 19; 21. 379B; 36. 423C = ed. Bidez-Cumont, 79. 60; 61. G. Dagron (1968), 181–2 shows that the balance of religions at city level was decisive.

[2] The local bishop remained the key figure. Libanius, *Or.* xxx *passim* (especially 11, 15, 19, 28) shows how the bishop of Antioch, in co-operation with monks, and encouraged by the praetorian prefect Cynegius, suppressed paganism in parts of the Syrian countryside on the pretext of enforcing the ban on animal sacrifices (*C.T.* xvi. 10. 9 of A.D. 385).

[3] On Themistius see G. Dagron (1968). The theory is absent from the verse panegyrics of Claudian. See A. Cameron (1970), 386–7.

[4] *Or.* xi addressed to Julian: 3. 2; 13. 2; 23. 2; 27. 2, 4; 28. 4; 32. 1.

[5] Ausonius, *Gratiarum Actio ad Gratianum*, i. 2: indulgentia divina; 7: consilium . . . ad deum retuli; 14: adorato dei numine; 18: aeterne omnium genitor.

of the Christian emperor Gratian's private life. His bedroom is as sacred as the altar of Vesta. His bed is as chaste as that of a *pontifex* or *flamen*.[1] It is not surprising that a Christian emperor, or indeed any emperor, should be praised for chastity. The surprising thing is that pagan priests should be used as a pattern of purity. Evidently the same standard was thought to apply to priests of all denominations.

In the same spirit Ausonius compares his own election to the consulate with the procedure by which the college of *pontifices* had long ago co-opted new members 'since you the *pontifex maximus* [Gratian had not yet repudiated the office] in partnership with God held the election'.[2] Thus the Christian emperor's God is represented as co-operating with him in the role of chief priest of the pagan religion.

Such passages imply that Christianity and paganism are worshipping the same God. Of course, Gratian soon after repudiated the title of *pontifex maximus* and rejected the practical expression of compromise when he removed the Altar of Victory from the senate-house, and withdrew public support from the state cults of the city of Rome.[3] Nevertheless, in the conservative medium of the Latin panegyric, religious neutrality is maintained a little longer.

The last panegyric in the collection was addressed in 389 by the Gallic orator Pacatus to the pious Christian emperor Theodosius. The orator too appears to have been a Christian. He relates that in worship (*divinis rebus operantes*) 'we' turn towards the rising sun. This was the Christian custom.[4] The pagan normally turned towards the cult image. Pacatus also draws an odd picture of the fates with writing-tablets sitting next to God and assisting his memory.[5] This looks like a translation into the traditional literary convention of the biblical concept of the angel who records the good and bad deeds of men in the Book of Life.[6] The image suggests familiarity with Christian writings. Nevertheless the speech gives expression to the same neutral monotheism as its predecessors. It goes

---

[1] Ausonius, *Grat. Act.* 14: operto conclavis tui non sanctior ara vestalis, non pontificis cubile cautius, nec pulvinar flaminis tam pudicum. On the literary convention, see A. Cameron (1975), 195.

[2] *Grat. Act.* 9. [3] A. Cameron (1968), 96–102.

[4] xii. 3. 2. [5] xii. 18. 4.

[6] Cf. Prudentius, *Per.* iv. 169–71; x. 1121.

without saying that sacred epithets are applied to the emperor, but the orator goes surprisingly far. The emperor's appearance, he writes, is fitting for one whom all nations adore, to whom all the world in a public or private capacity addresses prayers, from whom the sailor asks for fair weather, the traveller a safe return, and the soldier favourable auspices.[1] This passage, which seems to accept full worship of the emperor, is an expansion of a traditional theme. Pliny had said of Trajan: 'cuius dicione nutuque maria terrae pax, bella regerentur.'[2] Pacatus is just as far from implying that the emperor had power over nature as Pliny was. Nevertheless, the passage is astonishing, coming from a Christian.

The neutral monotheism of the panegyrics was of course a literary convention, but the convention reflected the fact that monotheism provided a wide area of common ground between Christians and pagans. This, as we have seen, had been the basic assumption of the apologetic writings of Arnobius[3] and Lactantius,[4] and Constantine himself had been a monotheist before he became a Christian.[5] As late as the last decade of the century the History of Ammianus was written from a neutral monotheistic point of view.[6] Even Symmachus, in spite of the extreme conservatism of his attitude to ritual, wrote about the supernatural power in language very much like that of Ammianus or Constantine.[7] On the other hand, caution in the face of persecution and desire to win educated converts had induced Christians to describe their religion in terms of traditional philosophical monotheism.[8]

---

[1] xii. 6. 4. Galletier concluded that the author was pagan. *Ed.* iii. 50–1.

[2] Plin. *Pan.* 4. 4. The τόπος probably originated at Alexandria. Cf. J. Gagé (1935), 88 ff. on Philo, *Leg. at Gaium*, 151 and temple of καῖσαρ ἐπιβατήριος at Alexandria, also Suet. *Aug.* 98. It is significant that Philo could use the τόπος, though a Jew.　　　　　　　　　[3] Arnob. *Adv. Nat.* i. 33.

[4] Lact. *Div. Inst.* i. 3.　　　　　　　　　[5] Euseb. *V.C.* i. 27.

[6] A. Demandt, *Zeitkritik und Geschichtsbild im Werk Ammians* (Bonn, 1965), 81 ff. P. M. Camus (1967), 133–48.

[7] Not only in the famous *Rel* 3 but also *Ep.* 8. 13, ope divinitatis; 9. 12; 6. 30, summa divinitas; 8. 5, praesidii caelestis; 9. 72, caelestis nutus; 8. 47, caelestem potestatem. Such impersonal monotheism is found together with impersonal polytheism as in 6. 75, caelestes; 7. 1, numinum. On Symmachus, see J. F. Matthews (1974), 58–99; R. H. Barrow (1973). J. F. Matthews (1973) comments on Symmachus' success 'in maintaining a front of senatorial unanimity and social cohesiveness at a time of great religious diversity within the upper class itself'. Cf. also the prayers of the still pagan Firmicus Maternus, *Math.* v praet. 3 and vii. 1.

[8] Lact. *Op. Div.* 1. 20; 21. 1.

But the circumstances which had produced the compromise were changing. Paganism was being steadily undermined. Temples had been destroyed. Temple estates had been confiscated.[1] The ruling classes of the empire were being steadily converted to Christianity.[2] What was more important, upper-class Christianity grew not only in numbers, but also in depth of conviction. Christianity received an infusion of radicalism through the ascetic movement. The sons of a man converted for reasons of secular advantages, or of a pagan father and a Christian mother were likely to grow up with deeply Christian convictions.[3] Around 380 the emperor Theodosius was a committed Christian, and many men of similar attitude held important positions at his court at Constantinople, and at that of Gratian in the West.[4]

These were the circumstances in which Gratian and Theodosius ended the Constantinian compromise. Not content with being Christians who happened to be emperors, they insisted on being Christian emperors.[5] This decision is reflected symbolically in literature and art. The oration of 389 is the last of the collection of *panegyrici veteres*. This is in a way an accident, but not altogether. The function of the secular festival speech was increasingly performed by a bishop's sermon. The sermons preached by Ambrose on the respective deaths of the emperors Theodosius and Valentinian II[6] are examples of the new type of religious court-celebration. At the same time, monumental art, like the column put up by Arcadius at Constantinople in 403, proclaimed to all who could see that a Christian emperor was ruling a Christian empire.[7] The first practical expression of the new temper was the complete separation of the Roman state from the old state religion by the disestablishment of the public cults of Rome.[8] There followed waves of legislation prohibiting

---

[1] H. Bloch (1945). Destroyed temples: *C.T.* xvi. 10. 3 (A.D. 342); Lib. *Or.* lxii. 8, *Ep.* 724. Confiscation of Temple estates: *C.T.* v. 13. 3; 8. 1. 8 (A.D. 364). Cf. treasures: Euseb. *V. Const.* iii. 54; Lib. *Or.* xxx. 6. 37; lxxii. 8; Jul. *Or.* vii. 228b; Anon. *de rebus bell.* ii. 1.

[2] P. Brown (1961), 1–11 = (1972), 161–82.

[3] Ibid. 6–7 = (1972), 172 on effect of intermarriage.

[4] J. Matthews (1975), v and viii.

[5] A. Cameron (1968); A. Piganiol (1972), 237–43, 246–51.

[6] *C.S.E.L.* lxxiii. 329–401.

[7] A. Grabar (1936), 74, pls. xiii–xv.

[8] A. Cameron (1968); R. Klein (1971) and (1972).

pagan cults.[1] Rome very soon became a Christian city. This was perhaps not so much due to the laws,[2] as to the fact that the tide was flowing very strongly for Christianity. Its strength can be judged from the fact that the calamities that broke over the western empire in the first decade of the fifth century did not discredit the new public religion.[3] On the contrary, the Romans of Rome united around their Church.[4] As the military situation steadily worsened, new church buildings[5] added their testimony to that of Constantinian structures, proclaiming—as in the time of Polybius or of Cicero—that no people surpassed the Romans in religious observance.

[1] *C.T.* xvi. 10. 7 of 381 opens the attack in the Code. It forbids sacrifices. Libanius, *Or.* xxx. 7, suggests that Valens and Valentinian had provided a precedent. Suppression of paganism became continuous with *C.T.* xvi. 10 (391). On Theodosius' religious policy and its temporary accommodations see J. Geffcken (1929), 145–62; H. Bloch (1945); W. Ensslin (1953); J. Matthews (1975), 121 ff., 227–47. Suppression of paganism was preceded and accompanied by an alliance with Catholic Christianity, and the suppression of other tendencies in the Church. See *C.T.* xvi. 5. 15 (379) and following laws. On the essential role of the local bishop see P. Brown (1972), 320–33.

[2] P. Brown (1961), 11, argues that the laws by provoking opposition may actually have delayed the conversion of the remaining pagan senators.

[3] The situation produced Augustine's defence of Christianity, the *De Civitate Dei* and Orosius' *Historiarum adversus paganos libri VII*. But it was not its literature that saved Christianity, but the fact that it had already achieved a position to provide reassurance and stability in a deteriorating situation. Military catastrophe could no longer shake it. On the judgement of God as a historical category see S. Mazzarino (1959), 58–70.

[4] P. Brown (1968) = (1972), 190 ff.

[5] R. Krautheimer (1965), 127: 'Never until the Seventeenth Century did church building flourish in Rome as it did in the century from 380–480.' See also A. Grabar (1966), 6 ff.

EPILOGUE

THE book ends in a paradox: the religion whose founder was crucified on the order of a Roman official has been accepted by the nobility at Rome itself as the successor of the religion of Jupiter. This was a long and complex development. Here it has been treated from one point of view: the interrelation of change in the political system and religious change.

Christianity began as an association of individuals for private religious ends. Christianity achieved much of its early progress through its ability to satisfy the religious needs of individuals,[1] not least by making them part of a closely knit religious community.[2] Nevertheless it was the conversion of Constantine which inaugurated the period of most rapid advance. It was only after the conversion of the emperor that Christianity arrived at all in large areas of the Balkan and western provinces. It was only from this time that it began to win significant numbers of converts among the peasantry and the nobility.[3] Even in the eastern provinces, which were much more strongly Christianized, large-scale conversion of the rural population was in many areas post-Constantinian.[4] But the conversion of Constantine had not been an expression of private religion. It had been the outcome of political concern. Constantine was converted because he required effective supernatural support, first to defeat his rivals, and then to safeguard the empire he had won.[5]

The rejection of the ancestral religion of Rome was not a consequence of its deficiencies as a personal religion. What gave Christianity the chance to become more than a very important sect was the crisis of the third century.[6] In the middle decades of the century plague, invasion, and civil war, in seemingly endless succession, suggested that the old public religion was failing in

---

[1] See the excellent analysis of A. D. Nock (1933).
[2] P. Brown (1971), 60–3, cf. above, p. 211.
[3] A. H. M. Jones (1949), ch. 16; *L.R.E.* 96.
[4] W. Liebeschuetz (1978).
[5] See above, pp. 277 ff.
[6] See above all the articles of G. Alföldy in the bibliography.

its role of securing effective support for the community. Epigraphic dedications ended abruptly.[1] But the dramatic decline in monumental demonstrations of traditional piety was not a purely religious phenomenon. It was one aspect of a general loss of confidence in the values of the city community in general and of historical Roman values in particular. Men of the monument-commissioning classes were becoming reluctant to hold office in their communities, and were much less eager to display their achievements to their fellow citizens.[2] At the same time, Rome, for so long the pattern for public life and worship in numerous provincial cities, ceased to be the permanent centre of the empire.[3] The late third century was a time when the ancestral worship received comparatively little support from the consideration that it was an essential part of the historical institutions of Rome.[4] It was in these circumstances that Christianity could win very large numbers of converts.[5] Shortly after, divine support for Christianity was dramatically demonstrated by the failure of the Great Persecution and the 'deaths of the persecutors'.[6] At this point Christianity could offer an alternative to the gods. It seemed to work. After all, ancestral worship too had always been justified pragmatically by success. So Constantine took up Christianity. It worked for him too. Once the emperor had been won over, Christianity expanded irresistibly with the help of imperial patronage, and its own organization and intolerant determination.[7]

Much has been written about the long drawn-out death of paganism.[8] Its supposed inadequacies have been pointed out by modern scholars as they had been by Christian apologists like Lactantius.[9] The fact is that the old religion of the Romans was extremely adaptable and for a very long time was able to meet most of the new demands made on it. Since it was tolerant, it could allow the ancestral rites to be supplemented by cults of loyalty,[10] by Stoic philosophy,[11] by the worship of new abstract

[1] See above, pp. 231–2.
[2] Cf. A. Mòcsy (1970), 199–212.
[3] See above, p. 236; cf. A. H. M. Jones, *L.R.E.* 366–7.
[4] See above, p. 204; A. D. Momigliano (1963).
[5] W. H. C. Frend (1965).   [6] See above, pp. 250–2.
[7] J. Matthews (1975), 154–60; P. Brown (1961), 1–11 = (1972), 161–2.
[8] e.g. K. Latte, *R.R.* 310, 327–31, 360.
[9] See above, p. 265.   [10] See above, pp. 63 ff.
[11] See above, pp. 112 ff., 169 ff., 188, 207 ff.

deities,[1] by mystery cults[2] and, in the later empire, by Neo-platonism.[3] But the ancestral rites always remained the central feature of Roman piety and the maintenance of divine support for the Roman people remained its central concern. It is significant that when, under the impact of barbarian invasions and the sack of Rome (A.D. 410), a religious debate was opened, the challenge to Christianity was made on the ground of public religion. Augustine has been criticized for directing his *City of God* against an out-dated paganism.[4] But he knew better. What troubled people at the time was not whether Christianity provided more satisfactory reassurance for the individual than Mithras, Isis, or Cybele, but whether it could mobilize divine support for Rome as effectively as the traditional gods of Rome had done. The Roman nobles had once again become extremely conscious of the historical roots of their culture, which they knew from Augustan literature, and consequently saw through the eyes of Virgil and Livy.[5]

A pagan ritual once established could not be changed, but pagan religious attitudes could and did develop. It has been suggested earlier that under the empire Romans had on the whole become more certain of the existence of a god beyond the universe,[6] more receptive of knowledge received through divination of various kinds,[7] and more convinced that the essence of worship was moral behaviour.[8] These attitudes were perfectly compatible with punctilious performance of the traditional religious duties. On the other hand, there is no doubt that in each area Christianity could 'outbid' the old religion with teachings that were simpler, more consistent, and more authoritative than any which pagan authorities could supply. Christianity was based on revelation. It was emphatically monotheistic. It upheld a morality based on divine teaching. Finally, it formed a community that existed independently of the Roman state. In the crisis of the fifth century Christianity

---

[1] See above, pp. 175 ff.
[2] See above, pp. 180, 220–3.
[3] P. Brown (1967), 90 ff., 301.
[4] e.g. F. Cumont (1972), 202–3.
[5] A. D. Momigliano (1963), 81, 86; P. Brown (1967), 305–6.
[6] See above, p, 118.
[7] See above, pp. 227–9, 234, 248, 266–7.
[8] See above, pp. 114 ff.; 175 ff.

was not vulnerable as the old religion had proved itself to be in the crisis of the third. When the political framework of the empire collapsed, the Church continued to provide a sense of community, while its bishops offered authoritative moral instruction and encouragement.[1] This was just what the shaken citizens of the overrun provinces needed.

[1] P. Brown (1967), 313 ff.

APPENDIX

Deposition of officials or interference with election:

I. DICTATORS

368 Liv. vi. 38. 9 (civic strife).
337 Liv. viii. 15. 6 (military failure, vestal scandal).
332 Liv. viii. 17. 4 (threat of war, plague).
325 Liv. viii. 29–37 (war, this *vitium* did not result in deposition).
321 Liv. ix. 7. 12–14 (Caudine forks disaster).
217 Liv. xxii. 33–4 (Punic war).
216 xxiii. 19 (Punic war; outcome: a renewal of auspices).

II. CONSULS

391 Liv. v. 31–2 (plague, war. Consuls deposed without *vitium*).
223 Liv. xxi. 63. 2 (consuls refuse to resign).
220 Broughton (1951), 235 (consuls resign because of *vitium*?).
215 Liv. xxiii. 31.
214 Liv. xxiv. 7 (election stopped on authority of president without religious cause, cf. x. 22 on election of 295).
210 Liv. xxvi. 22 (election stopped on authority of consul without religious cause).
202 Liv. xxx. 39 (weather prevents elections).
161 Cic. *N.D.* ii. 4 (10–11).

> second
> Punic
> war

III. OTHER MAGISTRATES

441 Liv. iv. 7. 3 (consular tribunes, the first college).
396 Liv. v. 17 (failure to capture Veii).
380 Liv. vi. 27. 5 (censor).
231 Broughton (1951), 226 (censor).
292 Liv. x. 47 (tribunes).
201 Liv. xxx. 39. 8 (plebeian aediles during second Punic war).

BIBLIOGRAPHY

ABAECHERLI, A. L. (1935). *The Institution of the Imperial Cult in the Western Provinces of the Roman Empire* (Bologna).

ABT, A. (1908, repr. 1967). *Die Apologie des Apuleius von Madaura und die antike Zauberei* (Giessen; Berlin).

AFRICA, T. W. (1965). *Rome of the Caesars* (New York).

AHL, F. M. (1974). 'Appius Claudius and Sextus Pompeius in Lucan', *Classica et Mediaevalia*, xxx. 331–46.

ALBRECHT, M. VON (1964). *Silius Italicus* (Amsterdam).

ALEXANDER, W. H. (1946). 'Cato of Utica in the Works of Seneca Philosophus', *Trans. Royal Soc. Canada*, 3rd ser., xl, sect. 2, 59–74.

ALFÖLDI, A. (1948). *The Conversion of Constantine and Pagan Rome* (Oxford).

—— (1967). 'Die Vorherrschaft der Pannonier im Römerreiche und die Reaktion des Hellenentums unter Gallienus', in *Studien zur Geschichte der Weltkrise des 3. Jahrhunderts*, 228–81.

—— (1967). *Studien zur Geschichte der Weltkrise des 3. Jahrhunderts nach Christus* (Darmstadt).

—— (1970). *Die monarchische Repräsentation in dem römischen Kaiserreiche* (Darmstadt).

—— (1971). 'Redeunt Saturnia regna', *R.N.* xiii. 76–89.

—— (1975). Review of S. Weinstock: *Divus Julius*, *Gnomon*, xlvii. 155–79.

ALFÖLDI, M. I. (1964). 'Die Sol Comes Münze vom Jahre 325', in *Mullus, Festschrift Theodor Klauser* (Münster), 10–16.

ALFÖLDI, M. R. (1963). *Die Constantinische Goldprägung* (Bonn).

ALFÖLDY, G. (1963). 'Geschichte des religiösen Leben in Aquincum', *Acta Arch, Acad. Sc. Hung.* xiii. 109 ff.

—— (1966). 'Barbareneinfälle und religiöse Krisen in Italien', *Bonner Historia-Augusta-Colloquium 1964–5* (Bonn), 1–19.

—— (1968). 'Septimius Severus und der Senat', *Bonner Jahrbücher*, clxviii. 112–60.

—— (1969). 'Die Generalität des römischen Heeres', ibid. clxix. 233–45.

—— (1971). 'Cassius Dio und Herodian über die Anfänge des neupersischen Reiches', *Rh. Mus.* cxiv. 360–7.

—— (1971). 'Zeitgeschichte und Krisenempfindung bei Herodian', *Hermes*, xcix. 429 ff.

—— (1973). 'Der heilige Cyprian und die Krise des römischen Reiches', *Historia*, xxii. 479–501.

—— (1974). *Noricum* (London).

—— (1974). 'The Crisis of the Third Century as seen by Contemporaries', *Greek, Roman and Byzantine Studies*, xv. 89–111.

—— (1976). 'Das neue Saeculum des Pescennius Niger', *Antiquitas*, Reihe 4, Beiträge zur Historia-Augusta-Forschung, 12 (Bonn), 1–10.

—— (1976). 'Zwei Schimpfnamen des Kaisers Elagabal: Tiberinus und Tractatitius', ibid. 11–21.

—— (1976). Soziale Konflikte im römischen Kaiserreich', *Heidelberger Jahrbücher*, xx. 111–25.

ALTHEIM, F. (1938). *A History of Roman Religion*, trans. by H. Mattingly (London).

AMIT, M. (1962). '*Concordia*, idéal politique et instrument de propagande', *Iura*, xiii. 133–69.

ANDERSON, A. R. (1928). 'Heracles and his successors', *Harv. St. Cl. Phil.* xxxix. 7–59.

APPEL, G. (1909, repr. 1975). *De Romanorum precationibus* (Giessen; New York).

ARMSTRONG, A. H. (ed.) (1967). *Cambridge History of Later Greek and Medieval Philosophy* (Cambridge).

ARNHEIM, M. T. W. (1972). *The Senatorial Aristocracy in the Later Roman Empire* (Cambridge).

ARNOLD, E. V. (1911). *Roman Stoicism* (Cambridge).

ASTIN, A. E. (1964). 'The leges Aelia et Fufia', *Latomus*, xxiii. 421–45.

—— (1967). *Scipio Aemilianus* (Oxford).

AUDOLLENT, A. (1904). *Defixionum Tabellae* (Paris).

AUERBACH, E. (1965). *Literary Language and its Public in late Latin Antiquity and in the Middle Ages*, trans. R. Manheim (London).

AUGUSTINE, *De civitate dei, C.S.E.L.* xl.

AVERY, W. T. (1940). 'The *adoratio purpurae* and the Importance of the Imperial Purple in the 4th Century', *M.A.A.R.* xvii. 66–80.

BABUT, E. CH. (1916). 'L'Adoration des empéreurs et les origines de la persecution', *Rev. Hist.* cxxiii. 225–52.

BÄCKER, J. (1970). 'Antike Heilsgötter und die römische Staatsreligion', *Philologus*, cxiv. 211–55.

BAGEHOT, W. (1964, first published 1867), *The English Constitution*, with introduction by R. H. S. Crossman (London).

BAILEY, C. (1935). *Religion in Virgil* (Oxford).

BALSDON, J. P. V. D. (1951). 'Sulla Felix', *J.R.S.* xli. 1–10.

—— (1969). *Life and Leisure in Ancient Rome* (London).

—— (1971). 'Dionysius on Romulus: a Political Pamphlet?', *J.R.S.* lxi. 18–27.

BARBIERI, G. (1952). *L'albo senatorio da Settimio Severo a Carino* (Rome).

BARDON, H. (1956). *La Littérature latine inconnue* (Paris).

BARDT, G. (1871). *Die Priester der vier grossen Collegien aus römisch-republikanischer Zeit* (Berlin).

BARLEY, M. W., and HANSON, R. P. C. (1968). *Christianity in Britain 300–700* (Leicester).

BARNES, T. D. (1968). 'Pre-Decian *Acta Martyrum*', *J. Theol. S.* xix. 509–31.

—— (1970). 'The Lost Kaisergeschichte and the Latin Historical Tradition', *Bonner Historia-Augusta-Colloquium 1968/9* (Bonn).

—— (1973). 'Lactantius and Constantine', *J.R.S.* lxiii. 29–46.

BARROW, R. H. (1973). *Prefect and Emperor: The Relationes of Symmachus A.D. 384* (Oxford).

BASCOM, W. (1969). *Ifa Divination* (Bloomington).

BASSETT, E. L. (1955). 'Regulus and the Serpent in the *Punica*', *Cl. Phil.* l. 1–20.

—— (1966). 'Hercules and the Theme of the *Punica*', in L. Wallach (ed.) *The Classical Tradition: Studies in Honor of H. Caplan* (Cornell), 258–73.

BATIFOL, P. (1920). Bréhier, L.: *Les Survivances du culte impérial romain* (Paris).

BAUMAN, R. A. (1967). *The Crimen Maiestatis in the Roman Republic and Augustan Principate* (Johannesburg).

—— (1974). *Impietas in Principem*: Münchener Beiträge zur Papyrusforschung und antiken Rechtsgeschichte, lxvii (Munich).

BAYET, J. (1937). 'Présages figuratifs déterminants dans l'antiquité gréco-latine', *Mélanges Fr. Cumont* (Brussels), 27–51 = *Croyances et rites*, 44–63.

- —— (1949). 'La Croyance romaine aux présages déterminants: aspects littéraires et chronologie', *Hommages Bidez-Cumont*, 13–30 = *Croyances et rites*, 73–83.

—— (1955). 'Les Sacerdoces romains et la prédivinisation impériale', *Bulletin de l'Académie royale de Belgique* (Classe des Lettres), xli. 453–27 = *Croyances et rites*, 275–336.

—— (1958). 'Prodromes sacerdotaux de la divinisation impériale, *Numen Suppl.* iv. 418–34 = *Croyances et rites*, 337–52.

—— (1959). *Histoire politique et psychologique de la religion romaine* (Paris).

—— (1960). 'Les Malédictions du tribun Ateius Capito', *Mélanges Dumézil* (Brussels) = *Croyances et rites*, 353–65.

—— (1961). 'Les Cendres d'Anchise, dieu, héros, ombre ou serpent (*Aen.* v. 42–103)', *Gedenkschrift für Georg Rohde* (Tübingen), 39–56 = *Croyances et rites*, 366–81.

—— (1965). *Littérature latine*, 2nd edn. (Paris).

—— (1971). *Croyances et rites dans la Rome antique* (Paris).

BAYNES, N. H. (1929 repr. 1934, 1972). 'Constantine the Great and the Christian Church', *Proceedings of the British Academy*, xv. 341–442 (London).

—— (1934). 'Eusebius and the Christian Empire', *Ann. de l'Inst. de Philol. et d'Hist. Orient*, ii. 13–18 = *Byz. Studies*, 168–72.

—— (1935). 'The Imperial Cult', from a review of J. Vogt and E. Kornemann, *Römische Geschichte, J.R.S.* xxv. 83–4 = *Byz. Studies*, 243–5.

—— (1939). 'Constantine', *C.A.H.* xii. 678–99, with bibliography, 796–9 (Cambridge).

—— (1955). *Byzantine and Other Studies* (London).

BEAUJEU, J. (1955). *La Religion romaine à l'apogée de l'empire* (Paris).

—— (1964). 'La Religion de la classe sénatoriale à l'époque des Antonins', *Hommages à J. Bayet* (Brussels), 54–75.

BECKWITH, J. (1970). *Early Christian and Byzantine Art* (London).

BEHR, C. A. (1968). *Aelius Aristides and the Sacred Tales* (Amsterdam).

BERNHARD, M. (1927, repr. 1965). *Der Stil des Apuleius von Madaura* (Stuttgart; Amsterdam).

BEUTLER, R. (1953). P. W. xxii. 1. 275–313, s.v. Porphyrios.

BICKEL, E. (1911). 'De Silii Punicorum libris VII post Domitianum abolitum editis', *Rh. Mus.* 505–12.

BICKERMANN, E. J. (1929). 'Die römische Kaiserapotheose', *Arch. f. Religions wissenschaft*, xxvii. 1–34.

—— (1973). 'Consecratio', in *Le Culte des souverains dans l'empire romain,* Fondation Hardt, *Entretiens*, xix (Geneva).

—— (1974). 'Diva Augusta Marciana', *A. J. Ph.* xcv. 362–76.

BIDEZ, J. (1913, repr. 1964). *Vie de Porphyre, le philosophe néoplatonicien* (Geneva; Hildesheim).

BINDER, G. (1974). 'Hercules und Claudius', *Rh. Mus.* cxvii. 288–317.

—— and MERKELBACH, R. (1968). *Amor und Psyche*, Wege der Forschung, cxxvi (Darmstadt).

BIRLEY, A. R. (1966). *Marcus Aurelius* (London).

—— (1969). 'The Coups d'État of the Year 193', *Bonner Jahrbücher*, clxix. 247–80.

—— (1971). *Septimius Severus* (London).

BLEICKEN, J. (1957). 'Kollision zwischen *sacrum* und *publicum*', *Hermes*, lxxxv. 446–80.

—— 'Oberpontifex und Pontifikalkollegium', ibid. 345–66.

—— (1962). 'Der politische Standpunkt Dios gegenüber der Monarchie', ibid. xc. 441 ff.

—— (1962). *Senatsgericht und Kaisergericht* (Göttingen).

BLOCH, H. (1945). 'A New Document of the Last Pagan Revival in the West 393–4 A.D.', *Harv. Theol. Rev.* xxxviii. 199–244.

BLOCH, M. (1973, first French edn. 1923). *The Royal Touch (Les Rois thaumaturges)*, trans. J. E. Anderson (London).

BLOCH, R. (1958). *The Etruscans*, Ancient Peoples and Places (London).

BLUMENTHAL, F. (1913). 'Der ägyptische Kaiserkult', *Archiv. für Papyrusforschung*, v. 317–45.

BODSON, A. (1967). *La Morale sociale des derniers stoïciens, Sénèque, Epictète et Marc-Aurèle* (Paris).

BOLL, F. J. (1926). *Sternenglaube und Sterndeutung*, ed. W. Gundel, 3rd edn. (Leipzig).

BÖMER, F. (1957–63). *Untersuchungen über die Religion der Sklaven in Griechenland und Rom*, Mainzer Akademie, geistes- und social-wissenschaftliche Klasse, 1957 no. 7; 1960 no. 1; 1961 no. 4; 1963 no. 10.

—— (1966). 'Der Eid beim Genius des Kaisers', *Athenaeum*, xliv. 77–133.

BONHÖFFER, A. (1890). *Epictet und die Stoa* (Stuttgart).

BONNER, C. (1946). 'Magical Amulets', *Harvard Theol. Rev.* xxxix. 25–53.

—— (1950). *Studies in Ancient Amulets chiefly Greco-Egyptian* (Ann Arbor).

BORN, L. K. (1934). 'The Perfect Prince according to Latin Panegyricists', *A. J. Phil.* lv. 20–35.

BOUCHÉ-LECLERCQ, A. (1871, repr. 1975). *Les Pontifs de l'ancienne Rome* (Paris; New York).

BOULANGER, A. (1923). *Aelius Aristide et la sophistique dans la province de l'Asie au 11ᵉ siècle de notre ère* (Paris).

BOURGERY, A. (1928). 'Lucain et la magie', *R.E.L.* iii. 299–313.

BOWERSOCK, G. (1969). *Greek Sophists in the Roman Empire* (Oxford).

—— (1972). 'Greek Intellectuals and the Imperial cult', in Fondation Hardt, *Entretiens*, xix (Geneva), 179–212.

—— (1975). 'Herodian and Elagabalus', *Yale Cl. St.* xxiv. 229–36.

BOWIE, E. L. (1970). 'Greeks and their Past in the Second Sophistic', *Past and Present*, xlvi. 3–41.

BOYANCÉ, P. (1950). 'Encore le *Pervigilium Veneris*', *R.E.L.* xxviii. 212–35 = *Études*, 359–82.

—— (1950). 'Properce aux fêtes de quartier', *R.E.A.* lii. 64–70 = *Études*, 291–7.

—— (1952). 'Les Pénates et l'ancienne religion romaine', *R.E.A.* liv. 109–15.

—— (1955). 'Sur la théologie de Varron', *R.E.A.* lvii. 57–84 = *Études*, 253–82.

—— (1962). '*Fides* et le serment', *Hommages à Albert Grenier* (Brussels), 329–41.

—— (1964). 'Les Romains, peuple de la *Fides*', *Bulletin de l'association G. Budé*, suppl. Lettres d'humanité, 4ᵉ série, xxiii. 419–35.

—— (1964). 'La Main de *Fides*', *Hommages à Jean Bayet*, Coll. Latomus, lxx (Brussels), 101–13.

—— (1965). 'La Science d'un quindécemvir au 1ᵉʳ siècle après J.-C.', *R.E.L.* 334–46.

—— (1966). 'Le *Pervigilium Veneris* et les *Veneralia*', *Mélanges offerts à André Piganiol* (Paris), 1547–63 = *Études*, 383–99.

—— (1972). *Études sur la religion romaine*, Collection de l'école française de Rome, xi (Rome).

——— (1972). '*Fides Romana* et la vie internationale', *Études*, 105–19.

BOYCE, G. K. (1937). *Corpus of the Lararia of Pompeii*, *M.A.A.R.* xiv.

BRAM, J. R. (1975). *Ancient Astrology: Theory and Practice (Matheseos Libri viii by Firmicus Maternus)* (New Jersey).

BRANDT, S. (1891). 'Lactantius und Lucretius', *Jahrbücher für classische Philologie*, xxxvii. 225–59.

BRENK, B. (1968). 'Die Datierung der Reliefs am Hadrianstempel in Ephesos und das Problem der tetrarchischen Skulpturen des Ostens', *Istanbuler Mitteilungen*, xviii. 232–58.

BRISSET, J. (1964). *Les Idées politiques de Lucain* (Paris).

BROCK, M. D. (1911). *Studies in Fronto and His Age* (Cambridge).

BROK, S. P. (1973). 'Early Syrian Ascetism', *Numen*, xx. 1–19.

BROUGHTON, T. R. S., and PATTERSON, M. L. (1951). *The Magistrates of the Roman Republic*, i (New York).

BROWN, P. L. (1961). 'Aspects of the Christianisation of the Roman Aristocracy', *J.R.S.* li. 1–11 = *Religion and Society*, 161–82.

——— (1967). *Augustine of Hippo: a biography* (London).

——— (1967). 'The Later Roman Empire', *Ec. Hist. Rev.* 2nd ser. xx. 327–43 = (1972), 46–73.

——— (1968). 'Approaches to the Religious Crisis of the Third Century', *Eng. Hist. Rev.* lxxxiii. 542–58 = (1972), 74–93.

——— (1968). 'Pelagius and His Supporters', *J. Theol. S.* n.s. xix. 93–114.

——— (1969). 'The Diffusion of Manichaeism in the Roman Empire', *J.R.S.* lix. 92–103.

——— (1970). 'Sorcery, Demons and the Rise of Christianity: from Late Antiquity into the Middle Ages', in *Witchcraft Confessions and Accusations* (Association of Social Anthropological Monographs, no. 9), 17–45 = *Religion and Society*, 119–46.

——— (1971). 'The Rise and Function of the Holy Man in Late Antiquity', *J.R.S.* lxi. 80–101.

——— (1971). *The World of Late Antiquity* (London).

——— (1972). *Religion and Society in the Age of Saint Augustine* (London).

——— (Spring 1975). 'Society and the Supernatural: a Medieval Change', *Daedalus*, 133–51.

BRUHL, A. (1953). *Liber Pater*, Bibliothèque des Écoles Françaises d'Athènes et Rome, no. 175.

BRUNT, P. A. (1961). 'Charges of Provincial Maladministration', *Historia*, x. 189–227.

——— (1971). *Italian Manpower 225 B.C.–A.D. 14* (Oxford).

——— (1973). 'Aspects of the Social Thought of Dio Chrysostom and of the Stoics', *Proc. Camb. Phil. Soc.* cxcix, n.s. 19. 9–34.

——— (1974). 'Marcus Aurelius and his *Meditations*', *J.R.S.* lxiv. 1–20.

BRUUN, P. M. (1966). *The Roman Imperial Coinage*, vii (London).

BUCHHEIT, V. (1963). *Vergil über Sendung Roms, Untersuchungen zum Bellum Poenicum und zur Aeneis*, Gymnasium Beiheft 3 (Heidelberg).

—— (1966). 'Christliche Romideologie im Laurentiushymnus des Prudentius', in *Polychronion*, Festschift F. Dölger (Heidelberg), 121–44 = R. Klein (ed.) (1971), 455–85.

BULARD, M. (1926). *Explorations archéologiques de Délos*, fascicule ix (Paris).

—— (1926). *La religion domestique dans la colonie italienne de Délos* (Paris).

BURCK, F. (1951). 'Die Schicksalsauffassung des Tacitus und Statius', in *Studies Presented to D. M. Robinson* (St. Louis), 693–706 = in *Das Menschenbild der römischen Literatur* (Heidelberg, 1969).

BURCKHARDT, J. (1949, first German edn. 1852). *The Age of Constantine the Great*, trans. M. Hadas (London).

BURDEAU, F. (1964). 'L'empereur d'après les panégyriques latins', in F. Burdeau, N. Charbonnel, M. Humbert: *Aspects de l'empire romain* (Paris), 1–60.

BURKERT, W. (1972). *Homo necans* (Berlin; New York).

BÜTLER, H. P. (1970). *Die geistige Welt des jüngeren Plinius* (Heidelberg).

CALDERONE, S. (1972). 'Superstitio', *A.N.R.W.* i. 2. 377–96.

Cambridge Ancient History, xii, *The Imperial Crisis and Recovery*, ed. by S. A. Cook, F. E. Adcock, M. P. Charlesworth, and N. H. Baynes (Cambridge, 1939).

Cambridge History of Later Greek and Medieval Philosophy, ed. by A. H. Armstrong (Cambridge, 1967).

CAMERON, ALAN (1967). 'The Date of Porphyry's *C. Christ.*', *C.Q.* n.s. vii. 382–4.

—— (1968). 'Gratian's Repudiation of the Pontifical Robe', *J.R.S.* lviii. 96–102.

—— (1970). *Claudian* (Oxford).

—— (1971). 'Why not Marius Maximus?', *J.R.S.* lxi. 262–7.

—— (1973). *Bread and Circuses: The Roman Emperor and his People* (London).

—— (1976). *The Circus Factions* (London).

CAMERON, ALAN and AVERIL (1966), 'The Cycle of Agathias', *J.H.S.* lxxxvi. 6–25.

CAMERON, AVERIL (1976). 'The Early Religious Policy of Justin II', *Studies in Church Hist.* xiii. 51–67.

CAMUS, P. M. (1967). *Ammien Marcellin, témoin des courants culturels et religieux à la fin du IVe siècle* (Paris).

CANCIK, HILDEGARD (1967). *Untersuchungen zu Senecas Epistulae Morales* (Hildesheim).

CARCOPINO, J. (1944). *La Basilique pythagoricienne de la porte majeure* (Paris).

—— (1953). *Études d'histoire chrétienne* (Paris).

CARDAUNS, B. (1960). *Varros Logistoricus über die Götterverehrung* (Würzburg).

—— (1976). *M. Terentius Varro: Antiquitates Rerum Divinarum*, 2 vols. (Mainz).

CARRATELLI, G. P. (1948). 'Tabulae Herculanenses', *Par. d. Pass,* iii. 165–84; and together with V. Arangio-Ruiz (1954), ibid. ix. 54–74.

CASTRITIUS, H. (1969). *Studien zu Maximinus Dia,* Frankfurter althistorische Studien, ii.

—— (1971). 'Zum höfischen Protokoll in der Tetrarchie: *Introitus (adventus)* Augusti et Caesaris', *Chiron,* i. 365–76.

CERFAUX, L., and TONDRIAU, J. (1957). *Le Culte des souverains dans la civilisation gréco-romaine* (Tournai).

CHADWICK, H. (1966). *Early Christian Thought and the Classical Tradition* (Oxford).

CHAMPLIN, E. (1974). 'The Chronology of Fronto', *J.R.S.* lxiv. 137–50.

CHARLESWORTH, M. P. (1925). 'Deus Noster Caesar', *C.R.* xxix. 13–16.

—— (1935). 'Some Observations on Ruler Cult', *Harv. Theol. Rev.* xxviii. 5–44.

—— (1936). 'Providentia and Aeternitas', ibid. xxix. 107–32.

—— (1937). 'Flaviana', *J.R.S.* xxvii. 54–62.

—— (1937). 'The Virtues of a Roman Emperor: Propaganda and the Creation of Belief', *Proc. Brit. Acad.* xxiii. 105–33.

—— (1939). 'The refusal of divine honours', *P.B.S.R.* xv (1939), 1–15.

—— (1943). 'Pietas and Victoria: The Emperor and the Citizen', *J.R.S.* xxxiii. 1–10.

CHASTAGNOL, A. (1966). *Le Sénat romain sous le règne d'Odoacre* (Bonn).

CIZEK, E. (1972). *L'Époque de Néron et ses controverses idéologiques* (Amsterdam).

CLARKE, G. W. (1972). 'Books for Burning', *Prudentia,* iv. 67–81.

CLOUD, J. D. (1971). 'Parricidium: from the *lex Numae* to the *lex Pompeia de parricidis*', *Zt. Sav. Stiftung,* lxxxviii. 1–46.

COHEN, C. J. (1964). *Behaviour in Uncertainty and its Social Implications* (London).

COMSTOCK, W. R. (1972). *The Study of Religion and Primitive Religions* (New York).

COULSON, F. H. (1926). *The Week* (Cambridge).

COURCELLE, P. (1946). 'Commodien et les invasions du Vᵉ siècle', *R.E.L.* xxiv. 227–46.

—— (1948). *Histoire Littéraire des Grandes Invasions Germaniques* (Paris).

—— (1953). 'Les sages de Porphyre et les *viri novi* d'Arnobe', *R.E.L.* xxxi. 257–71.

—— (1963). 'Anti-Christian Arguments and Christian Platonism, from Arnobius to St. Ambrose', in A. Momigliano (ed.) *The Conflict between Paganism and Christianity* (Oxford).

COVA, P. V. (1970). *I principia historiae e le idee storiografiche di Frontone* (Naples).

CRAKE, J. E. A. (1940). 'The Annals of the Pontifex Maximus', *C. Ph.* xxxv. 375–86.

CRAMER, F. H. (1954). *Astrology in Roman Law and Politics* (Philadelphia).

CRAWFORD, M. H. (1974). *Roman Republican Coinage*, 2 vols. (Cambridge).

CROOK, J. A. (1967). *Law and Life of Rome* (London).

CUMONT, F. (1912). *Astrology and Religion among the Greeks and Romans* (London).

—— (1922). *The Afterlife in Roman Paganism* (Yale).

—— (1923). 'La Théologie solaire du paganisme romain', *Mém. prés. à l'académie des inscriptions et belles-lettres*, xii. 2, 448 ff.

—— (1942, repr. 1969). *Recherches sur le symbolisme funéraire des romains* (Paris).

CURRIE, J. MACL. (1972). 'Seneca as Philosopher', in D. R. Dudley (ed.), *Neronians and Flavians*, Silver Latin, i (London), 24–6.

DAGRON, G. (1968). 'L'Empire au IVᵉ siècle et les traditions politique de l'hellénisme', *Travaux et Mémoires*, iii. 1–235.

DAHLMAN, H. (1935). 'Terentius Varro', P.W. Suppl. vi. 1172–276.

DALY, L. W. (1950). '*Vota*', *T.A.P.A.* lxxxi. 164–8.

DANIÉLOU, J. (1948). 'La Typologie de la semaine au IVᵉ siècle', *Recherches de science religieuse*, xxxv. 382–422.

DANIELS, C. M. (1975). 'The Role of the Roman Army in the Spread of the Practice of Mithraism', in J. R. Hinnels (ed.), *Mithraic Studies* (Manchester), ii. 249–74.

DAUBE, D. (1956). *Forms of Roman Legislation* (Oxford).

DEININGER, J. (1965). *Die Provinziallandtage der römischen Kaiserzeit von Augustus bis zum Ende des dritten Jahrhunderts n. Chr.*, Vestigia, vi (Munich).

DELATTE, L. (1957). *Recherches sur quelques fêtes mobiles sur le calendrier romain* (Liège).

DELLA CASA, A. (1962). *Nigidio Figulo* (Rome).

DEMANDT, A. (1965). *Zeitkritik und Geschichtsbild im Werk Ammians* (Bonn).

DE MARCHI, A. (1896–1903, repr. 1975). *Il culto privato di Roma antica* (Milan; New York).

DEONNA, W., and RENARD, M. (1961). *Croyances et superstitions de la table dans la Rome antique*, Coll. Latomus xlvi (Brussels).

DE RUGGIERO (1886). *Dizionario epigraphico di Antichità romana* (Rome).

DES PLACES, E. (1971). *Oracles chaldaïques*, Coll. Budé (Paris).

—— (1972). 'Les Oracles chaldaïques dans la tradition patristique africaine', in F. L. Cross (ed.), *Studia Patristica*, xi (Berlin).

DESSAU, H. (1892–1916). *Inscriptiones Latinae Selectae* (Berlin).

DE STE CROIX, G. E. M. (1954). 'Aspects of the "Great Persecution"', *Harv. Theol. Rev.* xlvii. 76–113.

—— (1963). 'Why were the early Christians persecuted?', *Past and Present*, xxvi. 6–38.

—— (1975). 'Early Christian attitudes to Property and Slavery', *Stud. in Church Hist.* xii. 1–38.

—— 'Political Elements in the Persecutions of and by the Early Christians', *Past and Present (forthcoming)*.

DIAMOND, A. S. (1971). *Primitive Law* (London).

DIHLE, A. (1955). P.W. viii, A, 637–59, s.v. Velleius Paterculus.

—— (1973). 'Zum Streit um den Altar der Victoria', in W. den Boer, P. G. van der Nat, C. M. J. Sicking, J. M. C. van Winden, *Romanitas et Christianitas* (Amsterdam and London), 81–94.

DILKE, O. A. W. (1972). 'Lucan's Political Views and the Caesars', in D. R. Dudley (ed.), *Neronians and Flavians*, Silver Latin, i (London), 62–82.

DILL, A. (1904, repr. 1956). *Roman Society from Nero to Marcus Aurelius* (London; New York).

DODDS, E. R. (1947), 'Theurgy and its Relationship to Neoplatonism', *J.R.S.* xxxvii. 55–73.

—— (1965). *Pagans and Christians in an Age of Anxiety* (Cambridge).

—— (1973). *The Ancient Concept of Progress, and Other Essays on Greek Literature and Belief* (Oxford).

DÖLGER, F. J. (1918). *Die Sonne der Gerechtigkeit*, Literaturgeschichtliche Forschungen, ii.

—— (1925). *Sol Salutis*, Literaturgeschichtliche Forschungen, iv–v.

—— (1940). 'Das Sonnengleichnis in einer Weihnachtspredigt des Zeno von Verona', *Antike und Christentum*, vi. 1 ff.

DOMASZEWSKI, A. VON (1895). *Die Religion des römischen Heeres* (Trier).

DÖRRIE, H. (1974). 'Die Solartheologie in der kaiserzeitlichen Antike', in H. Frohnes and W. Knott (eds.), *Kirchengeschichte als Missionsgeschichte*, i, Die alte Kirche (Munich), 262–92.

DÖRRIES, H. (1954). *Das Selbstzeugnis Kaiser Konstantins*, Abhandlungen der Akad. Wissenschaften Göttingen, Phil.-Hist. Klasse, 3. Folge, xxxiv (Göttingen).

—— (1960). *Constantine and Religious Liberty*, trans. by R. H. Bainton (Yale).

DOVER, K. J. (1974). *Greek Popular Morality* (Oxford).

DOWNEY, G. (1975). 'Tiberiana', in H. Temporini and W. Haase (eds.), *Aufstieg und Niedergang der römischen Welt*, ii (Principat), pt. 2 (Berlin), 95–126.

DUCHESNE, L. (1887). 'Le Concile d'Elvire et les *flamines* chrétiens', *Mélanges Renier* (Paris).

DUMÉZIL, G. (1966). *La Religion romaine archaïque* (Paris).

DUNCAN JONES, R. (1974). *The Economy of the Roman Empire* (Cambridge).

DÜRKHEIM, E. (1912, trans. 1926). *Les Formes élémentaires de la vie religieuse* (Paris) = *The Elementary Forms of Religious Life*, trans. by J. W. Swain (London).

DVORNIK, F. (1966). *Early Christian and Byzantine Political Philosophy* (Washington).

ECHOLS, E. C. (1961) (translator). *Herodian of Antioch's History of the Roman Empire* (Berkeley).

ECK, E. (1971). 'Das Eindringen des Christentums in den Senatorenstand bis zu Konstantin d. Gr.', *Chiron*, i. 381–406.

EDELSTEIN, E. J. and L. (1943–5). *Asclepius, a Collection and Interpretation of the Testimonies*, 2 vols. (Baltimore).

EDELSTEIN, L. (1966). *The Meaning of Stoicism* (Oxford).

EGGER, R. (1962). *Römische Antike und frühes Christentum* (Klagenfurt).

EHRENBERG, V. (1951). *The People of Aristophanes, a Sociology of Old Attic Comedy*, 2nd ᵉdn. (London).

—— and JONES, A. H. M. (1949). *Documents Illustrating the Reigns of Augustus and Tiberius* (Oxford).

EHRHARDT, A. (1955). 'Constantin d. Gr. Religionspolitik und Gesetzgebung', *Zt. Sav. Stift.* lxxii (= lxxxv *Zt. Rechtsgeschichte*), 127–90 = H. Kraft (1974), 388–456.

EITREM, S. (1933). 'Das Ende Didos in Vergil's *Aeneis*', in *Festskrift til Halvdan Koht* (Oslo), 29–41.

—— (1936). 'Religious Calendar concerning the Imperial Cult', *Papyri Osloenses*, iii. 77.

—— (1941). 'La Magie comme motif littéraire chez les Grecs et les Romains', *Symbol Osloenses*, xxi. 39–83.

—— (1942). 'La Théurgie chez les néoplatoniciens et dans les papyrus magiques, *Symbolae Osloenses*, xxii. 49–79.

—— (1947). *Orakel und Mysterien am Ausgang der Antike*, Albae Vigiliae, ser. ii, no. 5 (Zürich).

ELIADE, M. (1961). *The Sacred and the Profane* (New York).

ENSSLIN, W. (1923). *Zur Geschichtschreibung des Ammianus Marcellinus*, Klio, Beiheft, xvi.

—— (1948). P.W. 2. R. vii. 2. 2419–96, s.v. Valerius (Diocletianus).

—— (1956). *Die Religionspolitik des Kaisers Theodosius d. Gr.*, Sitzungsberichte der Bayerischen Akademie der Wissenschaften, Phil.-hist. Kl. 1953, 2, reviewed *J.R.S.* xlvi. 177–80.

ÉTIENNE, R. (1958). *Le Culte impérial dans la péninsule ibérique d'Auguste à Dioclétien* (Paris).

EVANS-PRITCHARD, E. E. (1937). *Witchcraft, Oracles, and Magic among the Azande* (Oxford).

FABIA, PH. (1914). 'L'Irréligion de Tacite', *Journal des Savants*, 250.

FANTHAM, E. (1975). 'Sex, Status and Survival in Hellenistic Athens: A Study of Women in New Comedy', *Phoenix*, xxix. 44–74.

FARQUHARSON, A. S. L. (1944). *The Meditations of the Emperor Marcus Aurelius*, 2 vols. (Oxford).

FERGUSON, J. (1970). *The Religions of the Roman Empire* (London).

FESTUGIÈRE, A. J. (1940). 'La doctrine des *viri novi* sur l'origine et le sort des âmes d'après Arnobe ii, 11–66', *Mémorial Lagrange* (Paris), 97–132.

—— (1944). *La Révélation d'Hermès Trismégiste*, i, 'L'Astrologie et les sciences occultes' (Paris).

—— (1946). *Epicure et ses dieux* (Paris).

—— (1953). *La Révélation d'Hermès Trismégiste*, vol. iii, 'Les Doctrines de l'âme' (Paris).

—— (1954). *Personal Religion among the Greeks* (Berkeley).

—— and NOCK, A. D. (1944–5). *Corpus Hermeticum*, ed. by A. D. Nock and trans. by A. J. Festugière. Collection des Universités de France (Paris).

FESTUS (1930, repr. 1965). *De verborum significatu*, ed. W. W. Lindsay, in *Glossaria Latina*, iv (Paris; Hildesheim).

FINK, R. O., HOEY, A.S., and SNYDER, W. F. (1940). 'The *Feriale Duranum*', *Yale Cl. St.* vii. 165–210.

FINUCANE, R. C. (1975). 'The use and abuse of medieval miracles', *History*, lx. 1–10.

FISHWICK, D. (1961). 'The imperial cult in Roman Britain', *Phoenix*, xv. 159–73, 213–20.

—— (1963). 'Vae puto deus fio', *C.Q.* n.s. v. 155–7.

—— (1964). 'The institution of the imperial cult in Africa Proconsularis', *Hermes*, xcii. 342–63.

—— (1969). 'The imperial *numen* in Great Britain', *J.R.S.* lix. 76–91.

—— (1969). 'Genius and Numen', *H. Theol. Rev.* lxii. 356–67.

—— (1973). 'The Severi and the provincial cult of the Three Gauls', *Historia*, xxii. 627–49.

FLACELIÈRE, R. (1965). *Greek Oracles*, trans. by D. Garman (London).

FLACH, D. (1973). 'Dios Platz in der kaiserzeitlichen Geschichtsschreibung', *Antike und Abendland*, xviii. 130–43.

FONDATION HARDT (1963, 1973). *Entretiens sur l'antiquité classique publiés par O. Reverdin*: xv, *Lucain* (Geneva, 1963); xx, *Le Culte des souverains dans l'empire romain* (Geneva 1973).

FONTAINE, J. (1968). *Aspects et problèmes de la prose d'art latine au IIIᵉ siècle*, La genèse des styles latins chrétiens (Turin).

FOWLER, W. WARDE (1914). *Roman Ideas of Deity* (London).

—— (1917). *Aeneas at the Site of Rome, Observations on the eighth Book of the Aeneid* (Oxford).

—— (1923). *The Religious Experience of the Roman People* (London).

FRAENKEL, E. (1927). 'Lucan als Mittler des antiken Pathos', *Vorträge der Bibliothek Warburg 1924–25* (Leipzig), 229–57 = *Kleine Beiträge zur Klassischen Philologie* (Rome, 1964), 243 ff.

—— (1957). *Horace* (Oxford).

FREND, W. H. C. (1952). *The Donatist Church, a Movement of Protest in Roman Africa* (Oxford).

—— (1955). 'Religion in Roman Britain in the Fourth Century A.D.', *J.B.A.A.* xviii. 1–19.

—— (1959). 'The Failure of the Persecutions in the Roman Empire', *Past and Present*, xvi. 10–30 = M. I. Finley, *Studies in Ancient Society* (London, 1974), 263–87.

FREND, W. H. C. (1965). *Martyrdom and Persecution in the Early Church* (Oxford).

—— (1968). 'The Christianisation of Roman Britain', in M. W. Barley and R. P. C. Hanson (eds.), *Christianity in Britain 300–700* (Leicester), 37–49.

FUCHS, H. (1958). 'Der Friede als Gefahr', *Harv. St. Cl. Phil.* lxiii. 363–85.

GABBA, E. (1974). *Per la storia dell'esercito romano in età imperiale* (Bologna).

GAGÉ, J. (1931). 'Observations sur le *carmen saeculare* d'Horace', *R.E.L.* ix. 290–300.

—— (1935). 'Actiaca', *Mélanges d'archéologie et histoire*, lii. 37–100.

—— (1936). 'Le *templum urbis* et les origines de l'idée de *renovatio*', in *Mélanges Fr. Cumont* (Brussels), 151–88.

—— (1938). '*Saeculum novum*', in *Transactions of the International Numismatic Congress 1936*, ed. J. Allan, H. Mattingly, E. S. G. Robinson (London), 179–86.

—— (1954). 'Hercule impérial et l'amazonisme de Rome', *R. H. Phil. R. (Strasbourg)*, v. 342–72.

—— (1955). *L'Apollon romain* (Paris).

—— (1961). 'Commodien et le moment millénariste du IIIe siècle (258–62 ap. J.-C.)', *R. H. Phil. R. (Strasbourg)*, xli. 355–78.

—— (1975). 'Programme d'italicité et nostalgies d'hellénisme autour de Gallien et Salonine. Quelques problèmes de paidéia impériale au IIIe siècle.' *A.N.R.W.* ii$_2$, 828–52.

GALLETIER, E. (1949–55). *Panégyriques Latins*, i–iii (Paris).

GANGHOFFER, R. (1963). *L'Évolution des institutions municipales en Occident et en Orient au Bas-Empire* (Paris).

GARNSEY, P. (1970). *Social Status and Legal Privilege in the Roman Empire* (Oxford).

GAUDEMET, J. (1958). *L'Église dans l'empire romain, IVe–Ve siècle* (Paris).

GEERTZ, C. (1966). 'Religion as a Cultural System', in M. Banton (ed.), *Anthropological Approaches to the Study of Religion* (London), 1–46.

GEFFCKEN, J. (1902, repr. 1967). *Die Oracula Sibyllina* (Leipzig).

—— (1902, repr. 1967). *Komposition und Entstehungszeit der Oracula Sibyllina* (Leipzig).

—— (1929). *Der Ausgang des griechisch-römischen Heidentums* (Heidelberg).

GETTY, O. J. (1941). 'The astrology of P. Nigidius Figulus', *C.Q.* xxxv. 17–22.

—— (1960). 'Neopythagoreanism in Lucan', *T.A.P.A.* xci. 310–23.

GILLIAM, J. F. (1954). 'The Roman Military *Feriale*', *Harv. Theol. Stud.* xlvii. 183–96.

GLOCK, C. Y., and STARK, R. N. (1965). *Religion and Society in Tension* (Chicago).

GLOVER, T. R. (1920). *The Conflicts of Religions in the Early Roman Empire* (London).

GLUCKMAN, M. (ed.) (1972). *The Allocation of Responsibility* (Manchester).

GNILKA, C. (1973). 'Götter und Dämonen in den Gedichten Claudians', *Antike und Abendland*, xviii. 144–60.

GOAR, R. J. (1972). *Cicero and the State Religion* (Amsterdam).

GOMME, A. W., ANDREWES, A., and DOVER, K. (1970). *A Historical Commentary on Thucydides*, iv (Oxford).

GOULD, J. B. (1970). *The Philosophy of Chrysippus* (Leyden).

GRABAR, A. (1936, repr. 1971). *L'Empereur dans l'art byzantin* (Strasburg; London).

—— (1966). *Byzantium from the Death of Theodosius to the Rise of Islam*, trans. by S. Gilbert and J. Emmons (London).

—— (1967). *The Beginnings of Christian Art*, trans. by S. Gilbert and J. Emmons of French edition of 1966 (London).

GREENSLADE, S. L. (1954). *Church and State from Constantine to Theodosius* (London).

GRÉGOIRE, H. (1913). 'Les Chrétiens et l'oracle de Didymes', in *Mélanges Holleaux* (Paris), 81–91.

GRIFFE, E. (1964). *La Gaule chrétienne à l'époque romaine*, i (Paris).

GRIFFIN, M. T. (1962). 'De Brevitate vitae', *J.R.S.* lii. 104–13.

—— (1972). 'The Elder Seneca and Spain', *J.R.S.* lxii. 1–19.

—— (1976). *Seneca, a Philosopher in Politics* (Oxford).

GRIMAL, P. (1948). *Sénèque: sa vie, son œuvre* (Paris).

—— (1960). 'L'Éloge de Néron au début de la Pharsale est-il ironique?', *R.E.L.* xxxviii. 296–307.

GRIMM, G. (1969). *Die Zeugnisse ägyptischer Religion und Kunstelemente im römischen Deutschland* (Leyden).

GRUEN, E. S. (1968). 'M. Antonius at the Trial of the Vestal Virgins', *Rhein. Mus.* cxi. 59–65.

—— (1969). *Roman Politics and the Criminal Courts 149–78 B.C.* (Cambridge, Mass.).

—— (1974). *The Last Generation of the Roman Republic* (Berkeley).

GSELL, S. (1922). *Inscriptions Latines de l'Algérie*, i, Inscriptions de la proconsulaire (Algiers-Paris).

GUEY, J. (1948). 'Encore la "pluie miraculeuse"', *Rev. de Phil.* xxii. 16–62.

GUNDEL, W., and GUNDEL, H. G. (1965). *Astrologumena*, Die astrologische Literatur in der Antike und ihre Geschichte (Wiesbaden).

GÜNTHER, R. (1963). 'Der politisch-ideologische Kampf in der römischen Religion im zweiten Jahrhundert von u. Z.', *Klio*, xli. 209–97.

GUTHRIE, W. K. C. (1967). *A History of Greek Philosophy*, i (Cambridge).

HABICHT, C. (1970). *Gottmenschtum und griechische Städte* (Munich).

—— (1973). 'Die augusteische Zeit und das erste Jahrhundert nach Christi Geburt', in Fondation Hardt, *Entretiens*, xix (Geneva), 41–88.

HADOT, L. (1969). *Seneca und die griechisch-römische Tradition der Seelenleitung* (Berlin).

HAGENDAHL, H. (1958). *Latin Fathers and the Classics* (Göteborg).

HAHN, D. (1963). 'The Roman Nobility and Three Major Priesthoods 218–167', *T.A.P.A.* xciv. 73–85.

HALLIDAY, W. R. (1913, repr. 1967). *Greek Divination* (Chicago).

HALSBERGHE, G. H. (1972). *The Cult of Sol Invictus* (Leyden).

HAMMOND, M. (1959). *The Antonine Monarchy* (Rome).

—— (1963). 'Liberty under the Early Roman Empire', *H. S. Cl. Phil.* lxvii. 93–113.

HÄNDEL, P. (1959). P.W. xxiii. 2. 2283–96 (Nachträge), s.v. Prodigium.

HANDS, A. R. (1968). *Charities and Social Aid in Greece and Rome* (London).

HANI, J. (1973). 'La Consolation antique', *R.E.A.* lxxv. 103–10.

HANSON, J. H. (1959). 'Plautus as a source-book for Roman Religion', *T.A.P.A.* xc. 48–101.

HARNACK, A. VON. (1905, repr. 1963). *Militia Christi, die christliche Religion und der Soldatenstand in den ersten drei Jahrhunderten* (Tübingen; Darmstadt).

—— (1906). *Die Mission und Ausbreitung des Christentums* (edn. 2, Berlin).

HARTMANN (1921). P.W. 2 R. ii. 1. 494–557, esp. 518–19, s.v. Schlange.

HECK, E. (1970). 'Scipio am Scheidewege', *Wien. St.* iv. 156–80.

HEIBGES, D. M. (1962). *The Religious Beliefs of Cicero's Times as reflected in his Speeches* (Diss. Bryn Mawr).

HEINRICHS, A. (1968). 'Vespasian's Visit to Alexandria', *Zt. f. Papyrologie und Epigraphie*, iii. 51–80.

HELLEGOUARC'H, J. (1963). *Le Vocabulaire latin des relations et des partis politiques sous la république* (Paris).

HENZEN, P. (1874). *Acta Fratrum Arvalium* (Berlin).

HERMANN, P. (1968). *Der römische Kaisereid*, Hypomnemata, 20 (Göttingen).

HERZOG-HAUSER, G. (1924). P.W. Suppl. iv. 806–53, s.v. Kaiserkult.

HEURGON, J. (1953). 'Tarquitius Priscus et l'organisation de l'ordre des haruspices sous l'empereur Claude', *Latomus*, xii. 402–17.

HICTER, M. (1944, 1945). 'L'Autobiographie dans l'*Âne d'or* d'Apulée', *Ant. Class.* xiii. 95 ff.; xiv. 61 ff.

HILD, J. H. (1896). Dar.S. 1490, s.v. Genius.

HOEY, A. S. (1939). 'Official Public Policy towards Oriental Cults in the Roman Army', *T.A.P.A.* lxx. 456–81.

HOFFMANN LEWIS, M. W. (1952). 'The Membership of the Major Colleges of Priests', *A. J. Phil.* lxxiii. 289 ff.

—— (1955). *The Official Priests of Rome under the Julio-Claudians* (Rome).

HOHL, E. (1938). 'Die angebliche Doppelbestattung des Antoninus Pius', *Klio*, xxxi. 169–85.

HOLLEMAN, A. W. J. (1973). 'An Enigmatic Function of the *flamen dialis* (Ovid, *Fast.* 2, 282) and the Augustan Reform', *Numen*, xx. 222–8.

—— (1973). 'Ovid and the Lupercalia', *Historia*, xxii. 260–8.

HOMMEL, H. (1972). 'Vesta und die frührömische Religion', *A.N.R.W.* i. 2 397–420.

HOMO, L. (1931). *Les Empereurs romains et le christianisme* (Paris).

—— (1948). *Vespasien, l'empereur du bon sens* (Paris).

HOPFNER, T. (1922–4). *Fontes Historiae Religionis Aegyptiacae* (Bonn).

—— (1928). P.W. xiv. 1. 302–93, s.v. Mageia.

—— (1935). P.W. xvi. 2. 2218–33, s.v. Nekromantie.

—— (1921, repr. 1974). *Griechisch-ägyptischer Offenbarungszauber*, Studien zur Palaeographie und Papyruskunde, ed. C. Wessely, xxi (Leipzig; Amsterdam).

HOPKINS, K. (1965). 'Contraception in the Roman Empire', *Comparative Studies in Society and History*, viii. 124–51.

HORNUS, J.-M. (1960). *Évangile et labarum* (Geneva).

HOSIUS, C. (1893). 'Lucan und seine Quellen', *Rh. Mus.* N.F. xlviii. 380 ff.

HOUT, M. P. J. VAN DEN (1954). *M. Cornelii Frontonis Epistulae* (Leyden).

HUBBARD, M. (1974). *Propertius* (London).

HÜBNER, W. (1970). *Dirae im römischen Epos*, Spudasmata, xxi (Hildesheim).

HUMPHREYS, S. C. (1975). 'Transcendence and Intellectual Roles: the Ancient Greek Case', *Daedalus*, 91–118.

JAHN, J. (1970). *Interregnum und Wahldiktatur*, Frankfurter althistorische Studien, iii (Kallmünz).

JAL, P. (1961). 'La Propagande religieuse à Rome au cours des guerres civiles de la fin de la république', *A.C.* xxx. 395–414.

—— (1961). 'Pax Civilis-Concordia', *R.E.L.* xxxix. 210–31.

—— (1963). *La Guerre civile à Rome* (Paris).

JOCELYN, H. D. (1966). 'The Roman Nobility and the Religion of the Roman State', *Journal of Religious History*, iv. 89–104.

JONES, A. H. M. (1940). *The Greek City from Alexander to Justinian* (Oxford).

—— (1949). *Constantine the Great and the Conversion of Europe* (London).

—— (1951). 'The Imperium of Augustus', *J.R.S.* xli. 112–19 = *Studies in Roman Government*, 1–17.

—— (1955). 'The Censorial Powers of Augustus', *J.R.S.* xlv. 9–21 = *Studies in Roman Government*, 21–6.

—— (1960). *Studies in Roman Government and Law* (Oxford).

—— (1963). 'The Social Background of the Struggle between Christianity and Paganism', in A. D. Momigliano (ed.), *Paganism and Christianity* (Oxford), 17–37.

—— (1964). *The Later Roman Empire* (Oxford).

—— and SKEAT, T. C. (1954). 'Notes on the genuineness of the Constantinian Documents in Eusebius' "Life of Constantine" ', *J. Eccl. H.* v. 196–200.

JONES, C. P. (1970). 'Licinius Sura', *J.R.S.* lx. 98–104.

KÄHLER, H. (1964). *Das Fünfsäulendenkmal für die Tetrarchen auf dem Forum Romanum* (Cologne).

—— (1973). *Die Villa des Maxentius bei Piazza Armerina* (Berlin).

KEYSSNER, K. (1936). P.W. xvii. 591–624, s.v. Nimbus.

KING, N. Q. (1961). *The Emperor Theodosius and the Establishment of Christianity* (London).

KIRSCHBAUM, E. (1948/9). 'Ein altchristliches Mausoleum unter der Peterskirche', *Das Münster*, ii. 400–6.

KLEIN, R. (1971) (ed.). *Das frühe Christentum im römischen Staat* (Darmstadt).

—— (1971). *Symmachus, eine tragische Gestalt des ausgehenden Heidentums* (Darmstadt).

—— (1972). *Der Streit um den Victorialtar.* Die dritte *Relatio* des Symmachus und die Briefe 17, 18 und 57 des Mailänder Bischofs Ambrosius. Einführung, Text, Übersetzung und Erläuterungen (Darmstadt).

KLINGNER, F. (1958). 'Tacitus und die Geschichtschreibung des ersten Jahrhunderts n. Chr.', *Mus. Helv.* xv. 194 ff. = *Römische Geisteswelt*, 469–89.

—— (1961). 'Die Einheit des virgilischen Lebenswerkes'; 'Virgil und die geschichtliche Welt', in ibid. (Munich), 274–92 and 292–311.

KLOSE, A. (1910). *Römische Priesterfasten* (Diss. Breslau).

KLUSSMANN, E. (1867). 'Arnobius und Lukrez, oder ein Durchgang durch den Epikuräismus zum Christentum', *Philologus*, xxvi. 362–7.

KNOPF, R., and KRÜGER, G. (1965). *Ausgewählte Märtyrerakten* (Tübingen).

KNOX, R. (1950). *Enthusiasm* (Oxford).

KOCH, C. (1954). 'Der altrömische Staatskult im Spiegel augusteischer Apologetik', in *Convivium*, Festschrift Konrad Ziegler (Stuttgart), 85–120.

KOESTERMANN, E. (1955). 'Die Majestätsprozesse unter Tiberius', *Historia*, iv. 72 ff.

KOHNS, H. P. (1971). 'Die tatsächliche Geltungsdauer des Maximaltarifs für Antiochia vom Jahre 362', *Rh. Mus.* cxiv. 78–83.

KORNEMANN, E. (1900). P.W. iv. 801–30, s.v. Concilium.

—— (1924). P.W. Suppl. iv. 914–41, s.v. Κοινόν.

KRAFT, H. (1955). *Kaiser Konstantins religiöse Entwicklung*, Beiträge zur historischen Theologie, xx (Tübingen).

—— (ed.) (1974). *Konstantin der Große*, Wege der Forschung, cxxxi (Darmstadt).

KRASCHENINNIKOFF, N. (1894). 'Über die Einführung des provinzialen Kaiserkultes im römischen Westen', *Philologus*, liii. 147–89.

KRAUS, F. B. (1930). *An Interpretation of the Omens, Portents and Prodigies recorded by Livy, Tacitus and Suetonius* (Diss., Philadelphia).

KRAUTHEIMER, R. (1961). 'The Constantinian Basilica', *Dumbarton Oaks Papers*, xxi. 115–40.

—— (1965). *Early Christian and Byzantine Architecture* (London).

KRETSKA, K. (1961). *C. Sallustius Crispus: Invektive und Episteln*, text, German translation, 2 vols. (Heidelberg).

KROLL, W. (1936). P.W. xvii. 1. 200–12, s.v. Nigidius Figulus.

KRUSE, H. (1934). *Studien zur offiziellen Geltung des Kaiserbildes im römischen Reich*, Studien zur Kultur und Geschichte des Altertums, xix. 3.

KUMANIECKI, F. (1962). 'Cicerone e Varrone', *Athenaeum*, xl. 221–43.

KURFESS, A. (1951). *Sibyllinische Weissagungen* (Berlin).

LABRIOLLE, P. DE (1934). *La Réaction païenne* (Paris).

LACOMBRADE, G. (1951). *Le Discours sur la royauté de Synesios de Cyrène* (Paris).

LAMBRECHTS, P. (1953). 'La Politique "apollinienne" d'Auguste et le culte impérial', *La Nouvelle Clio*, v. 65–82.

LANDSBERGER, H. A. (1974) (ed.). *Rural Protest: Peasant Movements and Social Change* (London).

LANGE, L. (1887). 'De legibus Aelia et Fufia commentatio', in *Kleine Schriften*, i (Göttingen), 274–341.

LARSEN, J. A. O. (1955). *Representative Government in Greek and Roman History* (Los Angeles).

LATTE, K. (1920). *Heiliges Recht*, Untersuchungen zur Geschichte der sakralen Rechtsformen in Griechenland (Tübingen).

—— (1950). 'Religiöse Begriffe im frührömischen Recht', *Zt. Sav. St.* lxvii. 47–61 = *Kleine Schriften*, 328–40.

—— (1960). *Römische Religionsgeschichte*, in Handbuch der Altertumswissenschaft (Munich).

—— (1968). *Kleine Schriften* (Munich), esp. 'Meineid', ibid. 376–9 = P.W. xvi (1931), 346–57.

LE BONNIEC, H. (1958). *Le Culte de Cérès à Rome* (Paris).

—— (1968). 'Lucain et la religion', in *Lucain*, Fondation Hardt, *Entretiens*, xv. 161–20.

LEGLAY, M. (1966). *Saturne Africain* (Paris).

LEMERLE, P. (1971). *Le Premier humanisme byzantin: notes sur enseignement et culture à Byzance des origines au Xe siècle* (Paris).

LENAGHAN, J. O. (1969). *A Commentary on Cicero's Oratio de Haruspicum Responso* (Paris).

LEWIS, M. J. T. (1966). *Temples in Roman Britain* (Cambridge).

LEWY, H. (1956). *Chaldean Oracles and Theurgy: Mysticism, Magic and Platonism in the Later Roman Empire*, Publications de l'institut français d'archéologie orientale, recherches d'astrologie, de philologie et d'histoire, xiii (Cairo).

LIEBESCHUETZ W. (1966). 'The Theme of Liberty in the *Agricola* of Tacitus', *C.Q.* xvi. 126–39.

—— (1967). 'The Religious Position of Livy's History', *J.R.S.* lvii. 45–55.

—— (1971). *Antioch* (Oxford).

—— (1978). 'Epigraphic Evidence on the Christianisation of Syria', Acts of the XIth International Congress of Limes Studies at Székesfehérvár (Budapest).

LIEGLE, J. (1942). *Zeitschrift für Numismatik*, xlii. 59–100 = H. Oppermann (ed.), *Römische Wertbegriffe* (Darmstadt, 1967).

LINDERSKI, J. (1966). *Rzymskie zgromadzenie wyborcze od Sulli do Cezara* (The Roman Electoral Assemblies from Sulla to Caesar) (Warsaw).

LINTOTT, A. W. (1968). *Violence in Republican Rome* (Oxford).

—— (1971). 'Lucan and the History of the Civil War', *C.Q.* n.s. xxi. 488–505.

—— (1972). 'Imperial Expansion and Moral Decline', *Historia*, xxi. 626–38.

LLOYD-JONES, H. (1971). *The Justice of Zeus* (Berkeley).

LODGE, G. (1924, repr. 1962). *Lexicon Plautinum* (Leipzig; Hildesheim).

LONG, A. A. (1974). *Hellenistic Philosophy, Stoics, Epicureans, Sceptics* (London).

L'ORANGE, H. P. (1934). '*Sol Invictus Imperator*, ein Beitrag zur Apotheose', *Symbolae Osloenses*, xiii. 86–114.

—— (1938). 'Tetrarchisches Ehrendenkmal auf dem Forum', *Mitteilungen des Deutschen Archaeologischen Instituts: Römische Abteilung*, liii. 1–34.

—— (1965). *Art Forms and Civic Life in the Late Roman Empire* (Princeton).

—— and VON GERKAN, A. (1939). *Der spätantike Bildschmuck des Konstantinbogens* (Berlin).

LUCK, G. (1956). '*Studia divina in vita humana*, Cicero's "Dream of Scipio" and its place in Graeco-Roman philosophy', *Harv. Theol. Rev.* xlix. 207 ff.

LUTERBACHER, F. (1904, repr. 1967). *Der Prodigienglaube und Prodigienstil der Römer* (Burgdorf; Darmstadt).

LUTZ, C. E. (1947). 'Musonius Rufus, the Roman Socrates', *Yale Cl. St.* x. 3–147.

MACBEATH, A. (1949). *The Relationship of Primitive Morality and Religion* (Glasgow).

—— (1952). *Experiments in Living* (London).

McCANN, A. M. (1918). *The Portraits of Septimius Severus A.D. 193–211*, *M.A.A.R.* xxx (Rome).

MacCORMACK, S. 'Change and Continuity in Late Antiquity in the Ceremony of the *adventus*', *Historia*, xxi. 721–52.

—— (1975). 'Latin Prose Panegyrics', in T. A. Dorey (ed.), *Empire and Aftermath* (London), 143–205.

McDONALD, A. H. (1957). 'The Style of Livy', *J.R.S.* xlvii. 155 ff.

McDONALD, W. F. (1929). 'Clodius and the *Lex Aelia Fufia*', ibid. xix. 164–79.

MACK, D. (1967). *Senatsreden und Volksreden bei Cicero* (Hildesheim).

McKAY, A. G. (1971). *Vergil's Italy* (Bath).

MacMULLEN, R. (1964). 'Some Pictures in Ammianus Marcellinus', *Art. Bull.* xlvi. 435–53.

—— (1967). *Enemies of the Roman Order* (London).

—— (1969). *Constantine* (London).

—— (1971). 'Social History in Astrology', *Anc. Soc.* ii. 105–116.

—— (1974). *Roman Social Relations* (New Haven and London).

MACROBIUS (1967). *Saturnalia*, ed. by N. Marione (Turin).

MAGDELAIN, A. (1962). 'Cinq jours épagomènes à Rome', *R.E.L.* xl. 202–27.

—— (1964). 'Note sur la loi curiate et les auspices des magistrats', *Rev. Hist. Droit Franc. et Étrang.* xlii. 198–203.

—— (1964). 'Auspicia ad patres redeunt', *Hommages à J. Bayet*, Coll. Latomus, lxx. 427–73.

—— (1968). *Recherches sur l'imperium, la loi curiate et les auspices d'investiture* (Paris).

MALAISE, M. (1972). *Inventaire préliminaire des documents égyptiens découverts en Italie* = *E.P.R.O.* xxi (Leyden).

—— (1972). *Les Conditions de pénétration et de diffusion des cultes égyptiens en Italie* = *E.P.R.O.* xxii (Leyden).

MARBACH, E. (1934). P.W. 2 R. v. 1, 781–4, s.v. Terminus.

MARGHITAN, L., and PETROLESCU, C. C. (1976). 'Vota pro salute imperatoris in an Inscription at Ulpia Traiana Sarmizegetusa', *J.R.S.* lxvi. 84–6.

MARKUS, R. A. (1974). 'Paganism, Christianity and the Latin Classics in the Fourth Century', in J. W. Binns (ed.), *Latin Literature of the Fourth Century* (London), 1–21.

MARQUARDT, J. (1881–5, repr. 1957). *Römische Staatsverwaltung*, 3 vols. (Darmstadt).

—— (1886, repr. 1964). *Das Privatleben der Römer*, 3 vols. (Darmstadt).

MARTI, B. M. (1945). 'The Meaning of the Pharsalia', *A. J. Ph.* lxvi. 352–76.

—— (1949). 'L'Hercule sur l'Oeta', *R.E.L.* xxvii. 189–210.

—— (1970). 'La Structure de la Pharsale', in *Lucain*, Fondation Hardt, *Entretiens*, xv (Geneva), 1–50.

MARTROYE, F. (1928). 'L'Épithète de *divus* appliquée aux empereurs chrétiens', *Bull. Soc. Antiq. Franc.* 297 ff.

MATTHEWS, J. F. (1973). 'Symmachus and the Oriental Cults', *J.R.S.* lxiii. 175–95.

—— (1974). 'The Letters of Symmachus', in J. W. Binns (ed.), *Latin Literature of the Fourth Century* (London), 58–99.

—— (1975). *Western Aristocracies and Imperial Court A.D. 364–425* (Oxford).

MATTINGLY, H. (1933). 'Fel. Temp. Reparatio', *Num. Chron.*, 5th ser., xiii. 182–202.

—— (1937). 'The Roman Virtues', *Harv. Theol. Rev.* xxx. 103–17.

—— (1950–1). 'The Imperial Vota', *Proc. British Acad.* xxxvi. 155–95; xxxvii. 219–68.

—— (1952). 'Jovius and Herculius', *Harv. Theol. Rev.* xlv. 131–4.

—— and SYDENHAM, E. A. (1962). *Roman Imperial Coinage*, ii (London).

MAZZARINO, S. (1959). *The End of the Ancient World*, trans. G. Holmes (London).

—— (1966). *Il Pensiero Storico Classico*, ii. 2 (Bari).

—— (1974). *Antico tardoantico ed èra constantiniana* (Rome).

MEIGGS, R. (1960, 2nd edn. 1973). *Roman Ostia* (Oxford).

MERGUET, H. (1887–94, repr. 1961). *Lexikon zu den philosophischen Schriften Ciceros*, 3 vols. (Jena; Hildesheim).

—— (1877–84, repr. 1962). *Lexikon zu den Reden des Cicero*, 4 vols. (Jena; Hildesheim).

MERTEN, E. W. (1968). *Zwei Herrscherfeste in der Historia Augusta*, Antiquitas iv, Beitr. zur Hist.-Aug. Forschung (Bonn).

MESLIN, M. (1970). *La Fête des Kalendes de janvier dans l'empire romain* = Coll. Latomus, 115 (Brussels).

MEYER, E. (1961). *Römischer Staat und Staatsglaube* (Stuttgart).

MEYER, H. D. (1961). *Die Außenpolitik des Augustus und die augusteische Dichtung* (Cologne).

MICHELS, A. K. (1967). *The Calendar of the Roman Republic* (Princeton).

MILLAR, F. (1964). *A Study of Cassius Dio* (Oxford).

—— (1965). 'Epictetus and the Imperial Court', *J.R.S.* lx. 141–8.

—— (1969). 'P. Herennius Dexippus', ibid. lix. 12–29.

—— (1973). 'The Imperial Cult and the Persecutions', Fondation Hardt, *Entretiens*, xix. 145–75.

MIX, E. R. (1970). *Marcus Atilius Regulus: exemplum historicum* (The Hague).

MÒCSY, A. (1970). *Gesellschaft und Romanisation in der römischen Province Moesia Superior* (Amsterdam).

—— (1974). *Pannonia and Upper Moesia, A History of the Middle Danube Provinces of the Roman Empire* (London).

MOINGT, J. (1966–9). *Théologie trinitaire de Tertullien*, vols. 1–4 (Paris).

MOMIGLIANO, A. D. (1955). 'Cassiodorus and Italian Culture of his Time', *Proc. of the British Acad.* xli. 207–45.

—— (ed.) (1963). *The Conflict between Paganism and Christianity in the Fourth Century* (Oxford).

—— (1963). 'Christianity and the Decline of the Roman Empire', ibid. 1–16.

—— (1963). 'Pagan and Christian Historiography in the Fourth Century', ibid. 79–99.

—— (1966). *Studies in Historiography* (London).

—— (1969). 'Seneca between Political and Contemplative Life', *Quarto contributo alla storia degli studi classici* (Rome), 239–56.

MOMMSEN, TH. (1890). 'Der Religionsfrevel nach römischem Recht', *Historische Zeitschrift.* lxiv. 389–429 = in *Gesammelte Schriften*, vol. 3 of *Juristische Schriften*, Berlin (1907, repr. 1963), 389–422.

—— (1897–8, repr. 1952). *Römisches Staatsrecht*, 3rd. edn. (Berlin; Graz).

—— (1899, repr. 1955). *Das römische Strafrecht* (Berlin; Graz).

—— (1913). 'Commentaria ludorum saecularium quintorum et septimorum', in *Gesammelte Schriften*, viii. 567–626.

Moreau, J. (1954). *Lactance, de la mort des persécuteurs*, introduction, texte, critique et traduction (Sources Chrétiennes, no. xxxix), 2 vols. (Paris).

—— (1961). *Die Christenverfolgung im römischen Reich* (Berlin).

—— (1964). *Scripta Minora* (Heidelberg). This includes: 'Krise und Verfall, das dritte Jahrhundert als historisches Problem', 26–41; 'Sur la vision de Constantin (312)', 76–98 = *R.E.A.* lv (1953), 307–33; 'Zur Religionspolitik Konstantins des Großen', 106–113.

Morford, M. P. O. (1967). *The Poet Lucan* (Oxford).

Motlo, A. L. (1970). *Guide to the Thought of Lucius Annaeus Seneca* (Amsterdam).

Müller, H. W. (1969). *Der Isiskult im antiken Benevent und Katalog der Skulpturen aus den ägyptischen Heiligtümern im Museo del Sannio zu Benevent* (Berlin).

Münzer, F. (1897). *Beiträge zur Quellenkritik der Naturgeschichte des Plinius* (Berlin).

Murray, G. (1946). 'Heracles "the best of men" ', in *Greek Studies* (Oxford), 106–26.

Murray, O. (1965). 'Philodemus on the Good King according to Homer', *J.R.S.* lv. 161–82.

—— (*forthcoming*). 'Panegyric and Advice to Rulers in Late Antiquity and the Early Middle Ages', *Journal of Warburg and Courtauld Insts.*

Musurillo, H. (1972). *The Acts of the Christian Martyrs* (Oxford).

Neugebauer, O. (1959). 'The Chronology of Vettius Valens' Anthology', *Harv. Theol. Rev.* xlvii. 65–7.

—— and Van Hoesen (1959). *Greek Horoscopes, Memoirs Am. Philosoph. Soc.* xlviii.

Newbold, R. F. (1974). 'Social and Economic Consequences of the A.D. 64 Fire at Rome', *Latomus*, xxxiii. 856–69.

Niemeyer, H. G. (1968). *Studien zur statuarischen Darstellung der römischen Kaiser* (Berlin).

Nikiprowetsky, V. (1970). *La Troisième sibylle* (Paris).

Nilsson, M. P. (1920). P.W. 2 R. i, A2, 1710–20, s.v. Saeculares Ludi.

—— (1950). *Geschichte der griechischen Religion*, ii, (Munich).

Nisbet, R. G. (ed.) (1939). *Cicero: De Domo* (Oxford).

Nock, A. D. (1927). 'Sarcophagi and Symbolism', *A.J.A.* l. 151–1 = *Essays*, 620–4.

—— (1928). 'Notes on the Ruler Cult I–IV', *J.H.S.* xlviii. 22–42 = *Essays*, 134–59.

—— (1928). 'Oracles théologiques', *R.E.A.* xxx. 280–90 = 160–8.

—— (1929). 'Greek Magical Papyri', *J.E.A.* xv. 219–35 = *Essays*, 176–94.

—— (1933). *Conversion* (Oxford).

—— (1933). 'Paul and the Magus', in Jackson-Lake (ed.), *The Beginnings of Christianity*, v. 164–88 = *Essays*, 308–38.

332   Bibliography

NOCK, A. D. (1934). 'A Vision of Mandulis Aion', *Harv. Theol. Rev.* xxvii.
52–104 = *Essays*, 357–400.

—— (1939). 'Conversion and Adolescence', in *Pisciculi*, Festschrift, F. J.
Dölger, 164–77 = *Essays*, 469–80.

—— (1941). 'Tomb Violations and Pontifical Law', *J. Biblical Lit.* lx. 88–
95 = *Essays*, 527–33.

—— (1944). 'The Cult of Heroes', *Harv. Theol. Rev.* xxxvii. 141–7 = *Essays*,
575–602.

—— (1947). 'The Emperor's Divine *Comes*', *J.R.S.* xxxvii. 102–16 = *Essays*,
653–75.

—— (1952). 'The Roman Army and the Roman Religious Year', *Harv.
Theol. Rev.* xlv. 187–251 = *Essays*, 736–90.

—— (1957). 'Deification of Julian', *J.R.S.* xlvii. 115–23 = *Essays*, 833–46.

—— (1972). *Essays on Religion and the Ancient World*, 2 vols. (Oxford).

NORDEN, F. (1924, repr. 1958). *Die Geburt des Kindes*, Geschichte einer
religiösen Idee (Stuttgart).

NORTH, J. (1968). *The Interrelation of State Religion and Politics in Roman Public
Life from the End of the Second Punic War to the Time of Sulla* (Diss. Oxford,
unpublished).

OGILVIE, R. M. (1961). 'Lustrum condere', *J.R.S.* li. 31–9.

—— (1965). *A Commentary: Livy 1–5* (Oxford).

—— (1969). *The Romans and their Gods* (London).

O'MEARA, J. J. (1959). *Porphyry's Philosophy from Oracles in Augustine*, Études
Augustiniennes (Paris).

—— (1969). *Porphyry's Philosophy from Oracles in Eusebius' Praeparatio Evangelica
and Augustin's Dialogues of Cassiciacum*, Études Augustiniennes (Paris).

OPELT, I. (1970). 'Die *Volcanalia* in der Spätantike', *Vigil. Christ.* xxiv. 59–63.

ORGELS, P. (1948). 'La Première vision de Constantin (310) et le temple
d'Apollon à Nîmes', *Bull. Acad. Roy. Belg.*, Lettres 5ᵉ ser., 176–202.

ORWELL, G. (1954). *Nineteen Eighty-Four* (London, Penguin).

OTTO, W. F. (1910). 'Augustus Soter', *Hermes*, xlv. 448–60.

—— (1912). P.W. viii. 1155–70, s.v. Genius.

PALMER, R. E. A. (1965). 'The Censors of 312 and the State Religion',
Historia, xiv. 319, 393–424.

—— (1970). *The Archaic Community of the Romans* (Cambridge).

—— (1974). *Roman Religion and Roman Empire* (Philadelphia).

PARK, G. K. (1963). 'Divination and its Social Contexts', *J. R. Anthrop. Inst.*
xciii. 195–209.

PARKE, H. W. (1967). *Greek Oracles* (London).

PASOLI, A. (1950). *Acta fratrum Arvalium quae post annum MDCCCLXXIV
reperta sunt* (Bologna).

PETER, H. (1897, repr. 1967). *Geschichtliche Literatur über die römische Kaiserzeit
bis Theodosius I* (Leipzig; Hildesheim).

—— (1914, repr. 1967). *Historicorum Romanorum Reliquiae* (Leipzig; Stuttgart).

PETIT, P. (1955). *Libanius et la vie municipale à Antioche an IVe siècle* (Paris).

—— (1974). *Histoire générale de l'empire romain* (Paris).

PFLAUM, H.-G. (1950). *Les Procurateurs équestres sous le Haut-Empire romain* (Paris).

PICHON, R. (1901). *Lactance:* Étude sur le mouvement philosophique et religieux sous la règne de Constantin (Paris).

—— (1906). *Les Derniers écrivains profanes* (Paris).

—— (1912). *Les Sources de Lucain* (Paris).

PIGANIOL, A. (1972). *L'Empire chrétien*, 2nd edn. (Paris).

PIGHI, I. B. (1965). *De Ludis Saecularibus Populi Romani Quiritium* (Amsterdam).

PIPPIDI, D. M. (1931). 'Le *numen* Augusti', *R.E.L.* ix. 83–111.

—— (1941). *Recherches sur le cult impérial* (Paris; Bucharest).

—— (1947–8). 'Apothéoses impériales et apothéose de Peregrinos', *S.M.S.R.* xxxi. 77.

PLEKET, H. W. (1965). 'An Aspect of the Emperor Cult: Imperial Mysteries', *Harv. Theol. Rev.* lviii. 331 ff.

POHLENZ, M. (1919). *Die Stoa* (Göttingen).

PORPHYRY (1969). *Πρὸς Μαρκέλλαν*, Greek text trans. and ed. by W. Pötscher (Leyden).

PORTALUPI, G. (1961). *Marco Cornelio Frontone* (Turin).

PÖSCHL, V. (1936, repr. 1962). *Römischer Staat und griechisches Staatsdenken bei Cicero* (Berlin; Darmstadt).

—— (1956, 4). *Horaz und die Politik*, Sitzungsbericht Heidelberger Akademie Phil. Hist. Kl.

PREIBISCH, P. (1874). *Quaestiones de libris pontificis* (Breslau).

—— (1878). *Fragmenta librorum pontificorum* (Tilsit).

—— (1975). *Two Studies on the Roman Pontifices* (New York), contains both studies.

PREISENDANZ, K. (1929, repr. 1974). *Papyri Graecae Magicae* (Leipzig; Stuttgart).

—— (1969). *R.A.C.* viii. 1–30, s.v. Fluchtafel *(Defixio)*.

PREISKE, H. (1927). *Christentum und Ehe in den ersten drei Jahrhunderten*, Neue Studien zur Geschichte der Theologie und Kirche, xxiii.

PRITCHETT, W. K. (1971). *The Greek State at War* (Berkeley).

PUTTEN, J. M. P. B. VAN DER (1971). 'Arnobe croyait-il à l'existence des dieux paiens?', *Vigil. Christ.* xxv. 52–5.

QUASTEN, J. (1960). *Patrology*, iii, The Golden Age of Greek Patristic Literature from the Council of Nicaea to the Council of Chalcedon (Utrecht).

RADKE, G. (1963). *P.W.* xxiv. 1114–48, s.v. Quindecimviri.

RAHNER, H. (1949). 'Das Christliche Mysterium von Sonne und Mond', *Eranos Jahrbuch*, x. 305–404.

RAHNER, H. (1963). *Greek Myths and Christian Mystery*, trans. by B. Battershaw (London).

RAWSON, E. (1971). 'Prodigy Lists and the Use of the *Annales Maximi*', *C.Q.* xxi. 158–69.

—— (1974). 'Religion and Politics in the Late Second Century B.C. at Rome', *Phoenix*, xxvii. 193–212.

—— (1975). *Cicero, a Portrait* (London).

REGEN, F. (1971). *Apuleius Philosophus Platonicus*, Untersuchungen zur Apologie (*De Magia*) and zu *De Mundo* (1971).

REHM, A. (1938). 'Kaiser Diokletian und das Heiligtum von Didyma', *Philologus*, xciii. 74–84.

REVERDIN, O., see Fondation Hardt.

REYNOLDS, J. M. (1962). 'Vota pro salute principis', *P.B.S.R.* xxx. 33–6.

RICHARD, J.-CL. (1966). 'Incinération et inhumation aux funérailles impériales', *Latomus*, xxv. 184–204.

—— (1968). 'Sur quelques grands pontifes plébéiens', ibid. xxvii. 786–801.

RIESS, E. (1939). P.W. xviii. 1. 351–78, s.v. Omen.

RINK, E. (1933). *Bildliche Darstellungen des römischen Genius* (Diss., Giessen).

RISTOW, G. (1971). *Mithras im römischen Köln* (Leyden).

ROBERT, L. (1948). 'Épigrammes du Bas-Empire', *Hellenica*, iv (Paris).

—— (1960). 'Recherches épigraphiques: Inscriptions d'Athènes', *R.E.A.* lxii. 316–24.

ROBERTS, A., and DONALDSON, J. (1871). *The Works of Lactantius*, Ante-Nicene Christian Library, xxi–xxii (Edinburgh).

ROBINSON, D. N. (1915). 'An Analysis of the Pagan Revival of the Late Fourth Century, with especial Reference to Symmachus', *T.A.P.A.* xlvi. 87–101.

ROGERS, R. S. (1935). *Criminal Trials and Criminal Legislation under Tiberius* (Middletown).

ROHDE, G. (1936). *Die Kultsatzungen der römischen Pontifices* (Berlin).

ROLOFF, D. (1970). *Gottähnlichkeit, Vergöttlichung und Erhöhung zu seligem Leben* (Berlin).

Roman Imperial Coinage (1962). Vol. ii by H. Mattingly and E. A. Sydenham (London).

—— (1962). Vol. v² by Percy H. Webb (London).

—— (1966). Vol. vii by P. M. Bruun (London).

—— (1967). Vol. vi by C. H. V. Sutherland (London).

ROSE, J. (1960). 'Roman Religion 1910–60', *J.R.S.* l. 161–72.

ROSE, K. F. C. (1966). 'Problems of Chronology in Lucan's Career', *T.A.P.A.* xlvii. 379–96.

ROSTOVTZEFF, M. (1926, 2nd ed. 1957). *The Social and Economic History of the Roman Empire* (Oxford).

RUTTER, J. (1968). 'The Three Phases of the Taurobolium', *Phoenix*, xxii. 226–49.

RUTZ, W. (1964). 'Lucan 1943–63 (Literaturbericht)', *Lustrum*, ix. 243–334.

—— (ed.) (1970). *Lucan*, Wege der Forschung, ccxxv (Darmstadt).

RYBERG, I. S. (1955). *Rites of the Roman State Religion in Art* (Rome).

RZACH, A. (1923). P.W. 2 R. A2, 2073–183, s.v. Sibyllen and Sibyllinische Orakel.

SAMBURSKY, F. (1959). *Physics of the Stoics* (London).

SAUTER, F. (1934). *Der römische Kaiserkult bei Martial und Statius*, Tübinger Beiträge zur Altertumswissenschaft, 21.

SCHEID, J. (1975). *Les Frères Arvales*, recrutement et origine sociale sous les empereurs Julio-Claudiens (Paris).

SCHILLING, R. (1942). 'L'Hercule romain et la réforme religieuse d'Auguste', *Rev. de Phil.* xvi. 31–57.

—— (1972). 'La situation des études relative à la religion romaine de la République', *A.N.R.W.* i. 2. 317–47.

SCHMIDT, P. L. (1968). *Julius Obsequens und das Problem der Livius Epitome*, Akademie Mainz, Abhandlungen der geistes- und sozialwissensschaftlichen Klasse, 5.

SCHOENEBECK, H. VON (1939, repr. 1962). *Beiträge zur Religionspolitik des Maxentius und Constantin (Klio*, Beiheft xliii n. Folge 30).

SCHOTES, H. A. (1969). *Stoische Physik, Psychologie und Theologie bei Lucan* (Bonn).

SCHWARTZ, E. (1913). *Kaiser Constantin und die christliche Kirche* (Berlin).

SCHWERTHEIM, E. (1974). *Die Denkmäler orientalischer Gottheiten im römischen Deutschland mit Ausnahme der ägyptischen Gottheiten* (Leyden).

SCOTT, K. (1933). 'Statius' adulation of Domitian', *A. J. Ph.* liv. 247–59.

—— (1936). *The Imperial Cult under the Flavians* (Stuttgart).

—— (1937). 'The Political Propaganda of 44–30 B.C.', *M.A.A.R.* 7–49.

SCOTT, R. T. (1968). *Religion and Philosophy in the Histories of Tacitus*, Papers and Monographs of the American Academy in Rome, xxii (Rome).

SCULLARD, H. H. (1951). *Roman Politics 220–150 B.C.* (Oxford).

SEAGER, R. (1972). *Tiberius* (London).

SESTON, W. (1940). 'De l'authenticité et de la date de l'édit de Dioclétien contre les manichéens', *Mélanges A. Ernout*, 345–54.

—— (1946). *Dioclétien et la tétrarchie* (Paris).

—— (1950). 'Jovius et Herculius ou l'épiphanie des tétrarques', *Historia*, i. 257–66.

SEVENSTER, J. N. (1961). *Paul and Seneca* (Leyden).

SEYRIG, H. (1971). 'Le culte du soleil en Syrie à l'époque romaine', *Syria*, xlviii. 337–73.

SHACKLETON BAILEY, D. R. (1960). 'The Roman Nobility in the Second Civil War', *C.Q.* n.s. x. 253–66.

SHERWIN-WHITE, A. N. (1966). *The Letters of Pliny: A Historical and Social Commentary* (Oxford).

SHOTTER, D. C. A. (1972). 'The Trial of M. Scribonius Libo Drusus', *Historia*, xxi. 88–98.

SIMPSON, A. D. (1938). 'The Departure of Crassus for Parthia', *T.A.P.A.* 511–32.

SIMON, M. (1955). *Hercule et le christianisme* (Paris).

SMALLWOOD, E. M. (1966). *Documents Illustrating the Principates of Nerva, Trajan and Hadrian* (Cambridge).

SMIT SIBINGA, J. (1970). 'Melito of Sardis, the Artist and his Text', *Vigil. Christ.* xxiv. 81–104.

SNELL, B. (1967). 'Ezechiels Moses-Drama', *Antike und Abendland*, xiii. 150–64.

SNYDER, W. F. (1940). 'Public Anniversaries in the Roman Empire', *Yale Classical Studies*, vii. 225 ff.

SODEN, H. VON (1950). *Urkunden zur Entstehungsgeschichte des Donatismus*, revised by H. von Campenhausen (Berlin).

SPIRO, M. E. (1966). Religion: Problems of Definition and Explanation, in M. Bantor (ed.), *Anthropological Approaches to the Study of Religion* (London).

STADE, K. (1926). *Der Politiker Diokletian und die letzte große Christenverfolgung* (Wiesbaden).

STAHL, G. (1964). 'Die Naturales quaestiones Senecas', *Hermes*, xcii. 425–54.

STARR, C. G. (1954, repr. 1965). *Civilization and the Caesars* (Cornell; New York).

STAVELEY, E. S. (1954–5). 'The Conduct of Elections during an Interregnum', *Historia*, iii. 201–11.

STEIDLE, W. (1971). 'Die dichtende Konzeption des Prudentius und das Gedicht *contra Symmachum*', *Vigil. Christ.* xxv. 241–81.

STEIN, A. (1927). 'Zur sozialen Stellung der provinzialen Oberpriester', in *Epitymbion Swoboda*.

STERN, H. (1953). *Le Calendrier de 354*, Bibl. Arch. Hist. lv (Paris).

—— (1954). 'Remarks on the *adoratio* under Diocletian, *Journal of Warburg and Courtauld Insts.* xvii. 184–9.

STEVENSON, J. (1957). 'The Life and Literary Activity of Lactantius', *Studia Patristica vol. I = Texte und Untersuchungen zur Geschichte der altchristlichen Literatur*, 63 (Berlin), 661–77.

STRACK, P. (1931–7). *Untersuchungen zur Reichsprägung im 2. Jahrhundert*, 3 vols. (Stuttgart).

STRASBURGER, H. (1965). 'Poseidonius on Problems of the Roman Empire' *J.R.S.* lv. 40–53.

STRAUB, J. A. (1939). *Vom Herrscherideal der Spätantike* (Stuttgart).

—— (1972). *Regeneratio Imperii* (Darmstadt).

—— (1972). 'Severus Alexander und die Mathematici', in *Regeneratio Imperii*, 383–409.

Bibliography 337

SUMNER, G. V. (1963). 'Lex Aelia, Lex Fufia', *A. J. Ph.* lxxiv. 337–58.

—— (1970). 'The Truth about Velleius Paterculus', *Harv. St. Cl. Phil.* lxxiv. 257–97.

SUTHERLAND, C. H. V. (1967). *The Roman Imperial Coinage* (R.I.C.), vi, A.D 294–313 (London).

SWAIN, J. W. (1946). 'The History of the 4 Monarchs, Opposition History under the Roman Empire', *Cl. Phil.* xxxv. 1–21.

SYDENHAM, E. A. (1958). *The Coinage of the Roman Republic* (London).

SYME, R. (1939). *The Roman Revolution* (Oxford).

—— (1958). *Tacitus* (Oxford).

—— (1959). 'Livy and Augustus', *H. St. Cl. Ph.* lxiv. 27–87.

—— (1964). *Sallust* (Cambridge).

—— (1970). *Ten Studies in Tacitus* (Oxford), 91–109.

—— (1971). *Emperors and Biography* (Oxford).

TAEGER, F. (1957). *Charisma*, i (Stuttgart).

—— (1960). *Charisma*, ii (Stuttgart).

TAYLOR, L. R. (1917, 1920). 'Augustales', *T.A.P.A.* xlv. li. 116–33, 231–53.

—— (1931). *The Divinity of the Roman Emperor* (Middletown).

—— (1949). 'Foreign Groups in Roman Politics', *Hommages Bidez-Cumont*, Coll. Latomus, 11, 323–30.

—— (1949). *Party Politics in the Age of Caesar* (Berkeley).

—— (1961). 'Freedmen and Freeborn in the Epitaphs of Imperial Rome', *A. J. Ph.* lxxxii. 113–32.

—— (1966). *Roman Voting Assemblies* (Ann Arbor).

TEMPORINI, H. (ed.) (1972). *Aufstieg und Niedergang der römischen Welt* = *A.N.R.W.* (Berlin).

TENGSTRÖM, E. (1964). *Donatisten und Katholiken* (Göteborg), Studia Graeca et Latina Gothoburgensia, xviii.

THEODORET. *Graecarum Affectionum Curatio, P.G.* lxxxiii.

THOMAS, K. (1971). *Religion and the Decline of Magic* (London).

THORNDYKE, L. (1913). 'A Roman Astrologer as a Historical Source: Julius Firmicus Maternus', *C. Phil.* viii. 415.

—— (1923). *History of Magic and Experimental Science*, i (New York).

THULIN, C. O. (1912). P.W. vii. 2. 2431–68, s.v. Haruspices.

TILLICH, P. (1960). *Christianity and the Encounter of the World Religions* (Chicago).

TOUTAIN, J. (1907). *Les Cultes païens dans l'empire romain* (Paris).

TRAUB, H. W. (1955). 'Pliny's Treatment of History in Epistolary Form', *T.A.P.A.* lxxxvi. 213–32.

TREGGIARI, S. (1969). *Roman Freedmen during the Late Republic* (Oxford).

TRENCSENYI-WALDAPFEL, I. (1958). 'Cicéron et Lucrèce', *Acta Antiqua*, vi. 342 ff.

TURCAN, R. (1967). 'Sénèque et les religions orientales', Coll. Latomus, xci (Brussels).

TURNER, V. W. (1963). *The Drums of Affliction* (Oxford).

ULRICH, TH. (1930). *Pietas als politischer Begriff im röm. Staat bis zum Tode des Commodus*, Hist. Untersuchungen, vi (Breslau).

USENER, H. (1905). 'Sol Invictus', *Rh. Mus.* lx. 465–91.

VAHLEN, I. (1928, repr. 1963). *Ennianae Poesis Reliquiae* (Leipzig; Amsterdam).

VALETON, I. M. J. (1891). 'De iure obnuntiandi comitiis et conciliis', *Mnemosyne*, xix. 75–113, 229–70.

VERGOTE, J. (1939). 'Les Principaux Modes de supplices chez les anciens et dans les textes chrétiens', *Bull. Inst. Hist. Belge de Rome*, x. 141–63.

VERNANT, J.-P. (1962). *Les Origines de la pensée grecque* (Paris).

—— (1965). *Mythe et pensée chez les grecs* (Paris).

—— VANDERMEERSCH, L., GENET, J., BOTTERO, J., and others (1974). *Divination et rationalité* (Paris).

VESSEY, D. (1973). *Statius and the Thebaid* (Cambridge).

VIDMAN, L. (1965). 'Die Isis- und Sarapisverehrung im 3 Jahrhundert u.Z.', *Neue Beiträge zur Geschichte der alten Welt*, ii, Römisches Reich (Berlin), 389–400.

VITTINGHOFF, F. (1953). 'Eusebius als Verfasser der *Vita Constantini*', *Rh. Mus.* xcvi. 330–73.

VOGLIANO, A., and CUMONT, F. (1933). 'The Bacchic Inscription in the Metropolitan Museum', *Am. J. Arch.* xxxvii. 215–70.

VOGT, J. (1944). 'Zur Frage des christlichen Einflusses auf die Gesetzgebung Konstantins des Großen', *Münchener Beiträge zur Papyrusforschung und antiken Religionsgeschichte*, xxxiv. 118–48.

—— (1968). 'Toleranz und Intoleranz im constantinischen Zeitalter', *Saeculum*, xix. 344–66.

VRETSKA, K. (1961). *C. Sallustius Crispus Invektive und Epistel*, edition with German trans., 2 vols. (Heidelberg).

WAGENVOORT, J. (1947). *Roman Dynamism* (Oxford).

—— (1972). 'Wesenszüge altrömischer Religion', *A.N.R.W.* i. 2, 348–76.

WALBANK, F. (1957). *A Historical Commentary on Polybius*, i (Oxford).

WALKER, B. (1952). *The Annals of Tacitus* (Manchester).

WALLACE-HADRILL, D. S. (1960). *Eusebius of Caesarea* (London).

WALLIS, R. T. (1972). *Neo-Platonism* (London).

WALSH, P. G. (1961). *Livy, his Historical Aims and Methods* (Cambridge).

—— (1970). *The Roman Novel* (Cambridge).

—— (1974). *Livy*, in Greece and Rome: New Surveys in the Classics (Oxford).

WALTERS, V. J. (1974). *The Cult of Mithras in the Roman Provinces of Gaul* (Leyden).

WALTZING, J. P. (1895–1900, repr. 1968). *Étude historique sur les corporations professionnelles chez les romains depuis les origines jusqu'à la chute de l'empire d'Occident*, 4 vols. (Louvain; Bologna).

WARMINGTON, B. H. (1954). *The North African Provinces from Diocletian to the Vandal Conquest* (Cambridge).

WARMINGTON, E. H. (1935). *Remains of Old Latin*, Loeb Classical Library, i, Ennius and Caecilius (London).

WARREN BONFANTE, L. (1964). 'Emperor, God and Man in the IVth. Century', *La Parola del Passato*, xix. 406–27.

—— (1970). 'Roman Triumphs and Etruscan Kings: the Changing Face of the Triumph', *J.R.S.* lx. 49–66.

WATKINS, O. D. (1920, repr. 1961). *A History of Penance*: being a study of the authorities for the whole church to A.D. 450, and for the Western church from A.D. 450 to A.D. 1215 (London; New York).

WATSON, G. R. (1968). 'Christianity in the Roman Army in Britain', in M. W. Burley and R. P. C. Hanson (eds.), *Christianity in Britain 300–700* (Leicester), 51–3.

WEBB, P. H. (1962). *Roman Imperial Coinage*, 2 (London).

WEBER, M. (1922–3). *Gesammelte Aufsätze zur Religionssoziologie*, 3 vols. (Tübingen).

—— (1965). *The Sociology of Religion*, trans. by E. Fischoff (London).

WEGENER, M. (1939). *Die römischen Herrscherbildnisse in antoninischer Zeit* (Berlin).

WEINREICH, O. (1969). 'Das Türmotiv im Prodigienglauben', *Religionsgeschichtliche Studien* (Stuttgart), 257–79.

WEINSTOCK, S. (1937). 'Clodius and the *Lex Aelia Fufia*', *J.R.S.* xxvii. 215–22.

—— (1946). 'Martianus Capella and the Cosmic System of the Etruscans', *J.R.S.* xxxvi. 101–29.

—— (1971). *Divus Julius* (Oxford).

WELLMAN, M. (1928). *Die φυσικά des Bolos Demokritos und der Magier Anaxilaos aus Larissa*, Abhandlungen der Preußischen Akademie, vii.

WHITE, L. (1966). *The Transformation of the Roman World: Gibbon's Problem after Two Centuries* (Berkeley; Los Angeles).

WHITE, P. (1974). 'The Presentation and Dedication of the *Silvae* and the Epigrams', *J.R.S.* lxiv. 40–61.

WHITTAKER, T. (1928, repr. 1961). *The Neo-Platonists* (Cambridge; Hildesheim).

WICKERT, L. (1954). P.W. xxii. 2. 1998–2296, s.v. Princeps.

WIGHTMAN, E. M. (1970). *Roman Trier and the Treveri* (London).

WILCKEN, U. (1912, repr. 1963). *Chrestomathie*, i. 2, in Wilcken and L. Mitteis, *Grundzüge and Chrestomathie der Papyruskunde* (Stuttgart; Hildesheim).

WILHELM, A. (1943). 'Zwei Inschriften aus Didyma', *Jahreshefte des östereich. archäolog. Inst. Wien*, xxv. 154–89.

WILHELM-HOOIJBERGH, A. E. (1954). *Sin and Guilt in Ancient Rome* (Diss. Utrecht, Groningen).

WILLIAMS, G. W. (1953). 'Some Aspects of Roman Marriage Ceremonies and Ideals', *J.R.S.* xlviii. 16–29.

—— (1968). *Tradition and Originality in Roman Poetry* (Oxford).

WINDISCH, H. (1929). *Die Orakel des Hystaspes*, Verhandelingen der Koninklijke Akademie van Wetenschappen te Amsterdam, vol. 28, pt. 3 (Amsterdam).

WINKELMANN, F. (1962). 'Zur Geschichte des Authentizitätproblems der *Vita Constantini*', *Klio*, xl. 187–243.

WISEMAN, T. P. (1969). *Catullan Questions* (Leicester).

—— (1969). 'The census in the First Century B.C.', *J.R.S.* 59–75.

—— (1974). *Cinna the Poet and other Roman Essays* (Leicester).

WISSOWA, G. (1895). P.W. ii. 2. 2313–44, s.v. Augures.

—— Ibid. 1463–86, s.v. Arvales fratres.

—— (1912). *Religion und Kultus der Römer*, Handbuch der klassischen Altertumswissenschaft (Munich).

—— (1932). P.W. 2 R. iv, A1. 942–51, s.v. *supplicationes*.

—— (1975). *Gesammelte Abhandlungen zur römischen Religions—und Stadtgeschichte* (New York).

WISTRAND, E. (1956). *Die Chronologie der Punica des Silius Italicus* (Göteborg).

WITT, R. E. (1971). *Isis in the Graeco-Roman World* (London).

WITTIG, J. (1932). P.W. xv. 1244–84, s.v. C. Messius Quintus Traianus Decius.

WLOSOK, A. (1960). *Laktanz und die philosophische Gnosis*, Abhandlungen der Heidelberger Akademie der Wissenschaften.

WOODMAN, A. J. (1975). 'Questions of Date, Genre and Style in Velleius', *C.Q.* xxv. 272 ff.

—— (1975). Velleius Paterculus in T. A. Dorey (ed.), *Empire and Aftermath* (London), 1–25.

WORTMANN, D. (1968). 'Neue magische Texte', *Bonner Jahrbücher*, clxviii. 57–111.

WRIGHT, J. R. G. (1974). 'Form and Content in the Moral Essays', in C. D. N. Costa (ed.), *Seneca* (London), 39–69.

WÜLKER, L. (1903). *Die geschichtliche Entwicklung des Prodigienwesens bei den Römern* (Leipzig).

YAVETZ, L. (1962). *Plebs and Princeps* (Oxford).

ZIEGLER, J. (1970). *Zur religiösen Haltung der Gegenkaiser im 4 Jh. n. Chr.* (Kallmünz) = Frankfurter Anthistorische Studien.

ZIEHEN, L. (1906). *Leges Graecorum Sacrae e titulis collectae* (Leipzig).

Translations

English translations together with the original texts of most of the works cited in this book can be found in the volumes of the Loeb Classical Library published by W. Heinemann, London, and by Harvard University Press, Cambridge, Massachusetts. The *Penguin Classics* of Penguin Books Ltd., London, have translations only.

The *Collection Budé* (Collection des universités de France publiée sous le patronage de l'Association Guillaume Budé, Paris: Les Belles Lettres) gives the original text with a French translation. English versions of Christian works are found in the Ante-Nicene Christian Library (A.N.C.L.), edited by A. Roberts and J. Donaldson, and published in twenty-four volumes at Edinburgh, 1867–72, and now reprinted in ten volumes by W. Eerdmans, Grand Rapids, Michigan, U.S.A.

Another series of early Christian works in translation are the *Fathers of the Church*, edited by R. J. Deferrari and published by the Catholic University Press, Washington. This includes translations of Eusebius' *Ecclesiastical History* and of Lactantius' *Divine Institutes*. Arnobius, whom I have cited from the A.N.C.L. edition, is also translated in vols. vii and viii of the *Ancient Christian Writer Series*: E. MacCracken, Arnobius, *The Case against the Pagans*, 2 vols. (London, 1949).

I have cited passages from the following books:

Apuleius, *Apologie, Florides* (Florida), ed. and Fr. trans. P. Valette, Coll. Budé (Paris, 1960).

—— *The Golden Ass*, trans. R. Graves, Penguin Cl. (Harmondsworth, 1951).

Arnobius, The Seven Books of Arnobius, *Adversus Gentes*, trans. A. H. Bryce and H. Campbell, A.N.C.L., vol. xix, Edinburgh, 1871 = vol. vi of reprint.

Cicero, *De Natura Deorum*, ed. and trans. H. Rackham, Loeb C.L. (London, 1951).

—— *De Senectute, De Amicitia, De Divinatione*, ed. and trans. W. A. Falconer, Loeb C.L. (London, 1946).

—— *De Republica*, and *De Legibus*, ed. and trans. C. W. Keyes, Loeb C.L. (London, 1928).

—— *The Speeches*: Pro Archia Poeta, Post Reditum in Senatu, Post Reditum ad Quirites, De Domo Sua, De Haruspicum Responso, Pro Plancio, ed. and trans. N. W. Watts, Loeb C.L. (London, 1923).

Eusebius, *Church History, Life of Constantine the Great*, and *Oration in Praise of Constantine*, trans. A. C. McGiffert, Post-Nicene Fathers, 1 (Oxford, 1890).

Horace, *The Odes and Epodes*, ed. and trans. C. E. Bennett, Loeb C.L. (London, 1946).

Lactantius, *The Works*, i: *The Divine Institutes*, ii: *On the Anger of God, The Manner in which the Persecutors Died*, etc., trans. W. Fletcher, A.N.C.L., vols. xxi–xxii (Edinburgh, 1871) = vol. vii of reprint.

Livy, *The Early History of Rome*, trans. A. de Selincourt, Penguin Cl. (Harmondsworth, 1960).

—— *The War with Hannibal*, trans. A. de Selincourt, Penguin Cl. (Harmondsworth, 1965).

Lucan, *Pharsalia*, ed. and trans. J. D. Duff, Loeb C.L. (London, 1943).

Marcus Aurelius, *Meditations*, trans. M. Staniforth, Penguin Cl. (Harmondsworth, 1964).

—— *The Meditations of the Emperor Marcus Antoninus*, ed. with trans. and commentary, A. S. L. Farquharson, 2 vols. (Oxford, 1968).

Pliny, The Elder, *Natural History*, ed. H. Rackham (vols. i–ix), and D. E. Eichholz (vol. x), Loeb C.L. (London, 1949–62).

Pliny, The Younger, *Letters and Panegyrics*, 2 vols. ed. and trans. B. Radice, Loeb C.L. (London, 1969).

Seneca, *Ad Lucilium, epistulae morales*, ed. and trans. R. M. Gummere, 3 vols., Loeb C.L. (London, 1953).

—— *Four Tragedies and Octavia*, trans. E. F. Watling, Penguin Cl. (Harmondsworth, 1966).

—— *Moral Essays*, ed. and trans. J. W. Basore, 3 vols., Loeb C.L. (London, 1928–58).

Silius Italicus, *Punica*, ed. and trans. J. D. Duff, 2 vols., Loeb C.L. (London, 1949).

Tacitus, *The Annals of Imperial Rome*, trans. M. Grant, Penguin Cl. (Harmondsworth, 1956).

—— *The Histories*, trans. K. Wellesley, Penguin Cl. (Harmondsworth, 1964).

Theodosius II, *Theodosian Code and Novels and the Sirmondian Constitutions*, trans. C. Pharr (Princeton, 1952).

Virgil, *The Pastoral Poems* (The Eclogues), ed. and trans. E. V. Rieu, Penguin Cl. (Harmondsworth, 1949).

INDEX